A HERCULES IN THE CRADLE

AMERICAN BEGINNINGS, 1500–1900

A series edited by Edward Gray, Stephen Mihm, and Mark Peterson

ALSO IN THE SERIES

Frontier Seaport: Detroit's Transformation into an Atlantic Entrepôt
by Catherine Cangany (2014)

Beyond Redemption: Race, Violence, and the American South after the Civil War
by Carole Emberton (2013)

The Republic Afloat: Law, Honor, and Citizenship in Maritime America
by Matthew Taylor Raffety (2013)

Conceived in Doubt: Religion and Politics in the New American Nation
by Amanda Porterfield (2012)

A HERCULES IN THE CRADLE

War, Money, and the American State, 1783–1867

MAX M. EDLING

THE UNIVERSITY OF CHICAGO PRESS
CHICAGO AND LONDON

MAX M. EDLING is Lecturer in North American History at King's College London and the author of *A Revolution in Favor of Government: Origins of the U.S. Constitution and the Making of the American State*.

The University of Chicago Press, Chicago 60637
The University of Chicago Press, Ltd., London
© 2014 by The University of Chicago
All rights reserved. Published 2014.
Printed in the United States of America

23 22 21 20 19 18 17 16 15 14   1 2 3 4 5

ISBN-13: 978-0-226-18157-8 (cloth)
ISBN-13: 978-0-226-18160-8 (e-book)
DOI: 10.7208/chicago/9780226181608.001.0001

Library of Congress Cataloging-in-Publication Data
Edling, Max M., author.
  A Hercules in the cradle : war, money, and the American state, 1783–1867 / Max M. Edling.
      pages ; cm. — (American beginnings, 1500–1900)
      ISBN 978-0-226-18157-8 (cloth : alk. paper) — ISBN 978-0-226-18160-8 (e-book) 1. United States—History, Military—To 1900—Economic aspects. 2. War—Economic aspects—United States—History—18th century. 3. War—Economic aspects—United States—History—19th century. 4. Finance, Public—United States—History—18th century. 5. Finance, Public—United States—History—19th century. 6. Fiscal policy—United States—History—18th century. 7. Fiscal policy—United States—History—19th century. I. Title. II. Series: American beginnings, 1500–1900.
HJ249.E35 2014
336.7309′034—dc23
                                                                     2014008019

♾ This paper meets the requirements of ANSI/NISO Z39.48–1992 (Permanence of Paper).

TO AUGUST AND LEOPOLD

Money is now the *sine qua non* of political existence. Power is measured by the amount that can be commanded.
— *New York Times,* February 25, 1862

CONTENTS

	Acknowledgments	ix
	Introduction: War, Money, and American History	1
1.	A More Effectual Mode of Administration: The Constitution and the Origins of American Public Finance	17
2.	The Soul of Government: Creating an American Fiscal Regime	50
3.	So Immense a Power in the Affairs of War: The Restoration of Public Credit	81
4.	Equal to the Severest Trials: Mr. Madison's War	108
5.	The Two Most Powerful Republics in the World: Mr. Polk's War	145
6.	A Rank among the Very First of Military Powers: Mr. Lincoln's War	178
	Conclusion: The Ideology, Structure, and Significance of the First American Fiscal Regime	222
	Notes	253
	Index	307

ACKNOWLEDGMENTS

In 2003, I published a book on the adoption of the United States Constitution. Even before the book was out, I had decided to write a sequel that would investigate what, if anything, came out of the urge to build a viable national government that I had identified in the ratification debates of 1787 and 1788. Intended as a short book, the project soon grew in scope, and then grew some more until it seemed at times interminable. It is therefore with a sense of both relief and incredulity that I write these acknowledgments. I never thought I would get this far.

As a non-American who has neither studied nor worked in the United States, I have marveled at the generosity with which my work has always been received by my fellow American historians there. Despite cultural and linguistic barriers and considerable geographic distance, they have made me feel part of their community. Their readiness to listen to what foreign voices like mine have to say about their nation's history never ceases to amaze and impress me. It ought to be a source of pride to all historians in the United States and a shining example to the rest of us. Two historians in particular have taken me under their wing, although neither was under the slightest obligation to do so. For their support and friendship, and for everything that I have learned from them, I will always be grateful. Peter Onuf has been a major influence on my understanding of the nature of the early American union, and he will no doubt recognize many of his ideas in the pages that follow. From Jack Rakove, I have taken the insight that for all their intellectual brilliance, the statesmen of the early republic were also politicians who faced practical problems of statecraft. I would also like to express my gratitude to Daniel Walker Howe, Richard John, the late Pauline Maier, and Gordon Wood for supporting my work. Many historians of the American state, public finance, and the Constitution have provided important help, insights and criticism over the years. They include Brian Balogh, Nicolas Barreyre, Richard Bensel, Roger H. Brown, Richard Buel Jr., Robin L. Einhorn, Woody Holton, Daniel J. Hulsebosch, John P. Kaminski, Richard Leffler, Marc-William Palen, Patrick O'Brien, Gautham Rao, Leonard Sadosky, Patrik Winton, and Martin Öhman.

A number of financial historians have encouraged and gently corrected me throughout as I ventured onto their turf. Chief among them are Richard Sylla and Edwin J. Perkins, but their number also include Robert E. Wright and Farley Grubb. I am aware that my relationship to these impressive scholars is best described by the term *commensalism*. But I hope that my work will at least help bring them to the attention of my fellow historians. They deserve a wide readership. At the University of Chicago Press I would like to thank the staff for their professionalism and hard work I am especially grateful to George Roupe for his first-rate copyediting and Bonny McLaughlin for an excellent job on the index. Closer to home Susanna Rabow-Edling has as always been a careful and constructive critic, and I have benefitted immensely from our many discussions about this project..

Central parts of the research for chapter 4 were conducted when I was a fellow at the Robert H. Smith International Center for Jefferson Studies. In Charlottesville, I was provided access to unpublished material of the Papers of James Madison project at the University of Virginia. I would like to thank Andrew O'Shaughnessy and his staff at the Jefferson Center for their hospitality and John Stagg and Angela Kreider at the Papers of James Madison for their invaluable help.

A fellowship at the Stanford Humanities Center in 2010–2011 made it possible to give my undivided attention to the manuscript. The SHC director, Aron Rodrigue, and his staff, together with the center's fellows and members of the Stanford University faculty, made my stay in Palo Alto a productive year and a wonderful experience. Not a day goes by when I do not wish that I was back in California. I would in particular like to thank Gordon Chang, Giorgio Riello, Richard White, and Caroline Winterer.

The book was brought to completion during a research leave in the fall of 2012. I am grateful to Paul Readman and Adam Sutcliff, respectively the outgoing and the incoming chair of the Department of History at King's College London when I joined the department, for providing me with this opportunity and for extending such a very warm welcome.

Many audiences have listened to presentations related to this book. I would like to thank the participants at the following venues for showing up, asking intelligent questions, and providing me the chance to test ideas and conclusions in front of an engaged and knowledgeable audience: the Atlantic

History Seminar, Harvard University; the American Political Science Association annual meeting; the German Historical Institute, Washington, DC; the Society for Historians of the Early Republic annual meeting; the Swedish Historical Association triennial meeting; the Robert H. Smith International Center for Jefferson Studies; the Omohundro Institute of Early American History and Culture annual meeting; the Library Company, Philadelphia; the American History Research Seminar at the University of Oxford; the Centre d'Étude Nord-Américaines, L'École des Hautes Études en Sciences Sociales, Paris; the Bay Area Seminar in Early American History and Culture; the Institute of Historical Research, London; and the University of Cambridge American History Seminar.

Material in chapter 1 has appeared in "A More Perfect Union: The Framing of the Constitution," in Edward Gray and Jane Kamensky, eds., *The Oxford Handbook of the American Revolution*, (New York: Oxford University Press, 2012), 388–406; and in "'A Mongrel Kind of Government': The U.S. Constitution, the Federal Union, and the Origins of the American State," in Peter Thompson and Peter S. Onuf, eds., *State and Citizen: British America and the Early United States* (Charlottesville: University of Virginia Press, 2013), 150–77, © 2013 by the Rector and Visitors of the University of Virginia. Chapter 2 is a revised and expanded version of an article coauthored with Mark D. Kaplanoff and published as "Alexander Hamilton's Fiscal Reform: Transforming the Structure of Taxation in the Early Republic," *William and Mary Quarterly*, 3d ser., 61, no. 4 (October 2004): 714–37. Chapter 3 appeared as "'So Immense a Power in the Affairs of War': Alexander Hamilton and the Restoration of Public Credit," *William and Mary Quarterly* 3d ser., 64, no. 2 (April 2007): 287–326. I am grateful to Oxford University Press, USA, to the University of Virginia Press, and to the editor of the *William and Mary Quarterly* for permission to reprint this material here. Research for this book has been made possible thanks to financial support from the Bank of Sweden Tercentenary Foundation, the Swedish Research Council, and the Swedish Foundation for Cooperation in Research and Higher Education.

I would like to dedicate this book to my sons August and Leopold for being such good fun and a source of pride, but also for their support over the last decade or so. It is not that I have been an absent father. Whatever flaws there are in the Swedish welfare system, it does allow parents who so wish to strike a balance between family life and work commitments. But my work has forced them to live away from our beloved Södermalm and Hammarby Football Club for long stretches of time. I am infinitely grateful to them not only for putting up with our nomadic existence but also for doing so with relatively good cheer, all things considered. A book on money and war may not be what they have most wished for in life. Indeed, they have always had a talent for putting my professional life in perspective, and not always in the most delicate manner. But I do believe that even though the days of American hegemony are now gone, an understanding of the history, politics, and culture of the United States remains essential to an understanding of the world they inhabit. For regardless of whether we celebrate it or regret it, it is a world that was largely made in the USA.

INTRODUCTION

War, Money, and American History

Sometime in the year 1791, the Swedish minister of the Gloria Dei Church in Philadelphia, Nils Collin, or Nicholas Collin as he was known in America, began an account of his new homeland. When he laid down his pen, Collin had filled 230 pages in his characteristic strong hand. In typical Enlightenment style, his account carefully considered the geography, natural resources, and agriculture; the political system; and the religion, education, and mores of the newly established United States of America. This was not a tract intended for an American audience. Collin wrote in Swedish, and his aim was to dissuade his countrymen from migrating to America. On the face of it, it seems a strange project. No more than a handful of Swedes had traveled across the Atlantic in the eighteenth century, and the great Swedish out-migration to the New World began only after the Civil War. However, it seems likely that Collin believed that America's political independence, which had been recognized by Britain in 1783, and the stability and prospects expected from the adoption of the Constitution of 1787 would make the United States appear an attractive country of residence to his fellow Swedes.

Writing to make people stay at home, Collin naturally painted a rather bleak picture of the new nation. Finding fault with its unhealthy climate, uncouth inhabitants, and dangerous wildlife and with the general neglect of everything from husbandry to religion and family relations, he also questioned America's political prospects. "The federal government *appears* to be a mighty sovereign," he wrote. "But it is a Hercules in the cradle, surrounded by serpents." Irrespective of Collin's ulterior motives, this image of the newborn United States as a defenseless infant surrounded by life-threatening snakes captures well the new nation's weakness and precarious existence on the eve of the world-shattering upheavals of the French

I

Revolution and ensuing global wars. But the image is even more pertinent because of the outcome of the story that Collin was referring to. In the ancient Greek myth the infant Hercules strangles the serpents sent by a jealous Hera to destroy him, and he grows up to be an invincible giant. In the same way, the United States survived the challenging decades following the Declaration of Independence and in a rapid and dramatic manner grew to achieve great-power status by the end of the nineteenth century.[1]

Collin was not alone in finding an appropriate metaphor for the new nation in the legend of Hercules. No matter how difficult the struggle for independence had been or how crisis-ridden the postwar years, the conviction that the United States was destined for greatness was widespread among the founding generation. John Adams wished to see the full-grown Hercules on the Great Seal of the United States, and Benjamin Franklin put the infant Hercules on the 1783 Libertas Americana medal struck to celebrate independence. In 1794, Alexander Hamilton alluded to the Hercules legend in a letter to George Washington, writing that the United States was "a people recently become a nation, . . . and as yet, if a Hercules—a Hercules in the cradle." In 1815, French émigré Julia Plantou painted an allegory entitled *The Peace of Ghent 1814 and the Triumph of America*. In this painting, later engraved by Alexis Chataigner, the American Hercules, representing the "force" of the United States, compels a prostrate Britannia to accept his peace terms after the War of 1812. Two decades later, artist Robert Sully suggested the infant Hercules for the state seal of Wisconsin, with the serpents slowly choking in the reflexive grasp of the precocious giant representing the Fox and the Sauk Indian nations, which had recently been routed by the US Army and the local militia in the Black Hawk War of 1832. Nor was this conception of the United States and its destiny embraced only by Americans. The Count de Aranda, Spain's ambassador to France, allegedly predicted the future rise of the United States during the peace negotiations in Paris in 1783 that ended the War of Independence. According to Aranda, the United States "has been born a pigmy" but "in the time to come, it will be a giant, and even a colossus, very formidable in these vast regions. Its first step will be an appropriation of the Floridas to be master of the Gulf of Mexico."[2]

Aranda's prescience was not nearly as remarkable as it first seems, however. In fact, he never made any prediction about the future fate of the United States at all, either in 1783 or later. The quotation comes from a spurious memoir that first appeared in France in 1827. Yet this makes the Aranda prophesy only more interesting. In the 1820s Spain was recovering from the loss of virtually all its American dominions in the Spanish

American struggle for independence. The United States had benefited handsomely from the disintegration of the Spanish Empire by acquiring the Floridas. Together with the Louisiana Purchase of 1803, the Florida Cession meant that the United States was indeed fast on its way to becoming master of the Gulf of Mexico and much more besides. This expansion forced America's neighbors to try to come to terms with the young and assertive nation. It was in this context that Aranda's forged memoir appeared and soon became popular. And so it remained as the United States grew in size and power. In 1850, Aranda's memoir was used by a group of Mexican intellectuals to analyze their nation's recent disaster in the US-Mexican War. Tellingly entitled *The Other Side*, their collective work explained Mexico's loss of half its national domain partly by pointing to the Mexican government's weakness but much more by drawing attention to an inherent American aggression, which had been present from the birth of the United States. From the moment of its independence, the document asserted, the United States had announced "that it was called upon to represent an important part in the world of Columbus."

> The North American Republic has already absorbed territories pertaining to Great Britain, France, Spain, and Mexico. It has employed every means to accomplish this—purchase as well as usurpation, skill as well as force, and nothing has restrained it when treating of territorial acquisition. Louisiana, the Floridas, Oregon, and Texas have successfully fallen into its power. It now has secured the possession of the Californias, New Mexico, and a great part of other States and Territories of the Mexican Republic. Although we may desire to close our eyes with the assurance that these pretensions have now come to an end, and that we may enjoy peace and unmoved tranquility for a long time, still the past history has an abundance of matter to teach us as yet existing, what has existed, the same schemes of conquest in the United States. The attempt has to be made, and we will see ourselves overwhelmed anew, sooner or later, in another or in more than one disastrous war, until the flag of the stars floats over the last span of territory which it so much covets.[3]

Similar views of America's rise to greatness were entertained also by the United States' northern neighbor. In the winter of 1865, as Union forces pressed hard on the embattled Confederate army in Virginia, delegates from Britain's North American provinces came together to debate the need for stronger union. The origins of the Canadian Confederation in the provinces' wish to protect themselves against US aggression has sometimes been downplayed in the historical literature, but it was never far from the minds of Canadian reformers. On February 9, 1865, during the confederation debates, the poet, publicist, agricultural minister, Canadian nationalist, and recent Irish immigrant Thomas D'Arcy McGee took a full swing at the United States, exclaiming that

> the policy of our neighbor to the south of us has always been aggressive. There has always been a desire among them for the acquisition of new territory, and the inexorable law of democratic existence seems to be its absorption. They coveted Florida, and seized it; they coveted Louisiana and purchased it; they coveted Texas, and stole it; and then they picked a quarrel with Mexico, which ended by their getting California. They sometimes pretend to despise these colonies as prizes beneath their ambition; but had we not had the strong arm of England over us, we should not now have had a separate existence.[4]

I

McGee's allegations in the Canadian Confederation debates and the Mexican lament in *The Other Side* show how in the course of the nineteenth century the conception of the United States as a Hercules destined for greatness was also adopted by America's neighbors. But Mexicans and Canadians gave the story of the rising giant a distinctive twist. They claimed that the United States grew to dominate the North American continent not because of its free institutions or its enterprising population but by its liberal use of state-sanctioned and state-directed aggression and violence.

Such an understanding goes against the grain of a strong indigenous tradition that sees the federal republic as fundamentally peaceful. In the early days of the American union, George Washington called on his countrymen to "observe good faith and justice towards all nations. Cultivate peace and harmony with all." Thomas Jefferson declared that the United States sought "peace, commerce, and honest friendship with all nations," and Andrew Jackson said that American policy was "actuated by the sincere desire to do justice to every nation and to preserve the blessings of peace." Even James Polk, perhaps the United States' least convincing peace apostle, made the point in his inaugural address that the essence of American foreign policy was "peace with . . . all the world," adding that "the world has nothing to fear from military ambition in our Government." This understanding of the United States as a peace project inspired not only political rhetoric but also the arts. When Henry Adams published his history of the United States in 1890, he noted that "the chief sign that Americans had other qualities than the races from which they sprang, was shown by their dislike for war as a profession, and their obstinate attempts to invent other methods for obtaining their ends." Two years earlier, John Fiske had concluded that the adoption of the Constitution of 1787 ensured that "the continent of North America should be dominated by a single powerful and pacific nation instead of being parceled out among forty or fifty small communities, wasting their strength and lowering their moral tone by perpetual warfare, like the states of ancient Greece, or by perpetual preparation for warfare, like the nations of modern Europe." In more recent years the idea that the early United States was a peace project has made a strong comeback in the social sciences, where specialists on international relations speak of the American union as the "Philadelphia system" or a "peace pact" intended to banish war from the New World.[5]

But on the question of whether the antebellum United States was more prone to peace than war, its neighbors seem to have got it more nearly right than the Americans themselves. War has been an important part of the nation's history from its inception. The claim that the nineteenth-century United States was inherently aggressive is more problematic, even if it should not be ruled out offhand. It seems much safer to say that the many wars and the stupendous territorial expansion of the United States in the century after its founding reflect no more than the fact that the nation is the most spectacular success story of the modern era. As two prominent American historians note, much as the national self-image and ideas of exceptionalism might deny it, the truth is that "the long-term pattern of America's development look[s] broadly similar to those of other large, successful nations." And like other successful nations, the United States has used war and military force as means to achieve policy goals. It has done so from the creation of the federal government in 1787, long before the Spanish-American War of 1898 or the Second World War, the two events that are conventionally used to mark America's imperial ascendancy.[6]

International events such as the French Revolution, the Jay Treaty, the Quasi War, the War of 1812, and the Mexican War have always figured prominently in the political history of the early republic and pre–Civil War America. Yet until quite recently historians were much more interested in the effects of these events on domestic politics—such as the rise of the first party system, the election of 1800, the decline of the Federalist party, and the fate of the Whigs—than in their effects on the United States' relations to foreign nations. Outside the subfield of diplomatic history, American historians typically showed little interest in foreign policy and international relations after the colonies' exit from the British Empire in 1783. Though no one denied the outside world's influence on the United States, it was quite legitimate to write the history of the early American republic with no more than passing reference to anything outside it. Nor was there much interest in studying the influence of the United States on the rest of the globe after the radical shock that the Revolution sent through the Atlantic world. In recent decades, however, there has been a great shift in perspective. With the growth of Atlantic and global history has appeared an awareness of the importance of foreign relations—such as war, commerce, and territorial expansion—to internal political and economic developments as well as a greater interest in how Americans affected the world around them. More important still is a new willingness to see the political history of the American union not only as the unfolding of democracy and freedom but also as the realization of "imperial ambitions" that were largely the legacy of the British Empire.[7]

The federal union created by the Declaration of Independence and the adoption of the Constitution was as much a peace pact intended to preserve harmonious relations among the member states as it was a sovereign state intended to defend and promote common interests against European powers and Native American polities on the North American continent. As a sovereign nation, the United States had to negotiate its political and commercial relationships with other nations. To do so it had to formulate policies and build institutions that would secure American interests in the international arena. On the North American continent, the young republic continued and accelerated the expansion of territory and settlement begun under British imperial rule. Its consequences—territorial expansion (through annexation, wars of conquest, and purchase), the subjection of foreign peoples, and the transformation of the natural environment—are all central aspects of the history of the United States.[8]

The general neglect of wars, military coercion, and diplomacy in the historiography of the early United States led to an unfortunate side effect that most American historians did not welcome. This neglect created a blind spot that served to maintain the myth that the rise of American power through territorial and commercial expansion somehow just happened, or worse, that the process was providential and peaceful. The neglect of wars and international relations also obscured the origins of what is perhaps the most interesting feature of the American polity today, namely the combination of, on the one hand, a fundamentally liberal regime in the domestic sphere with, on the other hand, a government possessing the ability and willingness to regularly mobilize and project powers of coercion on an enormous and unprecedented scale beyond the nation's pale. Today historians show a much greater appreciation for the role of the federal government in conquering the West, in transforming public lands into private property, and in binding the nation together through networks of communication. Nevertheless, despite a host of important new scholarship, we have yet much to learn about the governmental institutions that made such actions possible.⁹

II

Independence and union turned thirteen colonial dependencies into a sovereign nation within an intensely competitive transatlantic state system. It was a system largely governed by war and violence, and it remains so today. In this hostile environment, states that could mobilize resources and project military power were more successful in protecting their territorial integrity and in promoting their interests than states that could not. Very soon after independence, the United States acquired this ability and used it to gain an edge over its competitors in the struggle for dominance over the North American continent.

Including the Civil War, the American republic fought three major wars in the early and mid-nineteenth century. In addition to these full-scale wars, the federal government also intervened militarily outside the nation's borders on repeated occasions from 1798 onward. These actions took place all over the globe far and near, from Florida to the Barbary states of North Africa to Kuala Batee on the island of Sumatra in Indonesia. Within its own borders, the government engaged in numerous small-scale engagements and wars with American Indian nations throughout most of the nineteenth century. The gains made by being able to project military power onto neighboring states and peoples within and without the national domain were far from marginal. Each of America's major wars brought about important geopolitical reconfigurations that influenced the nation's future development. But the smaller conflicts, what the British poet Rudyard Kipling called "the savage wars of peace," were just as important as conventional wars.

The Paris Peace Treaty of 1783 awarded the United States a territory stretching from the Atlantic seaboard to the Mississippi River, encompassing roughly 820,000 square miles. In the next five decades, the American federal republic added more than two million square miles to the national domain. Another 570,000 square miles followed with the Alaska Purchase in 1867. This tremendous territorial expansion took place to a large extent through purchase and negotiation and has therefore been described as peaceful. But the threat of violence was never far away. France, Spain, and Britain preferred to sell or to settle peacefully over Louisiana, Florida, and Oregon rather than risk armed confrontation with the US government or American freelance agents. The same is true of the many smaller polities and groups that bent to the will of the United States. For although the endless supply of land may have made the United States the "best poor man's country" on earth, not a square mile acquired by the federal union was terra nullius. In some places the land was occupied by European descendants. Much more often the residents were members of American Indian nations. These polities had no say in the diplomatic negotiations that transferred land from European states and their successor regimes to the United States. Nevertheless, American Indians typically had a well-developed concept of territoriality and no inclination to give up their land freely. But give it up they were made to do. The American political project was premised on agrarian expansion, and a basic task of the federal government was to transform "unsettled" territories into freehold farms that could sustain a federal republic of citizen-farmers. Between the Paris Peace Treaty and the outbreak of the Civil War, the United States concluded more than three hundred treaties regulating Indian land cessions. It was a process no less important than the better-known international treaties to the history of American territorial expansion.[10]

By clearing the land of its previous inhabitants, the federal government played a crucial part in turning the national domain into agrarian republics. From the first Trade and Intercourse Act of 1790, the federal government tried to establish a physical separation of European Americans and American Indians by drawing and policing an Indian frontier. This shifting line was steadily pushed westward and was in reality much more porous than the legislation intended. It fell to the US Army to maintain the frontier, and the army frequently clashed with American Indians. Some of these conflicts are well known. There were Indian wars in the Old Northwest in 1790–1795, 1811, and 1832; in the Old Southwest in 1814 and 1837–1838; and in Florida in 1817–1818, 1835–1842, and 1855–1858. But these conflicts represent no more than the tip of the iceberg. Tension along the Indian frontier was frequent. An incomplete tally of clashes between the army and the Indians lists 309 armed encounters between 1790 and 1861. The situation escalated in the years between the Mexican Cession and the outbreak of the Civil War. "It would be quite a misnomer," the army's commanding general Winfield Scott wrote in 1849, to call the army "a *peace establishment*." He further noted, "About four-fifths of the regiments or companies are, under threats of hostilities, in a state of constant activity or alert on our Indian borders, in Florida, Texas, New Mexico, California, and between the basin of the Mississippi and the Rocky mountains, including the long lines of emigration across those mountains and the removal of the Menomonies from Wisconsin."[11]

The combined events of the mid- and late 1840s—the Texas annexation, the Oregon settlement, and the Mexican Cession—exploded both the concept and the reality of the Indian frontier. Migrants on the overland trails cut straight through Indian territory on their way to California and Oregon, and their protection from depredations of the powerful Indian nations that controlled the Great Plains became an important concern for the army and the federal government. The solution to this sudden and often violent comingling of the two peoples was the reservation system, which promised to restore the physical separation of Euro-Americans and Indians. Instead of withdrawing behind an Indian frontier, American Indians would now retreat into demarcated territories, forming little islands in a sea of European American settlement. Developed and initiated in the 1850s, its implementation belonged mostly to the post–Civil War period. But the forceful removal of Indian nations from choice agricultural land began long before the creation of the first reservations. The Indian removal of Andrew Jackson, which created the tragic diaspora of the five civilized tribes of the Old Southwest, is only the best-known instance of what was an established policy for clearing the land of unwanted elements. More often than not, Indian removal required coercion or the threat of coercion, and the army played a crucial role in carrying it out.[12]

The expansion of agriculture was intimately connected to the expansion of trade, as American farmers produced at least partly for the market and often for foreign markets. The promotion of international commerce was therefore another central task of the federal government. The United States treated with foreign nations not only to acquire land but also to acquire commercial advantage. Between 1783 and 1861, the Senate ratified over 160 international treaties, roughly half of which concerned trade. The government's commitment to commerce can also be seen in the network of consuls that by the middle of the nineteenth century stretched across the globe. Although concentrated in Europe and especially in Britain, there were consuls in faraway Zanzibar, Cape Town, Mumbai and Calcutta, Singapore, Manila, Canton, and Shanghai, as well as all over South America, the West Indies, Australia, New Zealand, and other Pacific islands. The government's commitment to trade is evident also in the naval squadrons that the United

States maintained on a permanent basis in the Mediterranean (from 1815), the Pacific (1821), the West Indies (1822), the South Atlantic (1826), and East Asia (1835).

In the eighteenth and nineteenth centuries international trade was not free, and nations had no natural right to sell their goods to other nations. Markets had to be opened through treaty, commercial and navigational information had to be collected, and trade had to be protected. The United States used its fledgling navy to perform these tasks. Some of its commercial and diplomatic activities, such as the two Barbary Wars or Commodore Matthew Perry's opening of Japan, are well known. But they constitute only a fragment of the navy's international policing and diplomatic activity. The navy used military force against other governments, such as in the occupation of the Falkland Islands in 1830–1831 or the bombardment of Chinese coastal fortifications outside Canton in 1852. More often the arms of the navy were directed against stateless pirates or robbers and, on occasion, even cannibals, to keep the sea lanes open to American merchantmen in the West Indies, the Mediterranean, Indonesia, and the Pacific. During domestic disturbances shore parties landed to protect American property and lives in foreign ports. In periods of international war, the navy protected the merchant marine by escorting American ships in and out of illegally blockaded ports. And by showing the flag in foreign harbors, the US Navy demonstrated the government's intention to defend its citizens and their interests in every corner of the globe.[13]

Yet more than the savage wars of peace and policing actions of the army and navy, it is the three major conflicts of the early and mid-nineteenth century that most dramatically demonstrate the significance of military power to the nation's development. Although the War of 1812 is generally considered an abject failure, it settled the long struggle over who would control the trans-Appalachian West. European empires had vied for power and influence over this region since the mid-eighteenth century, but superior population numbers and an advanced political organization meant that the Native Americans were the dominant military power in the area. The Treaty of 1783 awarded the territory to the United States, yet effective control remained in the hands of powerful Indian confederations and nations north of the Ohio River and in the Southeast. Until the War of 1812, these polities formed a formidable impediment to the expansion of European American settlement. Both Britain and Spain had an interest in maintaining an autonomous Indian territory as a barrier to US growth and did what they could to bolster the Indian nations occupying the Union's outer marches. Meanwhile the loyalty of the white settlers who moved into the western regions of the United States was limited at best, and numerous plans were hatched by westerners to break out of the Union. In the 1790s and early 1800s there was a real possibility that the United States would fail to become an interior power in North America and would remain an elongated federal union sandwiched between the Appalachian Mountains and the Atlantic Ocean—a North American equivalent of the Republic of Chile. Such a development would have had a profound impact on the nation's future history. Instead, the War of 1812 broke the resistance of the American Indians. Never again would Indian nations pose a serious threat to United States expansion, and not for half a century would the interior areas of the nation again contemplate secession.[14]

Three decades after the War of 1812, the US-Mexican War and the annexation of Texas transferred about half of Mexico's national domain to the United States. These vast new provinces turned the United States into a transcontinental power, whose future faced the Pacific Ocean as well as the Atlantic and the Gulf of Mexico. Mexico's loss of its northern provinces also marked the final demise of the control, such as it was, of the Spanish Empire and its successor state over North America north of the Rio Grande. Instead the continent would develop as a largely Anglophone and Protestant cultural and political sphere over the ensuing century, before immigration reintroduced a Hispanic influence in what is now the American Southwest. Like the War of 1812, the Mexican War also had its Native American dimension. Several Indian nations had established economically successful and politically powerful polities on the Great Plains. After the Mexican Cession and the beginning of migration to California and Oregon, these polities crumbled as the US Army established a presence along the overland routes and the border with Mexico and allowed buffalo hunters onto the prairies to destroy the ecological foundations of the Plains economy. This drawn-out process culminated in the decades following the Civil War when the government used its military capacity to hound the Native Americans into reservations.[15]

The Civil War, too, had important geopolitical consequences that are sometimes overlooked in the conventional rendition of the war as the traumatic finale to the struggle over slavery. Most obviously it prevented the disintegration of the federal republic into two powerful American states that would have coexisted in uneasy tension and conflict. The astounding military mobilization of the Union demonstrated that the American system of government, although in many ways a weak state, nevertheless had the capacity to raise enormous resources for war. The military buildup of the North was closely monitored by Europe's great powers, who took careful note of its effects on the balance of power on the North American continent. As early as 1863 the British ambassador to Washington reported home that should a war would break out between Britain and the United States "the relative positions of the United States and its adversary would be very nearly the reverse of what they would have been if a war had broken out three or even two years ago." Alongside other developments closer to home, this realization led British policy makers to pull the British army out of its North American provinces and offer home rule to the Dominion of Canada. The Colonial Office even vetoed an attempt to make Canada a kingdom, because it would be "too open a monarchical blister on the side of the United States." France, too, saw the scales tip in favor of the United States; Napoleon III aborted his Mexican adventure, and France withdrew permanently from the New World. In the same period, Russia decided to give up Alaska for a few million dollars. By 1867, the United States was the sole great power on the North American continent.[16]

Irrespective of the moral concerns historians raise about the stunning trajectory of the United States between the Revolution and the aftermath of the Civil War—and today, of course, the profession is wont to lament rather than celebrate this development—it is difficult to conclude other than that the remarkable growth of the physical size of the nation, and the growth in population and wealth that this made possible, were to a large extent the result of state-organized and state-directed violence. In short, war and violence helped lay the foundation for American greatness.

III

If war and violence made America great, that greatness rested on the ability of the American government to pay for soldiers, warships, military equipment, and supplies. As one British historian has remarked, "The capacity of any state to act and to realise its policy goals depends, more than anything else, on its financial resources." There is no question that the projection of military power is and has always been enormously expensive. To build and maintain for one year a single seventy-four-gun ship of the line, the standard battleship of eighteenth-century fleets, cost $550,000 in the 1790s. Paying and maintaining a regiment of light dragoons for one year in the early nineteenth century cost about the same. As a point of comparison, the Bank of New York, the largest private corporation in America before the establishment of the Bank of the United States, was capitalized at $500,000. To wield military force in the early modern era, or even to use military threat with any degree of credibility, governments had to have access to vast monetary resources. Even nonviolent territorial expansion was expensive. It is common to speak of the treaties that transferred Louisiana and other areas to the United States as "bargains." But the compensation paid to foreign governments nevertheless represented significant sums. The $15 million Thomas Jefferson paid for Louisiana amounted to 120 percent of the annual income of the federal government.[17]

A casual glance at the budget of the federal government in the period between the Revolution and the Civil War shows that items related in one way or another to the military and foreign affairs made up four-fifths of total expenditures. These items were the army, navy, foreign and Indian relations, military pensions, and charges on the public debt, which in this period overwhelmingly resulted from loans taken out to pay for wars and territorial acquisitions. The United States was not unusual in this respect. All over the world, central governments focused on warfare rather than welfare well into the twentieth century. But more than most other nineteenth-century governments, the national government of the United States became unusually good at finding the money it needed to pay for its territorial acquisitions, its military, and its wars.

This book sets out to explain how the federal government acquired its capacity to finance wars and territorial expansion and how it made use of this capacity in the nineteenth century up to and through the Civil War. It begins by showing how the federal government very soon after independence acquired the ability to finance extraordinary expenses such as war by issuing and selling long-term bonds. This method of financing government costs was characteristic of the most advanced states in Europe at the time, and it is still used by governments today to pay for wars and budget deficits. The Constitutional Convention and the First Congress are the crucial moments in the history of how the United States acquired the capacity to sell long-term bonds. The Constitution centralized fiscal powers and reorganized the Union, thereby laying the foundation for a functioning national government. George Washington's first administration and the senators and representatives of the First Congress next transformed the paragraphs and sections of the new Constitution into the institutions and policies of the new federal government. The nation's first secretary of the Treasury, Alexander Hamilton, looms large in this account. Yet Hamilton's greatness should not be exaggerated. Others could have achieved what Hamilton did, and the path he followed was well marked. But what he did was nonetheless of the highest significance. In a few years Hamilton engineered the transformation of the nation's public debt from a liability to an asset. In the 1780s the debt caused friction between the states and social unrest. By 1791 it had become an advertisement for America's creditworthiness.

As part of the reform of the nation's finances, the First Congress also transformed the nation's fiscal system and ensured that a steady income flowed into the federal treasury without much protest from taxpayers. Considering the difficulties Britain and the Continental Congress had experienced when trying to tax the American people, this was a considerable achievement. During Hamilton's tenure at the Treasury certain fundamental principles of American public finance were laid down. Extraordinary expenses were to be paid for by creating debt rather than taxing the people in order to spare the citizens the burdens of government as much as possible. But despite his infamous reference to the national debt as a "public blessing," Hamilton did not approve of a permanent debt. He believed that the government should constantly strive to pay down the debt in times of peace in order to avoid burdening the taxpayers with interest charges. These recommendations were duly followed. The debt from the War of Independence was repaid between 1795 and 1832, the debt from the War of 1812 in the 1820s, and the debt from the Mexican War in the 1860s. The debt from the Civil War was sharply reduced in the decades after 1865.

Ironically, it was not Hamilton's Federalists who made the most extensive use of the nation's public credit and productive revenue system to realize policy ends. Instead it was Thomas Jefferson and James Madison, both inveterate enemies of public debts, who borrowed to acquire Louisiana and to go to war against Britain. They started something of a tradition. James Monroe bought Florida from Spain. Andrew Jackson spent huge sums removing American Indian nations from the South and expanding the navy. James Polk conquered Mexico on credit and then paid compensation for the spoils with American taxpayers' money. Throughout the early republic and the antebellum era, it was the self-proclaimed enemies of central government and public indebtedness, politicians in the Jeffersonian and Jacksonian antietatist tradition, who made the most extensive use of the federal government and its capacity to raise money in order to realize policy objectives.

In the chapters that follow, the period from 1801 to 1867 is analyzed in separate studies of the War of 1812, the Mexican War, and the Civil War. The first of these conflicts was very much a failure from the perspective of American war aims. The execution of the war also left much to be wished for, and the government had its share of problems in the war's financial management. Yet the financing of the war represents a significant change compared to the chaotic and idiosyncratic methods used during the War of

Independence. The War of 1812 was paid for through a much more ordered process than the struggle for independence, using methods that were similar to those Britain had employed for over a century. The war also shows the extent of common ground between the Hamiltonians and the Jeffersonians. Under the directorship of Albert Gallatin, the federal government managed the war in ways that Hamilton could hardly have disapproved of had he lived to witness it. War finances were centralized, and extraordinary costs were met by selling long-term interest-bearing securities, or, in Jeffersonian parlance, by transferring the costs of the living to the next generation. Mr. Madison's War is significant to the history of American war finance because it was the first time the federal government made real use of the Hamiltonian system that had been established in the 1790s. In contrast to the financial chaos that had been the result of the War of Independence, the financing of the War of 1812 demonstrated the basic soundness of Hamilton's system of finance.

In comparison to the War of 1812, financing the Mexican War proved relatively unproblematic. This limited conflict was fought entirely on enemy soil. In contrast to the War of 1812, Mr. Polk's War was a land war that did not interrupt American trade or the government's income from customs duties. Led by Robert J. Walker, the government easily floated its loans. The Mexican War is of interest not for the United States' management of the war—the government mostly applied lessons learned in the previous conflict—but because it provides the opportunity to contrast the stable finances of the United States with the bankrupt Mexican treasury. Mexico's attempts to finance its opposition to the American invasion were the very reverse of US policy. The Mexican government relied on coerced loans and the expropriation of property rather than on voluntary investments in government loans. Rather than make property holders loyal supporters of the government, Mexican leaders turned them into bitter opponents who sponsored armed uprisings against the regime. The war against the United States was only one instance in a long period of national decline for Mexico in which the poor state of its public finances played a large part. In the United States the eight decades that followed after independence was a time of territorial expansion and growing strength. In Mexico, the postindependence period was a time of repeated insults to Mexican sovereignty, of political disintegration, and of constant civil strife. Perhaps nothing illustrates the weakness of the Mexican state more clearly than the government's need to sell off the national domain in order to cling to power.

In terms of resource mobilization, the nation's first two wars dwindle into insignificance in comparison to the Civil War. The War of 1812 and the

Mexican War were limited conflicts. The Civil War was war of a magnitude that the world had never witnessed before. Wartime mobilization was on a scale to match. The cost of the War of 1812 was $90 million. The cost of the Mexican War was ten million less. The cost of the Civil War, to the Union side alone, has been calculated at $2.3 billion. With an annual income of around $50 million to $55 million in the late 1850s, the Union government had no alternative to fighting the war on credit. The level of indebtedness skyrocketed. Less than two years into the war Secretary of the Treasury Samuel P. Chase remarked that

> Great Britain, in a century, has made a debt of $4,000,000,000, but the interest is only 3%, which however, makes the startling sum of $120,000,000. We, in two years, unless we entrench, are making a debt of $1,200,000,000 on which the interest if in Bonds, as usual will be at least 6% or $72,000,000. Thus in two years, you impose on the people, practically, six-tenths of the load British Statesmen have educated that nation to bear, in the course of near a hundred years.[18]

Chase in fact erred on the conservative side. In 1866, the national debt stood at $2.8 billion and the annual interest charge at $144 million. The United States had entered the Civil War virtually unencumbered by debt. It came out of the war the second-greatest debtor in the world, trailing only Great Britain.

It is easy to think that as the world's second-largest debtor, the United States was in severe distress. But the ability to sustain such an enormous debt is a sign of strength rather than weakness. Public credit is a vital resource that allows governments to do things they could not otherwise do. The Civil War therefore represents a coming of age of sorts, whereby the United States joined the family of great powers in large degree because of its ability to run up a huge debt to pay for an enormous war. In future years this was an ability that the United States would use to good effect, not least for foreign-policy ventures. It underpinned the nation's transition first into a superpower at the close of the Second World War and later into a hyperpower at the close of the Cold War.

This book is the history of how it all began.

CHAPTER ONE

A More Effectual Mode of Administration: The Constitution and the Origins of American Public Finance

"Money is with propriety considered as the vital principle of the body politic; as that which sustains its life and motion, and enables it to perform its most essential functions. A complete power therefore to procure a regular and adequate supply of it, as far as the resources of the community will permit, may be regarded as an indispensable ingredient in every constitution." This observation in one of Alexander Hamilton's essays in *The Federalist* suggests that fiscal and financial matters played a prominent role in the framing and ratification of the US Constitution. The troubled finances of the American union were a primary reason for the calling of the Philadelphia convention, and the fiscal and financial powers of the reformed national government were the subject of considerable interest both in the convention and in the ensuing struggle over ratification. But the reverse is even more true: the Constitution was of fundamental importance to the history of American public finance. It provided the authority for the creation of governmental institutions that would give the federal government the ability to draw forth the nation's resources and thereby realize ambitious policy goals.[1]

In 1787, the critical issues confronting the American federal union originated in the vast western reaches of the United States and on the boundless oceans. In the West, the Continental Congress had only nominal control over the American Indians and European Americans who resided there. Britain, the former mother country, violated the new nation's territorial integrity by maintaining military posts on American soil and diplomatic relations with Indian nations living within the borders of the United States. On the Atlantic Ocean and beyond, the expulsion of the American colonies from the common market of the British Empire had led to a sharp downturn in exports and shipping, which in turn had caused an economic depression. A third challenge lay in the cracks that had begun to appear in the federal union, where conflicts of interest between the member states over the Revolutionary debt, commercial regulations, and territorial claims were producing tension. If the term is defined broadly, to include the management of the western domain and its inhabitants as well as interstate relations within the American union, these issues can all be said to pertain to foreign affairs. They concerned questions that fell outside the internal politics of the states, although international commerce, the management of the western lands, and interstate conflicts had obvious impacts on economic and political life. The significance of the framing and adoption of the Constitution lies in the fact that it made possible the creation of an energetic national government that could begin to address issues facing the American nation in the international rather than the domestic sphere. The centralization of fiscal and financial powers that resulted from the framing and adoption of the Constitution is a crucial part of this story.

Historians have not always appreciated the importance of this change because they have insisted on seeing the Constitution as both originating in and aimed at domestic rather than international problems. The predominant interpretation centers on the question of popular political influence over American government and argues that the nationalists of 1787 entered the Philadelphia convention intent on depriving the people of political influence by transferring power from the states to a central government less receptive to the popular will. Far from being successful, however, the founders "failed miserably" in their task. In their new guise as the Federalist party, the heirs of the nationalist reformers struggled courageously through the 1790s to establish a central government that could reach deeply into society to regulate economic and social relations in accordance with the wishes of the elite. But their cause was doomed. Their program lacked the support of the broad layers of the population who still dominated the nation's politics. With the "Revolution of 1800," when Jefferson ascended to the presidency, the Federalist attempt at nation-state formation came crashing down. Thanks to Jeffersonian intransigence the American union returned to its pre-Constitution condition in which the states held "*sovereign status* in a *voluntary* and *conditional* union." States' rights advocates won the day, and the nationalist vision was expunged from the American political tradition. In the nineteenth century, "governance in Washington barely mattered in the lives of ordinary Americans," and the federal government dwindled to become no more than a laughing matter, the ludicrous spectacle of "a midget institution in a giant land."[2]

In recent decades, historians have begun to reinterpret the impulse behind the Philadelphia convention and the long-term impact of the Constitution on the course of American history. Starting with a resurgence of interest in the international history of the founding, key documents such as the Declaration of Independence and the Constitution are now seen less as the expressions of a liberal state-building project than as means designed to allow the American nation to interact with foreign powers. The low profile of the federal government in the regulation of the nation's social and economic relations in the nineteenth century need no longer be seen as evidence of its abject failure. Its mission lay elsewhere.

The founders never designed their national government to deal with what contemporaries called "internal police," a broad field of government activity that included the regulation of the economy and the health, morals, and general welfare of the citizens. This power was left with the states. The state-republics delegated only the responsibility for conducting foreign affairs and intraunion relations to a common national government. Foreign relations included activities such as defense and war making, relations with American Indians, the acquisition of territory, international trade regulations, and commercial treaty making. The most important intraunion task was the preservation of peace between the member states through the settlement of interstate conflicts, such as disputes over territory or, later, over the expansion of slavery. It also fell to the national government to create and maintain a common market by means of a customs union, a common currency, and the protection of contracts in transactions between the citizens of one state and those of another state or nation.[3]

At the conceptual level, the founding was no radical reformulation of American federalism. Although the Constitution altered the system of American government profoundly, it did nothing more than fine-tune an already established division of powers between the states and the national government. The real change from the Articles of Confederation, the compact that first created the American union, was that the Constitution provided the authority and blueprint for a national government that could act independently of the state-republics that together formed the Union. As Roger Sherman pointed out, the powers delegated to the members of Congress by the Constitution were basically "the same as Congress have under the articles of Confederation with this difference, that they will have the authority to carry into effect, what they now have a right to require to be done by the States."[4]

To the extent that historians have failed to appreciate the limited but nonetheless important powers that the Constitution invested in the national government, it is in large part due to the nature of the paper trail left behind by the nation's founders. Private and public commentaries during the framing and ratification of the Constitution are filled with insistent demands that the federal union be reformed. A consistent complaint was the claim that the state governments had neglected the common good of the Union. But these statements have very little to say about what the common good of the Union really was. Nor do they speak of what the national government was designed to do, or even why a federal union was needed. To recover this information it is necessary to return to the original union established by the Articles of Confederation. It is also necessary to pause at points in the Constitutional Convention debates that most historians hurry past on their way to the Connecticut Compromise and the other major decisions of the convention. For it is only when the function of the Union and the role of the national government within it are established that is it possible to fully appreciate the significance of the structural reorganization of the federal union that was brought about by the framing and adoption of the Constitution.

In *The Federalist*, Hamilton's coauthor of the series, James Madison, wrote what may well be the most astute observation on the nature of the constitutional reform of 1787 when he remarked that

> if the new Constitution be examined with accuracy and candour, it will be found that the change which it proposes, consists much less in the addition of NEW POWERS to the Union, than in the invigoration of its ORIGINAL POWERS. The regulation of commerce, it is true, is a new power; but that seems to be an addition which few oppose, and from which no apprehensions are entertained. The powers relating to war and peace, armies and fleets, treaties and finance, with the other more considerable powers, are all vested in the existing Congress by the articles of Confederation.

Properly speaking, the Constitution could not therefore be said to enlarge the powers of the national government, because "it only substitute[d] a more effectual mode of administering them."[5]

This chapter looks more closely at the Constitution as an organizational reform making possible "a more effectual mode of administering" the national government's powers. In large part a familiar story, the inflections and stress will nevertheless vary from the traditional rendition of the business of the Philadelphia convention. Organizational reform may sound dull and almost pedestrian. We are used to employing grander words to describe the achievements of the American founders. But what they did was of the utmost importance to the ability of the United States to shape its own destiny in a largely hostile world. It was only with the Constitution that the federal union acquired national cohesion and a central government with the capacity to act with determination and energy to defend and promote the national interest against other powers and peoples.

I

The United States willed itself into existence through the Declaration of Independence. Thomas Jefferson's bold statement not only justified the colonies' separation from the British Empire and signaled their claim to the status of "Free and Independent States" but also declared the intention of the "United Colonies" to enter into union. The Articles of Confederation, which followed rapidly on the Declaration, aimed to show the outside world that the thirteen new states stood united in their opposition to the former mother country and were now to all effects an independent nation in the international family of nations. The origins of the American "Confederate Republic" therefore lie in the need "to crush the pr[esent] & future foes of her Independence," as a contemporary congressional committee succinctly put it. Union and independence were intertwined goals from the very birth of the new nation. The same motion that called for a declaration of independence also moved that "a plan for confederation" should be prepared forthwith. In early July 1776 such a plan was presented to the Continental Congress, but the pressure of the War of Independence prevented immediate action. It was not until mid-November of the following year that the Continental Congress adopted "certain articles of Confederation and perpetual Union" tying the thirteen states "into a firm league of friendship with each other, for their common defence, the security of their Liberties, and their mutual and general welfare" and binding them "to assist each other, against all force offered to, or attacks made upon them, or any of them, on account of religion, sovereignty, trade, or any other pretence whatever." Because the Articles of Confederation were a compact of union between sovereign states, they could not take effect until ratified by all the state governments, a process not completed until March 1781.[6]

The importance of foreign relations and war making to the American union is evident in the language of the Articles of Confederation. In the Declaration of Independence, the state-republics had each claimed the "full Power to levy War, conclude Peace, contract Alliances, establish Commerce, and to do all other Acts and Things which Independent States may of right do." Articles VI and IX of the Articles of Confederation transferred the power of making war and peace, sending and receiving ambassadors, and entering into treaties and alliances from the state governments to "the united states in congress assembled." Congress was also invested with the power to arbitrate interstate conflicts among the members of the Union, to facilitate their commercial intercourse by determining the value of coins and fixing weights and measures, and to regulate member states' relations with American Indian nations. In effect the Articles established a division of labor between the states in their individual capacity and the states acting in their collective capacity "in congress assembled." In their former role, the states retained their internal police powers. In their latter role, the states dealt with foreign affairs, including war, and with relations between the member states. The Articles of Confederation did not establish a national government, however. Congress was not a legislature but a "plural executive" or a "deliberating executive assembly" made up by state delegations. It provided a forum in which the states could agree on common measures and coordinate their actions. But there were neither executive departments nor field agencies answering to Congress, nor was there a continental court structure. Under the Articles, the states served as the administrative agents of the Union.[7]

The distinction between internal and international affairs was well established in the late eighteenth century although there was no fixed nomenclature to designate these categories. John Locke distinguished between "executive" and "federative" power, where the latter referred to "the management of security and interest of the publick without, with all those that it may receive benefit and damages from" and included "the Power over War and Peace, Leagues and Alliances, and all the Transactions with all Persons and Communities without the Commonwealth." Montesquieu spoke of two forms of executive power, pertaining to "the things depending on civil rights" and to "the things depending on the rights of nations." By means of the latter, Montesquieu wrote, the magistrate "makes peace or war, sends or receives embassies, establishes security, and prevents invasions." A similar homegrown version of this distinction between different spheres of government action can be found in the so-called Essex Results, the response of the residents of Essex County to the Massachusetts Constitution of 1778, which explained that "the executive power is sometimes divided into the external executive, and internal executive. The former comprehends war, peace, the sending and receiving ambassadors, and whatever concerns the transactions of the state with any other independent states. The confederation of the United States of America hath lopped off this branch of the executive, and placed it in Congress."[8]

Not only was the external-internal distinction well known to the draftsmen of the American union; there was also widespread agreement that it was proper to invest "federative" or "external executive" powers in Congress. Radicals differed little from conservatives on this score. In his 1776 *Thoughts on Government*, John Adams said that Congress's "authority should sacredly be confined to these cases, namely war, trade, disputes between colony and colony, the post-office, and the unappropriated lands of the crown." Carter Braxton agreed that Congress should "have power to adjust disputes between colonies, regulate the affairs of trade, war, peace, alliances, &c. but they should by no means have authority to interfere with the internal police or domestic concerns of any Colony." Even an early states' rights ideologue such as Thomas Burke held that "the United States ought to be as One Sovereign with respect to foreign Powers, in all things that relate to War or where the States have one Common Interest." Placing these functions in Congress required no radical rethinking of American politics. The American revolutionaries maintained that this distribution of labor had always characterized the British Empire. Only with the acts of Parliament that began in the 1760s had the traditional order been undermined. All the Articles of Confederation did was put this institutional arrangement to paper. As one historian has written, the major duties of Congress—the creation and command of the army and navy, the establishment of diplomatic relations with foreign states, the printing of money, the issuing of requisitions on the states, and the management of the post office—all "belonged to the crown before 1774." In contrast, "Congress did not pass laws, levy taxes, or regulate trade—functions that Parliament had claimed within the empire." Under the Articles of Confederation, Congress assumed the powers not of Parliament but of the king and council.[9]

The former colonies' Articles of Confederation gave Congress the mandate to coordinate and manage the war against Britain. However, it soon became apparent that a structural flaw in the organization of the Union prevented Congress from doing so efficiently. In part the reason was the colonies' inexperience with international affairs. "Prior to the revolution," John Jay later remarked, international affairs "were managed *for* us and not *by* us." As he noted, "War and peace, alliances, and treaties, and commerce, and navigation, were conducted and regulated without our advice or control." But even more important than inexperience was the reluctance to invest a distant central government with powers that could not be checked by the states. After all, the Revolution was triggered by the perceived abuses of an imperial government beyond the control of the colonial legislatures. It would make little sense to erect a similar structure of government on

American soil. Taxation without representation played a large role in Parliament's abuse of power, and it was only natural that the revolutionaries would hesitate to centralize fiscal power. But this choice of institutional design led to constant difficulties as Congress proved unable to find the money it needed to pursue the war against Britain with efficiency and dispatch. Under the Articles of Confederation, Congress could declare and conduct war but not create or supply an army; it could borrow money but not provide for its repayment; it could enter into treaties with foreign powers but not prevent its own citizens from violating international agreements. On paper, Congress's powers were formidable. In reality, it was completely dependent on the cooperation of the states. The result was serious logistical and financial difficulties that hampered the war effort.[10]

When Congress began to organize the armed resistance to Britain, it resorted to a method of war finance that was already well established in the colonies: the printing of paper currency. On June 22, 1775, Congress resolved that "a sum not exceeding two millions of Spanish milled dollars be emitted by the Congress in bills of Credit, for the defence of America." Although Congress also issued and sold interest-bearing bonds, paper money would be the mainstay of the war effort throughout the early part of the conflict. When Congress stopped printing money in 1779, around $200 million had been emitted. Colonial governments had made use of fiat money when faced with extraordinary expenditures in the past. They typically made their paper money legal tender and levied extraordinary taxes payable in paper, thereby creating a demand for the notes that prevented their depreciation. During the French and Indian War, this method of "currency finance" had been employed on an unprecedented scale yet had proved largely successful. Against this background it was not unreasonable for Congress to resort to the same method to finance the War of Independence. But in contrast to the colonial governments during the French and Indian War, Congress had the authority only to print money, not to retrieve it. This division of power proved to be a recipe for disaster. More and more money was emitted, while hardly any was brought in in taxes. The prewar money stock in the colonies has been estimated at between $11 million and $30 million. When Congress emitted $200 million in paper currency, popularly called "Continentals," depreciation was inevitable. By late 1779, one well-placed critic said, "The Credit of this paper became so bad that the Cost of Manufacturing was nearly equal to the Value it wou'd circulate at." "It was ridiculous to behold," another observer later recalled, "how for instance a frying pan sold for three hundred of these dollars, which were supposed to equal Spanish piastres." In April 1780, $100 in paper money was worth only

$2.50 in specie, and soon afterward the Continentals passed out of circulation altogether.[11]

Because the states were unwilling to levy taxes, the Union's Treasury remained empty. Without income in specie, Congress could not pay interest on the bonds it had already issued and could find no takers for new emissions. Unable to emit more Continentals, Congress had to turn to extreme measures. The Continental army relied increasingly on expropriation to raise necessary services and supplies for the troops. Congress also transferred much of the responsibility for financing the war to the states. But the states were hardly in better financial shape than Congress, having also relied on paper currency rather than taxes to pay their expenses. By early 1780, state currencies had depreciated just as badly as the Continentals. Instead of paper money, the state governments turned to "military" or "depreciation" certificates to pay their contingents in the Continental army. These certificates were written promises of payment at a later date, and after the war they would make up the bulk of the states' debts. Congress also asked state governments to supply the army by answering drafts issued on state treasuries by the army. Again the states resorted to paper certificates for such payments.[12]

In addition to paper money, bonds, and certificates, a small but important income was also derived from foreign loans extended by Britain's enemies, who were not too particular about Congress's creditworthiness. These loans were instrumental because they enabled payment for supplies from abroad, where neither Continentals nor certificates were accepted as tender. Foreign loans also became important after Cornwallis's surrender at Yorktown and the cessation of hostilities. The new superintendent of finance, Robert Morris, was successful in financing the last stages of the war mostly with money borrowed in France and the Netherlands. But there is nothing to suggest that Morris would have been able to finance the war if military campaigns had resumed in earnest. Nor did he make any attempt to honor the enormous outstanding claims on the Confederation. When Britain recognized United States' independence in 1783, the new nation was in deep financial distress.[13]

On the surface it was a problem of money. But contemporaries had no difficulty discerning that the shortage of money arose from a structural flaw in the design of the American confederation. Although the Articles invested enough powers in Congress "to answer the ends of our union," the lexicographer and political commentator Noah Webster wrote in the mid-1780s, there was "no method of enforcing [Congress's] resolutions." In other words, the problem was not that the formal powers of Congress were insufficient but that the Union was organized in a manner that prevented Congress from exercising them. According to Article VIII of the Articles of Confederation, "All charges of war, and all other expences that shall be incurred for the common defence or general welfare, and allowed by the united states in congress assembled, shall be defrayed out of a common treasury." The same article also stated that the "taxes for paying that proportion shall be laid and levied by the authority and direction of the legislatures of the several states within the time agreed upon by the united states in congress assembled." There was therefore no question that the states were constitutionally bound to honor the requisitions and resolutions of Congress. Yet they did not. Critics of the Articles believed that the crux of the matter was the absence of a mechanism by which Congress could force states to comply with congressional demands. The confederation articles provided Congress with no sanction or means of coercion to employ against recalcitrant state governments. Instead, the Union rested on voluntary compliance. But the "idea of governing thirteen states and uniting their interests by mere resolves and recommendations, without any penalty annexed to a non-compliance," Webster remarked in no uncertain terms, "is a ridiculous farce, a burlesque on government, and a reproach to America."[14]

The lack of coercive power made it difficult for Congress to pursue the War of Independence efficiently. But after peace was concluded and formal recognition of independence secured, it grew even more difficult to ensure compliance with congressional decisions. By the mid-1780s, the United States faced a number of critical issues that arose out of the war with Britain and the separation from the British Empire: state governments refused to adhere to the terms of the peace treaty with Britain; Britain refused to give up military posts on US territory; public creditors went unpaid; Native Americans attacked European American settlers, and squatters occupied public lands; Spain closed the Mississippi to American commerce; Britain banned US vessels from trading with the West Indies; France refused to open its markets to American merchants; and the Mediterranean trade was brought to a standstill because of depredations by the Barbary powers. Congress had the formal responsibility to address these problems but lacked the practical power to do it effectively. The issues were of more than marginal significance. On the eve of the Revolution the standard of living of the European American population in the North American colonies was probably the highest in the world, and the inhabitants were habituated to economic growth. But the basis of their wealth was easy access to agricultural land and to foreign markets. Once liberated from the British Empire, the newly independent states could provide neither.[15]

Foreign observers sometimes doubted if the thirteen united states could even be considered a nation, at least in the context of international law. In 1778, France asked that the state governments ratify the treaties of alliance and of amity and commerce individually rather than as a union. With the Articles of Confederation not yet ratified, France could hardly have done otherwise. But after Britain had formally recognized the independence of the United States in 1783, its politicians also insisted that diplomatic agreements "must be made with the States separately," because "no treaty can be made with the American States that can be binding on the whole of them." International weakness fed into and exacerbated intraunion rivalries. In the face of congressional passivity, the states began to take individual action to defend and promote their interests. Georgia made war on and entered into treaties with the Creek Nation; Massachusetts raised and maintained troops to quell domestic disturbances; and Virginia and Maryland concluded a commercial agreement. Some states adopted commercial legislation that not only discriminated against foreign nationals but also against out-of-state citizens, thus creating a potential source of conflict. Emission of paper money and adoption of legal-tender laws were other sources of interstate and international conflict because they unilaterally altered contracts with foreigners and citizens of other states. When Congress did act, things did not always improve. The Jay-Gardoqui negotiations between the United States and Spain over the navigation of the Mississippi River gave rise to sectional discontent within and without Congress. Although the heated rhetoric of the time may have exaggerated the extent to which the 1780s were a "critical period," there is no question that the new American states confronted difficulties that were serious enough to call the future of their union into doubt. To nationalists like Alexander Hamilton it seemed that the United States had "reached almost the last stage of national humiliation. There is scarcely any thing that can wound the pride, or degrade the character of an independent nation, which we do not experience."[16]

The inadequacies of the Union were readily apparent both to members of Congress and to interested observers beyond. In one of the most comprehensive treatises on the problem of union from the early 1780s, the Philadelphia merchant and political economist Pelatiah Webster laid down as his "first and great principle" "that the constitution must vest powers in every department sufficient to secure and make effectual the ends of it."

> The supreme authority must have the power of making war and peace—of appointing armies and navies—of appointing officers both civil and military—of making contracts—of emitting, coining, and borrowing

money—of regulating trade and making treaties with foreign powers—of establishing post-offices—and in short of doing every thing which the well-being of the commonwealth may require, and which is not compatible to any particular state, all of which require money, and can't possibly be made effectual without it, they must therefore of necessity be invested with a power of taxation.

To ensure compliance with Congress's resolutions, Webster suggested that Congress should have the right to summon and convict any individual who in either a private or a public capacity disobeyed its authority. Should a state government resist by force any act or order of Congress, it would "be lawful for Congress to send into such state a sufficient force to suppress it."[17]

Written in the year of the Peace of Paris, Webster's strictures on the Articles of Confederation mirrored the reform movement within Congress. Even before Maryland had ratified the Articles, attempts to reform them had begun. They would continue right up to 1787, and the Constitutional Convention was but the last in a series of reform attempts. Invariably, these proposals focused in on four issues. The first concerned the organization of the federal union and called for a coercive mechanism to secure state compliance with congressional demands. The second concerned the need to organize the national domain in the trans-Appalachian west. The two remaining issues concerned the need to invest Congress with two additional powers: the right to regulate commerce and the right to collect taxes independently of the states. Increased fiscal powers of Congress and the coercion of state governments were closely related questions because the most serious and persistent state delinquency was the failure of state governments to comply with Congress's requisitions for money. With the exception of the management of the national domain in the West, there was little progress, however. Amendments addressing the other three issues faltered either because of insufficient support in Congress or because of the Articles' demand for unanimous approval of amendments.[18]

In the summer of 1783, two months before the signing of the peace treaty between the United States and Britain, a British Order in Council closed the British West Indies to American ships. In response Congress began to consider amending the Articles of Confederation to give Congress the right to regulate commerce. It seemed that strong countermeasures alone could give the United States "reciprocal advantages in trade." Inaction, in contrast, would lead to American commerce slowly expiring in the face of commercial discrimination by rival powers. But effective countermeasures required the coordination of thirteen disparate state policies into one common navigation act. An amendment giving Congress the right to prohibit foreign ships and merchants from trading in American ports was therefore adopted and sent to the states in the spring of 1784. It was never ratified, however, and the demand for the centralization of the power to regulate commerce was repeated in 1785 and 1786 in a more sweeping proposal to invest "the United States in Congress Assembled" with the power "of Regulating the trade of the States as well with foreign Nations as with each other and of laying such prohibitions, and such Imposts and duties upon imports, and exports, as may be Necessary for the purpose." On neither occasion did the proposal secure sufficient support in Congress.[19]

In contrast to commercial discrimination, which became an issue only after peace was secured, the problem of the Union's empty treasury and of state neglect of congressional demands had already begun in the midst of the War of Independence. As Pelatiah Webster's pamphlet suggested, the coercive mechanism needed to make states comply with congressional resolutions might have to take severe form. To address this issue Congress appointed a three-man committee, which included James Madison. The committee report dated March 1781 pulled no punches when suggesting

> that in case any one or more of the Confederated States shall refuse or neglect to abide by the determinations of the United States in Congress assembled or to observe all the Articles of the Confederation as required in the 13th Article, the said United States in Congress assembled are fully authorised to employ the force of the United States as well by sea as by land to compel such State or States to fulfill their federal engagements, and particularly to make distraint on any of the effects Vessels and Merchandizes of such State or States or of any of the Citizens thereof wherever found, and to prohibit and prevent their trade and intercourse as well with any other of the United States and the Citizens thereof, as with any foreign State, and as well by land as by sea, untill full compensation or compliance be obtained with respect to all Requisitions made by the United States in Congress assembled in pursuance of the Articles of Confederation.[20]

It was an extreme proposal that laid bare the inherent flaw of the requisitions system. Expropriating the property of individual citizens to compensate for the delinquencies of their governments was an exceptionally heavy-handed way of administering the nation's finances. It is hardly surprising that the proposal went nowhere. Nor is it surprising that later proposals to invest Congress with coercive power over the states took much milder forms.

The need to replenish the Confederation's Treasury was the principal reason for inserting a coercive mechanism in the Articles of Confederation. An alternative means to the same end was to bypass the states and the requisitions system altogether. If Congress were given the right to levy and collect taxes directly from the citizens, the finances of the Union could operate without the assistance of the states. This would be the method later favored by the Constitutional Convention in 1787. The ground for the convention's decision had been well prepared by a series of amendment proposals presented in Congress in the years leading up to the Philadelphia convention. In 1781, a committee charged with the preparation of "a plan for arranging the finances, paying the debts and economizing the revenue of the United States" advised that Congress be given the right to levy a 5 percent import duty and a 5 percent duty on lawful prizes captured by American privateers. The committee tied taxation directly to the nation's debt obligation by stating that "the monies arising from the said duties be appropriated to the discharge of the principal & interest of the debts already contracted or which may be contracted on the faith of the United States for supporting the present war." Eventually all states except Rhode Island ratified the amendment. Rhode Island remained adamant, and in December 1782 Virginia killed the proposal by rescinding its earlier ratification. The following spring another committee, which included both Hamilton and Madison, repeated the impost proposal as part of a more extensive tax package that also asked the states to contribute $1.5 million annually to Congress. Again the money would be reserved for payment of the Union's debt. To make the proposal more palatable to the state governments, this grant of power would run for only twenty-five years. The $1.5 million contribution proved unpopular, but this time both Rhode Island and Virginia accepted the proposal. The amendment now fell instead on New York's refusal to deliver up its lucrative customs income.[21]

After repeated failures to amend the Articles, the reform initiative finally passed from Congress to the states. In 1785, Virginia negotiated an agreement with Maryland over the navigation of Chesapeake Bay, and in the following year Virginia invited all states to meet in convention in Annapolis to consider the national regulation of commerce. Although the convention immediately adjourned because of insufficient attendance, it wrote a report to Congress that spoke of "important defects in the system of the Foederal Government" and of "national circumstances" serious enough "to render the situation of the United States delicate and critical." The Annapolis convention also recommended the calling of a second convention "to devise such further provisions as shall appear to them necessary to render the constitution of the Foederal Government adequate to the exigencies of the Union." After a brief debate Congress acceded to this request and called a convention "for the sole and express purpose of revising the Articles of Confederation." Under this mandate the Constitutional Convention assembled in May 1787.[22]

III

When the convention delegates gathered in Philadelphia, the ills of the Union had been debated for the better part of a decade. It was widely accepted that Congress had to acquire the right to regulate commerce and the right to bypass the state governments to raise revenue. The Constitution provided for these additional powers in what proved to be the less problematic part of the Philadelphia convention's work. The crux of the matter was not so much the need for additional powers as the fact that the "united states in congress assembled" could not exercise the powers it already possessed. Congress could only govern with the cooperation of the states and could not force their cooperation. In practical terms every state government therefore possessed a veto over national affairs. By means of a bold reorganization of the federal union, the Constitutional Convention replaced this system with a national government capable of acting directly on the American people without the assistance of the states. It was a contentious move, and the convention almost broke apart over the issue. The small states' delegations did not trust that the large states would respect their interests if given command of an independent national government. Only the famed Connecticut Compromise, which provided for the protection of the small states by giving them equal representation in the Senate, allowed the delegates to move forward with their reform of the federal union.[23]

As the leading mind of the reform movement, James Madison is the necessary starting point for any discussion of the Constitution. By the spring of 1787, Madison had concluded that the organizational structure of the federal union, which made Congress dependent on the voluntary compliance of the states, was the fundamental problem facing the American nation. In this he was far from alone. But Madison had thought further and harder than others about how to fix the problem. Commentators such as Noah and Pelatiah Webster saw the need for a coercive mechanism in the Union but had only begun to grasp the need for a separate federal administrative structure.

Madison, in contrast, had come to see that the federal government had to be designed so that it could "operate without the intervention of the states." The key to an efficient national government was to keep the states out of the administration of government at the national level and allow Congress to legislate directly on individuals. The national government also needed administrative agencies and a court structure to implement its decisions. Such a drastic change in the operation of government required that the equal representation of states in Congress be replaced by the proportional representation of the citizens. If the federal government would act independently of the states and directly on individuals, the people rather than the states should elect the new government. Finally, to counteract state legislation threatening the common good of the Union, the federal government had to have the power to veto state laws. All of these points made their way into the so-called Virginia Plan, which opened and set the agenda for the Constitutional Convention. The acceptance of its fifteen resolutions was arguably the most important decision of the convention. By this act, the delegates pledged themselves to transform the national government from a congress of member states to a tripartite government "consisting of a *supreme* Legislative, Executive & Judiciary."[24]

Madison devoted much effort to detailing the reorganization of the Union but was reticent about the specific powers that his new national government would wield. It would possess all the "federal powers" of the old—that much was clear—together with "positive and compleat authority in all cases which require uniformity, such as the regulation of trade, including the right to tax both exports & imports, the fixing the term and forms of naturalization &c. &c." The Virginia Plan bore the mark of its maker in this respect. It, too, concentrated on the reorganization of the federal union and said only that the national legislature "ought to be impowered to enjoy the Legislative Rights vested in Congress by the Confederation" along with an undefined grant "to legislate in all cases to which the separate States are incompetent, or in which the harmony of the United States may be interrupted by the exercise of individual Legislation." This silence has sometimes been interpreted to mean that the Virginia delegation was set on creating an unlimited national government. But Edmund Randolph, who as governor of Virginia introduced the plan, denied any intention to invest the government with "indefinite powers" and declared that "he was entirely opposed to such an inroad on the State jurisdictions." And Madison later argued that an enumeration of powers was in fact always "meant to be inserted in . . . the text of the Constitution." "If there could be any doubt that this was intended and so understood by the convention," he noted, "it would be removed by the course of the proceedings."²⁵

As Madison observed, the convention did eventually work out a list of the powers of the new national government. There is in fact nothing to suggest that a majority of delegates ever contemplated anything but a national government limited to its traditional concerns with foreign affairs and intraunion matters. The Virginia resolutions opened by stating that the "articles of Confederation ought to be so corrected & enlarged as to accomplish the objects proposed by their institution; namely, 'common defence, security of liberty and general welfare.'" In his accompanying speech, Randolph expanded on this recommendation. He spoke of the "defects of the confederation" pointing to the familiar financial and commercial difficulties that had plagued the Union over the last decade. The most pressing matters confronting the Confederation were the "inefficiency" of requisitions, "commercial discord" between the states, the urgency of the foreign debt, the violation of international treaties, and the recent tax revolt in Massachusetts associated with Daniel Shays. To address them it was necessary to set up a national government able to "secure 1. against foreign invasion: 2. against dissentions between the members of the Union, or sedition in particular states: 3. to p[ro]cure to the several States various blessings, of which an isolated situation was i[n]capable: 4. to be able to defend itself against incroachment: & 5. to be paramount to the state constitutions." Although the third item has an expansive ring to it, Randolph had quite specific blessings in mind, such as "a productive impost," "counteraction of the commercial regulations of other nations," and the ability to increase American commerce "ad libitum."²⁶

The Virginia Plan generated strong resistance from the so-called small-state delegates in the convention, but the propriety of the remit of the national government outlined by Randolph was not questioned. Roger Sherman, who was an outspoken critic of the Virginia resolutions, acknowledged that "the Confederation had not given sufficient power to Congs. and that additional powers were necessary; particularly that of raising money which he said would involve many other powers." A few days later he defined "the objects of the Union" in a manner quite similar to Randolph as "1. defence agst. foreign danger. 2. agst. internal disputes & a resort to force. 3. Treaties with foreign nations 4 regulating foreign commerce, & drawing revenue from it." It was these and "perhaps a few lesser objects alone" that "rendered a Confederation of the States necessary." The New Jersey Plan, finally, which was developed as the small states' counterproposal to the

Virginia resolutions, also focused on commerce and revenue as the critical issues that had to be addressed by the convention. Like the Virginia Plan it stipulated that the national legislature would posses "the powers vested in the U. States in Congress, by the present existing articles of Confederation." In addition to these inherited powers, it would also be given the right to levy import duties and a stamp tax and to regulate commerce with foreign powers and between the members of the Union, but it would not have the broad right to legislate on questions where the states were "incompetent."[27]

The Philadelphia convention saw only one early attempt to list the proper powers of the national government. Introduced by Charles Pinckney of South Carolina, the Pinckney Plan was largely ignored by the other delegates but later came to be used by the Committee of Detail in its draft constitution. By way of this draft much of Pinckney's enumeration of powers would eventually make its way into the finished Constitution. The South Carolinian's proposal further demonstrates how the convention worked with a rather conventional conception of the proper distribution of powers between the states and the national government. The Pinckney Plan repeated the battery of powers already wielded by Congress under the Articles of Confederation but added the right to levy taxes, including duties on exports and imports, and to regulate interstate and international trade.[28]

Any disagreement over the exact powers of the national government was kept in the background during the first half of the convention as delegates battled over the principle of representation. The story of the compromise that critics forced on the proponents of the Virginia Plan is well known and need not be repeated here. Of greater importance to the development of the national government's fiscal capacity was the solution to the problem of state delinquency that the delegates worked out in the shadow of their better-known conflict over representation. The Virginia Plan offered no less than three institutional solutions to this problem. The first was the creation of a separate national government that could act directly on the people without assistance of the states. If the states were simply left out of the implementation of the Union's decisions, there would be no need to coerce them. For this reason the Virginia Plan called for a national government that could both legislate and implement its legislation. This government had to possess executive and judiciary branches because a government "without a proper Executive & Judiciary," Madison said in a telling simile, "would be a mere trunk of a body without arms or legs to act or move." The proposal to establish a national government capable of acting independently of the states ran headlong into the problem of representation. How would the national government be constructed for the states to trust it with power to operate beyond their control? Here small states and large states reached different answers. Later the North and the South would clash over the same issue. Nevertheless, this was the mechanism that would eventually be adopted by the convention to overcome the problem of state delinquency.[29]

The Virginia delegation's other two proposals fared less well even though they did not raise the specter of representation. The sixth resolution proposed to invest the national legislature with the right "to negative all laws passed by the several States, contravening . . . the articles of Union." In Madison's mind this veto power would shield the Union from selfish and short-sighted state legislation. Without it, "every positive power that can be given on paper" to the national government "will be evaded & defeated" by the states. "The States will continue to invade the national jurisdiction, to violate treaties and the law of nations & to harass each other with rival and spiteful measures dictated by mistaken views of interest." The negative proposed by the Virginia Plan was actually a diluted version of Madison's original call for "a negative in *all cases whatsoever*," which his fellow Virginians presumably found too great an interference with state rights. Madison's later attempts to introduce this broader power were also unsuccessful. Although the convention at first accepted the resolution, this milder veto was eventually also rejected. Delegates believed that the negative would be both unpopular and impractical. "Are all laws whatever to be brought up" to the national legislature, Mason asked on one occasion. "Is no road nor bridge to be established without the Sanction of the General Legislature? Is this to sit constantly in order to receive & revise the State laws?"[30]

The convention delegates could reject the idea of the veto because they had begun to flesh out their concept of parallel structures of state and national governments. If the national government could act without the involvement of the state governments, the problem of their inaction, such as the noncompliance with congressional requisitions, would disappear. Positive state actions contrary to the interest of the Union would remain a problem, however. Had the convention aimed to set up a national government that would actively regulate the internal affairs of the states, this would have been a real concern. But Madison was one of the few delegates who had such an expansive government in mind. The majority of the delegates did not, and they preferred to trust to the judiciary to invalidate unconstitutional state laws. "A law that ought to be negatived will be set aside in the Judiciary departmt.," Gouverneur Morris said, "and if that security should fail; may be repealed by a Nationl. law." Sherman added that the veto involved "a wrong principle, to wit, that a law of a State contrary to the articles of the Union, would if not negatived, be valid & operative."[31]

In the finished Constitution the problem of unconstitutional state legislation was solved by the "supremacy clause," according to which the Constitution itself and all laws and treaties made under it became "the supreme Law of the Land," which "the Judges in every State" were bound to uphold. The right to appeal from state courts to the Supreme Court was implicit in the third article of the Constitution and made explicit in the 1789 Judiciary Act. The convention also wrote into the Constitution prohibitions against certain state laws that had appeared especially troubling to the delegates, including the printing of paper money and the infringement of contracts. With such safeguards Madison's veto became redundant.[32]

The third and final mechanism for making states adhere to congressional resolutions was military force. According to the Virginia Plan, the new national legislature would have the right "to call forth the force of the Union agst. any member of the Union failing to fulfill its duty under the articles thereof." It was not a new idea. The amendment proposal Madison had helped write in 1781 and the recommendations Pelatiah Webster had published in 1783 asked for the same thing. No sooner had the Virginia delegation presented its resolutions than its members began to have second thoughts, however. They came to realize that a separate national government acting directly on individual citizens would not need the assistance of the states and hence would have no need to coerce them. The very next day after Randolph had read the resolutions, Mason observed that "punishment could not [in the nature of things be executed on] the States collectively, and therefore that such a Govt. was necessary as could directly operate on individuals, and would punish those only whose guilt required it." Madison had reached the same conclusion. The "more he reflected on the use of force," he said, "the more he doubted the practicability, the justice and the efficacy of it when applied to people collectively and not individually." Using force against a member state "would look more like a declaration of war, than an infliction of punishment, and would probably be considered by the party attacked as a dissolution of all previous compacts by which it might be bound." Although the finished Constitution did give Congress the right to call out the militia "to execute the Laws of the Union," the convention's deliberations made clear that the new national government would not rest on such draconic means to administer its laws.[33]

Coercion was closely linked to revenue because it was the breakdown of the requisitions system that had provided much of the impetus for constitutional reform. The Virginia Plan had not mentioned taxation, but the New Jersey Plan did. It stipulated that beyond import duties and a stamp tax, the national government would have to continue to resort to requisitions to raise money. Obviously, this put the spotlight on the problem of state delinquency. William Paterson and the other draftsmen of the plan were well aware of the problem and provided for the right of the national government to collect taxes in states that failed to comply with requisitions. But the supporters of the Virginia Plan were not impressed. They had now embraced the concept of separate governments and had no patience with requisitions or state involvement in the national revenue system. "There are but two modes, by which the end of a Genl. Govt. can be attained," Randolph remarked. The first was coercion of states; the second was legislation for individuals. "Coercion he pronounced to be *impracticable, expensive, cruel to individuals*. . . . We must resort therefore to a national *Legislation over individuals*." Mason questioned the practicality of the New Jersey Plan. "Will the militia march from one State to another, in order to collect the arrears of taxes from the delinquent members of the Republic?" he asked. As Madison had done, Mason also pointed out that such a "mixture of civil liberty and military execution" was incompatible with a republican system of government resting on the consent of the governed. "To punish the nonpayment of taxes with death, was a severity not yet adopted by despotism itself: yet this unexampled cruelty would be mercy compared to a military collection of revenue, in which the bayonet could make no discrimination between the innocent and the guilty."[34]

In the course of its proceedings the convention therefore took a decisive stance against requisitions in favor of a broad grant of fiscal power to the national government. This centralization of fiscal power provided the foundations on which the First Congress would erect the national revenue administration. Requisitions, Hamilton plainly said, "can not be relied on." Gouverneur Morris even called them "subversive of the idea of Govt." Other delegates agreed. When Sherman tried to prevent the new Congress from levying direct taxes, he was voted down by eight states to two. And when Luther Martin reintroduced the idea that federal direct taxes would only be levied if requisitions on the states had first failed, there was even less support. Only one state voted in favor, with another divided. Madison noted that "there was no debate." In the draft constitution drawn up by the Committee of Detail, "the power to lay and collect taxes, duties, imposts, and excises" was placed first among the powers of the new national government. Both the wording and the elevated position of the tax power would remain in ensuing drafts and in the finished Constitution.[35]

IV

The Constitutional Convention began to address the powers of the new national government in earnest only after the Committee of Detail had made its report on August 6. Debate over taxation started in the broad grant found in Article VII of the Committee of Detail's draft constitution. In the fourth section of the article the government's fiscal power was restricted in ways designed to protect particular interests of the southern states, which were ultimately rooted in their slave economies. Although Congress's power to tax remained broad, these sectional restrictions formed the constitutional parameters within which the national fiscal regime had to operate. Expressing a southern agenda, the article was only marginally altered by the opposition of other delegates. Together with the right to tax, the Committee of Detail's constitution also gave Congress the right to "borrow money, and emit bills on the credit of the United States." The convention would modify this right by striking out the right to emit bills of credit, the effect of a strong aversion among the delegates to paper money as a method of financing extraordinary expenditures. Despite the importance of public credit to modern statecraft, delegates expressed little interest in its future use in facilitating war or territorial expansion. Instead their overwhelming concern was with the need to begin payment on the public debt inherited from the War of Independence.[36]

The sectionalism evident in the discussion of the fiscal clause reveals how the delegates saw the American union as a means to promote the interests of their respective constituencies rather than an imagined American nation. Because of its composition the Committee of Detail had been under the spell of southern influence. Its report proscribed Congress from taxing exports and from taxing, or otherwise interfering with, the slave trade. It also stipulated that Congress could only pass commercial legislation with the support of two-thirds of the members of both houses. Despite the fact that commercial regulation had been a primary reason for the calling of the convention, southerners now feared that a northern-dominated national council would betray their interests. The question of trade was deeply entwined with that of taxation because commercial regulation often took the form of prohibitive taxes on imports and exports rather than outright bans on foreign ships and goods.[37]

As staple producers, the southern states had an interest in free trade and cheap transportation. It was "the true interest of the S. States to have no regulation of commerce," as Charles Cotesworth Pinckney noted. Northern and middle states, in contrast, had extensive shipping interests that were threatened by international competition. Shipping was "the worst & most precarious kind of property. and stood in need of public patronage." Normally, this inherent conflict between North and South was defused by pointing to a sectional trade-off. The South and its slave economy could only be safe from external attack and slave insurrection with support from the naval and military capacity of the North. "A navy was essential to security, particularly to the S. States, and can only be had by a navigation act encouraging american bottoms [i.e., ships] & seamen," said Gouverneur Morris. It was a sign of the sectional tensions appearing in the convention that southern delegates now denied the truth of such assertions. "It had been said the Southern States had most need of naval protection," Maryland's John Mercer said. "The reverse was the case. Were it not for promoting the carrying trade of the North[er]n States, the South[er]n States could let their trade go into foreign bottoms, where it would not need our protection." Hugh Williamson of North Carolina feared no foreign invasion of the South, as "the sickliness of their climate for invaders would prevent their being made an object."[38]

When Article VII came up for debate, delegates from the middle states tried to roll back some of the South's gains. They were only partially successful. The taxing of exports seemed to these delegates both proper and necessary. Morris argued that a tax on the export of lumber, livestock, and flour would put pressure on Britain to open the West Indies to American trade because the islands could not survive without such imports. It was also "a necessary source of revenue." A coalition of southerners and New Englanders refused to budge, however. Because the "produce of different States is such as to prevent uniformity in such taxes," a duty on exports would be unjust and would therefore "engender incurable jealousies." The proscription against national export taxes was upheld by a vote of seven states to three, with only the small states of New Hampshire, New Jersey, and Delaware opposed to the measure.[39]

Luther Martin of Maryland next proposed to do away with the ban on interference with the slave trade. As could be expected, this was not well received by the delegations from the Lower South, whose constituents were dependent on the importation of enslaved Africans. The preservation of the slave trade was declared a sine qua non for the Carolinas and Georgia. Charles Pinckney made clear that "South Carolina can never receive the plan if it prohibits the slave trade." After several days of animated discussion Morris moved that the clause on the slave trade and the ban on export taxes be referred to a committee along with the demand for a two-thirds majority for all navigation acts. "These things may form a bargain among the Northern & Southern States," he suggested. Just before the vote on Morris's motion was taken, Massachusetts's Nathaniel Gorham reminded the southern delegates that "the Eastern States had no motive to Union but a commercial one. They were able to protect themselves. They were not afraid of external danger, and did not need the aid of the Southn. States."[40]

Morris was right. Within two days the committee came back with a watered-down version of Article VII. Congress would be permitted to legislate on the slave trade after the year 1800 and would be allowed to tax the importation of slaves. The sixth section, stating that "No navigation act shall be passed without the assent of two-thirds of the members present in each House" was struck out. The ban on export duties was left to stand. In the ensuing debate the protection of the slave trade was extended to 1808 and the import duty on slaves set to a maximum of ten dollars per imported slave. Some southern delegates made an effort to retain the qualified majority necessary to pass commercial legislation, but by now their compatriots were in a mellow mood. Charles Cotesworth Pinckney pointed to the northerners' "liberal conduct" on the slave question as sufficient cause to leave "the power of making commercial regulations" unfettered. Northern delegates meanwhile stressed that they could not agree to the Constitution unless they were "enabled to defend themselves against foreign regulations." "If the Government is to be so fettered as to be unable to relieve the Eastern States what motive can they have to join in it, and thereby tie their own hands from measures which they could otherwise take for themselves?" Nathaniel Gorham asked. The decision to strike out the demand for a qualified majority was accepted without a dissenting voice.[41]

The South had thus successfully blocked the right of the national government to tax exports. This constituted an important restriction to the fiscal system that could be introduced in the United States. The South also influenced the shape of future fiscal institutions in a more subtle way by linking direct taxes to representation. The origin of this link lies in the Virginia Plan, which suggested that representation be calculated either according to "the Quotas of contribution" or to "the number of free inhabitants." "Quotas of contribution" was a reference to the manner of apportioning expenditures between the states under the Articles of Confederation. In 1783 a committee had proposed that contributions no longer be based on wealth, which had been stipulated in the Articles, but on population. Under the new system, contributions would be "in proportion to the whole number of white and other free citizens and inhabitants, of every age, sex and condition, including those bound to servitude for a term of years, and three fifths of all other persons not comprehended in the foregoing description, except Indians, not paying taxes."⁴²

Through a long and tortuous process in which the delegates tried to accommodate southern interests without making use of the nefarious term slavery, the convention finally adopted the three-fifths rule for apportioning both representatives in the lower house and direct taxes. At first sight it may seem as if the South's disproportionate influence in the House of Representatives was a compensation for its willingness to foot the bill for the new government. As Morris, James Wilson, and other northerners knew, however, nothing could be further from the truth. No one expected the new government to introduce a program of direct taxation. The nation's primarily agricultural economy and the great diversity between its regions, along with a political culture saturated with antietatism and states' rights sentiment, made such a program utterly unlikely. It was "idle to suppose," said Morris, "that the Genl Govt. can stretch its hand directly into the pockets of the people scattered over so vast a Country. They can only do it through the medium of exports imports & excises." "For a long time the people of America will not have money to pay direct taxes. Seize and sell their effects and you push them into Revolts," he further noted. And of course direct taxes were made even less likely by the fact that the South, which now possessed a disproportionate influence over the formulation of the government's fiscal policy, would prefer duties on imports over taxes on wealth.⁴³

In contrast to the fiscal clauses of the Constitution, the question of the public debt did not align the delegates according to section. Southerners would later claim that they had been shortchanged by the federal assumption of state debts, but their representatives in the Constitutional Convention seemed unaware of the danger. Compared to the power to tax, the power to borrow was a relatively minor issue, and the delegates focused overwhelmingly on the existing debt rather than on future exigencies. Nevertheless, their decisions did place certain limits on the actions open to the national government, and their debate also signaled the expectation that a settlement of the Revolutionary debt would be high on the agenda of the new Congress.

The convention prevented future recourse to "currency finance" methods by striking out Congress's right to "emit bills on the credit of the U. States." There was some disagreement over the issue. Some delegates bravely declared themselves to be friends to paper money, but most found a constitutional right to print paper currency "as alarming as the mark of the Beast in Revelations." The vote nevertheless suggests that the matter was relatively uncontroversial. Nine states favored striking out the right, with only New Jersey and Maryland in opposition.[44]

The second important action was the guarantee that "all Debts contracted and Engagements entered into, before the Adoption of this Constitution, shall be as valid against the United States under this Constitution, as under the Confederation." This clause began life as a much stronger promise to pay off public creditors, including state creditors. When first introduced, this guarantee was placed in the enumeration of the powers of Congress and at one point made part of the opening tax clause. Again there was some disagreement among the delegates. Pierce Butler called public creditors "Blood-suckers who had speculated on the distresses of others," thus presaging the opposition to funding and assumption in the First Congress. Others rallied to the creditors support. In making the case for the assumption of state debts, John Langdon presented an argument that would later be heard in congressional debates. Assumption would be a just measure, he said, because the debt was contracted for the common cause. It would be a necessary measure because the Constitution would deprive the state governments of the income from import duties, their most important source of specie revenue. Finally, it would be a politic measure because the people would support the new government if it would relieve them from the heavy taxes needed to service the state debts.[45]

Those who wished to write into the Constitution a clause declaring that Congress "*shall* discharge the debts & fulfil the engagements [of the U. States]" argued that it would secure support for the reform of the Union. Rufus King pointed out that an explicit commitment to pay all creditors would win over the state creditors to the new Constitution. This group was "an active and formidable party" that "would otherwise be opposed to a plan which transferred to the Union the best resources of the States without transferring the State debts at the same time. The State Creditors had generally been the strongest foes to the impost-plan." Others countered that "shall" was too strong a word. The new government might not have the means to pay off the debt. The promise would also encourage speculation. In the end, Edmund Randolph suggested that the obligation to pay the debt be replaced with a general guarantee that "all debts contracted & engagements entered into, by or under the authority of Congs. shall be as valid agst the U. States under this constitution as under the Confederation." His motion was accepted by a vote of ten states to one and would become part of Article VI of the Constitution. Clearly a much weaker guarantee to the nation's creditors than a constitutional obligation to pay the nation's debts, the action was still not without consequence. It meant that default, the most drastic solution to the problem of the public debt, would not be open to Congress.⁴⁶

V

When the convention was about to wrap up its business in the second week of September, it appointed a Committee of Style and Arrangement to compose the finished Constitution. To this committee also fell the task to write a covering letter that would accompany the transmission of the Constitution to Congress, then sitting in New York. It was a brief letter, and like the Constitution it was drafted by Gouverneur Morris. The letter opened by declaring that "the friends of our country have long seen and desired, that the power of making war, peace and treaties, that of levying money and regulating commerce, and the correspondent executive and judicial authorities should be fully and effectually vested in the general government." It was a remarkably clear and concise statement of the rationale behind and outcome of the convention. Morris next went on to explain the complexity of the new tripartite government by pointing to "the impropriety of delegating such extensive trust to one body of men."

In the following paragraph, Morris argued that the states had to give up part of their sovereignty "for the interest and safety of all." In a thinly disguised reference to the protection of slavery and other state interests, he noted that the "difference among the several States as to their situation, extent, habits, and particular interests" had made it difficult for the convention to decide precisely which powers the states had to surrender to the national government. Only concern for the preservation of the Union, "in which is involved our prosperity, felicity, safety, perhaps our national existence," allowed the convention to overcome sectional conflicts of interest. The Constitution was thus the product of "a spirit of amity, and of that mutual deference and concession which the peculiarity of our political situation rendered indispensible." Morris ended by urging the state delegations in Congress to receive the document in the same spirit that it was produced.⁴⁷

Outside the convention, the Constitution met with enormous interest. Critical voices feared for the future of the states and their particular interests. They also feared that the national government would be so powerful and so far removed from the people that popular control would be impossible. True to the idiom of the dominant Country Whig rhetoric, the opponents of the Constitution believed that the reform would introduce a monarchy or an aristocracy that would gradually undermine the liberty of the people and degrade them to the status of the struggling masses of the Old World. This doomsday vision contrasted sharply with the upbeat prognostications of the Constitution's supporters, who took the name "Federalists." They typically focused on the new national government as a means to address the problems facing the American union, and they saw the Constitution as the herald of a better and brighter future. The petition from the inhabitants of Cumberland County to the Pennsylvania ratifying convention is a typical specimen of the genre. The "new federal government" carried the promise of "restoring system, firmness and energy, to the present embarrassed and relaxed Union," it said. Stronger government offered tangible benefits. It held out the prospect "of reviving our declining commerce, of supporting our tottering credit, of relieving us from the pressure of an unequal and inefficacious taxation, of giving us concord at home, and rendering us great and respectable in the eye of the world."[48]

As the Cumberland County petition suggests, the issues confronting the American nation did not change with the adoption of the Constitution. What changed was the ability of the government to address them. But before this could happen, the new compact of union had first to be adopted. This required a drawn-out process stretching over almost a year as the states, one by one, responded to the proposal of the Philadelphia convention. All states except Rhode Island called ratifying conventions, and eventually all conventions except North Carolina's voted in favor of the Constitution. In ratification conventions and in print discourse, the document was carefully scrutinized, and taxation and the public debt were issues of much concern. Opponents of the Constitution warned that heavy taxes and further indebtedness would follow from adoption. For the most part, the supporters concentrated on denying these allegations and warning about the consequences to the people of continuing under the Articles of Confederation. On occasion, however, more substantive comments were made.[49]

It is hardly surprising that the most substantive treatment of public finance was made in the pages of *The Federalist* the most extensive work written in support of the Constitution, or that it was authored by Alexander Hamilton, who had spent several years wrangling with questions of political power and public finance. A full seven essays, numbers 30 to 36, were devoted to taxation, and there were scattered remarks about fiscal and financial matters throughout the work. Much like the rest of the Constitution's supporters, the authors of *The Federalist* defended the Constitution from specific allegations of its critics. It is therefore much less of a timeless treatise on American government than readers have sometimes supposed. Yet there is enough material in the work to make possible the construction of something like a positive statement on the place of taxation and public debts in late eighteenth-century American statecraft. Compared both to the recent discussion in the Constitutional Convention and to the measures that Hamilton would soon engineer as secretary of the Treasury, *The Federalist*'s treatment of the nation's public finances displays some noticeable gaps. There was no hint about federal assumption of state debts beyond the opaque remark that these debts would soon be discharged, a statement that could mean either that the debts would be assumed by the Union or that they would be paid off by the states. Nor did Hamilton address the compromise over slavery, although James Madison defended it in essay 54.[50]

The most striking premise of Hamilton's discussion in *The Federalist* was his conviction that wars would be a recurrent feature in the national existence of the United States and that it fell to the citizens and their leaders to prepare for such exigencies. Mostly, wars would arise from external aggression. With uncanny prescience he warned about storm clouds gathering over Europe, whose fury might in part be "spent upon us." But they would also come from the nation's own ambitions. If the United States meant to continue as "a commercial people, it must form part of our policy, to be able one day to defend that commerce." This meant building a navy and engaging in naval wars. As Hamilton knew well, navies and naval wars were prohibitively expensive. All over Europe, the cost of armies, fleets, and war debts dominated state budgets. Britain's "ostentatious apparatus of Monarchy" accounted for no more than a fifteenth of the government's expenses, and "the other fourteen fifteenths are absorbed in the payment of the interest of debts, contracted for carrying on the wars in which that country has been engaged, and in the maintenance of fleets and armies." To Hamilton, war was by far the most important reason why the government had to possess adequate fiscal powers. Although he had no reason to present a detailed plan to deal with financial aspects of future contingencies, Hamilton made clear that public credit would be instrumental. "In the modern system of war," he said, "nations the most wealthy are obliged to have recourse to large loans." Taxes were a necessary foundation of credit because the "power of creating new funds upon new objects of taxation by its own authority, would enable the national government to borrow, as far as its necessities might require."[51]

The cost of war also explains why the national government had to possess "illimitable" fiscal powers. Again and again Hamilton returned to the basic maxim that a government's means had to be commensurate to its ends. There was no way of knowing how much money the government might need in a future war, and therefore "the exigencies of the Union could be susceptible of no limits, even in imagination." The most forceful statement of this logic is found in essay 31. Hamilton's starting point was the familiar idea that a "government ought to contain in itself every power requisite to the full accomplishment of the objects committed to its care." The Articles of Confederation gave to the national government the duty to protect the nation from external aggression and the public peace from domestic violence. This duty involved expenditures "to which no possible limits can be assigned," and therefore the ability to meet them "ought to know no other bounds than the exigencies of the nation and the resources of the community." Because revenue was "the essential engine" that would allow the government to respond to the exigencies of the nation, its power over taxation had to be without limits. Consequently a change in the organization of the federal union was necessary. Since both theory and practice demonstrated that "the power of procuring revenue is unavailing, when exercised over the States in their collective capacities, the Federal government must of necessity be invested with an unqualified power of taxation in the ordinary modes."[52]

An important part of Hamilton's defense of the Constitution's fiscal clause therefore rested on the inefficiency of the requisitions system. Requisitions were an *"ignis fatuus* in finance," a will-o'-the-wisp without substance or reality, which had offered "ample cause, both of mortification to ourselves, and of triumph to our enemies." It was a serious matter because a government without revenue was defenseless. "Destitute of this essential support, it must resign its independence and sink into the degraded condition of a province" governed by a foreign power. The problem was a structural one, and the solution therefore had to be structural too. Here Hamilton repeated the insights from Madison's preconvention writings, the Virginia Plan, and the debate in the Constitutional Convention. "The great and radical vice in the construction of the existing Confederation is in the principle of LEGISLATION for STATES or GOVERNMENTS, in their CORPORATE or COLLECTIVE CAPACITIES and as contradistinguished from the INDIVIDUALS of whom they consist." This vice could only be overcome by investing the national government with an unqualified power over taxation.[53]

Although Hamilton was insistent that the government possess unfettered fiscal powers, apart from the restrictions incorporated into the Constitution, he was also concerned to paint the new compact of union in the best possible light. If part of his message was a warning against the dangers of a weak union, the other part held out the hope for better times. Despite the creation of a more efficient and more active central government, the new system promised to reduce the tax burden on the people. Hamilton's promise made sense against eighteenth-century ideas of taxation and political economy. At the time, it was common to distinguish between direct and indirect taxes. The former fell on property, chiefly land, and persons, so-called poll or capitation taxes. The latter were duties on trade and were normally divided into internal duties, or excises, on the production, retail sale, and possession of goods on the one hand, and external duties on exports, imports, and tonnage on the other hand. In the postwar period, the state governments had relied mostly on direct property taxes. It had not been a happy experience, as Hamilton and his readers knew well. As Hamilton noted, "Tax laws have in vain been multiplied—new methods to enforce the collection have in vain been tried—the public expectation has been uniformly disappointed, and the treasuries of the States have remained empty." On the basis of this experience it seemed reasonable to conclude that direct taxes could never produce much revenue in the United States. But excise duties were no real alternative. Their administration required inspections and assessments of the citizens' property that were highly unpopular. This left the government with duties on imports and tonnage as the most acceptable forms of taxation.[54]

Adoption of the Constitution did not promise to reduce the total amount of taxes paid. As Hamilton put it, the "quantity of taxes to be paid by the community" would be the same whether or not the plan were adopted. But adoption nonetheless offered the possibility to shift the burden of taxation from land to trade, thereby easing the pressure on the taxpayers. There were several reasons why a national government would be able to make more money from trade duties than the state governments. To begin with, a more energetic government would adopt commercial legislation that would benefit trade. By increasing the volume of trade, the potential tax base would also increase. Second, the administration of the revenue would be more efficient if centralized in the national government. This was partly because a national customs service would use fewer officers than the combined services of thirteen states. Partly the reason was that the national service would not need to bother with smuggling across state borders. But more important than either of these reasons was the ability to increase the level of import duties, something that interstate competition would prevent under the old system. Hamilton estimated the average rate in the states at 3 percent. France, in contrast, taxed imports on average 15 percent and Britain even more. Without question American import duties could be trebled.[55]

To Hamilton's mind the key to a functioning fiscal system was to minimize friction. A smooth-running revenue service employed methods of taxation that were considered legitimate by the taxpayers and therefore gave rise to no opposition. "It might be demonstrated," Hamilton said at one point, "that the most productive system of finance will always be the least burthensome." Duties on trade constituted such a system as long as they avoided taxing basic consumer items, so-called necessaries. The citizen-taxpayers could then chose either to consume an item and pay the duty levied on it or abstain from consumption and not pay the tax. In other words, there was a voluntary element to such tax administration, which accorded well with republican ideas of rule by consent. By targeting luxury items, the tax could also be made to fall on those who could best afford to pay. The ideal system of taxation was therefore one that rested lightly on the citizens and in particular the members of the community with the least ability to contribute to the common good. "Happy it is when the interest which the government has in the preservation of its own power, coincides with a proper distribution of the public burthen, and tends to guard the least wealthy part of the community from oppression!" Hamilton asserted.[56]

VI

The Constitution invested Congress with a relatively broad power to "lay and collect Taxes, Duties, Imposts, and Excises." But some limitations existed. Exports could not be taxed, and direct taxes had to be apportioned according to population without any concern for the distribution of wealth. This meant that poor states would pay more than rich ones relative to their resources. These limitations affected the structure of the federal fiscal regime. But they are also important because they reveal the extent to which the federal union and national politics were shaped by considerations of state interests. Delegates to the Constitutional Convention acted as representatives of their constituents rather than of a unitary American people. In the First Congress, senators and representatives would continue to perceive their roles in such terms. The idea that the Union was foremost a means to provide for the safety and interests of the member states would affect the nature of national politics, perhaps nowhere more so than in the sphere of fiscal legislation.

Occasional remarks in the Constitutional Convention and the more systematic treatment in Alexander Hamilton's *Federalist* essays show how the people in power intended to tread carefully to avoid sectional clashes over taxation. Political controversy could be avoided by relying on duties on trade rather than direct taxes on property and persons. The tariff would certainly become a divisive issue later as the North and the South battled over protectionism. But as a revenue measure, the impost remained the most acceptable type of tax to northerners and southerners alike.

The debate in the Constitutional Convention was overwhelmingly focused on the ills of the Union and was silent on the future agenda of the new national government. The ratification debate is much more instructive in this respect. Proponents of the Constitution pointed to very concrete issues that Congress would now begin to address. Britain would be forced out of the Northwest Territory, and the Indian nations in the area would be pacified. Spain would be made to open the Mississippi to American navigation. The restrictions on the West Indies trade would be eased or lifted altogether. By means of a more energetic foreign policy, material benefits would accrue to the American people. Both the Constitutional Convention and the ratification debate held out the expectation that Congress would begin payments on the national debt, thereby restoring the credit, reputation, and strength of the United States.

But a more energetic foreign policy would be expensive, and payments on the debt would be even more so. The Constitution had placed the power to draw forth that money from the American people in Congress, and Hamilton and others had devised a blueprint for how to effect this. But it still remained to transform the plan into practice and to fulfill the promise that the Constitution would lift some of the burden of government off the shoulders of the citizens.

CHAPTER TWO

The Soul of Government: Creating an American Fiscal Regime

The background to and the debates in the Philadelphia convention suggested that a principal purpose of the Constitution was to create a government that could overcome the inefficiency of the requisition system and begin to act more forcefully in foreign affairs. These priorities remained when the first federal Congress convened in the spring of 1789. On April 8, on the very first day of business in the new House of Representatives, the first speaker to rise did so to make "a few observations on the state of our finances—the deficiencies of the federal treasury, and the necessity of immediately adopting some measures, on the subject of the national revenue." The speaker was none other than James Madison, and the question he introduced would dominate the proceedings of the House for its first six weeks, to May 18, when the representatives moved on to other subjects. In contrast to this extended fiscal debate, the discussion of the Bill of Rights, or the first ten amendments to the Constitution, often seen as the principal achievement of the First Congress, took no more than ten days, and the House only found time to address the question four months into its first session.[1]

The outcome of the fiscal debate was the Impost Act, which became the second law on the US book of statutes. Two related pieces of legislation, the Collection Act and the Tonnage Act, were the third and fifth statutes, respectively. There is no deep mystery about the attention paid to fiscal matters by the First Congress. "Of all the operations of government," Massachusetts representative Fisher Ames remarked, "it was admitted that those respecting revenue were the most delicate as well as most important. Revenue was the soul of government, and if such a soul had not been breathed into ours it would have been a dead body and fit only to be buried." Without money the new national government would have been paralyzed.

Setting up a functioning revenue system was therefore a prerequisite for every other government activity.[2]

The reform of the nation's finances that took place after the adoption of the Constitution has often been associated with Alexander Hamilton, Madison's close collaborator on *The Federalist*. But Hamilton had no direct influence on the Impost Act. In the spring of 1789 he was watching Congress from the sidelines, no doubt with considerable anxiety. It was not until September 11 that President George Washington appointed him secretary of the Treasury. By that time the first session of the First Congress was drawing to a close. But even as Treasury secretary, Hamilton's impact on fiscal policy was limited. None of his famous reports on public finance dealt directly with taxation. Fiscal legislation was a power that the Constitution had placed in the House of Representatives, and the lower house jealously guarded this privilege from executive influence. Hamilton's fiscal measures were instead appended to his reports on public credit and manufactures, and they did not signal any significant departure from the reigning ideas in the House.

The Impost Act of July 4, 1789, did breathe a soul into the national government. A steady income from customs duties allowed the government to begin payment on the public debt and to build a rudimentary army. But the actions of the First Congress also fundamentally transformed the structure of taxation in the states. In this development the much-maligned decision to assume the state debts was of decisive importance. When the First Congress convened in New York City, many representatives had had direct experience of strong popular opposition to taxation in their respective states. Tax resistance of course already had an impressive pedigree in America. Parliament's attempt to impose new taxes on the colonies after the French and Indian War had triggered the American Revolution, and after independence things did not improve. Having rebelled against Crown and Parliament in opposition to impositions from a distant government, the citizens of the new states were now asked to pay taxes several times higher than those levied before the Revolution. It was not a popular request. The Confederation Congress and the states soon found that many citizens could not or would not pay their taxes. When the state governments increased the pressure on the taxpayers, the people protested. They petitioned for relief, they voted governments from office, and they obstructed the administration of taxation in numerous ways. When nothing else worked, they turned to violence. Although Shays's Rebellion in Massachusetts is by far the best-known case, strong and sometimes violent protests against taxation occurred in the majority of the states in the 1780s.[3]

Within less than a decade this situation had changed completely. Late in 1796, Secretary of the Treasury Oliver Wolcott could remark that it "is known that the State taxes have generally been very inconsiderable." The previous year, the president had told Congress that the tax burden on the citizens was now "so light as scarcely to be perceived." The administration was well aware that this situation contrasted sharply with the one before the adoption of the Constitution. In 1795, Hamilton had written that state taxation in the 1780s had "embraced every object and was carried as far [as] it could be done without absolutely oppressing individuals." Indeed, in some of the states things had been even worse. In Massachusetts taxation "was carried still farther even to a degree too burthernsome for the comfortable conditions of the Citizens." This oppressive tax burden was caused in part by administrative mistakes—"that unskilfullness which was the common attribute of the State administration of Finance"—yet it was "still more owing to the real weight of the Taxes." Like so many of his contemporaries, Hamilton believed that Shays's Rebellion "was in great degree the offspring of this pressure."[4]

Hamilton had no difficulty explaining how state taxes could go from "oppressive" to "inconsiderable" in less than a decade. The federal assumption of state debts, which he had engineered in 1790, was the cause. "It is a curious fact which has not made its due impression," Hamilton wrote, "that in every state the people have found relief from assumption while an incomparably better provision than before existed has been made for the state debts." There were therefore two important consequences of the establishment of the first federal fiscal regime. On the one hand there was the creation of a federal revenue service built on customs revenue, which proved to be a long-lived order that remained in place up to the Civil War. On the other hand there was the transformation of the fiscal regime in the states resulting from the federal assumption of state debts.[5]

The creation of the federal revenue service is a relatively straightforward story. The First Congress built on the attempts to reform the Articles of Confederation by investing the Continental Congress with the power to raise an impost independent of the states. When Madison introduced the subject of taxation in the House of Representatives, he related that "he had availed himself of the propositions made by the late Congress, in 1783—and had taken from them the enumeration of articles, on which duties might be properly imposed." In fact, Madison had been a member of the five-man committee that drafted the propositions he was referring to, and he had even been responsible for writing its report. Thomas Fitzsimons, who would also play a leading part in shaping the Impost Act, had been another member. Although specific figures were rarely mentioned, reform-minded politicians had long argued that impost duties would provide the bulk of the national government's income. Their many promises that customs duties could be made a productive source of revenue turned out to be true. By the middle of the 1790s, the federal government raised around $5 million to $6 million per year from the impost.[6]

The second important consequence of Congress's fiscal reform is less visible because here the changes took place within the states rather than at the national level. In order to trace this development, it is necessary to compare state taxation before and after the adoption of the Constitution. The Constitution itself did not bring about changes in fiscal policy. But it made it possible for Congress to set up a productive revenue service, which in turn allowed the federal government to assume payment on the state debts. Federal assumption of state debts removed the need for heavy state taxation and considerably eased the fiscal burden imposed on the citizens. Because such taxes had been the cause of popular protest and unrest, the actions of the First Congress diffused a volatile political situation and brought about social stability.

From a bird's-eye view of the American system of taxation, the actions of the First Congress can be seen to have brought about two structural changes. First, the national government replaced the state governments as the most important agent in fiscal matters. Second, because the federal government could raise considerably more money from the impost than the states had been able to do, it was possible to replace direct taxes with indirect taxes as the main source of government revenue. Whereas the productivity of the impost has always been in plain sight, the fiscal consequences of federal assumption have been largely ignored in the literature on the Federalists. Historians have instead focused on the appreciation of previously worthless state securities and have ignored the sharp reduction of state taxation. But the changes in the fiscal burden and in the structure of taxation were just as important as securities appreciation, if not more so, to both the citizens and the state governments of the early federal republic.[7]

I

Taxation was not the only means by which American state governments raised money. In some periods, in some of the colonies and later states, it was not even the most important one. Colonial and state governments raised revenue from incomes on investments, from interest on loans issued through their loan offices, and from the sale of public lands and confiscated

Loyalist property. Many states also printed bills of credit, or paper money. But in the 1780s, when the states tried to pay the large public debt run up during the war against Britain, these sources proved insufficient, and it was necessary to resort to taxation. Table 2.1 shows that New York, Pennsylvania, and Virginia expected nontax income to yield less than 10 percent of total revenue in the years before the adoption of the Constitution. In contrast, South Carolina's Committee of Ways and Means estimated that more than 10 percent of government revenue in 1785 would come from the sale of land in Charleston and confiscated estates. But such assets would soon be exhausted. North Carolina apparently expected nothing at all from sources other than taxes, and in the same period, Maryland's Committee of Claims reported only negligible sums from nontax incomes. With the important exception of bills of credit, which were issued by seven of the states in the 1780s, nontax revenue was only marginally important to the states in the years between 1785 and 1787.[8]

State governments implemented three basic types of taxes in the 1780s. In the majority of the states, the most important type was direct taxes on property and persons. In the middle and northern states, tax laws stipulated the total sum to be raised in the state, and the individual tax rate was set according to the size and the wealth of the household. In the South, legislatures voted on tax rates rather than a total sum. In terms of government revenue, the most important taxes in the South were the land tax and the slave tax, with the exception of North Carolina, where the poll tax was more important. North Carolina was also unique in taxing land by acre, while the other states tried to assess land value by classing land rather crudely according to quality. Slaves within a certain age span were taxed at a flat rate.[9]

The second-most important type of tax—in some states the most important one—was duties on exports and imports. Although imported goods were sold to consumers throughout the Union, collections were made by the state in possession of the port of entry. This arrangement obviously benefited states possessing busy ports, such as Pennsylvania and New York, at the expense of those that did not. The third and final type of tax was fees and duties on the retail sale and sometimes production of consumer articles, so-called excises. Among the former, the most common were marriage and tavern licenses, court fees, and fees on certain professions, such as law and medicine. Pennsylvania fined its many conscientious objectors who refused to do militia service. Other states imposed duties on billiard tables, playing cards, and dice, on carriages, sales at auction, and on alcohol, whether imported brandy or wine or locally produced whiskey and rum. Before the Revolution, excises on spirituous liquors, which under federal

TABLE 2.1. The structure of government revenue, 1785–1787 ($ and percent of total)

Income	NY	PA	VA	NC	SC
Direct tax	83,000 (32%)	205,000 (42%)	828,000 (70%)	131,000 (77%)	324,000 (62%)
Customs	143,000 (55%)	162,000 (33%)	282,000 (24%)	30,000 (18%)	111,000 (21%)
Excises and fees	9,000 (4%)	80,000 (16%)	33,000 (3%)	10,000 (6%)	28,000 (5%)
Other	21,000 (8%)	47,000 (9%)	30,000 (3%)		56,000 (11%)
Total	257,000	494,000	1,173,000	171,000	519,000

Sources: New York: [New York, Session Laws (New York)], Apr. 29, 1786, Apr. 11, 1787; *Journal of the Assembly of the State of New-York* (Jan. 9–Mar. 22, 1788) (Poughkeepsie, 1788), 19, 21, 23. For direct taxes, see sources listed in Table 2.2. Pennsylvania: *State of the Accounts of David Rittenhouse, Esq., Treasurer of Pennsylvania; from January, 1785, till January 1786* (Philadelphia: Oswald, 1790), 8–19; *State of the Account of David Rittenhouse, Esq., Treasurer of the Commonwealth of Pennsylvania; from January, 1786, till January, 1787* (Philadelphia: Bailey, 1790), 3–35; *State of the Accounts of David Rittenhouse, Esq., Treasurer of Pennsylvania; from 1st January till 1st November 1787. Including His Continental and State Money Accounts for the year 1786* (Philadelphia: Aitken, 1790), 6–39; *State of the Accounts of David Rittenhouse, Esq., Treasurer of Pennsylvania; For the Year 1788* (Philadelphia: Aitken, 1791), 3–29. For direct taxes see sources listed in table 2.2. Virginia: W. F. Dodd, "The Effect of the Adoption of the Constitution upon the Finances of Virginia," *Virginia Magazine of History and Biography* 10 (1903): 366. North Carolina: Senate Journal, Dec. 11, 1787, in William L. Saunders and Walter Clark, eds., *State Records of North Carolina*, 26 vols. (Goldsboro: Nash Brothers, 1886–1907), 20:396, 398. South Carolina: *Second Report of Ways and Means* (Charleston, 1785).

Notes: Figures for direct taxes in New York and Pennsylvania are taxes levied, not taxes collected. Figures for Virginia are based on Treasury receipts. North and South Carolina figures are estimates by legislative committees. Arrearages for duties, fees, and so forth from years before 1785 are not included for any state. For New York and Pennsylvania figures are yearly averages for the period 1785–1787, although in New York the first year covers Sept. 21, 1784, to Dec. 31, 1785. Figures for Virginia are yearly averages for the period 1785/1786–1787/1788, except "Excises and fees" and "Other," which are yearly averages for 1786/1787–1787/1788. In North and South Carolina the figures are contemporary estimates for 1788 and 1785, respectively. Throughout this chapter all conversions from local currency to dollars are based on John J. McCusker, *How Much Is That in Real Money? A Historical Commodity Price Index for Use as a Deflator of Money Values in the Economy of the United States*, 2d ed. (Worcester, MA: American Antiquarian Society, 2001), 34, table 1; and Philo Copernicus [pseud.], *Folsom's New Pocket Almanac for 1789* (Boston, 1789), 35. Percentages may not add up to 100 because of rounding.

auspices would later become so controversial, were in effect in New Hampshire, New York, Pennsylvania, Maryland, Virginia, and North Carolina.[10]

The income from excises and fees was relatively modest compared to the money raised through direct taxes and customs duties. Table 2.1 shows that the ratio of fees and excises to direct taxes ranges from a high of more than 1:3 in Pennsylvania to a low of 1:25 in Virginia. The corresponding figures for New York, North Carolina, and South Carolina are, respectively, 1:9, 1:13, and 1:12. The aggregate figure for the five states is 1:10. The share of total revenue raised from fees and excises varies from 3 percent in Virginia to 16 percent in Pennsylvania. The aggregate figure for the five states is 6 percent. In contrast to many European states at the time, therefore, excises and fees generated only minor incomes for American governments in the mid-1780s.[11]

Export and import duties were much more important than excises and fees in producing revenue in the pre-Constitution years. New York was exceptional in raising 55 percent of its income from customs duties. But duties on international trade were an important source of revenue in other states too. Table 2.1 shows that Pennsylvania received 33 percent of its total income from customs duties. In the remaining three states, they contributed between a fifth and a fourth of total income. These figures underestimate the importance of customs duties to state finances, however. Whereas a large share of direct taxes could be paid in bills of credit, securities, or interest certificates, customs duties tended to be the state governments' major source of specie income. Thus in Massachusetts the government earmarked the income from the impost and excise fund for interest payments on the public debt in order to keep up the value of its public securities and placate the mood of its powerful public creditors. The significance of customs duties to the states is reflected in the refusal of Rhode Island and New York to accept the impost proposals of 1781 and 1783. It is also reflected in the concern that states would be unable to meet their revenue needs without the impost, which was often expressed in the debate over the ratification of the Constitution. This concern remained for a few years after the Constitution's adoption, before the consequences of Hamilton's funding and assumption plans were fully realized. Hence, although customs duties accounted for only about 20 percent of the revenue in the budget of South Carolina, the governor remarked in 1789 that "since the Duties on Tonnage and Impost have been received for the use of the United States—our public Funds have been in the most impoverished condition."[12]

With a few exceptions, state governments relied far more on direct taxes than on customs duties, excises, and fees. This was probably the least efficient branch of the fiscal administration. Direct taxes were often paid late, sometimes several years after the tax had become due. In the 1760s, Connecticut taxpayers were still making payments on taxes levied in the 1740s, and in 1767 a Massachusetts collector petitioned the General Court to be relieved from collecting taxes from the 1730s. As a result, there was a substantial difference between the amount of money levied by the state legislatures and the amount of money collected by the taxmen. Indeed, considering how difficult direct taxes were to collect, it is an indication of the desperate state of public finances in the 1780s that the state legislatures made such extensive use of them.[13]

Reliance on direct taxes varied from state to state. In New York, direct taxes accounted for no more than about a third of total revenue, and in Pennsylvania the figure was only slightly higher. In contrast, direct taxes accounted for 62 percent of the revenue in South Carolina, 70 percent in Virginia, and 77 percent in North Carolina. It has been estimated that the figure was about 90 percent for Massachusetts. New York and Pennsylvania differed from the other states, and it is not difficult to see why. Their busy ports ensured substantial incomes from customs duties. With the possible exception of Maryland, the other states were probably more similar to Massachusetts, Virginia, and North and South Carolina than to New York and Pennsylvania.[14]

On the basis of table 2.1 and the foregoing discussion, it is possible to offer a crude generalization about the structure of taxation in the state governments in the 1780s. First, with the exception of currency emissions, revenue from sources other than taxation was only marginally important. Second, direct taxes were by far the most important type of tax in the majority of the states. On average, state governments expected to receive somewhere on the order of two-thirds of their tax income from taxes on polls and property, about a quarter from duties on imports and exports, and the remainder from excises and fees.

II

It is well known that tax administration in eighteenth-century America was grossly inefficient. Tax arrears were the norm in most colonies before the Revolution, and matters did not improve when taxes rose after independence. In South Carolina and Massachusetts, for instance, tax arrears grew rapidly in the years preceding the adoption of the Constitution. By February 1787, South Carolina had collected no more than 41 percent of its 1785 tax; by October of the same year Massachusetts had collected no more than 16 percent of its 1786 tax. However, it would be a mistake to equate administrative inefficiency with tax relief. South Carolina and Massachusetts did not remit, respectively, 59 and 84 percent of the taxes for 1785 and 1786 simply because they were not paid on time. Instead, unpaid taxes became tax debts. On occasion it did happen that taxes were reduced or abolished, but it was not common practice. As a rule, once passed, a tax law was not rescinded. The money that went uncollected when the tax was due the taxman came back to claim on a later day.[15]

Nonpayment of taxes in fact incurred stiff penalties. Tax laws stipulated that delinquent taxpayers could be jailed and that their property and land could be foreclosed and sold at public auction. Nor were these empty threats. State governments applied considerable pressure on taxpayers in the postwar period and thereby caused many citizens considerable hardship. One study of rural Pennsylvania even speaks of "a statewide epidemic of foreclosures" in this period, although many if not most cases were the result of private debts. Far from reducing these hardships, the accumulation of tax arrears increased them. In 1786, Massachusetts levied a very heavy tax of more than $1 million. At this time, back taxes amounted to $1.4 million. In order to pay both back taxes and the 1786 tax, the inhabitants of Massachusetts would have had to contribute about $5.50 per person. Even compared to British taxes at the time, this was a considerable sum. The British government made annual impositions of about twice as much, but only a fifth, or roughly two dollars per capita, was raised from direct taxes.[16]

Despite arrears, the major part of a tax levy was in fact usually paid in the end. Thus, while South Carolinians had only paid 41 percent of the 1785 tax by February 1787, they had by then paid 70 percent of the 1784 tax and 62 percent of the 1783 tax. In the same way, Massachusetts had only collected 16 percent of the 1786 tax by October 1787, but the government had by then collected 65 percent of the 1784 tax, 78 percent of the 1783 tax, and 67 percent of the two taxes levied in 1782. The citizens of Massachusetts paid even more of their back taxes after the adoption of the Constitution, when they reduced back taxes from £494,474 to £33,847 in a few years. A similar development occurred in other states as well. In the late 1780s, Pennsylvania levied an annual tax of £76,946. In 1787, the taxpayers paid only £8,499 of the 1787 tax, but they paid a full £37,804 on the tax of 1786. In 1788, North Carolina's subcommittee on public revenue reported that the state had received £35,863 in taxes and £54,132 in back taxes. In 1783, Maryland's treasury stated that the total of unpaid taxes amounted to £66,933. By 1790, Marylanders had paid £38,935 of this sum, bringing their back taxes down to £27,998. In 1797, Virginians were still making payments on the revenue tax of 1783. Indeed, in that year the treasurer recorded payments on the annual revenue tax for every single year between 1783 and 1796. In short, administrative inefficiency did not allow the citizens to ignore the tax laws.[17]

III

An attempt to determine the burden of taxation in the Confederation period must consider that the main share of the taxes levied by the states was not paid in gold and silver coin but in different kinds of depreciated paper instruments. Neither Congress nor the states struck their own coin in the late eighteenth century, nor was British coin used either before or after independence. Instead, the American money stock was made up of a vast array of foreign gold and silver coin in addition to bills of credit issued by the state governments. Because the states often lacked cash, they also made frequent use of Treasury notes—a receipt that could be cashed at the Treasury—to pay for salaries and services. In the 1780s, another paper medium of exchange was made up of the public securities issued by the states and Congress during and after the War of Independence and the "indents," or interest certificates, these securities earned. According to Philadelphia's *Pennsylvania Gazette* of August 4, 1784, "Treasury notes, state money, and public securities of all kinds, pass daily in stores and shops, in town and in the country at their *real* value," thereby adding "a great deal to the quantity of circulating cash." In addition to being used in stores and shops, these kinds of money could also be used to pay taxes. As the mention of "real value" indicates, by the mid-1780s these bills of credit and securities were in different states of depreciation relative to gold and silver. Such depreciation obviously had an impact on the real burden of taxation.[18]

The major part of the taxes levied in the 1780s was intended to raise money for payments on the state and federal debts. Part of the public debt was held abroad, but the main share was owned by Americans. Some of them had loaned money to Congress and the state governments, but most of them had received securities as compensation for services and goods rendered during the war against Britain. These people were offered payment in securities rather than specie for the simple reason that neither the states nor Congress had the means to pay cash. Nor could the federal or state governments pay interest to more than a handful of creditors in gold or silver. Most of them instead received interest in bills of credit issued by the states or in federal or state indents. Both paper money and indents were acceptable for tax payments at face value, at least in part, in most of the states.[19]

A market existed in securities, indents, and bills of credit, and therefore not only public creditors had the option of paying taxes in paper. In 1786, a broker in Philadelphia offered the following list of securities for sale:

Militia certificates, of Pennsylvania, Depreciation funded on the excise, Ditto unfunded, but purchase land, Stelle's and Story's certificates, Loan-Office ditto of Pennsylvania, Nicholson's, or new loan, Dollar money, Shilling money, Indents or Facilities, Continental securities, Land-office papers, of Pennsylvania, Jersey finals that draw interest, Thompson's,

Virginia depreciation, finals, treasury land warrants, Maryland finals, Depreciation, Delaware finals, depreciation, Continental money, New York finals that purchase land, Nourse's certificates of Pennsylvania, Nourse's, not adopted by any state.

Dealing with such a variety of instruments is a challenge to any attempt to determine the real burden of taxation in the 1780s. It was a challenge to contemporaries, too. Even the brokers found it difficult to keep track of the many securities and their fluctuating value. One of them prefaced his attempt to write an account of the public debts of the Union and the states with the laconic remark that "he was not so fully aware that the field into which he was entering had been so extensive, or that the subject would have required so much attention."[20]

Not much is known about this early securities market. No price series for securities have been collected, and there have been no attempts to measure the volume traded. Clearly, however, the securities were never dead paper. Scattered information indicates that there were considerable fluctuations in value over time as well as significant variations in value between different localities. The value of bills of credit and indents depended to a large extent on the willingness of state legislatures to levy taxes payable in these mediums.[21]

Many of the tax programs adopted by the states in the 1780s were part of their debt management and aimed to tax in various paper instruments. For this reason, only part of the total taxes they levied was levied in specie; the remainder could be paid in bills of credit or indents. Congress began paying interest on the federal debt in indents in 1784. To create a demand for federal indents, Congress expected the states to tax them in at the same pace that they were paid out. In this way it would be possible for the recipients of indents to sell their surplus to taxpayers who were not creditors but had to pay taxes in federal indents. The scheme soon broke down, however, and the supply of indents came to exceed demand. Depreciation followed. In the wave of state assumption of the federal debt in the mid-1780s, several states exchanged federal for state securities. Among the northern states, Pennsylvania and New York did so, whereas New Jersey assumed responsibility for interest payments on federal securities held by its citizens. These states paid interest on the federal debt in state bills of credit and, in the case of New Jersey, in "revenue money," which was a form of state indent. For this reason, none of them levied taxes in federal indents. Federal indent taxes were levied by New Hampshire, Massachusetts, and Delaware. Based on contemporary price quotations, it has been estimated that federal indents could be bought and sold for a third of their face value in the mid-1780s. Aside from bills of credit and federal indents, Massachusetts also levied taxes in army notes, and New Hampshire in state indents. The former traded at a third and the latter at four-fifths of face value.[22]

Paper money was issued by Rhode Island, New York, New Jersey, and Pennsylvania. In New York, there was very little depreciation, and in New Jersey and Pennsylvania the bills sold at a discount of 25 to 30 percent at most. New Jersey also issued state certificates of interest. Since the entire issue was taxed in the same year it was paid out, however, and since the holders had the right to exchange the certificates for specie with the treasurer or any tax collector, it seems unlikely that the New Jersey indents depreciated more than 50 percent. In Rhode Island, the state bills of credit depreciated rapidly. Emitted in 1786, they had lost a quarter of their value the following year and 90 percent of their value the year after that.[23]

In the South, the Carolinas and Georgia emitted paper money in the 1780s. In South Carolina, the state currency traded at par, but in the other states the depreciation was significant, and their bills of credit fell in value by 50 and 75 percent, respectively. As in the North, currencies were accepted for tax payments in all states that issued them. South Carolina had assumed the federal debt held by its citizens and made payments on the debt in "special indents." Like the New Jersey indents, these were taxed in the same year they were paid out, and it seems unlikely that they would have depreciated by more than 50 percent. This in fact was the value quoted for South Carolina special indents in the fall of 1785 and winter of 1786. In the other states, taxes could be paid in part in federal or state indents. In the absence of price quotations, it is assumed that these indents could be bought and sold for a third of their nominal value.[24]

IV

Table 2.2 lists the direct taxes levied in the northern and middle states between 1785 and 1795. These taxes may be compared to tax levies in the period before the War of Independence. Colonial taxes had been very low in comparison to what British subjects in the mother country were paying at the same time. Estimates put the American tax rate at 20 to 25 percent of the British rate. Taxes increased in many of the colonies after the French and Indian War, but they had returned to their normal levels by the early 1770s. Compared to this period, the second half of the 1780s constitutes a sharp break. In the years before the Revolution, Massachusetts levied no direct tax at all in 1770 and 1771, and between 1772 and 1775

TABLE 2.2. Direct tax levies in northern and middle states, 1785–1795 ($)

Year	MA	NH	RI	CT	NY	NJ	PA	DE	Total
1785	—	73,000	67,000	161,000	—	110,000	205,000	28,000	664,000
1786	1,036,000	271,000	67,000	172,000	125,000	94,000	205,000	63,000	2,033,000
1787	—	67,000	166,000	172,000	125,000	155,000	205,000	28,000	918,000
1788	261,000	154,000	100,000	206,000	60,000	117,000	205,000	—	1,102,000
1789	125,000	74,000	67,000	137,000	—	143,000	205,000	34,000	784,000
1790	98,000	10,000	—	23,000	—	80,000	—	14,000	225,000
1791	98,000	—	20,000	34,000	—	40,000	—	—	192,000
1792	—	—	—	23,000	—	40,000	—	—	63,000
1793	111,000	—	20,000	23,000	—	—	—	—	153,000
1794	150,000	—	20,000	46,000	—	80,000	—	14,000	310,000
1795	150,000	27,000	—	23,000	—	40,000	—	10,000	250,000

Sources: Massachusetts: Joseph B. Felt, "Statistics of Taxation in Massachusetts, Including Valuation and Population," American Statistical Association, *Collections* 1, no. 3 (1847): 474, 543. New Hampshire: [New Hampshire, Session Laws (Exeter and Portsmouth)], Feb. 23, 1785, Feb. 28, 1786, Mar. 4, Sept. 14, Dec. 30, 1786, Jan. 18, Sept. 28, 1787, Feb. 9, 1788, Feb. 7, 1789, Jan. 22, 1790, Jan. 9, 1795. Rhode Island: [Rhode Island, General Assembly, Schedules (Providence and Warren)], August 1785, March, September 1787, June 1788, March 1789, June 1791, June 1793, October 1794. Connecticut: *The Public Records of the State of Connecticut* (Hartford, 1894–), 5:40–42, 122, 6:36, 173, 297, 414, 504, 505, 7:16, 121, 126, 260, 263, 497, 8:17, 143, 241; Henry F. Walradt, "The Financial History of Connecticut from 1789 to 1861," Connecticut Academy of Arts and Sciences, *Transactions* 17 (March 1912): 27. New York: [New York, Session Laws (New York)], Apr. 29, 1786, Apr. 11, 1787, Mar. 19, 1788. New Jersey: [New Jersey, Session Laws (Trenton, New Brunswick, and Burlington)], Dec. 20, 1783, Nov. 26, 1785, Nov. 21, 1786, June 7, Nov. 6, 28, 1787, Dec., 1, 1789, June 12, Nov. 18, 25, 1790, Nov. 22, 1791, Nov. 20, 1792, Feb. 17, 1793, Dec. 1, 1794, Nov. 11, 1795. Pennsylvania: [Pennsylvania, Session Laws (Philadelphia, 1785)], Mar. 16, 1785, Dec. 8, 1789, Apr. 6, 9, 1791. Delaware: [Delaware, Session Laws (Wilmington)], June 4, 1785, June 24, 1786, Feb. 6, 1787, June 4, 1789, Oct. 26, 1790, Feb. 7, 1794, Feb. 3, 1795.

Notes: All dollar figures have been rounded to the closest thousand. Tax levies have been credited to the year the tax law was passed, even though taxes were often scheduled for collection the following year. Connecticut taxes have been estimated on the basis of valuations for 1785 and 1796.

taxes amounted to $391,880. In contrast, total direct taxes between 1785 and 1788 amounted to $1,297,534. This is equivalent to a tax increase of 230 percent, even though Massachusetts had discontinued its ambitious fiscal program in the aftermath of Shays's Rebellion. Had the tax level of 1786 been maintained in the following years, the tax increase would have been more than twice as great. Rhode Island direct taxes amounted to £4,000 annually in 1773 and 1774. Between 1785 and 1788, the average annual direct tax was £27,500. Even if the depreciation of the paper currency is taken into account, this still represents an increase of almost 300 percent. New Jersey levied a property tax of approximately $40,000 per year before the Revolution. The average annual tax between 1785 and 1788 was three times as great, or about $120,000. New York levied no direct tax at all after 1767, and in Delaware direct taxes were infrequent and insubstantial. In contrast, between 1785 and 1788, New York levied $310,000 and Delaware close to $120,000.[25]

As table 2.2 shows, taxes had returned to their prewar level by the mid-1790s. In Massachusetts, aggregate direct taxes were $411,377 in the period 1792 to 1795. This sum was almost exactly the same as that levied between 1772 and 1775. The same development took place in other states, too. In Rhode Island, the annual tax for the 1792–1795 period was £3,000, and New Jersey levied an annual tax of $40,050. In a return to pre-Revolution practice, New York stopped levying direct taxes altogether. Delaware levied direct taxes of $14,000 and $10,500 in 1794 and 1795, respectively, but the state levied no direct tax at all from 1791 to 1793. Significantly, tax levels fell sometime between 1789 and 1791 in all states but one. The exception was Massachusetts, where the tax level fell after Shays's Rebellion. From 1787 onward, the annual tax in Massachusetts fluctuated between roughly $100,000 and $150,000—in other words, fairly close to prewar levels. It remained at this level until the 1820s, when the annual tax was reduced to $75,000.[26]

The scale as well as the timing of the tax reduction is seen more clearly in table 2.3, where the tax levies are presented in annual per capita figures for the four-year periods 1785 to 1788 and 1792 to 1795. The change is greatest in New York and Pennsylvania, where direct taxation was discontinued altogether. In Massachusetts, New Jersey, and Delaware, the tax reduction amounts to between 70 and 80 percent. In Rhode Island and New Hampshire, direct taxes were reduced by 90 and 95 percent, respectively. In the seven states collectively, the reduction was roughly 85 percent.

The figures in table 2.3 are calculated based on the sums mentioned in the tax laws. Part of these taxes could be paid in bills of credit and indents,

TABLE 2.3. Average annual per capita direct tax levies in the northern and middle states ($)

State	1785–1788	1792–1795
Massachusetts	0.73 (0.38)	0.20
New Hampshire	1.09 (0.56)	0.04
Rhode Island	1.45 (0.57)	0.14
Connecticut	0.76 (0.40)	0.12
New York	0.27 (0.27)	0
New Jersey	0.68 (0.39)	0.21
Pennsylvania	0.53 (0.45)	0
Delaware	0.52 (0.38)	0.10
Total	0.66 (0.39)	0.09

Sources: On taxation, see sources cited in table 2.2. On population, see *Historical Statistics of the United States, Colonial Times to 1970*, Bicentennial ed., 2 vols. (Washington, DC: Bureau of the Census, 1975), vol. 1, series A, 195, vol. 2, series Z, 9.

Notes: Per capita values are calculated on the basis of census data for 1790 and 1800, assuming a linear growth in population between 1785 and 1800 with the exception of New York. New York experienced a population boom far greater than any other state in the 1790s, and I have therefore used an estimate for 1780 together with the census from 1790 to calculate its population in 1785–1788. Figures in parentheses represent an attempt to calculate the specie value of tax levies, taking into consideration the possibility provided by the legislatures to pay taxes in depreciated certificates and bills of credit.

which often traded at prices far below their nominal values. The option to pay at least part of their taxes in depreciated paper amounted to a substantial tax discount for taxpayers. The figures in parentheses in the table represent an attempt to calculate the real, or specie, value of the taxes levied by assuming that the taxes were paid in paper money or securities to the full extent permitted by the tax laws. Because of the lack of price series for state and federal interest certificates, these figures cannot be considered more than a rough indication of the real burden of taxation. They suggest that in real terms the tax reduction in Connecticut, Rhode Island, Massachusetts, and New Jersey was approximately 75, 70, 50, and 45 percent, respectively. The latter two states allowed for a relatively large share of their taxes to be paid in securities, while Rhode Island accepted its heavily depreciated paper money for tax payments. In the other states, the difference between the nominal and the specie value of the taxes is more modest. In New York and Pennsylvania, taxes could be paid in paper money, but the currency depreciated hardly at all in the former and not heavily in the latter.[27] Delaware levied the bulk of its taxes in this period in "lawful money" and did not emit bills of credit. In New Hampshire, the tax cut remained substantial, because taxes were almost nonexistent in the 1790s. The tax reduction in the seven states together was 77 percent.

Table 2.4 compares the tax rates for the three most important direct taxes in the periods 1785–1788 and 1792–1795 in the South. Since the concern here is with the tax burden, no attempt has been made to estimate the total yield of these taxes, even though scattered figures in the state records would make this possible. As the table makes clear, there was significant fiscal change in the South, too. In the 1790s, the poll tax for whites had been abolished in all states except North Carolina, although South Carolina and Georgia retained it for free blacks. But in North Carolina, where the poll tax had traditionally been the most important tax, it fell by almost 90 percent. The slave tax fell by close to 90 percent in Virginia, by about 55 percent in Georgia, and by a little more than 60 percent in South Carolina. The land tax followed a similar pattern. Maryland abolished its general property tax completely, and Virginia and North Carolina reduced the land tax by about 85 to 90 percent. In South Carolina and Georgia, the reduction was somewhat smaller, 50 and 70 percent, respectively.

TABLE 2.4. Average annual tax rates in the southern states

State	1785–1788			1792–1795		
	Property	Slave ($)	Poll ($)	Property	Slave ($)	Poll ($)
Maryland	0.32% of value	—	0.50	—	—	—
Virginia	1.90% of value	2.36	1.67	0.25% of value	0.28	—
N. Carolina	$0.78/100 acres	—	2.30	$0.08/100 acres	—	0.25
S. Carolina	1.00% of value	2.00	2.00	0.50% of value	0.75	2.00
Georgia	1.25% of value	1.07	1.07	0.37% of value	0.47	0.47

Sources: Maryland: [Maryland, Session Laws (Annapolis)], November 1784, November 1785. Virginia: William Waller Henning, *The Statutes at Large; Being a Collection of All the Laws of Virginia, from the First Session of the Legislature in the Year 1619* (1819–1823), 13 vols. (Charlottesville, 1969), vol. 11, October 1782, chap. 8; May 1784, chap. 39; vol. 12, October 1786, chaps. 26, 28, October 1787, chap. 1, October 1788, chap. 12; vol. 13, October 1789, chap. 21, October 1790, chaps. 1, 3, 4, October 1791, chap. 1; October 1792, chap. 2, October 1793, chap. 4, November 1794, chap. 1, November 1795, chap. 6. North Carolina: [North Carolina, Session Laws (Newbern, Fayetteville, Edenton, and Halifax)], Dec. 29, 1786, Jan. 6, 1787, November, Dec. 22, 1788, November 1792, December 1793, December 1794, November 1795. South Carolina: [South Carolina, Session Laws (Charleston)], Mar. 20, 1785, Mar. 22, 1786, Mar. 28, 1787, February 1788, Dec. 1, 1792, Dec. 20, 1793, Dec. 20, 1794, Dec. 19, 1795. Georgia: [Georgia, Session Laws (Augusta)], Feb. 10, 1787, Dec. 22, 1791, Dec. 20, 1792, Dec. 19, 1793, Dec. 29, 1794.

Notes: The table lists average rates for laws passed in the two periods. The legislative record for Georgia is incomplete; figures are based on tax laws of 1787, 1792, 1793, and 1794. In 1791, Georgia altered the evaluation of land for purposes of taxation by reducing land values by half. I have therefore doubled the land tax for 1787.

As in table 2.3, these figures do not reflect that part of the taxes could be paid in currency and indents. Yet, even if taxpayers paid this share in full in depreciated paper, there would still be a substantial tax cut in Maryland, Virginia, and North Carolina. Maryland did not emit bills of credit in the 1780s, but a quarter of the annual levy of 2s. 6d. per £100 in property value could be paid in federal indents. The larger levy for 1786 could be paid in certificates received for provisions or for vessels rented or impressed or by offsetting the interest of state securities against the tax. The reduction of Virginia's land and slave tax would amount to approximately 75 percent if paid in securities rather than specie. Similarly, in North Carolina the reduction of both the land tax and the poll tax would be about 75 percent if paid in currency and securities. If South Carolina's special indents traded at half their nominal value, there was no difference in the real burden of taxation between the 1780s and the 1790s. The state debt remained fairly substantial well into the 1790s, however, and taxes could be paid in paper medium throughout the decade. By 1799, the tax rate had also been further reduced. The land tax was down to $0.25 for every $100 worth of land, and the slave tax decreased to $0.50 per slave. The poll tax for free blacks, on the other hand, had not been reduced but remained at $2.00.

Whereas the reduction in tax rates took place between 1789 and 1791 in North and South Carolina and in Georgia, this was not the case in Maryland and Virginia. Maryland's property tax had already fallen from 10s. to 2s. 6d. per £100 in property value in 1786. In Virginia the land tax had been reduced from a very high 2.5 percent in 1785 to a more reasonable 0.75 percent by 1789. The tax on town lots and slaves followed a similar pattern, and the poll tax was abolished in 1787. Virginia's tax reductions apparently owed little to the adoption of the Constitution, and this may be one reason for the state's tortured relationship with the federal government in the 1790s.

Tables 2.2, 2.3, and 2.4 show that, within merely a few years after the adoption of the Constitution, state direct taxation had fallen very significantly. Because taxes could be paid in part in depreciated securities and bills of credit, the sums stated in the tax laws are an imprecise guide to the actual tax burden imposed on taxpayers. Nevertheless, it appears that direct taxes were reduced by at least 75 percent in most states and were altogether abolished in three states. By the early 1790s, after a decade of heavy and unpopular taxation, state taxes had returned to the low level of the colonial period.

The explanation for the reduction in taxation can be found in reduced expenditures. With the adoption of Hamilton's funding and assumption proposals, the state governments could sharply reduce their spending. Table 2.5 shows that debt charges and Congress's requisitions made up the bulk

TABLE 2.5. Structure of government expenses, 1785–1787 ($ and percent of total)

Expense	NY	PA	SC
Debt charges and congressional requisitions	169,000 (56%)	423,000 (77%)	357,000 (80%)
Civil list and assembly	91,000 (30%)	65,000 (12%)	65,000 (15%)
Pensions	26,000 (9%)	9,000 (2%)	—
Internal improvements	3,000 (1%)	12,000 (2%)	6,000 (1%)
Other	10,000 (4%)	38,000 (7%)	17,000 (4%)
Total	299,000	547,000	445,000

Sources: New York: *Journal of the Assembly of the State of New-York* (Jan. 9–Mar. 22, 1788) (Poughkeepsie, 1788), 18, 20, 22. Pennsylvania: *State of the Accounts of David Rittenhouse, Esq., Treasurer of Pennsylvania; From January, 1785, till January 1786* (Philadelphia: Oswald, 1790), 22–52; *State of the Account of David Rittenhouse, Esq., Treasurer of the Commonwealth of Pennsylvania. from January, 1786, till January, 1787* (Philadelphia: Bailey, 1790), 36–63; *State of the Accounts of David Rittenhouse, Esq., Treasurer of Pennsylvania, from 1st January till 1st November 1787; Including his Continental and State Money Accounts for the year 1786* (Philadelphia: Aitken, 1790), 40–70. South Carolina: [South Carolina, Session Laws (Charleston)], An Act for Raising Supplies for the Year 1785, 12, An Act for Raising Supplies for the Year 1786, 13–14, An Act for Raising Supplies for the Year 1787, 13.

Note: Figures are yearly averages for the period 1785–1787, but for New York the first year covers Sept. 21, 1784, to Dec. 31, 1785, and for Pennsylvania 1787 covers only Jan. 1 to Oct. 31. The first category includes various compensations paid for goods and services rendered during the War of Independence. The table gives only a rough indication of spending patterns, since the categories have been imposed on the record. State governments kept their books differently, and often specific items can fit more than one category. Army pay for service during the war has been included in the second category. In both New York and Pennsylvania emissions of paper money have been omitted.

of expenditures in New York, Pennsylvania, and South Carolina from 1785 to 1787. Next to nothing was spent on internal improvements or, with the exception of New York, on pensions. The figure for the civil list (nonmilitary expenses) is unusually high in the case of New York because it includes compensation to veterans of the New York Line for services in the War of Independence. Between 10 and 15 percent of expenditures appears to have been the norm in most states. Internal improvements, pensions, and contingent expenses account for another 5 to 10 percent of government outlays. On the basis of these budgets, it would seem that 75 to 80 percent of government costs were related to debt charges and requisitions. Scattered evidence from other states confirms this observation.[28]

Despite making debt payments their top priority, the state governments had not managed to pay off more than part of their debts when Hamilton presented his assumption plan. According to one estimate, the state governments had collectively recognized a debt of somewhere between $35 million and $50 million after the War of Independence. Since the federal government assumed $18 million in state debts in 1790 and the remaining state debts totaled around $8 million, the states had paid off between $9 million and $24 million, or 25 to 50 percent of their debts by this time. However, accumulated interest had increased the federal debt by $13 million in the same period. The combined debt of the state governments and the Union had therefore been reduced only marginally, if at all. To pay this debt would require years if not decades of continued heavy taxation.[29]

In most of the states, however, such plans had been put on hold well before the Philadelphia convention met in May 1787. Hamilton's policy of gradual and slow debt redemption that was adopted by the First Congress merely continued a development begun in the states. The outline of his financial program is well known. The federal government assumed about 70 percent of the state debts and consolidated them with the federal debt. The consolidated debt was turned into long-term securities on which the government paid only interest. Because the interest rate was also cut, the cost of debt charges was considerably reduced. Another aspect of Hamilton's program is less often mentioned in the literature. Because the federal government assumed responsibility for the debt of both the Union and the states, state governments were relieved of payments both on Congress's requisitions and on their own debts. Freed from these expenses, the state governments could reduce direct taxation by as much as 75 to 90 percent.[30]

V

The transfer of responsibility for debt servicing from the states to the national government meant that the latter had to dramatically increase its tax intake. Although funding and assumption reduced the overall cost of the public debt, it remained a very substantial outlay. The national government found the means to meet its costs not by a heavy-handed fiscal program, as historians have sometimes alleged, but by introducing a tax regime that promised to be both popular and productive.

It has been said that the Federalists believed "in the rigorous collection of taxes" and "in strict payment of public and private debts." To realize their ideals, they thought it necessary to create "a central government with coercive authority." The failure of the states to raise sufficient tax revenue in the early to mid-1780s, one historian says, "created an impression that the state governments did not have the requisite force and firmness to compel an unvirtuous people to pay taxes in sound money." To rectify this situation, the Federalists created a government possessing coercive power, which allowed it to compel an unwilling people to pay their just dues. "In their view, the state governments were too weak and changeable to command respect and collect taxes, they espoused a stronger, more stable central government that could require obedience to the law."[31]

Such claims are exaggerated. The supporters of the Constitution and the majority of members in the First Congress certainly wished to provide the federal government with a reliable income. But as far as possible they sought to create a fiscal system that would leave the property of the citizens alone by taxing imported consumer articles in the ports of entry. The federal revenue administration would have little or no contact with the citizenry in its daily operations. For this reason, the fiscal reform brought about by the Constitution did not increase but eased the burden of taxation and thereby "brought tax relief to rural America."[32]

To the government, it was advantageous to tax trade rather than property or persons. Farmers and planters had their assets tied up in land and slaves, whereas merchants had ready access to specie. The federal revenue service would be present only in the ports, and the vast majority of the population of the United States would never have to confront a federal tax collector. From the perspective of the taxpayer, however, customs duties were not necessarily easier to bear than direct taxes. The common understanding in the eighteenth century, nevertheless, was that the impost fell on "luxuries" rather than so-called necessaries, things such as fuel, basic foodstuffs, and clothing. As long as the fiscal legislation respected this distinction, customs duties could even be regarded as a voluntary tax. As the Philadelphia merchant and political economist Pelatiah Webster wrote, no person was "compelled to pay any of the taxes, unless he chooses to be concerned in the articles taxed." Contemporaries also pointed out that duties on consumption were paid in small increments whenever a person bought an article on which the government imposed a duty, whereas direct taxes had to be paid in full when the taxman came to make his collection. Finally, it was claimed that buyers were often not aware of paying a tax when buying consumer articles. In contemporary terms, the duty was "confounded" with the price.[33]

In practice, the impost embraced items such as salt, which by no stretch of the imagination could be deemed a luxury. But even if customs duties fell in part on necessaries, they were still preferable to direct taxation. Duties on articles of consumption might affect the patterns of consumption of planters, farmers, and artisans, but they did not touch their property or persons. As Webster put it, when revenue is raised from indirect taxation, "lands, labor, and farmer's stock are not called on." There could be neither tax debts nor foreclosures if the government raised revenue from the impost. Nor was it likely that consumption would be much affected by customs duties, since they had an inherent protection against excessive rates. "Imposts, excises and in general all duties upon articles of consumption may be compared to a fluid," Hamilton wrote in *The Federalist*, "which will in time find its level with the means of paying them." To raise money from the impost, the government had to calibrate the duties so that the price on imported articles did not become prohibitive. For when the price became too high, consumption would decrease and smuggling would increase, thereby bringing the revenue down.[34]

The several proposals to amend the Articles of Confederation that were presented in the 1780s had all emphasized that the impost was the most proper tax to be levied by the national government. The discussions in the Constitutional Convention and the ratification debate confirmed that customs duties would form the mainstay of the federal fiscal regime. When James Madison rose to introduce his resolution that Congress levy duties on imports, it was no surprise that he claimed that such taxes would secure "the object of revenue" without being "oppressive to our constituents." The first federal Congress convened in April 1789, and in order to capture the spring imports it was imperative that Congress acted with dispatch. Madison therefore suggested that the House of Representatives simply adopt the "propositions made on this subject by Congress in 1783." The majority of the states had already agreed to the propositions, so adopting them now should not be controversial, and the tax bill could therefore be passed quickly, Madison thought. In 1783, Congress had proposed specific duties on no more than twelve articles. All other imports would be taxed by a general 5 percent ad valorem duty. The enumerated items were typical "luxury" products such as wine and spirits, tea, coffee, and cocoa, sugar products, and pepper, which could be taxed at more than 5 percent without a significant reduction in consumption. All of them were items of mass consumption, and the 1783 tax proposal had clearly looked first and foremost to the revenue needs of the government.[35]

Madison's hope that the House could act quickly ended when Thomas Fitzsimons responded to his proposal with a motion for a more expansive use of fiscal policy. Taxation should be used not only to raise revenue but also "to encourage the productions of our country, and protect our infant manufactures." To this end Fitzsimons introduced a list of over fifty items that he wished to add to the enumerated list from 1783, ranging from foodstuffs to clothing and diverse manufactured items such as nails, saddles, and carriages. Although he spoke of the manufactures of "our country," Fitzsimons unashamedly promoted the interests of his Pennsylvania constituents. Following his example, other representatives rushed to propose protection of their favorite items: anchors, wool cards, limes and lemons, window glass, paper, and much more. Before Fitzsimons's intervention, some representatives had hoped that framing an acceptable tax bill would be the work of a few hours. Instead the House found itself bogged down for six weeks debating the Impost Act and its accompanying legislation, the Tonnage Act.[36]

The new Congress's first fiscal debate reveals much about contemporary attitudes toward taxation and conceptions of the federal union. It is clear that a legitimate fiscal regime had to respect reigning ideas about just and proper taxation and cherished state interests. Framing a tax law for the Union proved to be difficult, and the debate was both long and occasionally acrimonious. Nevertheless, beneath the disagreements there was considerable consensus about the fundamental elements of the federal tax system. No representative proposed a fiscal regime built on direct taxes on property and persons rather than import duties. Nor did anyone propose to make extensive use of excise duties. According to Madison, excises were unpopular and would "be received with indignation in some parts of the union." By default, the congressmen settled on customs duties, as no other tax was "so safe, as an impost, none so easy, none so productive." Customs duties were also widely recognized as "a popular mode" of taxation. Despite disagreement on the length of the enumerated list and the exact duties on various items, no one claimed that it was illegitimate to use fiscal measures to achieve ends other than meeting revenue needs. When a coherent free-trade position developed in the nineteenth century, protectionism would become controversial, but it was not in 1789. Instead, the opposition to Fitzsimons's motion arose not from objections to protectionism but from the need to act quickly on the revenue bill. Later in the debate, when Madison tried to use tonnage duties to force Britain to offer commercial concessions, his proposal met with a similar response. Representatives questioned the wisdom of the measure but not the legitimacy of using taxation to further American commercial interests.[37]

Fitzsimons's call for an impost act that included a much-expanded enumerated list protecting manufactures proved successful. In contrast, Madison's proposal to discriminate against nations that refused to sign a commercial agreement with the United States, a measure directed principally at Britain, was defeated in the Senate. But Congress did not reject discrimination per se. The Tonnage Act levied considerably lower duties on American-owned and American-built vessels than on other ships. It therefore institutionalized a policy "in favor of our own navigation against all foreigners whomsoever" but did not discriminate "between foreign nations" on the basis of their commercial policy toward the United States. The aim was to promote American shipping but also to improve the military capacity of the United States. Were it not for the need to have "some naval strength," Madison said, he would have preferred to have left commerce completely free. "But we have maritime dangers to guard against, and we can be secured from them no other way, than by having a navy and seamen of our own, these can only be obtained by giving a preference." From naval strength would follow the "respect and attention" of Europe and protection of American interests. To make the tonnage duty more attractive, it was even presented as a tax to "prevent the horrors of war."[38]

The dominant idiom of the House fiscal debate, whether the topic was customs or tonnage duties, was the language of states' rights. As representatives worked tirelessly and quite openly to further the interests of their constituents, the House of Representatives continued a style of politics that had been prominent in the Constitutional Convention. Just as had been the case in Philadelphia, the major rift was between North and South, with attitudes to shipping determining the position of the representatives. Hardly had Madison offered his discrimination plan than Thomas Tucker of South Carolina protested that the Tonnage Act would "bear harder on some of the states than on others." Northerners had an interest in excluding foreign carriers, but southerners benefited from keeping tonnage duties "extremely light" to keep down the costs of freight. For this reason "it would be improper and imprudent to take a decisive step, which would affect the different parts of the union in so different a manner." Madison's response took the form of an argument that would be used frequently throughout the antebellum era to combat states' rights arguments in the halls of the national legislature: states' rights had to be moderated by a concern for the good of the Union. Although the interests of the states should certainly be secured, it "ought to be remembered that we had to protect our national, as well as local interests," he said. But Madison did not appeal only to Tucker's better nature. He also played down the importance of conflicting state interests by pointing to intersectional symbiosis. What the South lost in higher freight charges it would gain in naval protection from New England. To Madison it seemed that the "greatest sufferers by this system, were those very parts which stood most in need of the national protection." Yet Tucker was not easily swayed. He continued to move to reduce or strike out duties on South Carolina's principal articles of importation. Meanwhile, fellow South Carolinian William Smith openly questioned the idea of intersectional symbiosis, saying he "would as soon be persuaded to throw myself out of a two-story window, as to believe a high tonnage duty was favourable to South Carolina."[39]

But northerners were just as adept as southerners at playing the states' rights card. The Massachusetts delegation fought hard to reduce the duty on molasses, which hit their state harder than others, not least by increasing the cost of one of their common but rather unsavory products: spruce beer. Wildly exaggerating the effects of the tax, the delegates argued that a duty of six cents per gallon on molasses would make the people of Massachusetts abandon their farms and remove to Nova Scotia and other British provinces to better protect their property. At one point Elbridge Gerry bluntly stated that "if Massachusetts pays her proportion on other articles we will never consent to add 120,000 dollars more, when all the rest of the union will not pay half that sum." Not to be outdone, his fellow delegate George Thatcher asked what southerners would say if he were to propose a fifty-dollar "impost on negroes"?[40]

If southern opposition to the tonnage duty and Massachusetts's struggle to reduce the tax on molasses were indicative of a style of politics that would be dominant in the early republic and antebellum period, so too was the willingness to compromise that also featured prominently in the First Congress. Ultimately, it was the readiness to compromise on matters of state interests that would keep the Union together for seven long decades. In the course of the fiscal debate, the duty on molasses was brought down from six to five cents per gallon and later to two and a half cents as a result of Massachusetts's objections. Another example of the willingness to back down rather than challenge fundamental state interests can be found in the clash over the tax on slave imports. Although South Carolina did not succeed in reducing the tonnage duty, the state did secure tax exemption on slave imports. Relatively late in the debate Virginian Josiah Parker introduced a motion to levy a ten-dollar impost on imported slaves, as not so much a revenue measure as an attempt to "prevent, in some degree, this irrational and inhuman traffic." Like Fitzsimons's protective list and Madison's attempt to discriminate against British trade, Parker's motion demonstrates that congressmen were ready to use fiscal measures for nonrevenue ends. Georgians and South Carolinians immediately rose to protest the motion, however. Despite the fact that they had acceded to the ten-dollar duty in the Constitutional Convention, they now had no intention of honoring this agreement. James Jackson of Georgia accused Parker of acting from self-serving motives. Virginia had enough slaves already, and the natural increase of its slave population made further importation into that state unnecessary. But Virginians "ought to let their neighbours get supplied before they imposed such a burthen on their importation," Jackson argued, and he demanded that Parker withdraw his motion. If imported labor were to be taxed, that duty should "comprehend the white slaves as well as black, who were imported from all the gaols of Europe; wretches, convicted of the most flagrant crimes," who "were brought in and sold without any duty whatever." Tucker meanwhile denied that Congress even had the right "to consider whether the importation of slaves is proper or not, the Constitution gives us no power in that point, it is left to the states to judge of that matter as they see fit." Roger Sherman, who had opposed any federal interference with the slave trade in the Philadelphia convention, continued his support of the Lower South by arguing that a slave duty would be unjust "because two or three states would bear the whole burthen, while he [Sherman] believed they bore their full proportion of all the rest." In the end, it fell to Madison to rein in Parker and to persuade him to drop his motion in order to reintroduce it as a separate bill unconnected to the Impost Act. It was never heard of again.[41]

The Impost Act was signed into law on July 4, 1789. The inability to address pressing matters of public finance had been a major impulse behind the movement for the Constitution, and the successful adoption of a federal revenue act was an important step toward a stronger Union. Nevertheless, the prolonged debate in the House of Representatives also gave cause for concern. Representatives had consistently acted with the interest of their states in mind and had made clear that the range of acceptable fiscal measures was sharply limited despite the broad fiscal powers that were written into the Constitution. To the incoming secretary of the Treasury, the debate on the Impost and Tonnage Acts must have seemed ominous. A few days before the House of Representatives adjourned on September 29, it commissioned Alexander Hamilton to submit a report on the public debt. The request put the spotlight on the government's revenue needs. It was evident to all that the Impost Act would not generate the kind of sums needed to service the national debt. More money was needed. In mid-October Hamilton turned to his old ally Madison, asking him to "put to paper and send me your thoughts on such objects as may have occurred to you for an addition to our revenue." The difficulty, he said, seemed to lie not in the absence of suitable objects of taxation but "in the prejudices which may be feared with regard to almost every object. The Question is very much What further taxes will be *least* unpopular?"[42]

During his first months as Treasury secretary, Hamilton received advice about tax reform from several correspondents, including Madison. All were in basic agreement: the government could not expect to raise revenue from direct taxes on property. Requisitions on the states were also out of the question. Excise duties and the impost were the only taxes the people would accept. William Bingham, one of the directors of the Bank of North America, warned against a fiscal system built solely on import duties and called for an array of internal duties and fees on the retail sale of "all articles of general Consumption, Such as Wines, Rum, Brandy, Sugar, Coffee, Tea, Chocolate, Salt Pepper &c." Madison suggested a stamp act on proceedings in federal courts, an increase of the duty on imported alcohol, and an excise on domestically produced spirits. High taxes on imported alcohol required a tax on American distilled rum and whiskey to prevent consumers from turning from expensive imported liquor to cheaper domestic spirits. To stop prying excisemen from invading the privacy of the citizens, a chief reason for the popular opposition to excise duties, Madison argued that the tax could be "regulated by the size of the Still" rather than actual production. Alone among Hamilton's advisors, Madison further recommended a federal land tax, which seemed to him "to be recommended by its simplicity, its certainty, its equity, and the cheapness of collecting it. It may be well also for the General Govt. to espouse this object before a preoccupancy by the States becomes an impediment."[43]

Hamilton proved to be much more cautious than Madison. Although sometimes portrayed as a hardliner, he was in fact careful not to provoke popular opposition to a government he thought fragile at best. His *Report on Public Credit* mostly tinkered with existing duties instead of introducing new taxes. The Senate had sharply reduced many of the duties adopted by the House of Representatives, and Hamilton now adjusted them upward again, sometimes to levels that exceeded the rates originally set by the House. The tax on Madeira wine, for example, had been 25 cents per gallon in the House bill but had been reduced to 18 cents in the Senate. Hamilton now argued for a duty of 30 to 35 cents per gallon. In the same manner, the duty on distilled spirits had been 10 to 15 cents per gallon in the House bill and 8 cents in the Impost Act. Hamilton thought it could bear a duty of 20 to 40 cents. The only novel measure in the report was an excise on domestically produced alcohol, which was necessary to compensate for increased duties on imported spirits. Commercial producers would pay a duty on production, whereas private distillers would be taxed according to the size of their stills, much as Madison had advised. In a follow-up report detailing how the government would find the means to pay for the assumption of state debts, Hamilton suggested further internal duties and fees on carriages, snuff and manufactured tobacco, sales at auction, licenses for the retail sale of alcohol, and licenses to practice law. Although it would take several years for Congress to adopt all his measures, Hamilton's tax package was set out already in the early months of 1790. Before Oliver Wolcott drafted the direct tax of 1798, there was very little fiscal innovation in the Age of Federalism.[44]

Rather than breaking new ground, the *Report on Public Credit* built on the work of the First Congress. Hamilton agreed with the representatives that alcohol and other "luxury" items that Congress had singled out for higher duties were proper objects of taxation. They were "all of them, in reality—luxuries—the greatest part of them foreign luxuries; some of them, in the excess in which they are used, pernicious luxuries." In his *Report on Funds for the Payment of the Interest on the States' Debts*, Hamilton noted that wine and spirits were "certainly, among the most unexceptionable objects of Revenue." In contrast to Madison, who had called for a federal land tax, Hamilton was anxious to point out that the national government took pains to leave "real estate" untouched. Partly this was to avoid popular protest, but Hamilton provided a further rationale for not taxing property: it was vital to keep some of the nation's resources in reserve to be mobilized in the event of crisis. Foreign nations would learn to respect the United States if they saw the vast untapped resources that the government had at its command, whereas "the appearance of exhausted resources, (which would perhaps be the consequence of mortgaging the revenue to be derived from land, for the interest of the public debt) might tend to invite both insult and injury, by inspiring an opinion, that our efforts to resent or repel them were little to be dreaded."[45]

Eventually all of the measures Hamilton proposed in his reports on public credit would become law. On August 4, 1790, a new Impost Act replaced the law of the previous summer. It doubled the duties on alcohol and foodstuffs such as coffee and tea. Congress postponed action on the excise, however. Hamilton repeated his call for higher duties on alcohol and an excise on domestic spirits in late 1790 when the House of Representatives asked him for further sources of revenue. Grudgingly, Congress passed the Excise Act in March 1791, which introduced both higher rates on imported alcohol and an excise on domestically distilled spirits. Three years later, in June 1794, Congress passed a series of acts introducing a license fee on the retail sale of alcohol and duties on carriages, snuff, refined sugar, and sales at auction. Four years after he had first outlined the nation's fiscal system in the *Report on Public Credit* and the *Report on Funds for the Payment of the*

Interest on the States' Debts, Hamilton's tax package was finally in place. He would leave office eight months later.[46]

VI

The legislation of the First Congress and the follow-up measures proposed by Hamilton led to a rapid rise in federal revenue. Despite auxiliary legislation providing for excises, customs duties provided the bulk of the government's income. From 1792 to 1795, the federal government raised $18.1 million in customs duties and $1.2 million in internal revenue. This should be compared to the limited sums raised by the states in the 1780s. Table 2.6 compares customs collections in four major ports before and after the adoption of the Constitution. It shows that the income from customs duties increased dramatically after the federal government took over the customs collection. The total increase in the four ports was 600 percent between the periods 1785–1788 and 1792–1795. There are significant variations between

TABLE 2.6. Customs receipts in four major ports ($)

Port	1785–1788	1792–1795
New York	603,000	4,653,000
Philadelphia	622,000	4,299,000
Baltimore	346,000	1,829,000
Charleston	404,000	1,064,000
Total	1,975,000	11,845,000

Sources: 1785–1788: New York: *Journal of the Assembly of the State of New-York* (Jan. 9–Mar. 22, 1788) (Poughkeepsie, 1788), 19, 21, 23; *Journal of the Assembly of the State of New-York* (July 6–16, 1789) (New York: Loudons, 1789), 56. Philadelphia: *State of the Accounts of David Rittenhouse, Esq., Treasurer of Pennsylvania; from January, 1785, till January, 1786* (Philadelphia: Oswald, 1790), 19; *State of the Account of David Rittenhouse, Esq., Treasurer of the Commonwealth of Pennsylvania; from January, 1786, till January, 1787* (Philadelphia: Bailey, 1790), 23–24, 35; *State of the Accounts of David Rittenhouse, Esq., Treasurer of Pennsylvania; from 1st January till 1st November 1787; Including his Continental and State Money Accounts for the year 1786* (Philadelphia: Aitken, 1790), 29, 39; *State of the Accounts of David Rittenhouse, Esq., Treasurer of Pennsylvania; for the Year 1788* (Philadelphia: Aitken, 1791), 27–28; *State of the Accounts of David Rittenhouse, Esq. Treasurer of Pennsylvania; from September 1788, till September 1st, 1789, including his Continental and State money accounts for 1788* (Philadelphia: Aitken, 1791). Baltimore: *Votes and Proceedings of the House of Delegates of the State of Maryland, November Session, 1787* (Nov. 14, 1785–Mar. 12, 1786) (Annapolis, 1786), 12, 14; *Votes and Proceedings of the House of Delegates of the State of Maryland, November Session, 1786* (Annapolis, 1787), 40; *Votes and Proceedings of the House of Delegates of the State of Maryland,. November Session, 1787* (Annapolis, 1788), 27; *Votes and Proceedings of the House of Delegates of the State of Maryland, November Session, 1788* (Annapolis, 1789), 56–57; Charleston: R. Nicholas Olsberg and Helen Craig Carson, *Duties on Trade at Charleston, 1784–1789* ... (Columbia, SC, 1970). 1792–1795: "Statement of Receipts at the Treasury, from the Collectors of the Customs, from the Commencement of the Present Government to the Close of the Year 1799," *ASP: Finance,* 1:666–67.

the ports, however. Collections at Charleston increased by a comparatively modest 260 percent, whereas collections at Baltimore increased by 530 percent, at Philadelphia by 690 percent, and at New York by 770 percent. In 1785, the combined impost and excise fund of Massachusetts, which included not only income from excises but customs collections from all the state's ports, generated some $190,000. On average, the annual customs revenue collected in the port of Boston alone between 1792 and 1795 was about two and a half times as much.[47]

The increase in the yield from customs duties coincides in time with an upswing in the American economy. The War of Independence had serious economic consequences. It has been estimated that the war set back the level of the gross domestic product per capita by as much as fifty years. After a brief recovery in 1781 to 1782, growth was slow and perhaps even negative. The adoption of the Constitution had a positive effect on the business climate, and from 1789 the economy began to grow rapidly. With the outbreak of the French Revolutionary Wars in 1792, the pace of growth increased further, as American merchants encompassed more and more of the Atlantic trade. The European war heralded a period of steady and high growth rates. In the words of one economic historian, "There can be no doubt that the years 1793 through 1807 were extraordinarily prosperous for the American economy."[48]

Despite the economic recovery, the yield from customs duties grew faster than the value of imports. The most important explanation for the rising productivity of the impost, therefore, was not the rise in trade but increases in the tariff rates and in the efficiency of the Customs Service. This was made possible only because the government took pains not to alienate the merchant class. As a group, merchants certainly stood to gain from the creation of an energetic federal government, yet the long tradition of smuggling meant that respect for the revenue laws was not guaranteed. The Federalists secured the compliance of merchants by negotiation rather than coercion, and their accommodation of the merchant class made the administration of the impost proceed without serious disruptions.[49]

VII

Federal assumption of state debts combined with the simultaneous return of prosperity eliminated protests over state taxation. A study of the Chesapeake states shows that "economic issues appeared on the legislative agenda with less and less frequency during the 1790s." "And when they did appear, they were less likely to generate public roll calls." Massachusetts saw the same development. Soon after the adoption of the Constitution, "the twin problems of personal debts and state taxes began to disappear as political issues." In the 1790s, the taxpayers not only contributed to the federal treasury, they also rapidly reduced the back taxes they owed to the state governments. This was an important development to the future of the American union, for taxation—together with the closely intertwined questions of the public debt and paper money—had been one of the most divisive issues in state politics in the 1780s and had given rise to severe instability at the national level, too.[50]

At the level of national politics, taxation and public finance continued to generate conflict. Although the impost was not controversial—the tariff would not become a major issue in American politics before the 1820s—other elements of Federalist public finance caused contention. Hamilton's policies attempted to emulate certain institutions and practices that had been part of Britain's financial arrangements at least since the Glorious Revolution. The first Bank of the United States and the funded federal debt had their British counterparts, and there was a strong Anglo-American political belief that such institutions bred corruption, which would eventually lead to the downfall of the free institutions that were the birthright of Britons on both sides of the Atlantic. Both institutions were fiercely resisted by the political opposition. Protests over federal taxation flared up, too, although on no occasion was the impost the object of discontent. The Whiskey Rebellion was a protest against the excise on alcohol. Fries's Rebellion was a protest against a program of direct taxation that aimed to finance the military buildup during the Quasi War with France. Both protests were put down by force.[51]

Historians have sometimes taken the Whiskey Rebellion and Fries's Rebellion as indications that federal taxes in the 1790s were just as oppressive as state taxes had been in the 1780s. But such a view fails to recognize that these protests were isolated occurrences and, above all, that the taxes that provoked them made up only a small part of the Federalists' fiscal regime. Whatever we may think of these protests and of the way the government handled them, they hardly justify the conclusion that the federal tax burden was heavy or that the federal fiscal administration rested on force. Considering the aversion to taxation evinced by the American public ever since the Revolution, what seems distinctive about the Federalists' fiscal regime is rather the way it managed to raise so much revenue with so little protest.

From small beginnings the impost grew to generate large sums for the federal government. In 1789 customs duties brought in $830,000. Two years later that sum was $3.2 million. From there the customs revenue increased steadily so that by the end of the decade the government netted nearly $10 million. The successful reform of the nation's revenue system allowed for the creation of a small army and more energetic management of the western domain. Later in the decade, the national government would also embark on a modest but still expensive naval program. The new fiscal system, finally, allowed for the restoration of public credit, which was of immense long-term significance to the United States and undoubtedly Alexander Hamilton's greatest achievement as secretary of the Treasury.[52]

CHAPTER THREE

So Immense a Power in the Affairs of War: The Restoration of Public Credit

As its second session drew to a close, the First Congress passed one of its most controversial acts of legislation. Debate on the Funding Act had taken up most of the session. It had caused the authors of *The Federalist* to fall out and had resuscitated sectional feelings. To the secretary of the Treasury, the very existence of the Union seemed to hang in the balance. In the greater drama of American history, the funding and assumption of the Revolutionary debt was the moment that set the stage for the party struggles of the 1790s. Disagreement over the management of the public debt led to the rivalry between Alexander Hamilton and Thomas Jefferson, who became not only leaders of clashing parties but also symbols of two radically different visions of the destiny of the United States. Their conflict has dominated interpretations of Hamilton's financial program to the extent that the original rationale behind funding and assumption has become obscured. The origins of Hamilton's program lay in the United States' situation as a relatively weak power in a world of hostile empires and nation-states. Regardless of any other intentions Hamilton may have harbored, the Funding Act aimed to equip the fledgling national government with a crucial institution of the modern state: a well-managed public debt. Though few historians have altogether missed this dimension of the Federalist program, they have accorded it no more than fleeting interest. And they have paid much less attention than Hamilton himself did to the importance of public credit to a state's ability to act decisively in international affairs.[1]

The impetus for the Funding Act came right after Hamilton's appointment as secretary of the Treasury in September 1789, when the House of Representatives asked him to prepare a plan "for the support of the public credit, as a matter of high importance to the national honor and prosperity." Hamilton responded with his *Report Relative to a Provision for the Support of Public Credit*, better known as the *Report on Public Credit*, in mid-January of the next year. With some important changes, the report formed the basis of the act adopted by Congress on August 4, 1790. The Funding Act reformed the enormous debt the new government had inherited from the War of Independence. It stipulated that outstanding securities would be exchanged for a new emission that was funded, meaning that the government pledged to pay interest on the debt with earmarked, or mortgaged, tax incomes. The new securities had no fixed maturation date, and the government's right of redemption was restricted. Neither the *Report on Public Credit* nor the Funding Act offered more than limited means to pay off the principal of the debt. Failure to ensure repayment led contemporary critics to charge that Hamilton wished to prolong or even perpetuate the debt, a charge that has sometimes been repeated by modern historians. With the Funding Act, the federal government also assumed responsibility for the main share of the state debts run up during the War of Independence. In the end, the federal government assumed $18 million owed by the states, thereby nationalizing almost the entire Revolutionary debt.[2]

Though he later pointed to the Funding Act as the centerpiece of Hamilton's schemes to destroy the American republic, Jefferson did not immediately awake to the dangers of the public debt. Much to his surprise, Hamilton's first major critic was his erstwhile nationalist ally James Madison. Madison's position on funding arose from his wish to protect the interests of original security holders against the actions of speculators. Most of the outstanding securities had been issued as a form of payment to soldiers and military suppliers in the early to mid-1780s. These securities represented the government's promise to pay the holder in real money at a later date. Because the government's financial situation was desperate, many doubted that such a day would ever come, and therefore most original holders sold their securities to third parties, often at prices far below face value. If the government put its financial house in order, however, the value of the securities would rise, benefiting those who had bought securities from the people who had originally received them as compensation for their services. In what to Madison seemed a blatant injustice, the Funding Act disregarded the original holders' right to compensation. Historians have often been impressed by Madison's arguments and have sometimes repeated his charge that the funding plan generated "enormous profit" for undeserving speculators. It was an exaggerated charge, however, that held true only for public creditors who bought certificates cheaply in the late 1780s. Investors who bought securities around the time the army was disbanded in 1783 did not make significantly greater profits than they would have earned from private investments, and they were exposed to far greater risk.[3]

Support for Madison was only lukewarm in the House of Representatives, which voted 36 to 13 against his proposal to discriminate between present and original security holders. The question of federal assumption of state debt, however, generated much more animosity. When Hamilton presented his report, Congress was still auditing the respective contributions made by state governments to the American War of Independence. Madison believed that Virginia had paid off much of its debt and therefore that assumption would force his own state to pay more than its fair share of the total war costs. He also feared that federal assumption of state debts would unduly strengthen the central government at the expense of the state governments. Many others agreed, and the House deadlocked over the issue. It was at this point that Jefferson claims to have stepped in to arrange the famous dinner-table bargain by which Madison supplied enough southern votes to pass the Funding Act in return for a promise to locate the national capital on the Potomac River.[4]

Hamilton's report and the subsequent Funding Act aimed to modernize American public finances by introducing contemporary European practices of debt management. The most controversial measures—nondiscrimination between creditors, federal assumption of state debt, and restriction on the government's right to pay off the debt—all stemmed from this attempt. Though controversial, the reform was successful in rapidly restoring public credit. Despite its role in provoking the split between Federalists and Republicans, the Funding Act introduced policies and institutions of debt management that outlived the Federalist administrations of George Washington and John Adams. Republicans upheld the right of public creditors and managed the debt well after they assumed power in 1801. They accepted the importance of sound public credit as much as the Federalists did and made much more use of it than their predecessors. Federalists and Republicans also shared a concern about the uncontrolled growth of public indebtedness. In furnishing means for debt reduction, the American funding system constituted a major divergence from European practice. Contrary to his reputation as a friend of perpetual debt, the architect of this provision was none other than Hamilton, who initiated a program of debt redemption that set the Revolutionary debt on the road to extinction. It was a program that would be faithfully administered by the Virginia dynasty.

I

Broadly speaking, modern historians have identified two distinct but not incompatible motives behind the funding and assumption of the Revolutionary debt. The first was Alexander Hamilton and the Federalists' wish to use the debt to forge a link between public creditors and the new federal government for political ends. This interpretation originates in the Jeffersonian critique of Hamiltonianism and is based on the arguments of Hamilton's critics rather than his own words. The second motive historians have identified was Hamilton's belief that the debt could be used to promote the American economy. In contrast to the political interpretation of his aims, this interpretation finds much support in Hamilton's own writings on the funding and assumption of the Revolutionary debt.

In the early days of George Washington's administration, Thomas Jefferson shared the Federalists' belief in the importance of restoring public credit. As minister to France, he had personally experienced difficulties in borrowing money on the credit of the United States. Toward the end of Washington's first term, however, Jefferson had developed second thoughts. He now regretted his role in shepherding the Funding Act through Congress, describing it as the greatest error of his political life. In a letter to Washington, he claimed to have been "duped" by Hamilton and "made a tool for forwarding his schemes." By this time Jefferson was convinced that Hamilton meant to use the public debt to destroy the republic. "I would wish the debt paid tomorrow," Jefferson wrote to Washington. In contrast, Jefferson said, Hamilton "wishes it never to be paid, but always to be a thing wherewith to corrupt and manage the legislature." According to Jefferson there existed a Treasury faction in Congress that followed the Treasury secretary's every bid. These men were bound to the Treasury because as public creditors they had a vested interest in maintaining a system of public indebtedness and heavy taxes as a means to transfer the community's wealth into their own pockets. But to Jefferson the problem went deeper than an attempt by creditors to lay their hands on the taxpayers' money. The aim of this "corrupt squadron" was to undermine the Constitution and republican liberty and ultimately to establish a monarchy on the British model.[5]

Jefferson was not alone in raising such concerns about Hamiltonian finance. Nor was his critique original; he merely applied arguments derived from the British Country Whig tradition to Hamilton's measures. The intellectual origin of this ideology lies in a body of thought that first appeared in opposition to new governmental institutions established in England in the wake of the Glorious Revolution of 1688. One of the most striking novelties of the new system was the introduction of a large and seemingly ever-increasing public debt, which was believed to undermine the political independence of the House of Commons by introducing executive influence in the legislative branch of government. As historians have long pointed out, the Country Whig tradition was adopted wholesale in the American colonies before the Revolution, and it remained strong in the early national period. It furnished powerful arguments with which to fight Federalist policies because Hamilton seemed intent on imitating British developments. Thus when the Virginia House of Delegates protested against the Funding Act, they did so by making explicit comparisons with the former mother country. The delegates claimed there was "a striking resemblance" between the Funding Act and the system "which was introduced into England at the Revolution—a system which has perpetuated upon that nation an enormous debt, and has moreover insinuated into the hands of the Executive an unbounded influence."[6]

Modern historians have only rarely shared Jefferson's view of Hamilton's ultimate aims, though Hamilton has on occasion been referred to as a "true Machiavellian" and a closet "dictator." Rather, they tend to accept Jefferson's interpretation of Hamilton's intentions without questioning his loyalty to the American republic. By the time he wrote the *Report on Public Credit*, the public debt had concentrated in the hands of the social and economic elite. Hamilton's principal aim, most historians agree, was to ensure the stability of the new regime by giving the elite a reason to support it. The funding and assumption of the Revolutionary debt could help serve this purpose. Though Hamilton may have been skeptical about democracy, he never wished to replace the republic with a monarchy.[7]

Not surprisingly, Hamilton denied Jefferson's charge that he had used the debt to corrupt the republic. Yet the terms in which Hamilton framed his denial are intriguing. Looking back on the Funding Act half a decade later, Hamilton "frankly acknowledge[d]" that the public debt could "strengthen our infant Government by increasing the number of ligaments between the Government and the interests of Individuals." He seems to have found nothing wrong in principle with using the debt to buy the electorate's support, believing such support would help maintain the Constitution and the Union. The new government was weak and needed every assistance against "the excentricities of State ambition and the explosions of factious passions." But if funding and assumption would secure the support of public creditors, it also threatened to antagonize taxpayers. Such support would therefore be "in a considerable degree counterballanced by . . . the necessity which it imposed on the government of resorting early to unpalateable modes of taxation which jeopardized its popularity and gave a handle to its enemies to attack." Furthermore the debt was likely to be bought up by foreigners with little or no political influence in America. "Had this then been the weightiest motive to the measure," Hamilton wrote, "it would never have received my patronage."[8]

The alleged economic motive behind the Funding Act was to use the debt to improve the economy by creating new investment capital and increasing the money stock. Hamilton repeatedly spoke in such terms when he argued in favor of his measures. Funding would create capital out of thin air as almost worthless bonds suddenly appreciated in value and then stabilized around par. Because these securities had been bought up by merchants, this new capital was placed in the hands of the dynamic force of the American economy: men who were able to invest money productively. Part of the capital would go into banks, where it would support the issue of banknotes. Funding therefore promised to increase the money stock, an important achievement in a nation where wealth had long been abundant but money scarce. Finally, the federal assumption of state debts promised to increase the capital market by as much as 30 to 40 percent, thus further promoting the economy.[9]

Like the politics of corruption, Hamilton's economic ideas can also be traced back to England. After the Glorious Revolution, the English public debt had increased the amount of capital in the hands of merchants and had thereby spurred "phenomenal" economic development. But historians have pointed to a crucial difference between the policies pursued in Britain and in the United States. In Britain public finance was a way to raise money to wage wars. Even if the economic consequences of the government's actions were important, they were no more than "incidental" side effects. Hamilton reversed these priorities. To him financial policy was a means to strengthen the economy and not the state. His intention to actively manage the national economy is why he has appeared so modern to many interpreters, who claim that "few of the techniques available to modern finance ministers and central bankers" in managing a modern economy "were not known and used by Hamilton two centuries ago."[10]

Apart from the question of intellectual origins, both major interpretations of the rationale behind funding and assumption point to the domestic origins and consequences of Alexander Hamilton's policies, whether these are conceived to be mainly political or economic. But Hamilton and the Federalists were also concerned with the American union's relations to the outside world. Independence had made the United States a new member of the international state system and the heir to Britain's imperial aspirations on the North American continent. To defend and promote American national interests, it was essential that the republic acquire some of the features of contemporary European great powers.

Ever since Hamilton first began to think seriously about public finance, he had treated public credit as a crucial resource of the modern state, of "immense importance" to "the strength and security of nations." In an April 1780 letter to the newly appointed superintendent of finance, Robert Morris, Hamilton argued that independence would be secured "not by gaining battles" but "by restoreing public credit." Even "the most powerful and opulent" nations were "obliged to have recourse to loans, in time of war," he declared in "The Continentalist No. IV" a few months later. A state able to borrow money could mobilize resources far beyond what its tax base would allow. In contrast, a state unable to borrow would be left at the mercy of stronger states. Credit, Hamilton wrote in his unpublished "Defence of the Funding System," composed after his retirement from the Treasury, "is so immense a power in the affairs of war that a nation without credit would be in great danger of falling a victim in the first war with a power possessing a vigorous and flourishing credit." Elsewhere he wrote, "It is impossible for a Country to contend on equal terms, or to be secure against the enterprises of other nations without being able equally with them to avail itself of this important resource." Public credit allowed governments not only to raise unprecedented sums of money but to do so in ways that were less painful to the population and less disruptive of the economy than alternative means of resource mobilization. In modern wars, Hamilton wrote," the current revenues of a nation do not . . . suffice. Plunder or Credit must supply the deficiency." Since the first alternative was obviously unacceptable and entailed "a subversion of all social order," credit was the only option.[11]

Regardless of other political and economic effects, the government's ability to borrow money was an important end in itself. It equipped the United States with the means to compete in the international state system. In the decades that followed the Funding Act's adoption, government loans were used repeatedly to fund war and territorial expansion. In contrast to the familiar narrative of American political history, there was no great break in the nation's development when Federalists were replaced by Republicans. If anything, the Revolution of 1800 signaled an even more aggressive policy against Indian nations and an even more active policy against European states. These policies forced Republicans to make vigorous use of the governmental institutions created by their predecessors. For all the rhetorical steam, Jefferson's "Empire of Liberty" was made possible by a Federalist fiscal system and Federalist policies of debt management.[12]

II

The *Report on Public Credit* opened with a set of "plain and undeniable truths." Like every other nation, the United States would engage in wars in the future. In the modern age, even "the wealthiest" of nations were forced to finance their wars with loans. Since the United States possessed "little monied capital," it would be even more dependent on this resource than other nations. But it was not only necessary to be able to borrow money; such loans had to be made "upon *good terms*." Therefore it was "essential that the credit of a nation should be well established." The report thus clearly identified public credit as an instrument of war. From the struggle for independence to the Second World War, American statesmen and political thinkers have often claimed that the United States differs from Europe largely because it is far removed from European wars and power politics. There is some truth in this claim, yet it is also problematic. Political independence introduced a turbulent period of repeated international crises that peaked with the Quasi War against France and the War of 1812 against Britain. Only with the close of the Napoleonic Wars in 1815 did the international situation calm down. By then, however, the American union had begun a policy of expansion that generated its own conflicts. Though early American statesmen may have dreamed of political and commercial isolation, they knew that this dream was impossible. Western expansion and involvement in the Atlantic economy made conflicts and wars inevitable.[13]

During Alexander Hamilton's term as Treasury secretary, the United States managed to avoid a European war. Still Hamilton had to borrow to finance Indian wars and to pay for the army sent against the whiskey rebels in western Pennsylvania. Given the constant danger of war, it seemed clear to Hamilton that the United States "ought to aim at rendering its credit, that is its faculty to borrow, commensurate with the utmost extent of the lending faculties of the community and of all others who can have access to its loans. Tis then that it puts itself in a condition to exercise the greatest portion of strength of which it is capable and has its destiny most completely in its own hands." Failure to make provisions for the nation's credit would force the republic to "a mean surrender of our rights and interests to every enterprising invader." This argument did not convince everyone. In the congressional debate on the *Report on Public Credit*, Michael Jenifer Stone rejected all funding systems as "monuments of the folly and vice of mankind" precisely because they made nations able to wage war. They gave a government without "money of its own" the ability to pursue "mad schemes of ambition" and "the means of purchasing mercenary soldiers, of shedding the blood of their neighbors, and of cutting so many more throats than they would otherwise be able to do."[14]

Stone's critique pointed to the origins of funding systems in what one late eighteenth-century British writer called "the prevalence and extension of the war-system throughout Europe." Loans allowed nations to multiply their resources. Money could be had quickly and without the need to impose upon taxpayers. As Adam Smith pointed out, borrowing was a way for governments to avoid reforming the tax system: "By means of borrowing they are enabled, with a very moderate increase of taxes, to raise, from year to year, money sufficient for carrying on the war, and by the practice of perpetual funding they are enabled, with the smallest possible increase of taxes, to raise annually the largest possible sum of money." Only rarely did governments manage to reduce debts in peacetime. Hence their debts grew with every new war. By the mid- to late eighteenth century, Europe's rapidly growing public debts were seen as one of the foremost problems of political economy.[15]

In principle a government could reduce its debt by paying it off or by repudiating it, wholly or in part. In practice neither alternative was viable. Paying off the debt required greater incomes, which in turn required fiscal reform. Tax reform was difficult in part because the surplus generated by eighteenth-century economies was not large and because any substantial reform would have to tax powerful and privileged groups. Debt repudiation was not an attractive alternative because governments feared that such action would ruin their ability to borrow in the future. In Amsterdam, Europe's primary market for government loans in the eighteenth century, bankers assessed creditworthiness solely on the record of past debt management. Though public bankruptcies had been common in sixteenth- and seventeenth-century Europe and would become so again during the long and expensive wars that followed the French Revolution, the eighteenth century was a period when governments did their utmost to honor their debts.[16]

Unable to increase their revenue, unwilling to repudiate their debts, but still seeking to maximize their capacity for borrowing, European governments were caught in a fix. The solution lay in the renegotiation of interest rates and repayment terms. If the interest rate could be reduced and the principal need not be repaid, the amount of debt a government could sustain on a given income would increase. As interest rates on private loans fell in the eighteenth century and capital outlays in public funds gradually came to be regarded as low-risk investments, the interest on public loans fell too. Thus in Britain, where the government was exceedingly careful to service the public debt according to contract, the interest rate on government loans fell from 10 percent in the late seventeenth century to merely 3 percent by the middle of the next century. On the international securities market in Amsterdam, interest rates had fallen to between 4 and 5 percent by the second half of the eighteenth century. Governments were quick to take advantage of falling interest rates by replacing old, expensive loans with new, cheap ones.[17]

The cost of indebtedness was further reduced when governments stopped making repayments of the principal, a practice that had become common in most European nations by the late eighteenth century. Creditors accepted this arrangement because government bonds could be freely sold to third parties. Such a right may seem self-evident today, but making securities freely alienable was a major financial innovation. A creditor could always liquidate an investment in the public funds by selling the claims on the government in the securities markets that had sprung up in London and Amsterdam. The pressure on the government to repay the loan was thereby removed, and the state was able to carry a greater burden of debt.[18]

The management of public debts was widely discussed in economic treatises and newspapers in eighteenth-century Britain and Europe. These texts were also read on the American side of the Atlantic, and informed Americans knew much about European funding systems. At the same time, such systems were new to the United States and had not formed part of the colonial experience. As Fisher Ames remarked in the House of Representatives, the "science of finance is new in America," and among the population at large there existed a strong aversion to public debts as the herald of oppressive taxes and overbearing government. Though historians have discussed the extent to which Hamilton copied from European—primarily British—financial institutions, there is no question that he knew them well. The *Report on Public Credit* was his attempt to adapt European principles of debt management to an American setting It came to generate a good deal of controversy.[19]

Hamilton's plan to restore public credit began with the need to restore the faith of present and future creditors in the ability and readiness of the government to service its debts according to contract. Faith was the essence of public and private credit. In his 1786 *An Essay on Credit*, Pelatiah Webster defined credit "in a commercial sense" as "*the confidence which people place in a man's integrity and punctuality, in fulfilling his contracts, and performing his engagements.*" As Congress debated the *Report on Public Credit*, Elias Boudinot, an old friend of Hamilton, also pointed to trust as the crucial aspect of public credit, which amounted to "the confidence reposed in a state, or body politic, who are borrowing money." In a later report, Hamilton described the public debt as *"a property subsisting in the faith of the Government. Its essence is promise. Its definite value depends upon the reliance that the promise will be definitely fulfilled."* The *Report on Public Credit* therefore declared that a government could only hope to maintain a high credit rating by observing "good faith" and "a punctual performance of contracts." Hamilton concluded, "States, like individuals, who observe their engagements, are respected and trusted: while the reverse is the fate of those, who pursue an opposite conduct."[20]

Federalists in Congress opposed discriminating between the original and subsequent owners of securities by pointing to the sanctity of contracts. They did so to establish a moral position from which to counter James Madison's accusation that funding would defraud virtuous soldiers and suppliers and benefit self-interested speculators. But even if much of the funding debate was framed as a discussion of the justice or equity of the measure, there was also a debate over the policy, or practical implications, of upholding the rights of final security holders against the claims of original holders. In Hamilton's words, a breach of faith with creditors, whether just or unjust, "renders property in the funds less valuable; consequently induces lenders to demand a higher premium for what they lend, and produces every other inconvenience of a bad state of public credit." Federalists in Congress were more outspoken. On "principles of policy," the United States ought to honor its contract with creditors "in order, that when public exigencies require it, we may borrow money with greater facility; we have no right, by our conduct, to put it out of the power of the United States hereafter to defend themselves, and unless we support the credit of America by a just performance of our engagements, we shall depreciate her credit to so low a state, as to prevent her forever obtaining any future loan."[21]

To honor its contract with the creditors, the government needed sufficient revenues to service the public debt. Raising money had been a major problem for the Confederation Congress since its inception, and fiscal reform was central to the agenda of the nationalists and later the Federalists during the ratification of the Constitution. The tax system created after the adoption of the Constitution relied heavily on customs duties, supplemented by minor incomes from excises. Over time, customs duties would generate large incomes, but in 1790 these duties were new, and Hamilton did not expect them to yield enough to pay the Revolutionary debt's stipulated interest of 6 percent, much less the principal. The *Report on Public Credit* estimated the domestic debt, including unpaid interest, at more than $42 million. In addition there was the foreign debt of $11.7 million. Interest charges alone on the two debts amounted to around $3 million annually. For the debt to be paid off within a reasonable period of time, say twenty-five years, it would require an additional $1.2 million per year. Furthermore, the running costs of even the most limited national government would be some $600,000 every year. Annual expenses would therefore amount to about $4.5 million to $5 million. In 1790 Hamilton calculated that the income of the federal government would be no more than $2.8 million.[22]

The Federalists in general and Hamilton in particular are sometimes portrayed as friends of big government. In the fiscal sphere, however, most American statesmen and legislators seem to have shared the view that there were narrow limits to the amount of taxes American citizens were ready to pay in support of the federal government. During the debate on the Funding Act, congressmen at one point contrasted the high tax pressure in France to the low levels of taxation in America. To some this comparison suggested there was ample room for a tax increase in the United States. Others disagreed. To Hugh Williamson there was no doubt that American taxpayers would always flee from undue pressure from the government: "The people in England, France, and most parts of Europe, are surrounded by the sea, or by nations with whom they cannot mix; they cannot remove with any degree of ease, wherefore they groan and bear the oppression of taxes. Press the American in the same manner, and he will fly to the boundless wilderness, that he may be free as the original inhabitants."[23]

To Hamilton and other Federalists, emigration from the eastern states to the western territories was certainly problematic. Yet a more immediate threat to the American fiscal system stemmed from obstructions and even tax rebellions. From the crisis with Britain through the American War of Independence and the postwar fiscal crisis to Shays's Rebellion, resistance to taxation had been at the center of American politics for a quarter century. Contemplating taxes beyond customs duties in his fall 1789 letter to Madison, Hamilton had remarked that the difficulty lay "not so much in the want of [taxable] objects as in the prejudices which may be feared with regard to almost every object." About to retire from the Treasury five years later, he was of the same opinion. "To extinguish a Debt which exists and to avoid contracting more are ideas almost always favored by public feeling and opinion," he noted, "but to pay Taxes for the one or the other purpose, which are the only means of avoiding the evil, is always more or less unpopular." From this aversion to taxation came the habit of governments to "shift off the burden from the present to a future day" by acquiring more debt, "a propensity which may be expected to be strong in proportion as the form of the State is popular."[24]

But even if citizens had been willing to pay higher taxes, a high level of taxation may have proven detrimental to public credit. Should the state appropriate the entire surplus generated by the economy, there would be no funds on which to contract new loans in future crises. Some of the nation's wealth ought therefore to be held in reserve. "It will not be forgotten," Hamilton reminded Congress in the *Report on Public Credit*, "that exigencies may, ere long, arise, which would call for resources greatly beyond what is now deemed sufficient for the current service; and that, should the faculties of the country be exhausted or even *strained* to provide for the public debt, there could be less reliance on the sacredness of the provision." Faced with the choice between raising taxes to pay off the debt rapidly or accepting indebtedness for at least the foreseeable future, Hamilton opted for the latter.[25]

Despite the increased cost of indebtedness, the assumption of state debts was primarily a means to make ends meet. A well-running revenue service was essential to the restoration of public credit. Assumption would "leave the field of revenue more open to the US" by ensuring that the states were "under as little necessity as possible of exercising the power of taxation." Without assumption there would be "a conflict of interests and feelings among the public creditors," a point that had already been made in the Constitutional Convention. State creditors had an interest in seeing the states raise taxes to service their debts. They would therefore pressure state legislatures to adopt fiscal programs but would care little if such programs interfered with federal taxation. Hence there would be a danger that the state and federal fiscal systems would come into conflict, perhaps resulting in insufficient incomes for both governments. In the congressional debates, Federalists stressed this point repeatedly. The proposed solution to this potential conflict presented in the *Report on Public Credit* was to place the responsibility for debt servicing and taxation in the same hands. "If all the public creditors receive their dues from one source, distributed with an equal hand, their interest will be the same. And having the same interests, they will unite in the support of the fiscal arrangements of the government: As these, too, can be made with more convenience, where there is no competition: These circumstances combined will insure to the revenue laws a more ready and more satisfactory execution."[26]

Hamilton made no attempt to identify who the state creditors were. Elbridge Gerry, however, claimed it was "well known that the commercial interest throughout the union" held the "greatest part of the state securities." The fact that they did so supplied an additional reason in favor of assumption. Merchants were the chief source of loans "in cases of emergency," and for this reason "their friendship is cultivated by the governments of all commercial states." Merchants were the group from which the main part of the tax revenue would be collected. Because the means of coercion available to the United States revenue service were limited, tax collection could only succeed if taxes were regarded as legitimate and paid voluntarily. The Whiskey Rebellion and Fries's Rebellion may of course suggest otherwise. But they happened precisely because the taxes that were imposed, or at least the taxes that the people *thought* were being imposed, failed this test of legitimacy. The coercion involved in suppressing the rebellions was not typical of day-to-day Federalist tax administration, which rested on the taxpayers' "confidence in, and attachment to your government," as Gerry put it. "If you lose that confidence and attachment, what means have you to prevent their smuggling? Cruizers you have none; and if you had, it would be difficult to reconcile the citizens to coercion."[27]

III

In the fall of 1789, when working on the *Report on Public Credit*, Alexander Hamilton found himself in a predicament that would easily have been recognized by contemporary European financiers. On the one hand, he had to honor the government's contract with its creditors. On the other hand, he did not have the money to do so and doubted that he could find it. In one respect Hamilton was actually worse off than European finance ministers. In 1790 Britain was the most indebted nation in Europe in absolute terms and relative to tax income. Its debt was about fifteen times greater than its tax revenue. The public debt of the United States was much smaller than Britain's, $80 million compared with more than $1 billion. But so was the tax revenue. The British government could count on close to $70 million annually, whereas Hamilton expected to raise only $2.8 million. The American debt was almost thirty times greater than the expected annual income, which made its debt-to-revenue ratio twice as great as the British. The situation led Thomas Jefferson to anxiously compare levels of indebtedness in Europe and America, concluding that the United States was not just "the youngest nation in the world" but "the most indebted." In contrast to developments in Europe, however, the American debt stayed more or less constant during the next decade, whereas tax income grew rapidly. By 1800 the United States debt was less than eight times the annual tax revenue, lower than the debt of most European states. Yet when Hamilton wrote his report, this development lay in the future and could not be counted on with certainty. In 1790 the Treasury secretary looked forward to servicing a substantial debt with too little revenue.[28]

The course Hamilton followed out of this dilemma would also have been recognized by contemporary European statesmen. As European governments had done, Hamilton proposed to refinance the Revolutionary debt. He did not make any explicit reference to European practice, but other Federalists such as Fisher Ames did, and there is little doubt where Hamilton's models came from. By renegotiating interest rates and terms of repayment, the United States could reduce the cost of indebtedness and avoid a heavy tax burden. Whereas replacing expensive old loans with cheap new ones could reduce the cost of the foreign debt, the domestic debt required a different solution. Hamilton first redefined the outstanding debt as redeemable annuities without a fixed maturation date. The securities had been issued either with a fixed due date or with the assumption that they would be paid as soon as Congress could afford to, but Hamilton claimed that over time they had been "converted into a capital . . . without any definitive period of redemption." They were therefore redeemable at the pleasure of the government, and as long as the government took care to pay the promised interest, the creditor had no legitimate right to claim repayment of the principal. "For it seems to be a clear position," Hamilton reasoned, "that when a public contracts a debt payable with interest, without any precise time being stipulated or understood for payment of the capital, that time is a matter of pure discretion with the government, which is at liberty to consult its own convenience respecting it, taking care to pay the interest with punctuality." This move not only took care of the need to make installments on the principal but also gave Hamilton a bargaining position from which to negotiate a reduction of the interest rate.[29]

The change from fixed-term securities to securities without maturation date made it necessary to uphold the creditors' right to transfer their securities. If the government did not plan to repay the principal in the near future, public creditors could only liquidate their investments by selling them to third parties. Final settlement certificates as well as Continental loan office certificates stated that they were payable to bearer, and the right of a secondary holder could not "be disputed, without manifest injustice." Such a breach of contract would inevitably raise the price of future loans because it would add an element of risk to investments in the public funds. Here Hamilton followed the recommendations laid down by Malachy Postlethwayt, whose *Universal Dictionary of Trade and Commerce* Hamilton is known to have consulted. Postlethwayt was certain "that no body would lend their money to the support of the state under the most pressing emergencies, unless they could have the privilege of buying and selling their property in the public funds, when their occasions required. 'Tis certain, therefore, that the greatest delicacy and tenderness is to be observed, in laying any restraints upon these transactions, lest the public credit should be thereby irrevocably prejudiced." The right to sell securities was also an important inducement for men and women of capital to lend their money to the public. David Hume wrote that a holder of British "public securities" held "funds which will answer the most sudden demand that can be made upon him. No merchant thinks it necessary to keep by him any considerable cash. Bank-stock, or India-bonds, especially the latter, serve all the same purposes; because he can dispose of them, or pledge them to a banker, in a quarter of an hour." In the same way, Hamilton thought that "from their negotiable and easily vendible nature," American public securities could "at any moment" be applied "to any useful or profitable undertaking which occurs." The right to sell or transfer securities "without restriction" was therefore "an ingredient of value to the holder."[30]

Hamilton's next move was to reduce the interest rate. He believed that payment of the stipulated interest rate of 6 percent would require tax levels the people were unlikely to accept. It was therefore necessary to bring it down to a lower level. The offer eventually presented to creditors by the Funding Act, which was a simplified version of Hamilton's original proposal, was 4 percent rising to 6 percent in 1801. Two-thirds of the capital would start to earn a 6 percent interest immediately; one-third, the so-called deferred debt, would start to earn interest only after ten years. Because it was "evidently impracticable" to pay the $13 million of accumulated interest owed on the debt, Hamilton suggested that the outstanding interest, which had been paid in paper certificates called indents, also be converted into interest-bearing securities redeemable at the pleasure of the government. Congress accepted this proposal, but the Funding Act converted them into securities bearing 3 rather than 6 percent interest.[31]

Opponents inside and outside Congress had no difficulty detecting a breach of contract in this reduction of the interest rate. It appeared to be a clear example of an arbitrary change in the terms of the government's obligations. All of a sudden, the Federalists seemed to have abandoned every concern for the sanctity of contract. Some public creditors, as well as some of Hamilton's allies in Congress, also expressed their discontent with anything short of 6 percent. The charge that the government had broken the contract with the creditors was a serious one. Precisely because the *Report on Public Credit* suggested a partial debt repudiation in the form of a reduced interest rate, it was of great importance to Hamilton and his supporters that the reform of the debt was not the effect of a unilateral change in contractual terms but of a renegotiation of terms entered into voluntarily by the public creditors. As informed Americans knew, each of Britain's eighteenth-century debt conversions had taken place with the creditors' consent. Hamilton was therefore careful to stress that "no change in the rights of creditors ought to be attempted without their voluntary consent; and that this consent ought to be voluntary in fact, as well as in name." The perceived need to secure the consent of the creditors was why Hamilton's original proposal contained six different options to creditors to convert their old securities into a combination of new securities, tontines, and western land.[32]

In part Hamilton hoped that creditors would consent to new terms because as enlightened men they would realize that the original terms were not realistic. Heavy taxes were likely to produce tax resistance. It was essential that the government create a fiscal system that was "substantial, durable and satisfactory to the community." In a public but anonymous address to the creditors, Hamilton was even more straightforward. The Funding Act, he said, asked them to accept a temporary reduction of interest "in order to avoid the necessity of burthening the community, or carrying taxation to objects which might be displeasing to them. And you cannot wonder that a government, so lately formed, and not without considerable opposition, should be cautious in this respect." Yet he also held out a material incentive. If the creditors agreed to new terms, the government would be able to pay interest in "actual gold and silver" rather than practically worthless "paper money," as had hitherto been the case. The certain effect of such a change was rising security prices that would benefit public creditors.[33]

On its own, the hope of rising prices did not clear the government from the charge that it had arbitrarily broken the contract with its creditors. To secure the consent of the creditors, "a fair equivalent should be offered for what may be asked to be given up, and unquestionable security for the remainder. Without this, an alteration, consistently with the credit and honor of the nation, would be impracticable." The fair equivalent Hamilton offered the public creditors was to make their investments safer in two ways, both of which became controversial. First, the government's right of redemption was limited. Second, the debt was funded. Hamilton argued that the rate of interest in the United States was likely to fall to 4 percent in twenty years' time. Even if creditors lost on the reduced interest rate in the short run, they could look forward to a return on their investments considerably above the market rate of interest in the long term. If the government's right to redeem the debt was not restricted, however, nothing would stop it from taking advantage of the falling interest rate to refinance the debt at lower cost. It was therefore in the creditors' interest "to be able to arrest the hand of Government from paying him, when it is in his interest not to receive." For this reason Hamilton proposed that the combined annual payment on interest and principal should not exceed $7 on every $100 subscribed to the new loan. Payment on the deferred debt would not be allowed to start before it began to earn interest in 1801. Congress accepted Hamilton's reasoning, but the Funding Act increased the maximum annual payment "on account both of principal and interest" to "eight dollars upon a hundred of the sum" subscribed to the loan.[34]

The funding of public debts had been practiced in England since the late seventeenth century and meant that specific tax revenues were permanently allocated to service a contracted debt. As Hamilton was well aware, legislators found it easier to spend rather than to raise money. Permanently allocating specific tax revenues to debt servicing would ensure that the government would use its income toward interest payments. The alternative to funding was an annual provision for the debt, "with an intire uncertainty whether it would be continued." Because the "essence" of property held in the funds was "Contract," its value depended on the certainty that the contract would be honored. In Britain public credit had been established by curtailing the monarch's role in fiscal and financial matters. Parliament rather than the king guaranteed public loans. Whereas Hamilton spoke of the Revolutionary debt as the price of liberty, he knew there were people who favored the repudiation of the debt. At the time of his retirement from the Treasury, Hamilton had seen enough opposition to the public debt emanate from Congress to conclude that in the American republic the legislature was more likely than the executive to threaten public credit.[35]

In a revealing passage, Hamilton wrote that funding was necessary "to guard the Government and the Creditors against the danger of inconstancy in the public Councils." If debt service depended on annual appropriations, the support of both houses of Congress would have to be secured every year. There was a real risk that such support would not always be forthcoming. "Whoever has attended to the course of our public Councils and to the dispositions which have been manifested by a powerful party in them must be sensible that danger in this case was not ideal." In fact, "the accidental result of a single election" was enough to "violate the justice and prostrate the Credit of the Nation." When Congress debated the *Report on Public Credit*, Hamilton's allies made clear what a failure to fund the debt would mean. If the debt was not funded, "no exigencies however great, would enable government to command those resources which every country may be necessitated to apply to." Indeed failure to fund the debt would itself produce "exigence that would not otherwise take place" because it was likely "to induce powers to enter into contest with us that would not do it otherwise. They would see a possibility of making a conquest of [the] United States."³⁶

If specific revenues were pledged to service the debt until such time that the debt was repaid, investments in the public funds would be safe from contract violations. Repealing a funding law would require the support of not only the House of Representatives and the Senate but also the president or, failing that, a two-thirds majority in both houses. As Hamilton said, the American system of government with its checks and balances made it "far more difficult to *undo* than to *do*." To such a government, "a suspension of action is far more natural ... than action. It can hardly happen, that all the branches or parts of it can be infected at one time with a common passion, a disposition, manifestly inimical to justice and the Public good; as to prostrate the public Credit by revoking a pledge given to the Creditors."³⁷

IV

The restriction of the government's right of debt redemption and the Funding Act's failure to offer a timetable for debt repayment led to repeated accusations that Hamilton and the Federalists wished to saddle the nation with a permanent debt. Such accusations were not correct, however. Though it has often been overlooked, Hamilton in fact set the Revolutionary debt on the road to extinction before he left the Treasury. He had already declared in the *Report on Public Credit* a wish to "see it incorporated, as a fundamental maxim, in the system of public credit of the United States, that the creation of debt should always be accompanied with the means of extinguishment." It is true that the Funding Act did not supply such means. It did set aside proceeds from the United States Post Office in a sinking fund intended to reduce the debt through open market purchase, but this money would allow for only limited debt reduction. Midway into the 1790s, however, the nation's finances were "prosperous beyond expectation," and it now seemed possible for the first time to address the question of debt redemption.³⁸

George Washington asked Congress to adopt "a definite plan for the redemption of the public debt" in his annual message of 1794. As far as practicable, such a plan should place "credit on grounds which can not be disturbed" and "prevent that progressive accumulation of debt which must ultimately endanger all governments." In response to the president's message, Congress asked the Treasury secretary to work out a plan for debt redemption, and Hamilton communicated his *Report on a Plan for the Further Support of Public Credit* to the House of Representatives on January 19, 1795.³⁹

To the extent that the Federalists intended to use the debt to cement the public creditors to the federal government or to make public securities a substitute for money, the report signaled a reversal of their program. There were reasons for such a course change. The Federalists were well aware that the "funding of the Debt has unhappily proved an occasion of division and jealousy in the country." The debt was a recurrent theme in the Republicans' opposition to the administration. Adopting a plan for the repayment of the debt would deprive them of an important weapon in the ongoing party struggle and promised to restore unity and harmony to the political life of the nation. Federalists thus did not hesitate to declare that removing the causes of Republican objections was an "auxiliary motive" for extinguishing the debt. As far as the need to use the debt as a form of money is concerned, this approach may have been more pressing in 1790 than in 1795. During these years there had been a rapid growth of the money stock, which may have reduced the need for public securities to substitute for money. Yet it makes more sense to interpret the Federalist program of debt reduction as an attempt to strengthen the federal government's ability to borrow money. Seen in this context, debt repayment did not signify a policy reversal.[40]

The terms of the political debate on the debt changed from 1790 to 1795. In the 1790 *Report on Public Credit*, Hamilton had declared his wish to eventually extinguish the public debt, yet he had also said that "the proper funding of the present debt, will render it a national blessing." In Congress Federalists had also argued that the economic benefits of funding the debt would outweigh any drawbacks. By 1795 no Federalist spoke of the debt as a blessing. Instead they dreamed of "the novel spectacle of a great nation which has freed itself from debt." Hamilton sounded like a convert to Jeffersonianism as he recycled Country Whig doctrine. The "progressive accumulation of Debt" formed a "danger to every Government," Hamilton now declared. It was "the natural disease of all Governments; and it is not easy to conceive any thing more likely than this to lead to great & convulsive revolutions of Empire." Closer inspection shows that what the Federalists feared was not "a system of paper influence, of treasury corruption, of certificate nobility," which was the Republicans' great terror, but the demise of public credit. Fisher Ames made their point well: "I am one of those who believe a nation ought to cherish public credit, for the same reason it ought to have strength; for, in critical situations, credit is strength, and the want of it may happen to be not only weakness, but subjugation and ruin," he told the House of Representatives. "And it is my belief that although it may answer for a time to pay the interest, and neglect the principal, yet, at last, in the course of affairs, it will appear that a nation which neglects to pay its debts will have no credit."[41]

British writers had long warned about the dangers of a growing debt. By the late eighteenth century, this warning had become so common that it could be described as "a sort of national music" struck up by anyone attempting to curry favor with the English people. The growing indebtedness following the French Revolutionary Wars added fuel to the fears of national bankruptcy. By the mid-1790s, Thomas Paine noted that commentators on the "English system of finance . . . have been uniformly impressed with the idea of its downfall happening *some time or other*," and it now seemed that this moment had finally arrived. Famous eighteenth-century British writers on politics and political economy such as William Blackstone, David Hume, and Adam Smith, all of whom were widely read in the United States, denounced the public debt as a major danger to their nation's future. None of them, however, were alive when the French Revolutionary Wars broke out. Paine's *The Decline and Fall of the English System of Finance* was part of a polemic against a set of largely forgotten writers who questioned the assertion that the public debt would inevitably lead to the nation's ruin, at least in the foreseeable future. Compared with the usual complaints about the dangers of the public debt, their arguments sounded remarkably fresh. They pointed out that inflation had reduced the debt's real value over time; that public loans meant public spending, which supplied incomes for many subjects and increased their means to pay taxes; and above all that the proper measure of public indebtedness was the size of the debt relative to the size of the national economy. As long as the economy grew faster than the debt, all was well. "The situation of that country can never give ground for alarm," one of them asserted, "where the debt is increasing, but where the resources are also proportionally increasing."[42]

These defenders of the English system of finance were no friends to an uncontrolled growth of the public debt. Yet they believed that the policies introduced by William Pitt in 1792 established controls on the increase of indebtedness. "The system of borrowing money to carry on war is in itself one that tends ultimately to ruin any nation that adopts it," William Playfair wrote, significantly, however, adding, "unless a fund is assigned for paying it off by degrees, without which it would be perpetually augmented." From 1792 "every new loan" contracted by the British government had "a sinking fund attached to it." The sinking fund introduced by Pitt had old origins. Its best-known proponent was Richard Price, who had advocated its establishment in a series of writings in the 1770s. On every new loan, the House of Commons now pledged not only the means necessary to pay interest charges but also money for the gradual repayment of the principal. Repayment took the form of adding 1 percent of the principal to the annual interest charges on the loan. Similar to a modern fixed-rate mortgage, this annual payment would go toward a greater share of the principal every year and, given the British rate of interest, would fully repay a loan in forty-five years. The introduction of the sinking fund meant that government loans were given a fixed termination date and were no longer redeemable at the pleasure of the government, which in practice had meant the perpetuation of debt. As Playfair noted, "Our loans are not . . . now to be considered as perpetual ones, but as annuities for forty-five years only. *This is a very great difference, and if adhered to, will destroy entirely the fatal tendency of national debt.*"[43]

In Britain the redemption of the public debt was a means to preserve public credit to secure the nation's ability to continue its wars with France. On the other side of the Atlantic, the Federalists were much more traditional in their approach to the public debt than were the British defenders of the funding system. The American debt was small, and by the mid-1790s it must have been clear to everyone that the country was growing fast in population, land, and wealth. Indeed Hamilton was only too willing to take credit for the strong state of the economy. There should have been little doubt that the nation could sustain a far greater debt and that there was no real need to pursue debt redemption. Yet the Federalists rarely questioned the wisdom of this policy. Robert Goodloe Harper was one of the few who criticized proposed tax increases introduced to pay back the debt owed to the Bank of the United States. He pointed to the growth "beyond all former calculation in population, commerce, wealth, and all the pursuits of industry." In contrast to a "stationary" nation, the United States could expect the income from present sources of revenue to grow rapidly over time, thereby removing the need to impose new taxes. Why then "take the capital out of the pockets of our constituents, when an annuity equal to the interest would satisfy the creditor?"[44]

Influenced by the British experiment with a sinking fund and no doubt with Hume's famous discussion of the "natural death" of Britain's public credit in mind, Hamilton repeatedly declared in the *Report on a Plan for the Further Support of Public Credit* his wish to make American public credit "immortal" by avoiding the accumulation of debt. To give "immortality to credit," it was necessary "that with the *creation* of debt should be incorporated the *means* of extinguishment; which means are two fold, the establishing *at the time of contracting* a debt funds for the *reimburse-*

ment of the Principle [i.e., principal], as well as for the *payment* of Interest within a determinate period—The making it a part of the contract that the funds so established shall be inviolably applied to the object." The aim was to guarantee that public borrowing was sustainable by ensuring that every loan contract included the terms for its eventual liquidation, thus filling in the only gap in the provisions made for the Revolutionary debt by the Funding Act in 1790. Inevitably, Ames told Congress, the United States would be involved in war in the future. "Peace is the time to prepare for it by extinguishing the burdens of the last war." Should Congress fail in paying down the debt in "the interval of peace and prosperity," it would be impossible "to avoid the occasion of adding to it."[45]

The *Report on a Plan for the Further Support of Public Credit* and the debate it prompted have been overshadowed by the great turmoil about the Jay Treaty and have been little noticed by historians. But the report was adopted by Congress and formed the basis for two acts that made provisions for the gradual redemption of the public debt, which were passed on March 3, 1795, and April 28, 1796. Hamilton had left the Treasury by then and been succeeded by his close collaborator Oliver Wolcott Jr., who set up an amortization plan for the foreign debt, the 6 percent debt, and the deferred 6 percent debt. No provision was made at that time for the 3 percent indents. According to Wolcott's plan, there would be no further attempts to roll over or refinance foreign loans on their maturation date, but they would be repaid according to contract. The foreign debt would therefore be completely paid off in 1809. The 6 percent debt would be repaid by making use of the right to pay $8 on every $100 of original stock each year. With the help of compound interest, such payments would terminate the debt in twenty-four years, by 1818. Because the government was prohibited by the Funding Act from beginning repayment of the principal on the deferred 6 percent securities before they began to earn interest in 1801, this part of the debt would be repaid by 1824.[46]

The legislation passed on March 3, 1795, transformed the nature of the securities in the same way that British securities had been transformed after 1792. Wolcott pointed out that since the act had supplied "unconditional" instructions to the commissioners of the sinking fund, and since "permanent funds have been vested and appropriated, it is conceived that a successive reimbursement annually . . . has become an irrevocable stipulation with the creditors." The securities had thereby been converted from "an annuity of six per centum per annum, for an indefinite period, into an annuity of eight per centum per annum, for a period of somewhat less than twenty-four years, commencing with the year 1795."[47]

For political reasons Federalist critics focused on the overall growth of the public debt rather than on the program to extinguish the Revolutionary debt. The Federalists' record of debt redemption has also passed unnoticed by historians. Republicans argued that the public debt did not decrease but grew under Federalist administrations. They were correct about the first half of the 1790s but wrong about the second half. In 1795 the total public debt was $83.8 million. Six years later it was $80.7 million, suggesting a debt reduction of around $3 million. In reality the federal government paid off around $4 million of the 6 percent debt, $2 million of the foreign debt, and $5.5 million of its short-term loans as well as the debt to the Bank of the United States. This considerable achievement is hidden to anyone who focuses on the aggregate indebtedness of the United States because the government simultaneously increased the debt by borrowing around $7 million to pursue the Quasi War with France. In 1795 Hamilton had argued that war, at least against "Civalized [sic] powers," was a legitimate reason for increasing the long-term debt but that there "should be a steady effort, *as a rule of administration*, not to encrease the permanent Debt of the Country by permanent loans, except when it is inevitable by the existence of a war with some European power." Rather than signifying a break with the Federalist policy of debt management, the loans contracted during the Quasi War suggest adherence to the plan to repay the principal of old loans to maintain a credit rating that made it possible to borrow during wartime.[48]

V

Historians routinely give Republicans the credit for paying off the Revolutionary debt. To a large extent, they are right in doing so. Thomas Jefferson and his Treasury secretary, Albert Gallatin, certainly deserve top marks on debt redemption.[49] But they were not the initiators of the debt redemption policy. Rather, they implemented a policy formulated by the Federalists. The repayment of the Revolutionary debt actually followed the Federalist plan adopted in 1795 and 1796 closely (figures 3.1–3.3). Contrary to what may have been expected, there was no sharp break in the management of the debt after 1801. Only midway through his second term did Jefferson find the means to speed up debt repayment and to diverge significantly from the Federalist amortization plan.

Looking beyond political rhetoric to the governmental institutions and policies of the early republic allows historians to question the conception of Federalists as the advocates of big government and Jeffersonians as their antithesis. Federalists were not in favor of a permanent or growing debt. The

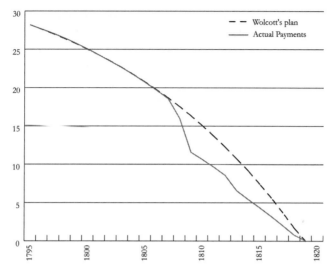

Fig. 3.1. Repayment of the 6 percent debt ($ million). The figure shows the status of the debt on January 1 of each year and compares the actual payments on the deferred 6 percent debt with the plan presented by Wolcott. In his plan, Wolcott printed the formula for his amortization plan rather than the sums of projected installments. This formula has been applied to Rafael A. Bayley's figure for the total debt on January 1, 1795. Sources: Wolcott, "Public Debt," ASP: Finance, 1:383; Bayley, History of the National Loans of the United States, from July 4, 1776, to June 30, 1880, in Report on Valuation, Taxation, and Public Indebtedness in the United States, as Returned at the Tenth Census (June 1, 1880) (Washington, DC: Government Printing Office, 1884), 403–4.

debt funded in 1790 was inherited from the Revolution and was not their own creation. In 1795 they developed and adopted a plan for the debt's eventual redemption. Yet they also embraced public credit and the government's ability to borrow money as a crucial instrument of modern war.[50]

The Jeffersonian attitude toward public debt is more complex. There is no doubt that Republicans wished to see their country free from debt and that many of them subscribed to Country Whig arguments condemning public debts, central banks, and public creditors. But their actions sometimes ran counter to their words. In his first inaugural address, Jefferson promised "the honest payment of our debts and sacred preservation of the public faith." Before his election was confirmed, as Congress struggled to break the deadlock between Jefferson and Aaron Burr, Alexander Hamilton had suggested that Federalist congressmen "make it a ground of exploration with Mr. Jefferson or his confidential friends" to obtain "some assurances of his future conduct." To Hamilton there were "three essential points" that

Federalists should try to secure. They concerned "the maintenance of the present system especially on the cardinal articles of public Credit, a *Navy, Neutrality*." "Other matters," he added, "may be left to take their chance." Whether or not a deal was ever struck with Jefferson, his politics upheld most of the Federalist system, suggesting a significant amount of common ground between Federalists and Republicans with regard not only to foreign policy and defense but also to principles of public finance.[51]

At several junctures Republican leaders were instrumental in realizing important financial policies and institutions associated with the Federalists. James Madison was crucial to the creation of the Treasury Department and especially to the elevation of the Treasury secretary to a powerful position. For all their later opposition, the Funding Act would never have passed Congress without the support of both Madison and Jefferson. When Jefferson came to power, he upheld the contract with the creditors and made no attempt to repudiate the debt. Though the Virginia dynasty presided over

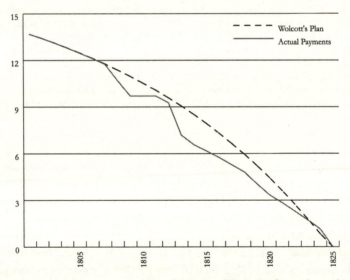

Fig. 3.2. Repayment of the 6 percent deferred debt ($ million). The figure shows the status of the debt on January 1 of each year and compares the actual payments on the deferred 6 percent debt with the plan presented by Wolcott. In his plan, Wolcott printed the formula for his amortization plan rather than the sums of projected installments. This formula has been applied to Rafael A. Bayley's figure for the total debt on January 1, 1801. Sources: Wolcott, "Public Debt," *ASP: Finance*, 1:383; Bayley, *History of the National Loans of the United States from July 4, 1776, to June 30, 1880*, in *Report on Valuation, Taxation, and Public Indebtedness in the United States, as Returned at the Tenth Census (June 1, 1880)* (Washington, DC: Government Printing Office, 1884), 403–4.

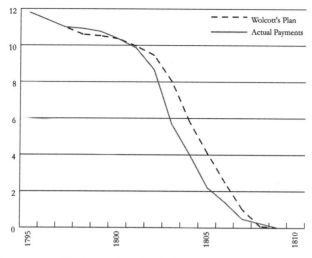

Fig. 3.3. Repayment of the foreign debt ($ million). This figure compares the repayment plan presented by Wolcott to the actual repayments made on the foreign debt. The foreign debts included in the figure are the Amsterdam and Antwerp loans; the French loans had been liquidated when Wolcott presented his plan. Sources: Wolcott, "Public Debt," in *ASP: Finance*, 1:374–76; Rafael A. Bayley, *History of the National Loans of the United States from July 4, 1776, to June 30, 1880*, in *Report on Valuation, Taxation, and Public Indebtedness in the United States, as Returned at the Tenth Census (June 1, 1880)* (Washington, DC: Government Printing Office, 1884), 468–89.

the liquidation of the Revolutionary debt, Jefferson, Madison, and James Monroe actually administered a Federalist repayment plan. There was also continuity in fiscal policies. Both Federalists and Republicans preferred low taxes and gradual debt repayment to high taxes and rapid debt liquidation. Furthermore Republicans followed Federalist precedent in their approach to the financing of extraordinary expenditures with loans rather than increased taxation. Fisher Ames's idea that wars should be financed with loans to be paid off in times of peace and plenty, which Hamilton subscribed to, was echoed almost verbatim by Madison and Gallatin a decade later, forming the policy followed during the War of 1812.

When it came to using public credit to realize policy aims, however, and quite in contrast to what most historians have assumed, the Republicans proved to be much more active than their more cautious predecessors. Both the purchase of the Louisiana territory from France in 1803 and the war against Britain that broke out nine years later were financed with borrowed money, made available thanks to Federalist reforms.[52]

CHAPTER FOUR

Equal to the Severest Trials: Mr. Madison's War

Thomas Jefferson came to power after almost a decade of sustained criticism of the policies pursued by the administrations of George Washington and John Adams. Convinced of the significance of his election, Jefferson described his rise to the presidency as a revolution, as real "in the principles of our government as that of 1776 was in its form." To Jefferson and his supporters, the "Revolution of 1800" heralded a radical change of course for the national government. The expansion of the bureaucracy, of the armed forces, of the fiscal system, and of the public debt would now come to a close, and so would the Federalists' attempts to transform the American republic into a European-style "fiscal-military state." As Jefferson made clear in his inaugural address, his would be "a wise and frugal government, which shall restrain men from injuring one another," but which would otherwise leave the citizens "to regulate their own pursuits of industry and improvement, and shall not take from the mouth of labor the bread it has earned." In contrast to his etatist predecessors, Jefferson's national government would be both cheap and of clearly delimited scope.[1]

Jefferson's portrayal of the election of 1800 as a watershed in the development of the early republic has been readily accepted by most historians, who routinely contrast a Jeffersonian with a Hamiltonian vision of the nation's future. Had the election not gone Jefferson's way, they say, the United States would likely have developed into something much more similar to nineteenth-century European states and societies. But such sweeping assertions are seldom founded on actual examinations of how the size and scope of Jefferson's government differed from that of the Federalists. This is an unfortunate oversight because such examination would force historians to moderate Jefferson's bold claims. In terms of the policy and institutional makeup of the federal government, continuity much more than change characterized the transition of power from Adams to Jefferson, especially in the realm of public finance. Albert Gallatin, Jefferson's Treasury secretary and trusted advisor on government finance, was much more of a Hamiltonian than either he or Jefferson would let on. And at the same time, Hamilton himself was rather less of a Hamiltonian than most historians have realized.[2]

Continuity does not mean a total absence of change. Gallatin streamlined Hamilton's fiscal system and reduced spending on the army and navy during Jefferson's first administration, after which the international situation once more led to mounting costs. Jefferson and Gallatin were also successful in paying down the public debt, although in this area they administered an amortization plan drawn up and adopted by a Federalist administration and Congress. But the principal institutions of the Hamiltonian system—the tariff, the funded debt, and the national bank—all remained. Jeffersonian policy choices, too, tended to continue Federalist practice rather than break new ground. Like Hamilton before him, Gallatin tried to keep taxes low, rely on customs duties for revenue, and resort to loans rather than taxes to finance extraordinary expenditures. In fact, the major difference between the Jeffersonians and the Federalists was not that Jefferson and James Madison dismantled a "fiscal-military state" of Hamilton's creation but that they were far more willing than either Washington or Adams to use the power of the national government to realize ambitious foreign policy goals.

I

Like Alexander Hamilton, Albert Gallatin was of foreign extraction. He arrived in America as a young man toward the end of the War of Independence. A Swiss aristocrat who despised Joseph Bonaparte for his middle-class ways and confessed to "a strong affection for the House of Bourbon," Gallatin was on the surface an unlikely champion for democracy. He was propelled into the political limelight soon after his election to the House of Representatives in 1795, where he became the leading critic of Federalist public finance. Thomas Jefferson and James Madison were elated when the new representative for western Pennsylvania made his appearance. Here at last was a man who not only understood the machinations of Treasury secretary Hamilton but could also offer stinging rebuke and popular countermeasures. In the spring of 1796, while still relatively new to the House, Gallatin launched a frontal assault on Hamilton's management of the public debt. Ever since Washington's first administration, he claimed, the government had outspent its tax income and made up the deficit with bank loans. Because of such spendthrift ways, the nation's debt had increased by as much as $16 million to $25 million since the First Congress met in 1789. Even worse, he warned, this ruinous habit was likely to continue until Congress began to employ its power over taxation and appropriations to halt public spending. Hamilton's supporters in the House strenuously denied Gallatin's charges, but the session ended before any agreement could be reached on whether or not the debt had grown in the past half decade. During the ensuing summer, Gallatin went to work on preparing evidence to vindicate his accusations. The result was published in November 1796 as *A Sketch of the Finances of the United States*, probably Gallatin's best-known political tract.[3]

Because Gallatin is habitually presented as Hamilton's opposite, it is seldom recognized that his *Sketch of the Finances* provided a rather limited and nuanced critique of Hamilton's reforms and by no means propagated their wholesale dismissal. Gallatin did challenge some of the contentions Hamilton had made in his 1790 *Report on Public Credit*. He denied that the appreciation of government bonds amounted to the creation of capital that would stimulate the economy. To the contrary, all debt payment represented a transfer of wealth from productive farmers, artisans, and merchants to an idle and corrupt rentier class. Government bonds would neither increase the money supply nor attract foreign capital to the United States, two other claims Hamilton had made in his report. Gallatin further questioned Hamilton's belief that the debt would serve to strengthen the government by providing ligaments between society and the national government. Public creditors were an "artificial interest," Gallatin said, which was just as likely to act against as for the true interests of the nation. Although Gallatin accepted that the creation of debt might sometimes be necessary, in itself a debt could never be a good thing. To the contrary, he affirmed, "It requires no argument to prove, it is a self-evident truth, that, in a political point of view at least, every nation is enfeebled by a public debt."[4]

Yet for all his aversion to public indebtedness, Gallatin readily acknowledged that the debt incurred during the War of Independence had been unavoidable. The war was expensive and "it is well known that the beginning of a revolution was a most unfavorable moment to raise any considerable taxes." Nor did Gallatin oppose the funding of what he called "the proper part" of the Revolutionary debt. He found it "attended with no immediate evil, except that arising from the taxes necessary to pay the interest" and felt no need to censure it. In contrast to Madison, he did not make much of discrimination either. Whether the original or the secondary holders were paid, "the general effects would have been nearly the same." The central issue was that either the principal or at least the interest had to be paid to one group or the other "unless the American government had chosen to forfeit every claim to common honesty." Regardless of past events and disagreements, both the Revolutionary debt and later loans had to be honored, or the government would commit "the most flagrant and pernicious breach of public faith and of national morality." The *Sketch of the Finances*, then, was not as hostile to Hamilton's management of the debt as could be expected from one of Jefferson's closest collaborators. Indeed, Gallatin did not even object to the creation of the Bank of the United States, which he believed to be both useful and beneficial to the national government and the economy. In their private correspondence, Gallatin tried to explain to Jefferson that banks in general, and the Bank of the United States in particular, provided the government with three "great advantages": it offered a safe place for the deposit of public money, it provided "instantaneous transmission" of government funds "from any one part of the continent to another," and it issued banknotes and provided discounts that facilitated tax collection by making money more readily available. Elsewhere he added that banks were also the natural source of government loans whenever extraordinary expenditures became necessary.[5]

Rather than distancing himself from the fundamentals of Hamiltonian finance, Gallatin objected to two specific measures. First, he believed that the national government had been overly generous to debtor states when assuming state debts. As a result, assumption had become an unfair measure because the citizens of creditor states were made to pay taxes to serve the debts of debtor states. Assumption had also made the national government take on too much debt—the *Sketch of the Finances* said $10.9 million—which increased the tax burden on the people and transferred the earnings of their industry to bondholders. Second, Gallatin claimed that the Washington administration had failed to balance its budget because of waste, miscalculations, and needless spending on the army and navy. The effect of such mismanagement was an increase of the public debt of several million dollars.[6]

The *Sketch of the Finances* was published after John Adams had been elected to the presidency and Hamilton had left the direction of the Treasury to Oliver Wolcott Jr. Under Adams, the Federalists paid off the government's short-term obligations to the Bank of the United States and began repayment of the debt from the War of Independence. But the Quasi War forced Adams to take up new loans, and consequently the government's total indebtedness fell only slightly between 1795 and 1800. When Gallatin was given command of the Treasury in March 1801, the public debt therefore remained foremost in his mind, and he would later say that debt reduction was "the principal object in bringing me into office." He took considerable pride in the retrenchment effected under his watch. Between 1801 and the outbreak of the War of 1812, the debt shrank from $83 million to $45 million, an achievement that together with his service in the House of Representatives Gallatin claimed to have cost him "the eighteen best years of [his] life."[7]

Undeniably, this was an impressive achievement. It should be remembered, however, that Gallatin implemented Federalist legislation passed in 1795 and 1796 and that he introduced no novel measure other than an increase of the permanent appropriation for debt service. Even in his autumn years, Gallatin sometimes maintained that "the debt had been increased" under the Federalists and that his term as Treasury secretary had consequently made a great difference. But at other times he admitted that Federalist and Jeffersonian debt policy was actually one and the same. The "maxim" that "a nation never ought to contract a debt in ordinary times" and that "it must provide by taxes for its annual expenditures" had been obeyed "by the government of the United States from its organization, or at least from the year 1796." In the first half century of the Union's existence there had been only two exceptions to this rule: the Louisiana Purchase in 1803, for which Jefferson and Gallatin were responsible, and the mistaken decision in the mid-1830s to deposit the Treasury surplus in the states when, soon after, the government ran a deficit and was forced to borrow. Still more revealing was Gallatin's admission to his relative Madame de Staël in 1814 that even "in the midst of all our party differences, no matter which party was in power, the same spirit as regards finance has always animated our country."[8]

A principal reason Gallatin wished to repay the public debt was because it would improve the nation's security. The United States "would not be much exposed to the wanton attacks, depredations, or insults of any nation was it not known that our revenue and resources are palsied by an annual defalcation of five millions of dollars," he claimed. In fact, repayment was a more effective means of "adding to our external security and respectability" than would be the creation of a navy. No doubt Hamilton would have agreed with much of this. A nation unencumbered by debt was in a better condition to defend itself than a nation struggling under heavy indebtedness.[9]

Even though there was considerable continuity in the practical policies of public finance pursued by Federalists and Jeffersonians, Gallatin was certainly not a mere carbon copy of Hamilton. In contrast to Hamilton, Gallatin mistrusted public creditors, who he thought were more likely to promote private benefits than the common good. Gallatin also disliked debts for reasons of political economy. Public debts were mementos of past wars, and wars in Gallatin's mind equaled destruction of capital. On one occasion he compared the social resources spent on war to a merchant inventory lost in a fire. Even if debts did not cause wars, public credit facilitated "the means of raising capital" and thereby tended "to enlarge the scale of expenses" and encourage "unnecessary ones." The ability to borrow therefore "indirectly promotes a greater destruction of capital than would otherwise have taken place." The fundamental problem with wars was that they required new taxes to service the resulting public debt. To Gallatin and Jefferson, such taxation represented a transfer of capital from the productive to the unproductive classes of society. A public debt therefore reduced the resources available for productive purposes. Hamilton believed that most public creditors were merchants who were likely to invest their money in productive ventures. Gallatin did not agree. He thought public creditors squandered their rents on the ostentatious consumption of foreign luxuries. The money paid to them was lost to the nation.[10]

For all his dislike of debts, Gallatin nevertheless accepted and understood the importance of public credit to modern statecraft. He never suggested that the government disown or renegotiate debts already contracted. As he made clear in the *Sketch of the Finances*, even in opposition Gallatin held that the federal government was honor bound to service its debts according to contract. During his tenure at the Treasury Department he continued to give the civil list (nonmilitary expenses) and debt charges priority over other public expenses. Even in the darkest moment of the War of 1812, when in the fall of 1814 the situation of the United States looked truly desperate, Gallatin maintained that the government had to pay its creditors before its soldiers. No longer in charge of the Treasury, he still worked diligently to uphold the nation's credit. It was thus on Gallatin's initiative that Baring Brothers of London was prompted to advance the funds necessary to pay European holders of American bonds in late 1814. Jefferson generally agreed with Gallatin about the importance of maintaining public credit. When he outlined his "political faith" to Elbridge Gerry in 1799, Jefferson noted that as soon as the funding system was "adopted by the constituted authorities, I became religiously principled in the sacred discharge of it to the uttermost farthing." And when he came to power, Jefferson explicitly promised as early as his inaugural address that "the honest payment of our debts and sacred preservation of the public faith" would be an "essential principle" of his administration. That Jefferson chose to stand by his word despite his profound aversion to public debts was of immense importance to the long-term development of American public credit.[11]

Even though debt reduction was a central goal to Jefferson and Gallatin, they began their tenure by undermining the government's capacity to repay its loans. In his first annual message, Jefferson informed Congress that "an augmentation of revenue" from the impost would "be sufficient to provide for the support of government, to pay the interest of the public debts, and to discharge the principals in shorter periods than the laws, or the general expectation had contemplated." As a result, the president suggested that "we may now safely dispense with all the internal taxes, comprehending excises, stamps, auctions, licenses, carriages and refined sugars," because "sound policy will not justify taxing the industry of our fellow-citizens" unnecessarily. Given his reputation as a champion of a perpetual debt, it is surprising to find Hamilton complaining that Jefferson's proposal would endanger the prompt repayment of the nation's debt. Hamilton nonetheless excoriated Jefferson's message in a series of essays under the title "The Examination," which were published in the *New-York Evening Post*. According to the former Treasury secretary, it was only so much better if the government could "discharge the debt faster than may have been contemplated." While in opposition Jefferson had constantly accused Hamilton of trying to perpetuate the debt. Was it not wonderful, Hamilton asked, that his fiscal measures were now "discovered to have done too much for the speedy discharge of the debt"?[12]

It is of course tempting to conclude that in December 1801 Jefferson the politician got the better of Jefferson the philosopher. Faced with the opportunity to gratify the present generation of citizen-taxpayers, Jefferson overcame his scruples about burdening future generations with a public debt. But there are actually more intriguing reasons behind Jefferson's tax break than short-term political gain. To begin with, Jeffersonian political economy saw taxes as a reduction of productive capital and government spending as unproductive investment. Government was certainly necessary, but as a rule, government spending represented "a destruction of the capital employed to defray them." As Jefferson said in his first annual message, governments had an inborn tendency to "increase expence to the ultimate term of burthen which the citizen can bear." An important part of Jefferson's revolution in the principles of government was to put an end to this trend so "that it never may be seen here that, after leaving to labour the smallest portion of it's earnings on which it can subsist, government shall itself consume the whole residue of what it was instituted to guard."[13]

There was another and perhaps more important reason that Jefferson had to abolish internal taxes, a reason that points to the president's concern that his "Revolution of 1800" was anything but irreversible. Although it might one day be necessary to reintroduce internal taxes if the nation found itself involved in war again, Jefferson nonetheless warned that the accumulation of funds in preparation for war was dangerous because the "temptations offered by that treasure" might themselves lead to war. In other words, if the government's fiscal and financial capacity was too well developed, its leaders were likely to pursue an ambitious and adventurous foreign policy that would cause government to expand in size and cost. Gallatin made the point more forcefully in a private comment on the draft version of Jefferson's first annual message. The Treasury secretary told the president that he was "firmly of opinion" that unless the present administration took measures to ensure the repayment of the public debt, it would "be entailed on us & the ensuing generations." Yet, dismantling the Federalist fiscal system was equally important, because

> if this administration shall not reduce taxes, they never will be permanently reduced; to strike at the root of the evil, & avert the danger of encreasing taxes, encroaching government, temptations to offensive wars, &a., nothing can be more effectual than a repeal of *all* internal taxes; but let them all go, & not one remain on which sister taxes may be hereafter engrafted. I agree most fully with you that pretended tax-preparations, treasury-preparations, & army preparations against contingent wars tend only to encourage wars.[14]

At stake was something more significant than a mere tax cut: Jefferson and Gallatin were actively shaping governmental institutions in order to limit the choices open to future administrations. They deliberately tied the hands of the national government to prevent the United States from assuming the shape of the warmongering monarchies of the Old World. Not surprisingly, Congress was only too happy to follow the recommendations of the president. It abolished internal duties on retail licenses, sugar, snuff, carriages, paper, and sales at auction, as well as the excise on alcohol production in April 1802. The repeal of the duty on salt followed five years later. Meanwhile the Federalists' direct tax of 1798 was allowed to quietly expire. Within little more than a year of taking power, the Jeffersonians had scaled down the diversified Federalist revenue system to a customs service.[15]

As Hamilton pointed out in "The Examination," abolishing taxes would hardly facilitate debt retrenchment. But Jefferson was convinced that a

Treasury surplus could be created through a reduction of expenditures. It remains a deeply entrenched myth in the literature that Jefferson sharply reduced the cost and size of the national government. The figures suggest otherwise. While in opposition Gallatin had believed that substantial savings could be made on the civil list. Once in office, the Treasury secretary had to concede that this was impossible. Because the charges on the debt were sacrosanct, reductions of expenditure could only be made on the army and navy. At first Gallatin thought that an annual appropriation of $670,000 for each service would suffice. This estimate was soon revised upwards to $900,000 for the army and $1.1 million for the navy. Yet despite Gallatin's vigilant watch over his fellow cabinet members in the Navy and War Departments, these caps could never be imposed. On average, the army cost $1.1 million per year during Jefferson's first administration and $1.5 million during his second. The corresponding figures for the navy are $1.4 million and $1.7 million. During the first years of Jefferson's presidency, military expenditures were almost halved and naval spending reduced by a third compared to the previous Federalist administration. But it must be remembered that John Adams had mobilized for an undeclared war with France, whereas the international situation was far more peaceful in the first few years of Jefferson's administration. When hostilities resumed in Europe, the federal government began to expand again. During Jefferson's second term, combined military and naval expenditures exceeded those of the Washington administration by $800,000 annually. In the first three years of Madison's presidency, before the outbreak of the war against Britain, naval expenditure had again reached the level of the Adams's years, whereas the annual military cost was about $500,000 more than the cost of the Federalists' army.[16]

In the end, it was not reduced expenses but increased income that allowed Gallatin to pay down the debt. A splenetic Hamilton raged that "the LITTLE POLITICIANS" now harvested the "benefits of a policy, which they had neither the wi[s]dom to plan nor the spirit to adopt." The charge was not without a grain of truth, for the discharge of the debt *was* made possible by the fiscal and financial reforms of the Federalists, and to this extent the Republicans built their success on the institutions and policies of their predecessors. Jefferson's administration saw a substantial growth in customs income from $9.1 million in 1800 to $16.4 million in 1808. This wealth resulted not from new rates or duties. Gallatin's only positive fiscal measure was an additional 2.5 percent ad valorem duty on imports, which was earmarked for the Mediterranean Fund, intended to provide means to fight the Barbary powers of North Africa. The rise in income was rather the effect of a rising volume of trade. It is well known that from the 1790s onward

American merchants benefited from the French Revolutionary Wars and the Napoleonic War. From 1802 to 1807, exports rose by around 50 percent, and imports more than doubled.[17]

Although their record in the sphere of fiscal legislation is a negative one in the sense that they repealed taxes rather than devised new revenue measures, the actions of the Jeffersonian Republicans still had important consequences. In "The Examination," Hamilton warned that "more than in any other country" the "opinions and habits" of the American people formed obstructions to all attempt to impose new taxes. In Hamilton's view the Federalists had surmounted considerable difficulties, including a full-scale tax rebellion, in order to create their fiscal system. Eventually the citizens had come to regard the taxes imposed by the government as legitimate demands. When Jefferson became president, there was no "colourable pretence of there being a grievous or undue pressure on the community." Against this background, the Jeffersonian decision to abolish internal taxation was highly imprudent. If these taxes had to be reintroduced in an hour of need, the government was bound to suffer from "a repetition of the obstacles which have been before encountered and overcome." The internal revenue ought therefore "to be carefully preserved" rather than abolished. To Hamilton's mind this was particularly important, as internal duties were not "exposed to the casualties incident to our intercourse with foreign nations, and therefore the most certain." As Gallatin would learn during the War of 1812, Hamilton's warning was only too prescient.[18]

Modern scholars have echoed Hamilton's critique in arguing that a more responsible administration would have retained the system of internal taxation even at greatly reduced rates. This would have left the machinery for levying and collecting excises and property taxes intact, and the fiscal system would have had the flexibility to expand rapidly and relatively smoothly in the event of a war or major crisis. But this, of course, was precisely what Jefferson and Gallatin wished to avoid. Although they had faith in their own virtue, they could never be sure that the next incumbent in the White House would not be another Adams or Hamilton. Rather than trust to the virtues of future leaders of their country, they created a fiscal system that would make war more difficult. The downside of this policy was that they also created a fiscal system entirely dependent on the actions and goodwill of the great naval powers of Europe, powers over which the United States at best had only limited influence. To this extent, the Republicans' fear of energetic government undermined the nation's self-determination. This was readily demonstrated during the embargo of 1807 when the Treasury went from a large surplus to a $2.5 million deficit virtually overnight.

It would become even more evident when the United States went to war against Britain in 1812.[19]

II

Opposition to war comes natural to Treasury secretaries. Hamilton regularly advised against military conflict, pointing to the enormous cost and to the fact that the United States was not ready for a major war. Thus he promoted a prudent foreign policy, which his critics believed bordered on the pusillanimous. But Hamilton was also a soldier who gloried in military valor and eagerly accepted a general's commission in the army of 1798. Gallatin in contrast found little to celebrate in war. On the eve of the embargo he remarked that war might bring out "nobler feelings and habits than avarice and luxury," preventing the American people from "degenerating, like the Hollanders, into a nation of mere calculators." And after the War of 1812, in an oft-cited letter to Matthew Lyon, Gallatin argued that the war had strengthened "national feelings" and countered excessive local and state attachment. But such statements are rare.[20]

To Gallatin war was an enormous waste of money. Late in life he was an outspoken critic of the Mexican War, in part because he found the war deeply immoral but also for the familiar reason that "almost the whole capital applied to war expenses is destroyed because it is expended on unproductive objects." He claimed that Britain's growth in status and territory after the Napoleonic Wars amounted to little when compared to the "addition of five hundred millions sterling to her former debts, which imposes an enormous weight of oppressive taxation on the people, and has already crippled her resources and her power." War also meant a dangerous concentration of executive power. In his letter to Lyon, Gallatin noted that not only had the war caused the loss of life and property. It had also laid "the foundation of permanent taxes and military establishments, which the Republicans had deemed unfavorable to the happiness and free institutions of the country." When the storm clouds gathered in the spring of 1812, it is hardly surprising to find that Gallatin was less interested in facilitating the war than in ensuring "that the evils inseparable from [war] should, as far as practicable, be limited to its duration, and that at its end the United States may be burdened with the smallest possible quantity of debt, perpetual taxation, military establishments, and other corrupting or anti-republican habits or institutions."[21]

Given his attitude to war, there is considerable irony in the fact that it was Gallatin rather than Hamilton who became the nation's first wartime secretary of the Treasury. But this was hardly of Gallatin's own doing. He continued to warn of the consequences of a conflict with Britain right up to the outbreak of hostilities. Unlike Hamilton, Gallatin served a president and a party far more belligerent than Washington and the Federalists. Furthermore, the global crisis that began with the French Revolution escalated over time. The great European war had barely begun when Hamilton left the Treasury. His successor, Oliver Wolcott, suffered much more from its effects than Hamilton ever did, and when hostilities resumed after the brief Peace of Amiens, the situation grew increasingly worse. Nevertheless, the Republican triumvirate of Gallatin, Jefferson, and Madison managed to keep the United States out of the European conflict for nine long years before the nation finally descended into the maelstrom of war. It was a record that both Hamilton and Washington would have taken pride in.

It has often been remarked that the nation was ill-prepared to take on the world's most powerful state when Congress declared war on Britain on June 18, 1812. The American army was small, the navy nonexistent, and war plans rudimentary. Poor preparations were matched by an even poorer execution of the war effort. Congress has been called "negligent," commanding generals "incompetent," and President Madison "one of the weakest war leaders in the nation's history." In every respect the bungling and inefficient American republic appears the opposite of the methodical and efficient British fiscal-military state. Gallatin and the Treasury have come in for their fair share of criticism, too. The secretary's principles of war finance have been described as "essentially unsound" and the administration of the war as "even more bungled financially" than militarily.[22]

It is difficult to quarrel with many of these assertions and all too easy to understand why, from an American perspective, the War of 1812 best remains "a forgotten conflict." In the sphere of war finance there is nevertheless reason to qualify this bleak picture somewhat. The war finance plan drawn up by Gallatin, which drew heavily on principles laid down by Hamilton and the First Congress, constituted a conscious attempt to break with a previous tradition of American war finance in favor of a British, or modern, way of financing war. The administration would adhere to Gallatin's plan until the fateful fall of 1814, when the government's credit no longer sufficed to raise more loans. Rather than a resounding failure, Mr. Madison's War represents the first attempt by the United States to finance war by the sale of long-term securities. In 1812 this was the most advanced method of war finance available, and ever since, it has been the means by which all subsequent American wars have been funded. The introduction of this technique, which has underpinned the unequaled war-making capacity of the United States for the last two centuries, represents a significant step on the nation's road to world dominion. Admittedly the financing of the War of 1812 was only a small step on this journey. But because it was the first step and, despite great difficulties, a largely successful one, it was perhaps the most important.

III

In the sphere of public finance, the administration was not completely unprepared when the declaration of war came in June 1812. At the time of the embargo, war with one of the major European powers had seemed likely, and Gallatin was prompted to prepare a war finance plan, which he presented as part of his Treasury report for 1807. In its basic outlines, the plan would often reappear in the letters and reports of the Treasury secretary and his successors, and it would serve as the blueprint for administration policies throughout the first two years of the War of 1812. The plan began with Gallatin's rather hopeless task of trying to guess the cost of a major war, something no Treasury secretary has ever successfully done. In an 1807 memorandum to Jefferson, Gallatin nevertheless ventured the assumption that in the event of war total government costs would be about $18 million annually. This figure included ordinary costs but excluded amortizations on the public debt. At such cost the expected yearly deficit would be around $7 million. To this sum had to be added the amount necessary for the payment of the principal of the existing debt. On several other occasions Gallatin estimated the annual deficit at $10 million.[23]

The second step in the plan was to determine methods of resource mobilization. In the choice between loans and taxes, Gallatin came down squarely on the side of loans. It was a standing principle in American public finance to limit the burdens on the population, even in time of war. Undoubtedly, the war itself would have economic consequences, and "the losses and privations caused by the war should not be aggravated by taxes beyond what is strictly necessary." Without a navy to protect American trade, war with a European maritime power such as Britain or France was bound to cut off American producers from foreign markets. This would have negative effects on the economy far beyond the port cities and the shipping industry. If the war was financed from loans rather than taxes, at least the further stress on the citizenry of new and heavy taxes could be avoided. William Jones, Gallatin's successor at the Treasury, noted that "in a country like ours, where, from the lightness of the demands made upon the People, during the continuance of peace, the extraordinary expenses of a state of war can be supplied only by a resort to . . . credit."[24]

But Gallatin worried that the government would not be able to borrow on acceptable terms. If the war lasted for five years and the yearly deficit was $10 million, the Treasury would have to create a $50 million debt. From a twenty-first-century perspective this figure hardly looks daunting, but Gallatin was venturing into unchartered waters. Hamilton's major measure had been to refinance an existing debt rather than create a new one. Admittedly, he had borrowed extensively as secretary of the Treasury, but the sums had always been small. Gallatin's experience of borrowing was limited to the engineering of the Louisiana Purchase. But the Louisiana Stock had been sold abroad and not by the agency of the Treasury but through the private firm Baring Brothers of London. In 1812 such help was no longer available, as international capital markets had closed down because of the European war. Although Gallatin was convinced that the American people would fight and risk their lives for their country, he was equally convinced that they would "never give their money for nothing." Patriotism and loyalty would not fill the coffers of the Treasury, Gallatin said. Thus, he concluded, "We must buy money at its market price." But what that price might be was impossible to say.[25]

At first sight the Bank of the United States looks like the obvious source of government loans. Historians have made much of Congress's narrow decision in 1811 not to recharter the bank and have pointed to the absence of the bank as a major reason for the financial difficulties experienced during the War of 1812. To a large extent this is correct, yet the role of the Bank of the United States in American war finance has often been misunderstood. Originally, the bank was chartered to provide a number of different services to the government. Bank stock was intended to sink a substantial part of the public debt and to raise the price of government bonds. The Bank of the United States would also issue banknotes that could serve as a nationwide circulating medium and increase the economy's money stock. Apart from providing a general service to society, the banknotes would also facilitate tax collection. Furthermore, the bank would provide a place of deposit for public money and would transfer public funds between branches or to private banks. Finally, the Bank of the United States could offer loans to the government. Although a semiprivate institution, the services provided by the bank made it an important auxiliary institution in the fiscal and financial operations of the national government with close links to the Treasury Department.[26]

For all its uses, the Bank of the United States was not intended as the source of war loans, however. Although the bank was free to lend the government money, it was prohibited by its charter from acquiring additional long-term public bonds beyond the original subscription of $8 million unless it received authorization to do so from Congress. In any event, the Bank of the United States was prohibited from holding assets greater than $15 million in total. Hamilton repeatedly borrowed small sums from the bank to cover budget deficits, and the bank also advanced $1 million to finance the expedition that put down the Whiskey Rebellion. But the Treasury secretary never expected the Bank of the United States to be able to contribute the kind of sums necessary to wage war. In this respect, the institution was no different from its model, the Bank of England. When the United States issued its declaration of war, Britain had over a century's worth of experience with financing war through the sale of long-term securities. During this period, the Bank of England became the central institution in administering the national debt—in taking in subscriptions, maintaining the books, supervising transfers, and paying out interest—but it was rarely the source of long-term loans. The bank gradually increased its holdings of long-term debt from £1.5 million to £11.7 million, but this was typically done in return for the recharter that the bank had to seek every few decades. As a rule, these loans were created when the Bank of England absorbed outstanding short-term debt after or in the latter stages of a war, not because it offered new loans allowing the government to go to war. In fact, by the end of the eighteenth century, the most important role of the Bank of England was to serve private customers, not the government.[27]

In the United States the public debt was managed not by the Bank of the United States but directly by the Treasury Department and the various loan offices located in each state. Had it been in operation during the War of 1812, the bank could have managed loan subscriptions, but numerous private banks provided this service just as well. Instead the administration suffered from the loss of the bank in two other respects. In the summer of 1814, the nations' banks suspended the conversion of their banknotes to specie. When the banks no longer exchanged their notes for gold and silver coin or discounted the notes of other banks, the result was the creation of a host of local currencies in place of a nationally circulating medium because banknotes only circulated in the vicinity of the bank of issue. The suspension of specie conversion, Treasury Secretary Alexander Dallas remarked in October 1814, "has suddenly broken the chain of accommodation that previously extended the credit and the circulation of the notes which were emitted in one State into every State of the Union. It may in general be affirmed, therefore, that there exists at this time no adequate circulating medium common to the citizens of the United States." Because specie was in short supply, the government had to continue to accept banknotes in payment for taxes, bonds, and public land. As a result the Treasury accumulated money in local currencies at places of tax collection rather than places of disbursement. The money on hand was difficult to transfer because there were no national banknotes and a shortage of hard money. All transfer of money therefore involved negotiations over the terms of exchange between private banknotes. As Dallas wryly noted, suspension transformed "the public revenue, which is destined for general uses abroad as well as at home, into a local fund that may not be wanted where it exists, and cannot be applied where it is wanted." The difficulty in transferring money led to a failure to pay dividends on the public debt to creditors in Massachusetts and to a close call in Amsterdam. In both cases the sums were small but the symbolic importance enormous. The possibility that faith in the government's ability to honor its debts would disintegrate was very real and would have meant an instant end to further government loans.[28]

The second consequence of Congress's refusal to recharter the Bank of the United States was perhaps even more important. It was certainly more significant to Gallatin's war finance plan. Initially, the need to recharter the bank in 1811 must have appeared a godsend to the hard-pressed secretary of the Treasury. Gallatin proposed the creation of a much larger bank than the First Bank of the United States, recapitalized at $30 million, or three times the size of the original bank. Furthermore, a clause of the charter required the bank to lend the government half its capital on demand. Because Gallatin was convinced that a larger Bank of the United States would be capable of lending even more than this, his war finance plan counted on the new bank as the source of a $20 million loan. The expiration rather than recharter of the Bank of the United States was therefore a double setback for Gallatin. Not only would a possible war be more difficult to administer. He would also have to find a lender willing to advance $20 million in a nation where the government had never before borrowed substantial sums at home.[29]

The fact that loans rather than taxes were the backbone of Gallatin's war finance plan did not mean that taxes were unimportant. To the contrary, taxation was a crucial part of the plan because the government's ability to borrow depended on its ability to service its debts. Many years after the war, Gallatin gave a lucid definition of the essence of public credit when he noted that credit rested on two factors. First of all, credit depended on the "opinion entertained" of the government's "fidelity in fulfilling its engagements" and of its stability. In this regard, the United States had had an excellent record ever since the settlement of the debt created by the Revolution. But credit also depended on "the wealth and resources of the State" issuing securities "compared with its expenditures and debt." For loans to succeed, they had therefore to be backed by adequate taxation. The basic formula of Republican war finance, as devised by Gallatin, was that loans should pay only for the extraordinary expenses caused by the war effort. Taxes should continue to pay for all ordinary expenditures, including interest on new loans. To succeed in this the government had to impose taxes "at least equal to the annual expenses on a peace establishment, the interest of the existing debt, and the interest on the loans which may be raised [during the war]." Initially Congress responded favorably. The House Ways and Means Committee stated that failure to provide enough revenue to allow the government to service old and new debts would "sap the foundations of its credit." If the Treasury had to borrow to cover interest charges on the public debt, it would introduce a system "altogether unprecedented in the financial history of any wise and regular Government, and must, if yielded to, produce, at no distant period, that general state of public discredit which attended the national finances during the war of the Revolution, and which nothing but the peculiar circumstances of the country, and the want of a well-organized and efficient Government, during the period of that Revolution, could at all justify."[30]

For obvious reasons the ability of the United States to weather a war with a European naval power was severely restricted by the government's dependence on income from international trade. Any doubts about this flaw in the fiscal system had been removed by the experience of the embargo, and Gallatin was acutely aware of the problem. In his annual report for 1811, he remarked that the "most formidable objection" to the American fiscal regime was that it could not answer wartime needs: "In time of peace, it is almost sufficient to defray the expenses of a war; in time of war, it is hardly competent to support the expense of a peace establishment." Nevertheless, despite his conviction that the people would pay war taxes "cheerfully" and that the fiscal burden would remain light even with additional taxation, "when compared either with the population and wealth of the United States or with the burdens laid on European nations by their governments," the Treasury secretary hesitated to propose new taxes. In 1808 he was confident that no tax increase would be necessary other than a doubling of the import duties, at least for the first four years of a major war. He continued to urge that the duties be doubled, but by 1812 he had become convinced that additional taxes would also be necessary. Gallatin therefore suggested the reintroduction of the salt duty and that $2 million be raised from indirect taxes and $3 million from direct taxes. By his own admission Gallatin was no innovator in the fiscal sphere. The indirect taxes that he proposed included duties on distilled domestic spirits, refined sugar, licenses to retailers of spirits, sales at auction, and carriages and a stamp tax. In other words, Gallatin's proposal simply resurrected the Federalist taxes repealed in 1802. To the secretary it did not "appear necessary to resort to any other than those which had been formerly levied by the United States," nor for that matter did it seem that "any other equally productive could be substituted with any real advantage." The one substantial difference to the Federalist system was the proposal that the direct tax "should be laid and assessed in each State upon the same objects of taxation on which the direct taxes levied under the authority of the State are laid and assessed."[31]

The final element of Gallatin's plan was debt repayment. The Republicans' fear of a "system of perpetual and increasing debt" meant that Gallatin had his eyes on debt redemption even before the government advertised for its first loan. Costs had to be kept down in order to restrict borrowing. Congress should keep up repayments on the old Revolutionary debt throughout the war, by means of new loans if necessary, while giving "such a form" to the new debt "as may not impede its redemption." Although he became increasingly concerned about the terms on which new war loans could be secured, the Treasury secretary remained confident that the government could pay off its debt rapidly on the return of peace. From 1796 to the outbreak of the War of 1812, the public debt had been halved. This was sufficient to show that the United States was capable of rapid debt retrenchment so "that neither a perpetual and increasing public debt nor a permanent system of ever-progressing taxation shall be entailed on the nation." The time it would take to pay off the new debt obviously depended on the sums borrowed. Yet Gallatin ventured to guess that it would take no more than fifteen years after the return of peace to repay both the new debt and what remained of the 6 percent bonds from the War of Independence, thus reaching his and Jefferson's cherished goal of ridding the United States from public debt.[32]

In comparison to the financing of the French and Indian War and the War of Independence, two things in particular stand out in Gallatin's plan. The first is the fact that he made no mention of "currency finance" measures, that is, the emission of fiat currency such as the so-called Continentals that were emitted during the War of Independence. Even when Jefferson and his son-in-law, chairman of the Ways and Means Committee John Eppes, had begun to favor the issue of fiat money in the critical year of 1814,

Gallatin remained a convinced opponent of "paper money, so called." He called himself an "ultra bullionist" and in 1830 even argued for prohibiting all banknotes other than those of the Second Bank of the United States. There would be no return to the practices of the War of Independence while Gallatin remained in charge of the Treasury. The second difference from earlier practice was the reliance on long-term bonds. Not only was this the established method in Britain and Europe and a break with the established American method, it also rested firmly on the financial institutions and policies with which the Federalists and in particular Alexander Hamilton had equipped the American national government. Centralized finance and public credit would be the main pillars of Gallatin's method of war finance. To what extent they would suffice in seeing the United States through a war with the former mother country was anybody's guess.[33]

IV

The plan that Gallatin began to sketch in 1807 guided the government's financial management of the War of 1812. Through a process of trial and error, the Madison administration found a formula for raising loans that proved to be both workable and durable and served as the model for the financing of both the Mexican War and the early stages of the Civil War. After troubled beginnings, the high point of Treasury operations was reached in the early fall of 1813. By then Gallatin had left for Europe on a peace mission and had been replaced by William Jones, who for a few months doubled as Navy secretary and Treasury secretary. From this point, the public finances began to turn sour. The demand for loans seemed endless, the outcome of the war doubtful. In the summer of 1814, investors had grown wary of government loans, and further bond emissions proved to be impossible. In the fall, Gallatin's master plan was radically revised as the administration turned to a different strategy of war finance.

During the war, the government made use of three types of loans: temporary bank loans, short-term Treasury notes, and long-term securities. Bank loans were comparatively unimportant. The government borrowed a little more than $2 million in 1812 and a little less than $3 million in 1814 and 1815. In the latter stages of the war the money was advanced by banks in Baltimore and New York on condition that it was earmarked for local defense preparations. Much more important than bank loans were Treasury notes. These notes have sometimes been compared to the paper money issued during the War of Independence, and the opposition press quickly branded them "Continentals." As Gallatin admitted, however, they had little to do with American traditions of war finance but were "a mere transcript of the Exchequer bills of Great Britain." Like their British counterparts the notes bore interest, were payable to bearer, and were redeemable in order of issue one year after emission. Treasury notes were used directly by government agents to pay suppliers and contractors or sold to banks, which resold them to customers. The character of the Treasury notes meant that they were likely to replace banknotes "to a certain degree," and for this reason Gallatin warned that "the issue must be moderate, and never exceed the amount which may circulate without depreciation." In total the Treasury issued $36.7 million Treasury notes during the conflict and its immediate aftermath. Because of continual redemptions the amount outstanding at any point in time was much smaller, however. At the start of 1813, $2.8 million was outstanding. One year later the figure had climbed to $4.9 million. Under increasing pressure in the critical year of 1814, the Treasury allowed the redemption of notes to fall gradually into arrears. On January 1, 1815, $10.6 million in Treasury notes was in circulation. Over the ensuing year the amount increased to $17.1 million as the government grappled with the money shortage resulting from the banks' suspension of specie conversion.[34]

By far the most important type of loan was the sale of long-term interest-bearing bonds. Between 1812 and 1815, the government issued bonds at a face value of close to $73 million. The Constitution invested the power to "borrow Money on the credit of the United States" in Congress, which meant that every loan required legislative sanction. Altogether five loan acts were passed during the War of 1812. These acts determined the maximum amount the administration could borrow and sometimes constricted the Treasury's freedom of action by stipulating the maximum interest or the minimal sales price of securities. All the acts made the securities issued irredeemable for twelve years. This was in order to make bonds more attractive to investors by preventing the government from refinancing war loans at lower interest upon the return of peace.[35]

The loan act was only the first step in the borrowing process. The next and much more difficult one was to find willing investors. Here there were few precedents for the government to rely on. As Gallatin remarked in January 1812, the success and terms of a loan could "be ascertained only by experiment." The United States had never been able to borrow "considerable loans" at 6 percent other than from the now defunct Bank of the United States, and at no point had the government owed more than $7 million to the bank. In Britain, the government normally sold its loans to closed lists of underwriters, including Treasury officials, members of Parliament, and

City of London financiers, who made a profit by reselling securities to other investors. Eventually the securities found their way to the London securities market, where the general public could invest in the debt. Gallatin's first loan attempt did not follow this model. In anticipation of war Congress had authorized an $11 million loan in March 1812, and the following month the Treasury secretary advertised the loan in the major newspapers. Investors were invited to subscribe to the loan at a number of banks, from Portsmouth, New Hampshire, to Charleston, South Carolina. On payment of one-eighth of their subscription, the bank issued "scrip," short for subscription, which was a receipt for the first payment. After an additional seven monthly installments, duly noted on the scrip, creditors collected the actual bonds, or "stock certificates," at the Treasury or one of the loan offices in the states. The scrip could be sold and transferred by endorsement at any time, and the bonds once issued were "transferable by the creditors, or their attorneys, duly constituted, at the treasury and loan offices respectively, in the same manner as the present funded debt of the United States."[36]

The newspapers took an immediate interest in the loan. Editors were well aware that faith was the essence of public credit, and favorable reports about investments and investors were soon circulated by proadministration papers, which promised that the "stock will be undoubtedly good" and urged that "patriotism calls for the fulfillment of the loan." Soon misgivings were expressed, however, and before long these misgivings were confirmed. When the books closed after the stipulated six weeks, no more than $6 million had been offered. About a third had come from subscriptions by individuals, the remainder from banks. Republican newspapers blamed the failure on the willful sabotage of "federal Brokers," who were seen "running up and down our Stock exchange and Coffee Houses, offering large amounts of Government Stock to sell below par, and when called upon to take cash for their Stock at their own price, *they had it not.*" Such men deserved to have their "nose[s] tweaked and [their] seat[s] of honor well kicked." The Federalist press responded by questioning the patriotism of the prowar party, who seemed unwilling to put their money where their mouths were. Gallatin meanwhile did what he could to present the loan as a success. He noted that the $2 million subscribed by private individuals was more "than the aggregate of all the loans at six per cent. ever before obtained by this Government from individuals in the United States." Although the observation was true enough, it did not alter the fact that the subscription had fallen $5 million short.[37]

Gallatin reopened the books in August, but investors still did not come forward. In a private memorandum he informed the president that the prospects for a loan for 1813 were not good. "From banks we can expect little or nothing, as they have already lent nearly to the full extent of their faculties," the Treasury secretary said. Private individuals were an even less likely source of funds. When Congress authorized a new loan of $16 million on February 8, 1813, Gallatin knew that he had to find new ways to tap into the money market. He therefore opened negotiations with the New York merchant and German immigrant John Jacob Astor in the hope that Astor would put together a list of investors. But negotiations broke down, and the Treasury again had to advertise the loan offer in the newspapers. Then Astor suddenly made an abrupt about-face and declared that he was now willing to lend the government the money. Unfortunately for Gallatin, who would much have preferred a closed list, Astor's offer came too late.[38]

When the loan closed on March 13, 1813, the government was faced with yet another failure. Only 25 percent of the requested $16 million had been offered. The Federalist press was jubilant. Challenging the administration to dare impose new taxes, the *New York Gazette* quipped, "To BORROW—not to TAX—the GOVERNMENT was prone: The People, not Subscribing, left it quite ALONE." Clearly, a new strategy was called for. The books reopened between March 25 and 31, but this time the government auctioned off the bonds to the highest bidder. Any "person or persons, body or bodies corporate, who may offer, for themselves or others" were invited to submit proposals stating "the amount offered to be loaned, the species of stock or stocks, which the parties wish to obtain, and the price they will allow for the same." Although the Republican press liked to portray loan subscriptions as acts of patriotism undertaken by ordinary citizens, the minimum offer accepted by the government was $100,000, a sum that very few citizens could produce. Apart from the newspaper ads, the procedure resembled British Treasury practice. In London an investor in the funds would form "his list of friends, who are to take different proportions with him in case he succeeds" and then submit his offer to the government. Each interested "party offers as low as he can venture with a fair prospect of profit, and the most advantageous to the public is accepted."[39]

With the second offer for the $16 million loan Gallatin had found a working system. When the bids were opened in early April, the loan had been oversubscribed. Two "lists of friends" took close to $9 million. Astor's list in New York City was instrumental in securing acceptable terms from the list headed by Stephen Girard and David Parish of Philadelphia. Proadministration papers now got back at the opposition and ridiculed the Federalists' "flattering hopes" "that the *war would stop for want of funds.*" Early in 1812, Gallatin had believed that the real difficulty awaiting the government in the event of war would not be to procure loans but to procure loans on reasonable terms. The $16 million loan confirmed his view that there was enough money in the country but that investors were not ready to part with it at 6 percent interest. Subscribers to the $16 million loan offered to pay $88 for a 6 percent $100 bond redeemable after twelve years. This amounted to a current yield of 6.8 percent and a true yield of close to 8 percent on their investment. Hard pressed for money, the government had no choice but to accept these terms.[40]

Only four months after the sale of the $16 million loan, Congress authorized a third loan, this time for $7.5 million. The new secretary of the Treasury, William Jones, was optimistic about the government's prospects. To Madison he wrote that "I look forward with great solicitude for the close of the new Loan, the invitation to which I am more and more satisfied is calculated to bring forward the best bidders and excite the fairest competition." Jones followed the successful procedure laid down for the $16 million loan. Again the loan was oversubscribed, this time by a full $5 million. It was sold at $88.25, a slightly higher price than the price offered for the $16 million loan. Future prospects looked promising.[41]

Jones's annual Treasury report submitted to Congress in January 1814 still exuded optimism. Not only had the $7.5 million loan been filled, but Congress had finally passed new tax legislation in the summer of 1813. Furthermore, news had reached the president that the British were willing to open peace negotiations. An end to the hostilities therefore looked near. But over the spring and summer, hope turned to despair. Preparatory negotiations with creditors in New York and Philadelphia stalled. George W. Campbell, who critics said did not have "two distinct ideas about finance," replaced Jones at the Treasury. Although a $10 million loan offered in April sold at $88, the subscription was filled by a new investor of highly disreputable renown. Jacob Barker of New York had subscribed $1.5 million to the $7.5 million loan and now offered the government $5 million. Without his bid, the Treasury would have had to settle for a bond price of $85. The news worried Jones, who as Navy secretary had tried to help by subscribing $200,000 on account of the Navy and Privateer Pension Fund. He wrote to Madison, "I am humbled when I reflect that this great nation had to depend for one half of the Loan upon a speculative individual who may or may not fulfill his contract for in him I view it as the bold effort of a gambler." The administration had every reason to be concerned. Barker would find it difficult to raise money for his installments and eventually defaulted on $1.5 million of the payments. But this was not the end of the Treasury's troubles. Congress had authorized the Treasury to borrow $25 million, but

Campbell offered investors only $10 million. He feared that there would be insufficient demand for a larger offering and that, as a consequence, the price of a $100 bond would fall below $88, the price government bonds had previously sold at. But investors realized that a new offering was likely to follow later in the year. To guard their investment they forced Campbell to accept that if the Treasury sold another loan below $88 in 1814, the sales price of their bonds would be reduced to the same price as the new bonds. Meanwhile the international situation had deteriorated. The British government had not shown much interest in peace negotiations, and the end of the European war meant that Britain could now concentrate on its enemy across the ocean.[42]

When the Treasury advertised the $10 million loan, Gallatin had arrived in London on his peace mission. There he could witness firsthand the danger caused to the United States by Napoleon's abdication and surrender on April 11, 1814. "The numerous English forces in France, Italy, Holland, and Portugal ready for immediate service, and for which there is no further employment in Europe, afford to this government the means of sending both to Canada and to the United States a very formidable army," Gallatin wrote to his former cabinet colleagues. He estimated that Britain could land an army of fifteen to twenty thousand men anywhere on the Atlantic seaboard. The United States could also expect the British to "turn against us as much of their superabundant naval forces as they might think adequate to any object they have in view." Most likely the British would attack New York, Baltimore, Washington, and New Orleans. They might also aim to separate the New England states from the Union in order to restore them to the British Empire. Gallatin's predictions proved accurate enough. In the summer of 1814, the Royal Navy mounted a series of coastal raids culminating in the sack of Washington on August 24. A few weeks later an attempt was made to capture Baltimore, but Fort McHenry, which protected the city's approach, withstood the assault. In late December a major British invasion force landed at New Orleans.[43]

Although peace talks began in August 1814, they proceeded slowly, and the government was in desperate need of money to keep up the war effort throughout the summer and fall. The timing of Campbell's attempt to float a new $6 million loan could not have been worse, however. Subscription books were to close on August 25. On the night of August 24 the capital's public buildings, including the Treasury, were put to the torch by a British landing party. With the outcome of the war so obviously in doubt, interest in the funds plummeted. Only $2.8 million was offered, almost all of it at $80. In accordance with the loan contract, the price of the $10 million loan of May 1814 now had to be reduced to $80 also. At this price the premium was 25 percent. If the bond was paid for in depreciated banknotes at 80 percent of par, the true yield on a twelve-year bond would amount to about 14 percent. The $6 million loan of August 1814 represents the low watermark in Treasury operations during the War of 1812. It ended further attempts to finance the conflict by selling long-term bonds. It also heralded the abandonment of Gallatin's war finance plan.[44]

When the Thirteenth Congress met for an extra session in September 1814, the financial situation had become critical. Barker and other investors had defaulted on $1.9 million of their payments on the $10 million loan and $410,000 worth of subscriptions to the $6 million loan had been withdrawn. Unless the nation's credit was improved, loans were no longer an option to finance the war. Yet somehow Congress had to close a deficit of almost $12 million for the last half of 1814 alone. Campbell saw no choice but to announce the failure of the administration's method of war finance. From then on, it would be necessary to "provide, by means other than loans, for at least a portion of the extraordinary expenditures." "Means other than loans" of course meant new taxes. But Campbell did no more than suggest that the direct tax introduced the previous year be continued, after which he promptly resigned from the Treasury. It was left to his successor, Alexander Dallas, to draw up a new plan for financing the war.[45]

Dallas argued that in future the government had to rely more on the "national wealth" and less on the "national faith." He estimated that no less than $21 million per year had to be raised from taxes. Of this sum only $4 million would come from import duties, the traditional source of American tax revenue. Dallas justified this change of course by pointing out that the "wealth of the nation in the value and productions of its soil, in all the acquisitions of personal property, and in all the varieties of industry, remains almost untouched by the hand of government." The new Treasury secretary called for an increase in the rate of existing taxes and the introduction of a series of new duties and property taxes, including a truly intrusive tax on household furniture. The national government would now become precisely the sort of inquisitive and demanding state that the Antifederalists had warned against during the debate over the ratification of the Constitution and that the Jeffersonian Republicans had feared in the 1790s. Despite his call for new taxes, Dallas did not give up on loans altogether. Gallatin's plan had stipulated that taxes pay the $5.9 million necessary to cover the cost of the army and navy peace establishment. Dallas's plan did not propose any substantial increase over this sum but provided only for the payment of $2 million in tax revenue toward actual war expenses. The aim of the new taxes was rather to restore public credit by earmarking funds for charges on the old and new debt, for the payment of Treasury notes, for a sinking fund, and for a substantial contingency fund. Credit would continue to finance the war. According to the Dallas plan, the principal source of new loans would be a reestablished and much larger Bank of the United States capitalized at $50 million. Not only would the bank sink $44 million of outstanding 6 percent bonds, it would also be required to lend the government $30 million.[46]

Dallas's plan was a bold one. Faced with the seriousness of the situation Congress now proved willing to pass new fiscal legislation. In December 1814 and January 1815, the direct tax was increased to $6 million annually. Existing internal duties were also increased and others added (see table 4.1). New loans of $12 million altogether were authorized upon the pledge of internal duties and the direct tax, and the Treasury was given the right to issue and reissue Treasury notes to the value of $25 million. Congress proved more reluctant to charter a new bank, however. The financial situation therefore remained critical when the new year began. Dallas refrained from attempting to float a new loan in the fall of 1814 and instead allowed payments on Treasury notes and charges on the Treasury to fall in arrears. In January 1815, public securities were quoted at seventy-seven dollars on the Philadelphia securities market. Madison had proclaimed January 12 a day of "public humiliation and fasting and of prayer to Almighty God for the safety and welfare of these States, His blessing on their arms, and a speedy restoration of peace." Five days later, Dallas presented his budget to Congress. His estimates showed that government expenses would exceed income by $41 million and that the deficit had to be closed by new loans. It was reported that a stunned silence followed on the reading of the report in the House of Representatives.[47]

Had the war continued, it is doubtful if even stringent fiscal measures would have sufficed to restore the government's ability to borrow, especially without the creation of a new national bank. There was no upward movement in bond prices as a result of the new tax laws, and Dallas did not dare to try the loan market. But peace saved the government from possible ruin. Gallatin and the other members of the American peace commission concluded negotiations on Christmas Eve 1814, and news of the peace treaty reached New York on February 11, 1815. News of Andrew Jackson's victory at New Orleans arrived at about the same time. The success of American arms and the restoration of peace had an immediate effect on the price of government bonds, after "markets of every kind experienced a sudden and to many a shocking change." In one week bond prices in Phila-

TABLE 4.1. Fiscal system of the federal government in January 1815

Tax	Date enacted, increased, or proposed
Customs and tonnage duties	Increased Jan. 31 and July 1, 1812
Postage	Increased Dec. 23, 1814
Salt duty	Enacted July 29, 1813
Direct tax	Enacted July 22, and Aug. 2, 1813. Increased Jan. 9, 1815
Income tax*	Proposed Jan. 17, 1815. Not enacted
Duty on carriages	Enacted July 24, 1813. Increased 15 Dec. 1814
Duty on harnesses	Enacted Dec. 15, 1814
Duty on household furniture	Enacted Jan. 18, 1815
Duty on gold and silver watches	Enacted Jan. 18, 1815
Duty on refined sugar	Enacted July 24, 1813
Duty on licenses to distillers of spirits	Enacted July 24, 1813
Duty on licenses to retailers of wines, spirits, and foreign merchandise	Enacted Aug. 2, 1813. Increased Dec. 23, 1814
Duty on distilled spirits	Enacted Dec. 21, 1814
Duty on sales at auction of merchandise and ships and vessels	Enacted July 24, 1813. Increased Dec. 23, 1814
Duty on banknotes and financial instruments	Enacted Aug. 2, 1813.
Duty on the manufacture of iron	Enacted Jan. 18 and Feb. 27, 1815
Duty on the manufacture of nails	Enacted Jan. 18 and Feb. 27, 1815
Duty on the manufacture of candles	Enacted Jan. 18 and Feb. 27, 1815
Duty on the manufacture of hats and caps	Enacted Jan. 18 and Feb. 27, 1815
Duty on the manufacture of umbrellas	Enacted Jan. 18 and Feb. 27, 1815
Duty on the manufacture of paper	Enacted Jan. 18 and Feb. 27, 1815
Duty on the manufacture of playing and visiting cards	Enacted Jan. 18 and Feb. 27, 1815
Duty on the manufacture of saddles and bridles	Enacted Jan. 18 and Feb. 27, 1815
Duty on the manufacture of boots	Enacted Jan. 18 and Feb. 27, 1815
Duty on the manufacture of beer, ale, and porter	Enacted Jan. 18 and Feb. 27, 1815

TABLE 4.1. *continued*

Tax	Date enacted, increased, or proposed
Duty on the manufacture of tobacco, cigars, and snuff	Enacted Jan. 18 and Feb. 27, 1815
Duty on the manufacture of leather	Enacted Jan. 18 and Feb. 27, 1815
Duty on the manufacture of gold and silver plate, jewelry, and paste work	Enacted Jan. 18 and Feb. 27, 1815
Tax of one dollar of every barrel of wheaten flour*	Proposed Jan. 17, 1815. Not enacted
Tax upon inheritances and devices*	Proposed Jan. 17, 1815. Not enacted
Tax upon bequests, legacies, and statutory distribution*	Proposed Jan. 17, 1815. Not enacted
Auxiliary tax upon all testamentary instruments*	Proposed Jan. 17, 1815. Not enacted
Tax upon legal process and proceedings in federal courts*	Proposed Jan. 17, 1815. Not enacted
Tax upon conveyances, mortgages, and leases*	Proposed Jan. 17, 1815. Not enacted
Stamp tax on bonds, penal bills, warrants of attorney, etc.*†	Proposed Jan. 17, 1815. Not enacted
Tax upon dividends and upon the sale and transfer of stocks*‡	Proposed Jan. 17, 1815. Not enacted

Sources: "State of the Finances," December 8, 1815, *ASP: Finance*, 3:2–5; George Mifflin Dallas, ed., *Life and Writings of Alexander James Dallas* (Philadelphia: J. P. Lippincott, 1871), 268.

*Taxes proposed in the annual report of January 17, 1815, but not enacted.

†The full title of this tax proposal is "a stamp tax on bonds, penal bills, warrants of attorney, notarial instruments, policies of insurance, all negotiable notes, protests of bills of exchange, and promissory notes, bills of sale, and hypothecations of vessels, bottomry and respondia bonds."

‡The full title of this tax proposal is "a tax upon dividends and upon the sale and transfer of the stocks of banks, insurance companies and other corporations, operating for profit, upon a money capital."

delphia climbed 16 percent. On the last day of May, the government press could exclaim "'*Tis done. The long agony is over.* Public credit is restored." The administration responded to the good news even faster than the securities market. Within two weeks of the arrival of the news of peace, Dallas reported to Congress that "after the present year, there is reason to presume that the public revenue will considerably exceed the public expenditure, and, consequently, that the necessity of borrowing will cease." The Treasury secretary could now turn his attention to the absorption of the short-term or "floating" debt and the repayment of the war loans, and Congress could concentrate on the rapid dismantling of its wartime fiscal program.[48]

V

As previously noted, historians have not been impressed with the manner in which "the central government barely muddled through the War of 1812." The administration's attempt to finance the war has been described as "a pitiful failure." Yet few if any major wars in history have been devoid of difficulties of resource mobilization. Failure rather than success tends to dominate accounts of past war finance, and the judgment on the government's record in the War of 1812 may therefore be overly harsh. Our understanding of how American state capacity developed over time is hardly improved by comparing the record of the Madison administration with the manner in which the present-day federal government manages its bond sales. It is more enlightening to compare the administration's record to Gallatin's original war finance plan, to the British record during the Napoleonic Wars, and to the performance of the Continental Congress during the War of Independence.[49]

Gallatin's war finance plan stipulated that the government pay peacetime expenditures and interest on the war loans from its tax income. Before the war he assumed that the government had to raise around $9 million a year to do so. As was his habit, the Treasury secretary made overly pessimistic projections about government income and doubted that this would be possible without the addition of new taxes. In fact, the Madison administration managed to raise the money needed to follow Gallatin's plan without great difficulty. Tax income amounted to $9.8 in 1812, $14.3 million in 1813, $11.2 million in 1814, and $15.7 million in 1815. Gallatin's principal mistake was instead a far too optimistic calculation of war costs. Rather than $10 million annually for a war lasting four years, extraordinary military expenditures amounted to $20 million in 1813, $30 million in 1814, and a projected $40 million in 1815. Borrowing needs were therefore much higher than Gallatin's plan had assumed. The Treasury's position was undermined by Congress's refusal to double the duties on imports in advance of the declaration of war and to recharter the Bank of the United States. Instead of a $20 million war chest and an expanded national bank able to lend $20 million, Gallatin went to war with a Treasury surplus of less than $4 million and no central bank. Had Gallatin possessed his $40 million in cash and bank credit, he would not have had to float a loan until April 1814 (see table 4.2), and the financial situation would not have become precarious as early as the fall of 1814. Until that fateful fall, however, the administration managed its securities issues surprisingly well given its lack of experience. Gallatin was well aware that "the fact that the United States may easily, in ten years of peace, extinguish a debt of forty-two millions of dollars, does not necessarily imply that they could borrow that sum during a period of war." But only when the fortunes of war turned against the United States, when the government had sold $45 million in long-term securities, and when its rapidly growing Treasury-note debt was falling into arrears did the government's credit become exhausted.[50]

According to an oft-repeated claim, the credit of the national government was so poor during the War of 1812 that it sold $80 million in securities for no more than $34 million in gold and silver. The claim seems to have originated in an 1830 report prepared by the House Committee of Ways and Means on the Second Bank of the United States. This report supported the recharter of the bank and used the War of 1812 to show the hazard of going to war without a national bank. It was quite correct in stressing that the primary problem of Treasury operations caused by the dissolution of the Bank of the United States was the lack of a nationwide circulating medium. This lack forced the government to accept heavily depreciated banknotes in payment for securities, which, according to the report, were worth on average only 50 percent of face value. After the Mexican War, Treasury Secretary Robert J. Walker relied on this report to depict his management of the nation's war finances in a favorable light. In the twentieth century historians have taken it as evidence of the dismal failure of the Madison administration.[51]

There is no question that the banknotes issued by the Bank of the United States were sorely missed during the war and that their absence caused the government considerable difficulties. Some of the claims of the 1830 Ways and Means Committee report nevertheless seem exaggerated. Gallatin, who had inside information, if also a reputation to protect, certainly thought so. Although he confessed to being "an ultra-bullionist" and was strongly in favor of the Second Bank of the United States, he questioned the accuracy of the 1830 report, claiming that "the loss arising from the suspension of specie payments, which was incurred by government during the war, is overrated in the report." A careful reading of the record suggests that Gallatin was more nearly correct than the Ways and Means Committee. Specie conversion was suspended only in August 1814 and did not affect the early loans. The $10 million loan of 1814 would have been two-thirds paid by then. Two of the loans of 1815 were floated to absorb the short-term debt and were payable in Treasury notes only. This leaves the $6 million loan of

TABLE 4.2. Long-term securities emissions, 1812–1815

Date authorized	Proposals accepted	Amount offered ($)	Nominal value securities sold ($)	Price ($)	Real value of securities sold ($)	Price old 6 percent/ war loans (Philadelphia) ($)	Nominal interest (%)	Effective interest (%)
Mar. 14, 1812	—	11,000,000	8,134,700	100	8,134,700	—	6	—
Feb. 8, 1813	Mar. 25 to 31, 1813	16,000,000	18,109,377	88.00	16,000,000	91	6	6.8
Aug. 2, 1813	Aug. 30 to Sept. 25, 1813	7,500,000	8,498,582	88	7,500,000	93/90	6	6.8
Mar. 24, 1814	Apr. 4 to May 2, 1814	10,000,000	9,919,476	80	7,935,581	92/87	6	7.5
Mar. 24, 1814	July 25 to Aug. 25, 1814	6,000,000	5,384,135	80	3,445,846	88/80	6	9.4
Feb. 24, 1815	—	—	1,505,352	100	1,354,817	—	6	6.7

Feb. 24, 1815	—	—	9,070,386	100	—	8,163,347	7	7.8
Mar. 3, 1815	Apr. 15 to July 13, 1815	12,000,000	12,288,148	95.20	98.50/95.50	9,972,815	6	7.4
Total			72,910,157			62,480,106		7.1

Source: Rafael A. Bayley, *History of the National Loans of the United States from July 4, 1776, to June 30, 1880*, in *Report on Valuation, Taxation, and Public Indebtedness in the United States, as Returned at the Tenth Census (June 1, 1880)* (Washington, DC: Government Printing Office, 1884), 353, 416–17, 418–19, 420, 421, 422, 426, 428, 430; Richard Sylla et al., "The Price Quotations in Early U.S. Securities Markets, 1790–1860," database available at http://eh.net/database/early-u-s-securities-prices/.

Notes: The real value of securities sold for the loans of 1814 and 1815 are estimates. Because the loans were payable in banknotes that traded at a discount once the banks suspended specie payments in the summer of 1814, the real discount was greater than indicated by the sales price. The $10 million loan was paid in four equal installments on May 25, June 25, July 25, and August 25, 1814. It was therefore paid before the banks suspended specie payments. I have assumed that the $6 million loan was paid only in banknotes and that the real value of these notes was 80 percent of par value. This gives the following real value of the loan: $0.8 \times 0.8 \times 5,384,135 = 3,445,846$. The loans authorized on February 24, 1815, were sold at par and payable in Treasury notes only. In the summer of 1815 both the old and the new debt traded at between $89 and $100. It seems unlikely that the Treasury notes would have fallen below this price, especially considering that the government was able to reissue Treasury notes received. I have therefore estimated that Treasury notes traded at $90. This gives the following real value of the loan: $0.9 \times 1,505,352 = 1,354,817$ and $0.9 \times 9,072,815 = 8,163,347$. The $12 million loan was payable in banknotes and Treasury notes. Of the first $9.2 million subscribed, for which there are available figures, $3.2 million, or 35 percent, was paid for in Treasury notes. I have assumed that the share of Treasury notes were the same for the remainder of the $12 million loan and have estimated the price of banknotes at 80 percent of par value. For the $12 million loan, this gives the following real value: $[[0.35 \times 0.9 \times 12,288,148] + [0.65 \times 0.8 \times 12,288,148]] \times 0.952 = 9,972,815$. Bayley's figure for this loan is $11,699,327. According to Bayley, the average discount on the $12 million loan was 4.8 percent. The price of 1812 securities is based on securities prices in Philadelphia and Baltimore as recorded in Sylla et al.

1814 and the $12 million loan of May 1815 as the loans principally affected by the depreciation of banknotes. Treasury records show that two-thirds of the latter loan was paid for in banknotes. A recent estimate of banknote depreciation argues that banknotes never depreciated more than 20 percent. It is also unlikely that Treasury notes fell more than 20 percent. If we assume these figures to be correct, the Treasury's loss from currency and Treasury-note depreciation was around $6.3 million. This figure represents around 8.5 percent of the total borrowed during the war.

The $7 million that the government lost by selling securities at a discount in fact represents a greater loss than it suffered from the depreciation of Treasury notes and banknotes. As price series of securities in Philadelphia, the securities market with the fullest data, make clear, the sales price of new bonds reflected fluctuations in the price of old bonds in the nation's securities markets. Compared to the prices of old bonds, new loans were not sold at significantly cheaper rates than the market price of old government bonds. If the estimated effect of depreciation is added to the discounted sales price, the $73 million in bonds netted approximately $60 million in specie. The loss to the government from depreciation and discounts was close to 18 percent. Unquestionably, this was a substantial figure, but it was a far cry from the 58 percent loss presented in the Ways and Means Committee report of 1830.[52]

To contemporaries, the sale of securities below par did not necessarily amount to a failure in managing the nation's finances. Intervening in the debate over the Mexican War more than three decades after he had brokered the Peace of Christmas Eve, Gallatin explained the basic pattern of war bond emissions. It was a "general and invariable law" that as "war continues, and as new annual loans are required, Governments are compelled to pay dearer every successive year for the money borrowed; or, which is the same thing, the marketable price of their stocks is lessened every successive year." This pattern had "taken place everywhere," even in Britain, where "perfect confidence has always been placed in the good faith of the Government, and in its ability to pay at least the interest." Informed Britons writing at the turn of the eighteenth century confirmed the truth of Gallatin's "general and invariable law." The British public debt chiefly consisted of 3 percent bonds called "consols," which in the second half of the eighteenth century fluctuated between £90 and £106 6s. in peacetime, depending on the interest rates on private loans. When war broke out and the government entered the money market in search of new loans, the price of the securities plummeted. In wartime, British consols traded for between £60 and £70. As soon as peace returned, prices rebounded. Economic writers such as Thomas Mortimer therefore denied that falling bond prices suggested "either that the finances of the State are in a bad condition, or that its credit is on the decline. On the contrary, the immense sums annually subscribed for the support of Government, and the defence of the country, are demonstrative proofs of the strength of both."[53]

In the final years of the Napoleonic Wars, when the nation was also struggling to keep the United States at bay, Britain sold its securities at prices between £54 and £75. The average price in the period 1812 to 1815 was £61. These figures can be compared to American securities, which were sold at prices from $80 to $88. At 3 percent interest, the current yield of British bonds ranged between 4 and 5.5 percent. The current yield of American 6 percent bonds ranged between 6.8 and 7.5 percent. Although American loans were therefore considerably more expensive than British loans, the practice of selling loans at an increasing discount was similar in the United States and in Britain. In this respect the young republic's management of war finance conformed closely to the practice of the richest and financially most advanced monarchy in the Old World.

Compared to the War of Independence, finally, Mr. Madison's War represents an important step in the development of American public finance. The issue of $73 million in long-term bonds and $37 million in Treasury notes was a significant achievement, considering that the government's ability to finance war was previously untested. Although bond prices fell and Treasury notes depreciated, the financing of the War of 1812 was far more orderly than the financing of the first war against Britain. During the War of Independence, the Continental Congress tried to sell interest-bearing bonds but could only issue a small amount and soon had to suspend interest payments on the few bonds that were issued. Instead, most of the funds needed to wage the war were raised by means of the printing press. Altogether, Congress issued $200 million in fiat currency. The money depreciated rapidly and eventually became worthless.[54]

The War of Independence created a debt about equal to the size of the war loans floated during the War of 1812. Attempts to pay off the debt in the immediate postwar years created serious economic hardships and political tensions in the mid-1780s. Heavy taxes gave rise to demands for paper money and debt renunciation. They also gave rise to protests, obstructions, and, in the case of Massachusetts, a full-scale tax rebellion. The critical financial situation led to a reorganization of the American union and the creation of the national government through the drafting and adoption of the Constitution. When Alexander Hamilton became the nation's first Treasury secretary, he effectively addressed the government's fiscal and financial ills, but his policies also generated new controversy which helped generate the bitter party struggle of the 1790s.

The financial settlement of the War of 1812, in contrast, resulted in neither another Shays's Rebellion nor an age of passions. Instead, the war and the defeat of the Federalists ushered in an "Era of Good Feelings." No demands that the government should scale down the debt were heard. No complaints about the excessive profits of public creditors were made. The Treasury soon got the short-term debt under control by converting Treasury notes to bonds. On October 1, 1815, $16.2 million in Treasury notes was outstanding. Two years later this figure was down to $635,963. The following year these notes too were liquidated. The long-term debt took longer to reduce. Because the loans were not redeemable until the mid-1820s, there was no need to impose high taxes on the people to pay off the war loans. Instead, Congress abolished its war taxes and returned to the low prewar tax regime. The major exception to this policy was customs duties. The tariff of 1816 was considerably higher than the prewar tariff. By the mid-1820s, the tariff would become contested, but in the immediate postwar period it produced much-needed revenue but few objections. In June 1816, Gallatin could write to Madison that "the present state of the currency is the only evil of any magnitude entailed by the war." This last difficulty found its solution with the establishment of the Second Bank of the United States and by pressuring private banks to resume specie conversion. By April 1817, Treasury Secretary William Crawford noted that "specie payments have everywhere been resumed."[55]

Large Treasury surpluses made possible the reduction of the war loans when they began to fall due in 1824. The administrations of John Quincy Adams and Andrew Jackson paid off most of the loans from the War of 1812. Postwar administrations thereby carried through the final element of the original war finance plan by rapidly repaying the war loans during a period of peace and prosperity (see figure 4.1). Thus they made sure that the citizens of the American republic would not be permanently saddled with the burdens that pressed upon the subjects of Old World monarchies in the form of standing armies, high taxes, and public debts. By January 1, 1831, only $500,000 of the war debt remained unpaid. Gallatin's claim that the war loans could be paid off in fifteen years had thereby been vindicated. Three years later, Secretary of the Treasury Levi Woodbury could announce in his annual report that not only the war loans but the entire public debt had been terminated. Gallatin's and Jefferson's dream from the Revolution of 1800 had finally come true. The United States presented to the world the "unprecedented spectacle" of a government "virtually without any debt."[56]

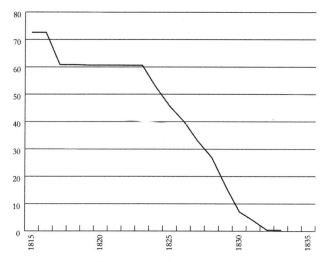

Fig. 4.1. Repayment of War of 1812 debt ($ million). *Source*: Rafael A. Bayley, *History of the National Loans of the United States from July 4, 1776, to June 30, 1880*, in *Report on Valuation, Taxation, and Public Indebtedness in the United States, as Returned at the Tenth Census (June 1, 1880)* (Washington, DC: Government Printing Office, 1884), 353, 416–17, 418–19, 420, 421, 422, 426, 428, 430.

The money raised by the Treasury during the War of 1812 did not win the war. At best it helped prevent the United States from losing it. As is well known, the Madison administration never attained its war aims, and to this extent the war must be deemed a failure. Yet by putting the republican experiment through the most severe test imaginable, Madison secured something more important than immediate war aims: faith in the ability of the United States to survive in an international state system of predatory monarchies. The war, Madison told Congress, had proved "that our political institutions, founded in human rights and framed for their preservation, are equal to the severest trials of war, as well as adapted to the ordinary periods of repose." Gallatin was of one mind with the president. On Christmas Day 1814, he wrote to Secretary of State James Monroe that the war had proved "our ability to resist alone the now very formidable military power of England" and to obtain unassisted "peace on equal terms." This, Gallatin was sure, would "raise our character and consequence in Europe" and "make us to be courted as much as we have been neglected by foreign governments." The first generation of American statesmen never doubted that sooner or later the United States would face war with a major European power. What they did not know was how well their federal union of state-republics would withstand the strains of modern war. Although the management of the War of 1812 is largely a history of failure, it also demonstrated the capacity of the United States to mobilize substantial resources, to create an efficient navy, and to recruit, train, and field an army of several thousand men. In this sense, the war vindicated the republican form of government and held it up as a viable alternative to the monarchies of Europe.[57]

In the sphere of public finance the War of 1812 represents a shift in American methods of war finance from an indigenous tradition relying on fiat currency and rapid debt redemption through high postwar taxes to a British method of bond emission and the acceptance of long-term indebtedness. However, an important difference between the United States and Britain was that the relatively small American debt made it possible to strive toward and realize the repayment of war loans within a few decades after the restoration of peace. Although it was a close call, the financial institutions put in place by Hamilton and nurtured by Gallatin held fast. The War of 1812 thereby demonstrated the ability of a republican society to develop a state capacity sufficient to withstand the might of the world's most powerful monarchy. It also demonstrated the readiness of leaders steeped in the antietatist tradition of Jefferson to employ the full range of state power to advance the interests of their republic at the expense of other nations. Three decades after the War of 1812 that readiness would again be demonstrated as the United States trained its resources not on a European monarchy but on an American republic.

CHAPTER FIVE

The Two Most Powerful Republics in the World: Mr. Polk's War

Annual Treasury reports rarely make for enticing reading. But Robert J. Walker's reports may well be the exception that proves the rule. Walker, who served as James K. Polk's Treasury secretary used his reports for bold projections of the future greatness that awaited the United States if only the nation would play its cards right. In December 1846, Walker dreamed of American deep-water harbors in California, and particularly of San Francisco Bay, that would capture the trade of the Pacific Ocean. If the United States could establish a presence on the Pacific Coast, if a canal could be cut or a railway constructed across the Mexican isthmus of Tehuantepec, and if American entrepreneurs could produce more steam ships, the combined effect of these actions would "more rapidly advance our greatness, wealth and power, than any event that has occurred since the adoption of the constitution." Within less than two years, as a result of the territorial conquest following on the Mexican War, the United States' possession of California had become a reality, and Asia had "suddenly become our neighbor." As Walker noted in his report for fiscal year 1848, this development was of momentous significance. Ever since ancient times, "the cities and nations that secured the trade of Asia were greatly enriched." Placed between the wealth of Asia and the markets of Europe, the United States was in position to dominate world trade and through that domination to become a nation of global significance.[1]

Mid-nineteenth-century reflections on the state of the nation in Mexico were far less happy. When a group of Mexican statesmen and army officers tried to explain the calamity that had befallen their republic in the *Guerra del '47*, they pointed to "the spirit of aggrandizement of the United States of the North, availing itself of its power to conquer us." On gaining independence, the United States had "appeared at once as a powerful nation" whose citizens "desired from the beginning to extend their dominion in such manner as to become the absolute owners of almost all this continent." With the "insatiable ambition" of the United States "favored by our weakness," the outcome of the war had been inevitable. Although the nineteenth century was widely praised as an age of enlightenment, it was really an age "of *force and violence*," where the strong conquered the weak at will.[2]

American historians of the Mexican War have also tended to present United States expansion at midcentury as unavoidable, if for different reasons than the authors of *The Other Side*. "Few things are inevitable," one of them has written, "but the inclusion of Texas into the United States comes very close to being one of those things." Until recently it has also been possible to argue that the United States and Mexico shared responsibility for the outbreak of war. The leaders of the Mexican republic should have accepted that the United States could not be contained. Instead, driven by foolhardy pride and "an almost oriental obsession" to "save face," they made a vain attempt to oppose demands for territorial concessions. Because Mexican statesmen embraced such flawed perceptions of their nation's strength and interest, the Mexican War became the most "inevitable war" in American history. Whereas historians south of the border have always seen the conflict as an "unrighteous war of conquest," north of the border the war has quite effortlessly been presented as a chapter of America's "democratic expansion" driven by the nation's "Manifest Destiny."[3]

The view from the other side highlights a dimension of US territorial expansion that has not always received the attention it deserves. Whereas the "spirit of aggrandizement" has long been the principal explanation of territorial expansion, usually under the rubric of "Manifest Destiny," it has been less common to note that expansion ultimately occurred because the United States had at its disposal a considerably stronger state apparatus than its neighbor. There is a romantic notion that the expansion of the federal union was achieved by settlers unaided by government—the rugged frontiersmen who populate the myth of the West. This notion distorts the historical record. When Polk was elected president, what is now the mainland United States was under the jurisdiction of five sovereign nations: three republics (the United States, Mexico, and Texas) and two monarchies (Great Britain and Russia). Several Indian nations, some with considerable military strength and organizational complexity, also resided in this domain. Within three short years there occurred a complete geopolitical realignment on the continent as the United States acquired title to almost all of its present-day North American possessions, a process completed by the Gadsden Purchase in 1853 and the acquisition of Alaska in 1867. In a process where sovereign states disappeared (Texas), contracted (Mexico), gave up their colonial possessions (Russia), or offered them home rule (Great Britain), and where Native Americans were dispossessed of their territory, the United States picked up the spoils.[4]

This process was as much the result of power politics as of migration, of diplomacy and war as much as of endless trains of covered wagons moving steadily westward. The United States expanded through annexation in the case of Texas; diplomatic settlement with Britain in the case of Oregon; war with Mexico in the case of California and the Southwest; and purchase from Russia in the case of Alaska. Against the American Indian nations, the full range of government action was employed: war, diplomacy, and land purchases, which together amounted to an efficient policy of ethnic cleansing. In the competition with European states and successor states and with Indian nations in North America, the United States came out ahead because it could bring to bear on its competitors a stronger and more efficient state. Compared to the great powers of Europe, the federal government may not have looked daunting, but in the eyes of Mexicans, British North Americans, and American Indians it appeared anything but weak and insignificant. By the middle of the nineteenth century the United States' capacity to mobilize and project military power vastly exceeded those of its neighbors. The significance of such capacity to the historical trajectory of nations is vividly demonstrated by the outcome of the war between Mexico and the United States.[5]

The US-Mexican War of 1846–1848 was a considerably smaller conflict than the War of 1812 and cost only a fraction as much as the War of Independence and the Civil War in terms of per capita expenditure or share of national economic output. In contrast to Mr. Madison's War, the sea lanes remained open, and the revenue flowed uninterruptedly into the Treasury. The American financial system had also matured rapidly in the previous decades. Funding the conflict with Mexico by selling long-term bonds therefore proved to be relatively unproblematic. The war nevertheless demonstrated the ability of the United States to mobilize resources and carry out a war of conquest. It thereby further confirmed the viability of the republican form of government and improved the international status and renown of the federal union. But the astounding success of American arms and finances also awoke traditional fears of the growth of state power. Public credit allowed the government to act forcefully without having to demand contributions from the people in the form of increased taxation, something that might have undermined support for the war. Yet in the minds of many Americans, and not least among the Democrats, a public debt had long been regarded as a central pillar of monarchical government and a threat to republican liberty. The postwar reduction of the debt was therefore a central concern to the administration even before it contracted its first loan.

Whereas the financial institutions and policies put in place in the 1790s again proved sufficient for the wartime expansion of the American state, Mexico's inability to mobilize for war led to the loss of half the nation's territory and what little remained of its honor and international standing. The war with the United States was only one of several deep crises in an age of national decline during which foreign powers repeatedly violated Mexican sovereignty. In the United States the pre–Civil War era was an age of consolidation and expansion. In Mexico, the period between 1821 and 1877 was characterized by political turmoil and territorial disintegration. A decade or so after the war with the United States, the London *Economist* wrote that Mexico "is not a nation; it is not a State; it is not a Government at all;—it is simply a vast territory overrun by armed bands, and in which the very elements of society seem to be dissolved." Ruinous public finances were at the root of many of Mexico's difficulties, leading to political instability, a weak military, foreign interventions and invasions, and the alienation of the national domain.[6]

I

James Polk was elected to the presidency on a platform promising an ambitious foreign policy, tariff reductions, and reform of the Treasury. Many years after his retirement, Polk's naval secretary, the historian George Bancroft, remembered that the president had entered the White House with "four great measures" on his administration's agenda: the settlement of the Oregon question, the acquisition of California, the introduction of a "revenue tariff," and the establishment of the "Independent Treasury." These measures were potentially in conflict. Polk's foreign policy goals were likely to lead to increased expenditures, whether through territorial purchase or war. In contrast, his financial reforms threatened to reduce the government's revenue and ability to meet extraordinary expenses. Polk's solution to this dilemma was to pursue an aggressive diplomacy on the cheap by refraining from making any preparations for war. If Britain could be bullied to yield Oregon and Mexico to give up California, Polk might achieve his aims at next to no cost.[7]

True to the principles of the Democratic Party, Polk was a determined opponent of the protectionist politics of the Whigs. To Polk and his Treasury secretary, Robert Walker, protectionist tariffs were unconstitutional and served to favor the industrialized North at the expense of southern planters. In their eyes the only legitimate function of customs duties was to generate government income. Walker therefore proposed that the protective tariff of 1842 be replaced with a "revenue tariff" that calibrated duties to maximize income without regard to their effect on domestic manufactures. Polk's second domestic measure was the creation of the "independent" or "constitutional" Treasury Department. From its inception, the national government had always used banks to deposit and transfer funds. When available, the first and second Bank of the United States had been the preferred institutions; at other times the government relied on private banks. Polk's mentor Andrew Jackson had violently opposed the Second Bank of the United States, and Congress had refused to renew its charter in 1837. As president, Jackson had moved government business from the Bank of the United States to numerous smaller banks. Gradually, however, the Democrats grew averse to any and all intermingling between public finances and banks. When Polk came to power, he pushed for a completely self-contained Treasury Department that would operate on a specie-only basis and make no use of banks for either deposits or transfers of government funds, an idea that had originated but not been realized under the presidency of Martin Van Buren. Like the tariff reform, the reform of the Treasury began in 1845 and kept Walker occupied during much of the Mexican War.[8]

On assuming the presidency Polk inherited from his predecessors conflicts of interest with Mexico and Great Britain. The annexation of Texas was completed only days before Polk's inauguration, and it saddled the United States with a decade-old conflict between Texas and Mexico over the border between the two republics. Texans held the Rio Grande to mark the border, Mexicans the Nueces River, 150 miles to the north. Polk promised to uphold the Texan claim and in the spring of 1845 sent an envoy to Mexico City hoping to secure Mexican recognition of annexation and to settle the border dispute. The president was also eager to acquire California and Nuevo Mexico, the extensive province between Texas and California. American interest in California arose principally from the expectation that Pacific harbors would play an instrumental role in the burgeoning Asia trade. Britain and France were both believed to share these aspirations with the United States, and competition with European powers therefore added a sense of urgency to the American mission to Mexico.[9]

The American envoy, William S. Parrot, arrived in Mexico City with instructions to demand Mexican recognition of the Texas annexation and the Rio Grande border and an offer to purchase California for $20 million and New Mexico for another $5 million. Parrot would later be replaced by the controversial John Slidell, who presented similar demands. In order to put pressure on Mexico, the United States demanded repayment of debts that Mexico owed American citizens. These debts had their origin in the chaotic times of Mexico's struggle for independence, and the terms of the debts had been settled in 1841. Although the sums were small, in the spring of 1845 they amounted to no more than $3,336,837.05, Mexico had been unable to honor the claims of its American creditors. It was "too well known to the world, that the Mexican Government are not now in a condition to satisfy these claims by the payment of money," Secretary of State James Buchanan remarked to Slidell. The administration therefore suggested that the debts be exchanged for recognition of the Texas annexation and the settlement of the border issue.[10]

War with Britain over the Oregon Territory meanwhile presented a more pressing danger. Thanks to skilful and somewhat devious diplomatic maneuvering, this danger was neutralized, and the Oregon question was settled in the spring of 1846. Polk could now increase the pressure on Mexico. There was no longer any danger of a two-front war or even of British assistance to Mexico should the relationship between the United States and Mexico deteriorate into armed confrontation. As the *New York Herald* put it, the United States could now "thrash Mexico into decency at our leisure." In the spring of 1846, the US Army was ordered to the disputed territory between the Nueces River and Rio Grande. On the Mexican side, the Army of the North was ordered to push the American troops back across the Nueces. In late April, American and Mexican troops clashed on the northern side of the Rio Grande. The news was rapidly relayed to Washington, and on May 11 Polk submitted his war message to Congress, claiming that "Mexico has passed the boundary of the United States, has invaded our territory and shed American blood upon American soil." After a brief debate, Congress declared war on Mexico and directed the president to mobilize the army, navy, and militia of the United States.[11]

II

Polk presented his plans for financing the war in mid-June. He proposed that the regular army be doubled to fifteen thousand men and that an additional twenty-five thousand volunteers be recruited. The cost of this increase was estimated at $24 million for the budget year ending June 30, 1847. The administration remained hopeful that the conflict would be short and Mexico would be overcome at limited expense. According to Walker the recently passed new tariff would increase the customs revenue by $12 million. Despite his opposition to debts and a high tariff, the secretary did not recommend the introduction of excise duties or direct taxation to generate additional income. Creating an internal revenue service would take time, and most likely the conflict would be well over before receipts from internal taxes would begin to reach the Treasury. But it is worth noting that Walker also advised against internal taxation because it would be unpopular. "A system of direct taxes and excises, it is believed, would not meet the sanction of the people, unless in the emergency of a war with some great maritime nation." Walker thus subscribed to two basic principles that had been characteristic of American fiscal arrangements since the First Congress: government impositions should rest lightly on the shoulders of the citizens, and the taxes that were levied should be regarded as legitimate. In place of excises and direct taxes, Walker suggested a 5 to 50 percent increase on import duties on a range of enumerated goods ranging from brandy to mother of pearl. To the administration, the practical advantages of the impost trumped the wish to establish a free-trade regime. But Walker's new duties would generate only part of the money needed to chasten Mexico. The principal means to do so would be a $12.5 million loan.[12]

Although the Polk administration opted for loans rather than taxes, the president and the cabinet subscribed to a view of public debts that had changed little since the days of Thomas Jefferson, James Madison, and Albert Gallatin. Debts were a feature of European monarchies and grew out of the frequent wars that were such a prominent part of international relations in the Old World. "The war-system," wrote the chairman of the American Peace Society, George Beckwith, in 1848, "with its debts and its current expenses, has become a mammoth incubus on the bosom of all Christendom." *American Cottage Library*, a modestly priced little book that aimed to provide facts "on great and important subjects," trumpeted that the "war debts of the European nations amount to $10,000,000,000 (ten thousand millions)." Under the headline "Peace and war—The difference" it printed a table of Britain's public debt from 1689 to 1815, which showed that a single year of war cost the taxpayers the equivalent of eighteen years of peace. Costly wars led to high taxes, and in Britain even the poor suffered from duties on their "bread, and meat, and coffee, and tea, and sugar, and fuel, and clothing." This dystopian view of European politics was found across the political spectrum. *The Whig Almanac for 1852* published a tabular cross-country comparison of government expenditure and indebtedness under the heading "The Cost of Kings," which contrasted frugal republican regimes like the United States and Switzerland with wasteful monarchies such as Britain and France (table 5.1). Reasoning in a similar manner, *The American*

TABLE 5.1. "The Cost of Kings"

Countries	Yearly expenditure per head ($)	Court		Army and navy		Debt
		Per head (¢)	Proportion of expenditure (%)	Per head ($)	Proportion of expenditure (%)	Per head ($)
Great Britain and Ireland	6.27	17⅓	2¹⁄₁₀	2.56	31	126
France	7.20	1½	⅕	2.10	29	32.80
Germany	5.53	23⅓	4¼	2.28	41½	26.11
Belgium	4.67	13⅓	2⁶⁄₇	1.10	23³⁄₇	22.40
United States (federal and state together)	3.60	⅑	¹⁄₃₂	.67	18½	2.60
Switzerland (federal and cantons together)	2.66⅔	¹⁄₁₅	¹⁄₄₀	.34	12¾	.67
Norway	2.06⅔	7⅓	⅗	.80	38⅔	Nothing

Source: Adapted from "The Cost of Kings," *The Whig Almanac and United States Register for 1852* (New York: Greeley and McElrath, 1851), 46, table.

Almanac and Repository of Useful Knowledge for the Year 1847 excluded spending on the American debt from its comparison of government expenditure in Britain and the United States. For whereas the "normal condition of Great Britain is one of indebtedness; that of the United States is freedom from debt."[13]

These popular views were echoed in the writings of political economists, who inherited from previous generations of political commentators an intense dislike of taxes to finance military establishments and debts run up by unnecessary wars. Public expenditures were seen as unproductive investments, a view also reflected in the table "The Cost of Kings." In his 1834 *Manual of Political Economy*, Thomas Cooper explained that most tax money "was so much money thrown away," since "all the persons employed by governments are unproductive consumers." Admittedly, some public services were useful, but "utility consumes no very large part of Government expenditure." Eight years earlier, Cooper's *Lectures on the Elements of Political Economy* had concluded that "as taxes are an evil, the fewer we have of them and the smaller in amount, the better. That government is best, and those political institutions are most eligible, that are efficient at the cheapest rate."¹⁴

Since war was by far the greatest expense of governments, political economists tended to be critical of military outlays. The occasional dissenting voice objected that "a nation which does not make an adequate preparation for its own defence, risks the loss of everything, even its national existence." To Friedrich List, the author of the *National System of Political Economy*, there was no excuse for unnecessary public expenses, "particularly those occasioned by war or the keeping of great armies." But List could not accept that military expenditure was unproductive by definition: "Military preparations, wars, and the debts, which they involve, may in certain cases, as is shown in the case of England, contribute to increase the productive powers of the country."¹⁵

Such ideas belonged to the minority view, however. Military expenditure and public debts were almost everywhere condemned in the mid-nineteenth century. People who defended active government could see the value of public investments in communication and transportation, in banking, and in education but retained the traditional jealousy of government. Albert Gallatin, for example, made a distinction between investments in canals, on the one hand, and "military establishments in times of peace," "unnecessary pensions, high salaries, sinecures," and "ill-digested and unproductive plans of improvements" on the other. The latter he regarded as "useless and unproductive," representing only "so much capital actually destroyed." The 1847 *American Almanac* made the same distinction in contrasting Britain's debt, the result of "*unproductive expenditure,*—the cost of wars," with American state debts, which were due to "*reproductive investments.*" The states "have borrowed money only for the purpose of constructing railroads, canals, and other productive public works, or of furnishing capital for banking objects." The return from such investments did not increase the burden on the people. To the contrary, because many public works generated income from fees, they made it possible to reduce taxes.¹⁶

Polk's vision of the national government was a minimalist one that had room for neither infrastructural investments nor a large military establishment or a public debt. In his inaugural address he noted that a "national debt has become almost an institution of European monarchies. It is viewed in some of them as an essential prop to existing governments." This was not the case in America, where government drew its strength from popular participation and acted in the interest of the common good. "Melancholy is the condition of that people whose government can be sustained only by a system which periodically transfers large amounts from the labor of the many to the coffers of the few," the new president declared. "Such a system is incompatible with the ends for which our republican Government was instituted."[17]

War against Mexico therefore posed a problem to Polk because the war loans would increase the public debt and perhaps also lead to increased taxation. Critics of the war noted that "Mexico, our own country, and France, bear witness that monarchs and nobles are not the exclusive devotees of war." Even a popularly elected president could endanger popular liberty by engaging in wars that made heavy demands on the citizens. When the *American Cottage Library* quoted the eighteenth-century English poet William Cowper's words that "war is a game which, were the people wise, Kings would not play at," it tellingly added "nor republics either." Polk and Walker dealt with this potential threat of the war to republican liberty in a manner similar to Gallatin and Madison some thirty years earlier. The administration tried to keep down costs and make rapid repayment of the war loans an integral part of the financing of the Mexican War.[18]

When Congress received the president's plan for financing the conflict with Mexico, the legislators willingly endorsed the administration's request for a loan but were less interested in adopting new tax legislation. The 1846 loan act gave the president the right to issue either short-term Treasury notes or long-term bonds. Walker had sought this flexibility in order to facilitate borrowing, but he had also asked Congress to set the maximum interest rate at the usual 6 percent and to prohibit the sale of bonds under par. In this way, lenders could not press the government to sell the loan at a discount, as had happened during the War of 1812. The administration hoped to be able to borrow $10 million by issuing Treasury notes redeemable in one or two years. A major advantage of the Treasury notes was that, in contrast to long-term bonds, they could be paid off as soon as the Treasury ran a surplus. Experience had shown that investors were not interested in bonds with a shorter maturity date than ten years. If the war could be financed by selling Treasury notes instead of bonds, the increase of the public debt would only be temporary. This choice made particular sense given the administration's expectation that the conflict with Mexico would soon be over.[19]

Opposition to the loan bill came from Whigs, who took the opportunity to air their discontent with the Walker tariff and the Independent Treasury Act. Their criticism reveals how, in the opening stages of the Mexican War, tariff and currency legislation seemed more important than the war to many congressmen. By demanding taxes instead of loans, the Whigs hoped to force the Democrats to revise their free-trade position. In demanding bond sales instead of Treasury note issues, they hoped that the administration would have to reestablish its cooperation with the nation's banks. Since the Independent Treasury could only accept payments in specie, a large loan would deplete the nation's specie supply and force Walker to accept banknotes in payments to the government. Although they did not always vote against government measures, preferring to see the follies of the Democrats produce a backlash at the polls, Whig rhetoric denounced the administration's ambition to finance the war with Treasury notes as an "unmanly" attempt to "humbug the people." But to Polk and Walker, the notes provided a means to pay for war without increasing taxes or running up the public debt.[20]

Hoping for a rapid settlement of the conflict, Walker financed the first months of military build up by tapping Treasury reserves. By the end of the year, a surplus of $11 million had been reduced to less than $3 million. In August, a total of $2.8 million in Treasury notes was issued to supply officers to pay for goods and services delivered to the army. Polk's diary shows that the cabinet did not discuss the financing of the war until September 29, 1846, more than two months after the adoption of the loan act. Walker then reported that a loan had become necessary and that he intended to sell one-year Treasury notes bearing 6 percent interest. Soon afterward, the Treasury secretary departed for New York to negotiate a loan from the city's bankers. Negotiations in New York City as well as Philadelphia and Boston proved fruitless, however, as the banks were not willing to accept Walker's terms. Back in Washington, the Treasury secretary tried to sell $3 million in notes through newspaper advertisements. When this too failed, Walker consulted Polk and decided to turn to the sale of long-term bonds. The administration thus fell back on the method of war finance used during the War of 1812. It was doubtless a setback for the government, although neither Polk nor Walker expressed much disappointment in surviving documents.[21]

Without any preparatory negotiations with bankers, Walker placed a newspaper ad declaring the government's intention to sell $5 million in 6 percent bonds with a ten-year maturity date. Investors were asked to submit sealed bids to the Treasury stating the amount of bonds they wished to buy and the price they were willing to pay. The ad appeared in the *Washington Union* on October 30, and Walker asked proadministration papers in Charleston, Washington, Baltimore, Philadelphia, New York, and Boston to reprint it. When the bids were opened two weeks later, the sum subscribed was considerably above the $5 million asked, and the Treasury secretary accepted bids totaling $5,146,000. A number of large institutional investors dominated the subscription. All of them were ready to pay the nominal price or a tenth of 1 percent more. Corcoran & Riggs, the Washington bank that would completely dominate the loans of 1847 and 1848, now made its first appearance in the bond market with an order for $350,000. The bankers and brokers who subscribed to the loan of 1846 acted much like modern investment bankers. They never intended to retain the bonds but aimed to sell them to third parties as soon as possible. Most of their bids were made on behalf of partners; the remainder of the bonds they acquired were soon sold to clients or brokers acting on the securities markets in the major cities. Corcoran & Riggs, for example, sold their share of the 1846 and 1847 loans within mere months. The 1848 loan took somewhat longer, and the firm made its last bond sales in the winter and spring of 1850.[22]

As the loan of 1846 was being completed, a new session of Congress began. When the second session of the Twenty-Ninth Congress met in December 1846, the administration's hope for a rapid settlement with Mexico had turned to dust. General Zachary Taylor had followed up his victory at Palo Alto by taking Monterrey on September 25, after which his offensive had stalled. In the West, both New Mexico and California had been occupied. Nevertheless, Mexican leaders showed no inclination to sue for peace. In the fall of 1846, Polk's cabinet decided to take the war closer to the Mexican politicians by opening a second front. Their plan was to land an army at the port city of Veracruz and march inland toward Mexico City, repeating the feat of Hernán Cortés over three hundred years previously. They assumed that, faced with the threat of losing its capital, Mexico's government would accept American peace terms. In his second annual address, Polk announced that the war had "been carried into the enemy's country and will be vigorously prosecuted there with a view to obtain an honorable peace." But the continuation and expansion of the intervention meant a longer war and greater costs. The $24 million granted by the previous Congress would not suffice to bring Mexico into submission.[23]

The Treasury report for 1846 estimated that a further $23 million would cover additional war costs to June 30, 1848. Most of this sum would have to be borrowed. Nevertheless, the administration did not lose sight of the need to limit the public debt. Polk stressed that had it not been for the conflict with Mexico, "the whole public debt could and would have been extinguished within a short period" and that his idea of good government still involved reductions of both the citizens' tax burden and the government's expenditures. Although Walker now asked for authorization to sell twenty-year bonds, Polk insisted that peace would create a Treasury surplus that would ensure the redemption of the debt "in a much shorter period than that for which it may be contracted." In order to reduce the need for loans, the administration again proposed new taxes and argued that Mexico should be made to pay part of the government's "extraordinary expenses," which according to the administration were the result of Mexico's unjust aggression and refusal to end the war.[24]

As early as September 1846, Secretary of War William Marcy had told Zachary Taylor that "the President hopes that you will be able to derive from the enemy's country, without expense to the United States, the supplies you may need, or a considerable part of them." In the eyes of the War Department, the American occupation seemed a blessing in disguise to the Mexican people. Not only did the troops guarantee the personal safety of the population and provide markets for their produce, thanks to the troops the Mexican people were also "shielded from the burdens and exactions of their own authorities." It was a "state of things so favorable to their interests" that it might "induce them to wish the continuance of hostilities." In order to force an end to the war, it was desirable to the American nation to remove the burden of war, "as far as practicable, from itself by throwing it upon the enemy." In the latter stages of the war, the administration's tone hardened. In his third annual message of December 1847, Polk suggested that the US Army "levy such military contributions on the enemy as may, as far as practicable, defray the future expenses of the war." American commanders in Mexico were unwilling to alienate the civilian population by living off the land, however, and largely chose to ignore Washington's directives.[25]

Apart from levies, the army and navy also administered taxes in the conquered territories. Walker's early projections of the income expected from commercial duties and internal taxes in Mexico were overly enthusiastic. He hoped that these taxes would reduce the need for "new loans and increased taxation" in the United States and thus help keep down the public debt. But the Mexican assessment never generated the kind of money Walker had hoped for. Altogether, American troops collected $4.1 million in taxes in Mexico, 85 percent of which came from customs duties. Yet the intention to finance the war by taxing Mexico rather than the United States is nevertheless indicative of the principle that as far as possible the federal government should spare its citizens the burden of war.[26]

In addition to shifting the burden of the war onto Mexico, the administration also asked Congress to raise the duty on coffee and tea and to introduce a graduated price scale on public-land sales. These reforms would provide an annual income of some $2.5 million to the Treasury. Even though the sum was relatively modest, Walker believed it to be important. With additional revenue, the loan proposed for 1847 could be reduced to $19 million and would prove easier to float. In the following year the secretary's report explained that it was "a sound rule, when contracting a public debt, to provide at the time, such revenue as will be adequate for the prompt payment of the interest, and the gradual but certain extinction of the principal of the debt." Readers who knew their nation's financial history no doubt recognized this as a paraphrase of Hamilton's first report on public credit. "So long as this rule is pursued," Walker continued, "there is no danger of any alarming accumulation of public debt, nor any apprehension that the public credit will be impaired or embarrassed." The same point had been stressed repeatedly during the War of 1812, but the limited nature of the Mexican War made it even more difficult for the Polk administration than it had been for Madison to convince Congress that new taxes were needed.[27]

During the war the opposition typically demanded that the conflict should be paid for at least partly from taxation, although such demands did not prevent Whig congressmen from regularly voting with the majority against the administration's proposal to tax tea and coffee. The aim of the Whigs was to challenge the administration to dare test the popularity of the war by introducing property or income taxes. "Fighting seemed to many people a very agreeable thing," said John Gorham Palfrey, as long as they did not experience "how expensive a luxury it was." He was seconded by Caleb Blood Smith, who claimed that "the boasted popularity of this war would not survive the first visit of the tax collector." Indirect imposts and excises might make the people "growl a little and cry hard times," one newspaper wrote, but direct taxes were disliked much more strongly because they made the cost of government so evident. When the tax collector appeared on the citizens' doorsteps, they became inclined to "carefully scan the policy of their servants and the expenditure of their money," another paper said. Let "Uncle Sam" present "Mr. Constant Harddigger" with a bill for $6 to cover government per capita expenses, the paper continued. Faced with the evidence that $5.70 of this money had been spent on guns, munitions, and soldiers, Mr. Harddigger's eagerness to finance a war of conquest against a weak neighbor would soon be dampened. "Then how shall we ever be able to get up another war?"[28]

In 1847 Polk was never forced to test the war's popularity, as the House of Representatives refused not only to increase the duty on coffee and tea but even to debate the need for new taxes. A large majority adopted the resolution that "it is impolitic to introduce a duty on tea and coffee." In order not to appear flailing in their support for the war, the representatives immediately afterward adopted a unanimous resolution that the people of the

United States were nevertheless "too patriotic to refuse any necessary tax in time of war." In the Senate there was some criticism of the administration's exclusive reliance on loans. In principle both parties subscribed to the idea that "a national debt is a national curse, and should be avoided, if possible to be avoided." It was hardly reasonable that a limited conflict such as the Mexican War should be financed almost solely with borrowed money. Whig senator Reverdy Johnson called it "a libel upon the patriotism of the people to suppose that they would not bear any amount of taxation deemed to be necessary for the vindication of the national honor."[29]

The opposition also argued that the administration's policies endangered the nation's credit. With every new loan and every new issue of Treasury notes, the price of bonds was further depressed. Potential investors needed to know the total cost of defeating Mexico. "They will tell you that they will not purchase this stock," one senator said, "because in a year's time, there would be other stock issued, which would reduce the price of it in the market, and insure to them a loss." Investors would also wish to know "whether there was any provision made for the repayment of the principal and interest accruing thereon." The lack of any intention "to lay taxes for that purpose" would discourage capitalists from buying bonds. According to their critics, Walker and Polk's tax measures were simply insufficient to safeguard the public credit. Instead of providing for a substantial increase of tax revenue, the administration "preferred to borrow, from day to day, not even looking thirty days ahead. Could they then expect that our stocks would maintain themselves at par?"[30]

Senate Democrats responded to the opposition by ridiculing Whig objections. "What government had ever existed in time of war without having to resort to loans?" Ambrose Sevier asked. "He knew of none." James Westcott believed $23 million was a "paltry sum" and Jesse Speight that "no more than the faith of this great nation" was necessary to guarantee the loan. Lewis Cass, an enthusiastic supporter of territorial aggrandizement, argued that the Whigs confused American public finances with conditions in Britain. The British Parliament had in the past been forced to "combine every loan with a specific tax" because it was then at war with "the whole civilized world—with a debt out of all proportion." American conditions were completely different. Could anyone really believe "that the faith of this great nation was not sufficient to raise this twenty-three millions?" There was no need for a tax on coffee and tea to secure the loan. "They could easily get it without." With reference to the reduction of the Revolutionary debt and the loans from the War of 1812, he reminded the Senate that the

United States "had paid off two debts, and they could pay off another." In the end, the Senate followed the lead of the House of Representatives and refused to vote for new taxes.[31]

Congress remained unwilling to adopt new fiscal measures even after the Democrats had lost control of the House of Representatives in the election to the 30th Congress. The US-Mexican War therefore became the only nineteenth-century war that did not lead to significant tax increases. As one senator pointed out, in this respect, at least, the conflict was a new departure representing "an example . . . unparalleled in the history of warfare." The Democrats' resistance to new taxes is not difficult to explain, however. The outbreak of the war had coincided with the introduction of the Walker tariff. Any discussion of increased taxation would inevitably have turned into a debate over free trade and protectionism. It was a debate that neither congressmen nor the administration wished to revisit, even if silence meant an increased public debt. When the Whigs gained a majority in the House, none of their dire predictions of economic disaster had been fulfilled. The Walker tariff had had a positive effect on government revenue and had caused little harm to the nation's manufacturers.[32]

Because Congress had refused new taxes, the administration had no choice but to turn to loans in order to finance the continuation of the war. The hope that the war could be paid for with Treasury notes was now abandoned. Walker asked permission to sell bonds with a twenty-year maturity date because "all experience, at home and abroad, proves that a loan for a long term will save a large amount to the treasury, compared with one of shorter date." After less than a day's debate, Congress passed a law that gave the president the right to issue $23 million in Treasury notes, which could be exchanged for twenty-year bonds at par. Because the 1846 Treasury notes could also be traded for twenty-year bonds, the law gave the administration the right to sell over $28 million in securities. In place of an increased duty on coffee and tea, Congress earmarked the income from public-land sales to pay interest charges and repay the new loan.[33]

The 1847 loan was marketed in the same way as the loan of 1846. Walker's advertisement inviting subscriptions to an $18 million issue of exchangeable Treasury notes appeared in the *Washington Union* on February 9. In order to allow the people at large the chance to support the war effort, the Treasury would accept bids as low as fifty dollars. This attempt to market government loans directly to the people would later be used with great success by the Union in financing the Civil War. When the sealed bids were opened on April 12, private citizens and financial institutions had offered the government close to $58 million. Corcoran & Riggs purchased 90 percent of the bonds, most of them at $1.25 above par. Another $5 million in Treasury notes was sold to a closed list in February 1847 and the final $5 million a year later after an open bidding process.[34]

Government finances prospered in 1847. Not only was the loan a success, but large imports led to increased customs revenue in the summer and made it possible for Walker to afford Corcoran & Riggs postponements on their loan installments, thus providing them with time to resell their Treasury notes to investors in the public funds. Prosperous finances were matched by success on the battlefield. Taylor defeated Mexico's president and military commander, Antonio López de Santa Anna, in the battle of Buena Vista on February 23. Further south, Scott marched on Mexico City after having taken Veracruz in an amphibious assault on March 28. A series of victories on the road from the coast to the Mexican heartland was crowned with entry into Mexico City on September 14. But if the Treasury secretary was successful in mobilizing resources and the nation's generals were successful in defeating the enemy army, the administration was still unable to force the Mexican government to the peace table. It was becoming clear that in order to end the war, the United States had not only to defeat the Mexican army but also to establish a Mexican government that was strong enough to negotiate and uphold a treaty of peace.[35]

Polk was well aware that no Mexican administration voluntarily ceding territory to the United States could hope to remain in power. In his annual message of 1847, he warned that "with a people distracted and divided by contending factions and a Government subject to constant changes by successive revolutions, the continued success of our arms may fail to secure us a satisfactory peace." Mexico's government had not dared to enter into negotiations "lest, from this very cause, a rival faction might expel it from power." Furthermore, the men who signed their name to a treaty alienating Mexican territory risked being "shot as traitors to their country."[36]

According to the president, the crucial element determining the stability of every Mexican administration was military support. A few months before the signing of the Treaty of Guadalupe Hidalgo, the cabinet contemplated a continued military presence in Mexico in order to prop up an indigenous puppet regime that could guarantee a peace treaty. The president had told Congress that American troops might have to give "assurances of protection to the friends of peace in Mexico." The people of Mexico would thereby have the chance to establish "a free republican government of their own choice, able and willing to conclude a peace which would be just to them and secure to us the indemnity that we demand." Meanwhile cabinet meetings discussed whether or not to write into the peace treaty "a stipulation that a sufficient portion of our army should remain in Mexico for a year after peace was concluded to afford the desired protection, and to enable any new Government which may be formed to execute the Treaty."[37]

The cabinet's original plan had been for the Mexican government to rely on the Mexican military rather than the US Army, however. Beginning in July 1846, Polk asked Congress to authorize funds that would allow him to pay cash for a peace treaty. Given "the present impoverished condition of Mexico, the knowledge that such a sum would be paid in hand might induce Mexico to Treat, when she might not otherwise do so," he said. Polk's request is best known for giving rise to the Wilmot Proviso, which split Congress along sectional lines. The president was puzzled and disappointed by the response from the House of Representatives and felt compelled to set down the real reasons behind his request in his diary. It was clear to everyone, Polk wrote, that no Mexican government "is strong enough to make a treaty ceding territory and long maintain in power unless they could receive, at the time of making the treaty, money enough to support the army. Whatever party can keep the army in its support can hold the power." He repeated this message to a group of Democratic representatives and senators in December 1846, saying that "no party which might be in power in Mexico was strong enough to make peace and still retain power, without money to feed, clothe, and pay the army." If the Mexican rulers knew that a peace treaty would be worth $2 million to $4 million, they would be ready to enter into negotiations "because with the money they could secure the support of the army and be able to retain power."[38]

When the Thirtieth Congress convened in December 1847, the administration was noticeably frustrated. "No change has taken place in our relations with Mexico since the adjournment of the last Congress," Polk informed the legislators. Military victory had not led to political progress, which led the president to ask "in what manner the war ought to be prosecuted and what should be our future policy." He answered that the war should be pursued with "increased energy and power until a just and satisfactory peace can be obtained." The occupation would continue, and if Mexico refused to compensate the United States for its just demands, the United States had to "indemnify" itself "by appropriating permanently a portion of her territory." With or without Mexico's concession, New Mexico and California would become part of the United States.[39]

In order to keep down the cost of war, Polk urged that more requisitions and taxes be levied on the Mexican people, and he renewed his recommendation that Congress introduce a tax on coffee and tea and a graduated price on public lands. Without these reforms, the government would have to borrow $18.5 million to keep up the war. The president confessed that another $20 million might be needed by December of the next year. Despite Polk's optimistic tone, the situation was becoming awkward if not yet critical. Mexico had been soundly beaten militarily, yet an end to the war was nowhere in sight. The United States faced the risk of a permanent state of war and an annual budget deficit of $20 million. Either the war had to end or the American republic would have to abandon its traditional low-tax regime and accept the existence of a large public debt as the price of empire. The situation was not improved by the fact that the administration now faced a Whig majority in the House of Representatives and therefore Walker had to work with a Ways and Means Committee led by the Ohio Whig Samuel Finley Vinton. When Congress postponed action on the administration's recommendations, Polk and Walker immediately concluded that the Whigs aimed to undermine the government's credit by seeking to "produce a panic in the money market and thereby, if possible, to break down the Treasury, and thus compel the inglorious withdrawal of our army from Mexico."[40]

In fact, the opposition had begun to play down its objections to the government's economic and commercial policies and to increase its attacks on the acquisition of territory. But to many Whigs, all of the Democrats' measures remained vexing and to a large extent interrelated. "The war, the sub-treasury, and the tariff of 1846," one newspaper said, were like "the triple-headed Cerberus, whose fangs are now felt in the side of the republic." The president undoubtedly wanted peace with Mexico, William Duer told the House of Representatives and then punningly asked, "How much piece?" Did Polk intend to take half its territory? Two-thirds? David Fisher called the conflict "ungodly," a war "conceived in sin, and brought forth in iniquity, and I fear its end will be destruction." Congress had a moral responsibility to end this crime by refusing to vote further means to support the war effort. To Fisher it was obvious that *"now* is the time to stop the war, or never." Attacks on the administration's "mischievous free trade policy" also continued. Whigs pointed to "the pernicious effects of the tariff of 1846" and warned the Democrats of their intention to return to protectionism by creating "a tariff on the basis of the act of 1842." By refusing Walker the right to issue Treasury notes and forcing him to sell long-term bonds, the Whigs hoped as before that the government's need for money would lead to increased import duties and a return to the use of banknotes in government transactions.[41]

The House of Representatives began debating a new loan act only in February 1848, and for the first time since the beginning of the war, the Democrats were not in position to force an immediate vote on the bill. Although the bill was adopted by the House on February 17, the Senate did not vote until March 29. In contrast to previous loan acts, the loan of 1848 contained no provision for Treasury notes but gave the president authority to borrow $16 million, rather than the $18.5 million originally asked for, through a straight bond sale. In December and January, the papers were rife with speculations that the loan would fail. Britain and Europe were suffering from a financial crisis, there was a slump in the price of cotton, and there was a negative balance of trade. Furthermore, words of warning were raised that an indefinite war would consume an indefinite amount of money.[42]

What could have developed into a precarious situation was avoided by the news of the Peace of Guadalupe Hidalgo. Peace meant that the loan of 1848 would be the last loan of the war, which had a positive effect on investors. Awaiting news of Mexican ratification of the peace treaty, Walker delayed the advertisement of the loan to April 17. When the bids were opened two months later, total subscriptions for the $16 million offered amounted to $30,393,890. Although the loan was not as oversubscribed as the loan of 1847, the price was higher, and the loan was sold at a 3 percent premium. Again Corcoran & Riggs became the major buyer. The administration was heartened by the news that the Washington bank acted in partnership with the British firm of Baring Brothers, one of the greatest actors on the world's securities markets. There could be no stronger endorsement of American public credit.[43]

Initially, Corcoran & Riggs made good profit on the resale of the loan. By late summer the market was becoming saturated, however, and with official blessing from Walker, William Corcoran went to London to find buyers for American war bonds. The bank was also forced to ask for postponements on their monthly installments. To Corcoran & Riggs the summer and fall of 1848 was therefore a dramatic period. But to the government it was anything but critical. Corcoran & Riggs paid its installments, and an upswing in international trade saw customs revenue rise from $23.7 million to $31.8 million. When Walker submitted his financial report to Congress in December 1848, he told the senators and representatives that the nation's finances were in sound condition. "Unless new and extraordinary expenditures are authorized by Congress," he reported, "no further loans will be required, and the public debt will be reduced."[44]

III

The Mexican War was a considerably smaller affair than the War of 1812. Total costs have been estimated at about a third those of the previous war.

Nor was funding hampered by the breakdown of the fiscal system as had been the case during Mr. Madison's War. To the contrary, the customs revenue grew during Polk's administration. A further difference between the two wars was that the United States now fought a war of conquest in foreign lands and far from its own territory. Finally, peace in Europe and the rapid development of the financial sector in the period between 1815 and 1845 made it much easier for Walker to float government loans than it had been for Gallatin and his successors. The financing of the Mexican War therefore proved to be an affair singularly lacking in drama.[45]

Nevertheless, like the War of 1812, the Mexican War demonstrated that the national government possessed a considerable flexible capacity for war making. The army swelled from 20,000 in 1845 to 40,000 in 1846 and 60,000 in 1847 and 1848, before it was scaled back to prewar levels in 1849 and 1850. As in all wars there was a considerable increase in expenditure. Total government costs in the three-year period beginning July 1, 1846, was $74.6 million more than in the three-year period immediately preceding the war. Of this sum, increased military expenditures accounted for $64.8 million and increased interest charges on the public debt for $3.6 million. The remaining increase is explained by the first indemnity payment to Mexico in 1848 and 1849. Growing costs were met by the sale of $49 million in long-term bonds and $33 million in Treasury notes (see table 5.2). Taxes contributed little to the war effort, as the income from customs duties increased only a modest $3.4 million in the period 1846 to 1849 over the previous three-year period. In contrast, the 1850s would see a trade boom

TABLE 5.2. US long-term securities issued during the US-Mexican War

Date authorized	Proposals invited	Amount authorized ($)	Amount issued ($)	Price ($)	Interest (%)
July 22, 1846	Oct. 30	10,000,000	4,999,149.45	100 to 100.28	6
Jan. 28, 1847	Feb. 9	23,000,000	28,230,350	101.25 to 102	6
March 31, 1848	Apr. 17	16,000,000	16,000,000	103.20 to 104.05	6
Total		49,000,000	49,229,499.45		

Source: Rafael A. Bayley, *History of the National Loans of the United States from July 4, 1776, to June 30, 1880*, in *Report on Valuation, Taxation, and Public Indebtedness in the United States, as Returned at the Tenth Census (June 1, 1880)* (Washington, DC: Government Printing Office, 1884), 364–67, 437–42.

that caused government income to triple from an annual average of $18.7 million in the early 1840s to $54.5 million in the early 1850s. In total, Mr. Polk's war pushed up the public debt from $15.5 million in 1846 to $63 million in 1849. In per capita terms it jumped from 77 cents to $2.81. The effortlessness with which the United States financed the conflict testifies to the growth of the American economy and to the development of the financial system in the decades after the War of 1812, but it also demonstrates the basic soundness of the nation's public finances.[46]

If financing the war proved easy to the United States, things looked very different on the other side of the border. The American mobilization for the Mexican War may have been minimal compared to what would follow in the Civil War, but it was a formidable demonstration of strength in the eyes of the Mexican government and people.

IV

It has been said that Mexico went to war with the United States not despite but because of its weakness. A militarily and administratively stronger Mexico would have been able to settle and defend its northern provinces and thereby block American expansion. A politically more stable Mexico would have been able to negotiate a settlement with the United States over Texas and American access to the Pacific that would have retained more of the nation's territory. But in 1846 Mexico was militarily weak, while any concessions involving alienation of the national domain amounted to political suicide. Both conservatives and liberals had publicly declared their refusal to give in to American demands. In Mexican politics, contemporary commentator José Fernando Ramirez remarked, the conflict over Texas and the ensuing war had come to serve "as a weapon that each of the quarreling factions wants to get hold of in order to wound its opponents to the death. The first one who talks about peace will lose that weapon, and, therefore no one wants to utter the fateful word." Mexican politicians were therefore as desirous to retain Texas, New Mexico, and California as Polk was to acquire them. The crucial difference between the combatants was not political will so much as the capacity to realize it. In this respect, the Mexican War serves to demonstrate the advantages of well-ordered public finances and the dangers springing from a weak state. As Ramirez continued, the inefficiency of the Mexican government had "plunged us into a war with regard to which we can say that it has begun, is going on, and will finally drag us on to its conclusion still unprepared."[47]

Mexico was far from poor in natural resources. At the time of independence, many commentators thought the new nation faced a glorious future. As late as the 1840s they could still speak of Mexico's "immense territory," "bathed by two great oceans" and crossed by "a multitude of navigable rivers"; its "varied climates in which all the fruits of the globe can be produced"; its "virgin territories" of "astonishing fertility"; and its "great hills and mountains loaded with the most precious metals." Modern historians, in contrast, have been more prone to point to the new nation's difficulties. Productive farmland was limited, and the mountain ranges and river courses made communication and transportation difficult. In any event, it is clear that the promises of independence were not realized. At the turn of the eighteenth century, Mexico's population was roughly equal to that of the United States and its national income about half that of its northern neighbor. But in the decades that followed, the United States grew, while Mexico was at a standstill. In 1845, the Mexican national income was less than a tenth that of the United States. Whereas the population in the United States had grown to over 20 million, the population of Mexico stood at 7.5 million.[48]

Against this background, the outcome of the Mexican War might seem a foregone conclusion. There is no question that the American government could draw on a far greater resource base than Mexican rulers could. Yet Polk made a very limited draft on the nation's resources. American armies were small. Winfield Scott entered Mexico City with no more than eight thousand men, and Zachary Taylor's command fluctuated between two thousand and six thousand troops. Mexico therefore faced only a fraction of the United States' military might and nothing near the coercive power mobilized by the Union during the Civil War. Nevertheless, Mexico could offer no effective resistance. The modest size of neither the economy nor the population fully explains why the Mexican government could not respond more energetically to the small-scale American invasion. Such an explanation has instead to be sought in the inability of the government to tap into the considerable societal resources that actually existed.

As a result of reforms undertaken after the Seven Years' War, Spain created a highly productive revenue system in its American possessions in the late colonial period. In 1760, the mother country collected $4.7 million annually in New Spain. Three decades later tax reforms had increased collections to $10.5 million a year. For good reason, the British were envious of Spanish achievements. In 1770, Britain collected no more than $150,000 in the thirteen colonies that would become the United States. Although the new national government was more successful in taxing the American people after independence, the United States did not reach the levels extracted from New Spain. In the early 1790s the national government raised on average less than $5 million in taxes every year. Meanwhile pressure to fund the Napoleonic War further boosted tax collections in New Spain, which reached an annual average of $20 million between 1801 and 1810. In the peak year of 1809 the tax revenue was $28 million. The United States would not reach such per capita levels before the Civil War. In addition to tax revenue, the viceroyalty also borrowed around $25 million to $30 million in the late eighteenth and early nineteenth century, or roughly half of what the Polk administration borrowed to finance the Mexican War half a century later.[49]

New Spain's revenue system did not survive the transition to Mexican independence. Although historians have traced the advent of its demise to the 1790s, the real crisis began with the outbreak of the Hidalgo revolt in 1810 and the ensuing decade of struggle for independence and civil war. Central rule disintegrated, and the provincial regions stopped remitting funds to Mexico City. Average annual tax collection fell to $8.5 million, and by 1817 revenue had returned to the prereform levels of the 1750s. The civil war ended with the acceptance of the compromise Plan of Iguala in 1821, which made Augustín Iturbide the head of the first government of independent Mexico, first as president and then as Emperor Augustín I.[50]

It is helpful to take a closer look at Augustín's administration because it suffered from several difficulties that would continue to plague Mexican politics up to the establishment of the Porfiriato in 1877, not least during the *Guerra del '47*. The legitimacy of the emperor's regime rested on his promises to restore peace and remove the hardships of war, including extraordinary taxes and levies. The administration thus began by abolishing most of the taxes introduced during the civil war. It was hoped that the economy would recover with peace and that revenue yields would return to prewar levels. Within a year it became clear that instead of recovering, the tax yield continued to fall. New taxes were sorely needed, but the congress refused to follow the recommendations of the finance minister. Instead it authorized the government to seek foreign loans amounting to approximately three years of government expenditure. If successful, the loans would remove the need for the new regime to tax a war-weary people and thereby buy the time necessary to create political stability, promote economic growth, and, the legislators hoped, increase revenue. Although the congress's refusal to adopt new taxes was irresponsible, the policy of complementing tax income with loans was similar to that pursued in the United States by Alexander Hamilton after the inauguration of the new national government in 1789.[51]

Because a European loan was not immediately forthcoming, the legislators' refusal to impose new taxes forced Augustín to resort to involuntarily loans and expropriations. When legislators opposed these measures, the emperor simply adjourned the recalcitrant congress. Turning his back on rule by law, Augustín ruled instead by decree with the support of a small *Junta Instituyente*. When the junta ordered further forced loans and imposed capitation and property taxes, it triggered a revolt that became the downfall of Iturbide's government in March 1823, less than ten months after he had been crowned emperor.

The presidency of Guadalupe Victoria, who served from 1824 to 1829, proved to be a rare period of stability in Mexico's early history. In fact, Victoria was the only president to serve out his term before the election of Porfirio Díaz in 1876. But Victoria did not address the government's financial problems. By the second half of the 1820s, the annual tax revenue had declined to around $7 million, but expenses were about twice that. Political stability rested on Victoria's being able to postpone difficult fiscal reforms with the help of borrowed money. In 1824 and 1825, Mexican agents finally managed to secure two loans in London brokered by separate British firms. The loan terms reflected the risk of investing in a newly independent nation, but the poor terms on the first loan were also the result of the fraudulent actions of the Mexican loan agent. In return for a total of $32 million worth of bonds, Mexico's government received only $17.7 million in cash. The balance was retained by the banking houses as commissions and funds for interest payments to the British-based investors. Victoria's policy was hardly sustainable in the long run, and the option of financing government from foreign loans was already closed off in 1827 when Mexico defaulted on its foreign debt.[52]

By the late 1820s, Mexico's government had made very little progress toward a balanced budget and a stable income. Thus, in contrast to the United States, the nation never managed to overcome the difficult critical period that followed after the achievement of independence. Instead, a destructive pattern of public finance was established that had serious consequences for the nation's ability to defend its interests and independence. Every attempt to reform the fiscal system, or even to balance the budget by reducing expenditure, invariably led to opposition, political crisis, and extralegal regime change. Disordered public finances therefore led to extreme political instability, which is most clearly demonstrated in the high turnover of governments. Between the abdication of Augustín I in March 1823 and the installation of Mariana Paredes y Arrillaga in January 1846, no less than twenty-seven different administrations governed Mexico. The office of finance minister changed hands fifty-two times. In the United States there were only four presidents between 1825 and 1845, and this number was only reached because single-term presidents were a common phenomenon in the middle decades of the nineteenth century. Mexico also saw instability in fundamental political arrangements. The federal constitution of 1824 was replaced by a centralist constitution in 1836, which was overturned by a federalist regime in 1846. In vain efforts to secure stability and an efficient government, the new nation oscillated between monarchy, republicanism, and dictatorship. Although the United States experienced the rise of the second-party system and much conflict surrounding the controversial Andrew Jackson in this period, political struggles nonetheless took place within the framework of stable and generally acceptable ground rules. There were, for instance, no amendments to the US Constitution between 1804 and the Civil War.[53]

If political stability was one victim of disordered finances, credit was another. Insufficient and irregular income made it impossible for the government to honor its debts. Despite European and American accusations to the contrary, Mexican statesmen accepted the sanctity of contract and well understood the importance of public credit. Creditor claims were repeatedly arbitrated and recognized, debts were renegotiated, and attempts were made to pay interest to public creditors. As late as the 1850s, the Mexican government used one installment of the United States indemnity to pay interest charges on its 1820s London loans. But without money and with the demands of the army taking precedence over the rights of public creditors, the government inevitably defaulted on its loans. To protect their investments, foreign creditors called on their governments to put pressure on Mexico in an early version of gunboat diplomacy. For example, before he learned of the skirmishes at the Rio Grande in late April 1846, Polk had planned to justify a declaration of war against Mexico with the country's failure to pay debts owed to American citizens. In fact, as early as 1837 Andrew Jackson had declared that Mexico's unpaid debts constituted a just cause for war. But it was not only United States citizens who complained about the behavior of the Mexican republic. In 1838, France blockaded Veracruz and landed an expeditionary force to exact payment of French claims. In 1861, only a decade after Scott had left Mexico City, the Tripartite Convention between Britain, France, and Spain decided to "seize and occupy the several fortresses and military possessions on the Mexican coast" to force Mexico to pay debts owed to its subjects. Their intervention soon developed into the French invasion and occupation of Mexico and the creation of the Second Empire under Maximilian I.[54]

The third victim of poor finances was the military. At first sight this appears contradictory because the national accounts show that Mexico spent considerably more on its army than the United States did in the years leading up to the US-Mexican War. Mexico's problem was therefore not only that the government's income was insufficient but also that a bloated officer corps and widespread corruption meant that the money expended on the military did not translate into an efficient army. Yet reform of the army proved to be as difficult as reform of the fiscal system. It is noteworthy that when Mexico finally got its financial house in order toward the end of the nineteenth century, the government had for a long time opted to neglect the army. Despite considerable investment in the military, Mexico's Northern Army was in a deplorable state when war over Texas threatened in 1845. One contemporary described it as "an insufficient force, poorly clothed and without equipment." There was no gunpowder for the artillery, no horses for the cavalry, and barely enough food for the troops. In December 1845 the war minister reported that war against the United States would require a 160 percent increase of the army at very heavy cost. In the same report the finance minister revealed that the Treasury was virtually empty. Meanwhile the city of Veracruz informed the government that it had neither soldiers nor artillery, and in a circular report the foreign minister told the state governors and legislators that California was impossible to defend and that a war with the United States would require untold sacrifices "simply to avoid annihilation." What Mexico needed in order to halt United States' encroachment was "money, money, and more money." But money was nowhere to be found.[55]

Without credit there was no possibility for the government to fund or execute any kind of extraordinary military endeavor. As a result the troops that Mexico managed to field against the United States were poorly fed, led, trained, and equipped. In the spring of 1847, Ramirez claimed that "strictly speaking, the army does not exist. What today bears that name is only a mass of men without training or without weapons." Despite isolated instances of individual bravery, the quality of Mexican troops was significantly inferior to that of the American soldiers. On repeated occasions Mexican commanders were unable to turn superiority in numbers or advantageous deployment into victory. Even before the war broke out, military weakness in the border areas had made Mexican sovereignty tenuous. The Mexican government could not stop the inflow of emigrants from the United States into Texas even when it tried to. In Texas and the northern provinces, the government could neither protect the population from Indian depredations nor provide them with access to markets. The Texas revolt in 1835 was neither the first nor the only case of regional discontent with the policies of Mexico City. Several other outlying provinces also resisted the central regime. In the south, Yucatán seceded in 1843 and again in 1846. Well before the American invasion, the Mexican nation was falling apart because of a weak central government with insufficient financial resources and consequent military incapacity. As a result, a substantial portion of the residents in the border areas, of both Mexican and American descent, accepted United States' occupation.[56]

When the American invaders swarmed across the Rio Bravo del Norte, Mexico had been an independent nation for a quarter of a century. Yet it was still struggling to establish political institutions that could provide for ordered conflict resolution and a political practice allowing for the peaceful transition of power. In the financial sphere, Mexico had yet to create a viable fiscal regime and reform its public debt. Finances were so strained that the government could not even meet ordinary expenditures. There was no possibility of financing the war with either taxes or loans in the way that Polk and Walker did in the United States. Instead the government had to resort to ad hoc solutions, forced loans, and army requisitions. Familiar difficulties were aggravated during the war. In the twenty-one months between the Battle of Palo Alto and the Treaty of Guadalupe Hidalgo, the presidency changed hands ten times and the Ministry of Finance twenty-three times. Within the span of four days in September 1846 three different finance ministers served, a pitiful record that was repeated over Christmas the same year.[57]

Mexico began its preparations for war by canceling all payments on the public debt and slashing all nonmilitary salaries by 25 percent. These moves reduced expenses but also ruined the government's credit and sowed discontent among government dependents. As it had in the past, the administration turned to the Church for support. The Church was asked to contribute $2 million to the war effort but grudgingly provided only half the amount. Instead of fitting out an army, however, the administration used up these proceeds to put down an indigenous rebellion. In September 1846 negotiations with Mexico City financiers for a $2 million loan yielded only $27,000 plus a week of supplies for the army. Under the direction of Valentín Goméz Farías the congress decreed stringent new fiscal measures on September 17. But Farías was met by massive resistance and was soon forced to step down. His measures were immediately repealed, possibly as a result of bribes paid to the new minister. Legislation passed on October 2 imposed a property tax on house owners but yielded little, as there was neither a fiscal administration to collect the tax nor much money to collect from the house owners.[58]

In the fall of 1846, unable to borrow or to reform the tax system, the government began to consider the expropriation of Church property, the nation's major untapped asset. A first attempt was a $2 million forced loan imposed on a group of *agiotistas*, or public creditors, and secured on Church property. Opposition from the clergy forced the government to back down, however. In December the government reached an agreement with the Church whereby it promised a loan of $1.85 million in return for guarantees against further disentailment. The government's guarantee proved to be of little worth. Within a month, a new administration headed by Santa Anna and Farías decided to expropriate $15 million of Church property. Faced with such a threat, the Catholic leadership mobilized in earnest and instigated the so-called revolt of the *Polkos*, which saw the capital erupt in civil war. Santa Anna now acted rapidly. He dismissed Farías and in an abrupt about-face declared his opposition to the expropriation of Church property. Grateful bishops offered him a further $1.5 million loan guarantee in return. By January 1847 the Church had contributed altogether $4.35 million toward the war effort. Although it was a substantial sum to the Church, it was far short of what was needed to meet the needs of the armed forces. Without money Mexican commanders had to resort to expropriation and forced requisitions in order to feed their troops. When news of Scott's victory at Cerro Gordo reached Ramirez in Mexico City, he wryly noted that not only did the enemy have seven thousand men and "an immense artillery train for their military operations," they also had $2 million "in their coffers and pay cash for their subsistence and transport." Mexican troops, in contrast, had "nothing and use force in obtaining what they need, either paying nothing at all or pay[ing] only grudgingly." In the spring and summer of 1847 the government authorized loans of up to $20 million secured on Church property, an action that caused the Church serious financial problems long after the war was over.[59]

The details of Mexico's war financing are of less significance than the overall pattern. Every step of Mexican resource mobilization depended on coercion rather than voluntary action. The pitiful sums raised were secured by force and broken promises. Such heavy-handed rule alienated the population and the moneyed elite and gave rise to opposition and armed rebellions. But even coercive measures could not raise enough money to field an adequate army. In the United States, in contrast, voluntary loans gave the national government abundant resources with which to finance military expeditions to New Mexico and California; a naval presence off the Pacific Coast; the occupation of northern Mexico; and, finally, the offensive that would take Scott and the US Army from Veracruz over Cerro Gordo and Chapultepec to Mexico City.

V

The defense of the sovereignty and territorial integrity of the nation is the primary responsibility of all states. Although it is not the only explanation, Mexico's failure to do so was caused by unstable and dysfunctional governmental institutions, among them an unproductive revenue system and a mismanaged public debt. Faced with an expansive and aggressive neighbor, Mexico could not prevent the partition of the national domain. The impoverished state of the finances also made the government voluntarily alienate territory in return for pecuniary compensation. The indemnity paid by the United States after the peace of Guadalupe Hidalgo created a few years of political stability in Mexico resembling the rule of Victoria in the 1820s. Investments were made in the army. Order was restored in Yucatán, and the province was reincorporated with the Mexican nation. Between June 1848 and January 1853, only two presidents governed Mexico. But in 1853, American payments had come to an end, and the Treasury was once more empty. Again the solution proved to be the sale of territory, and again the United States proved to be a ready customer. The Gadsden Purchase gave the United States thirty thousand square miles of present-day southern Arizona and New Mexico in return for $10 million. An attempt to sell transit rights to the United States over Mexican territory a few years later came to naught when Mexico descended into civil war followed by occupation by France. Nominally an independent nation, Mexico's destiny was in reality determined by the caprice of the European great powers and its powerful American neighbor. Unable to maintain its sovereignty and territorial integrity, the Mexican republic lost its power of self-determination, the very essence of republicanism.

Contemporary observers hardly found this development surprising. Republics were still regarded as unstable political entities prone to fall victim to foreign aggression or domestic discord. When the American South seceded to form the Confederate States of America in 1861, it only confirmed what many Europeans believed to be the inevitable fate of all America's federal republics. In Mexico, conservative politicians saw the reintroduction of monarchy as the solution to their nation's ills, and some of them welcomed the arrival of Napoleon III's puppet emperor Maximilian in 1862.[60]

In his wartime correspondence with Mexico's minister of foreign affairs, Secretary of State James Buchanan at one point referred to the United States and Mexico as "the two most powerful Republics in the world." In view of their radically divergent wartime records, this statement at first appears strange, if not perverse. Yet Buchanan was right. In the middle of the nineteenth century, the United States and Mexico were in fact the principal republican alternatives to a world of monarchies. But whereas the Mexican performance in the US-Mexican War confirmed European prejudice against a republican form of government, the American performance challenged it. The United States' successful pursuit of the war demonstrated that in terms of state capacity there need not be any significant difference between a republic and a monarchy. Underlying the performance of the United States in the Mexican War was precisely what was missing in Mexico but present in every European great power: stable and functional governmental institutions, not least in the sphere of public finance. These allowed the United States not only to avoid the destiny of Mexico and retain its independence but also to master the North American continent and dictate terms to its weaker neighbors.[61]

In 1790, the federal government had adopted crucial institutions, such as a funded public debt, from Europe's warring monarchies. The United States therefore benefited from innovations in the European war system that American statesmen habitually decried. To Polk and his sympathizers, the Mexican War represented a demonstration of the strength and basic soundness of the American union. In many ways their sentiments echoed those heard after the War of 1812. When the president submitted the Treaty of Guadalupe Hidalgo to the Senate, he remarked that the war had granted "the United States a national character abroad which our country never before enjoyed. Our power and our resources have become known and are respected throughout the world." In his third annual message delivered seven months earlier, James Polk had declared that "history presents no parallel of so many glorious victories achieved by any nation within so short a period." Robert Walker supported his chief and predicted that the United States could expect to be at peace with the world "as the result in part of our wonderful military power displayed in our recent glorious achievements and unparalleled victories, as well as from the development of our extraordinary moneyed resources." Even the president's critics maintained that the US Army in Mexico had outperformed the British in India and that "the British mind especially appears to have derived new impressions from these manifestations." The war, Polk said, had demonstrated that the United States was a power to be reckoned with. With the Mexican Cession the United States had become "nearly as large as the whole of Europe." Furthermore, the successful conclusion of a war of conquest showed that New World republics could be as capable as the powers of the Old World. "The war with Mexico," Polk concluded, "has thus fully developed the capacity of republican governments to prosecute successfully a just and necessary foreign war with all the vigor usually attributed to more arbitrary forms of government."[62]

The increase of the republic's war-making capacity was a dangerous development, however, because modern war and the institutions that made it possible—bloated armies, heavy taxes, and permanent debts—had long been identified as particular threats to republican liberty. For this reason Polk's pride in his administration's achievement did not quiet his fear of public debts and political corruption. It is of course ironic that this proponent of small and frugal government caused the greatest expansion of the public debt between the presidencies of Madison and Lincoln. But it would be wrong to dismiss Polk's concern with the debt as insincere. The president took the repayment of the Mexican War loans very seriously. In his inaugural address he referred to the "wise policy" of liquidating "the debts contracted in our Revolution and during the War of 1812," which he considered an important tradition in American statecraft. Obviously, Polk's intention of paying down the public debt was frustrated by the war, but he remained an opponent of permanent debts. He pointed to the importance of reducing the war loans when he submitted the peace treaty to Congress, saying that it was "against sound policy and the genius of our institutions that a public debt should be permitted to exist a day longer than the means of the Treasury will enable the Government to pay it off." He returned to the problem of the debt in his final annual message to Congress. Although the American debt was small compared to the debts of other nations, it was nevertheless "our true policy, and in harmony with the genius of our institutions, that we should present to the world the rare spectacle of a great Republic, possessing vast resources and wealth, wholly exempt from public indebtedness. This would add still more to our strength, and give us a still more commanding position among the nations of the earth."[63]

As an opponent of high taxes, the only means open to Polk to rapidly reduce the debt was by cutting expenditures. If Congress could only avoid appropriating funds for expenses that were not "of absolute necessity" and make sure that "the earliest practicable payment of the public debt" became "a cardinal principle of action," the war loans could be paid off "without any increase of taxation on the people long before it falls due." A start was made in 1848 when $2 million of the American claims against Mexico, which had been assumed by the United States as part of the Treaty of Guadalupe Hidalgo, were paid without the introduction of new taxes. In his testament to Congress and the incoming administration, Polk insisted that American political leaders should make debt retrenchment by means of reduced expenditure a priority. If this could be accomplished, the United

States would be able to combine the power of Old World monarchies with the republican liberty of the New World and thereby realize a future "without a parallel or example in the history of nations."[64]

When Polk wrote his farewell address, it seemed that the Mexican War had once more vindicated the institutions set up in the 1790s and tested in the War of 1812. Little did he know that his war and the territorial expansion that followed from the Treaty of Guadalupe Hidalgo would set in motion a train of events that would lead to the severest test yet to the viability of the American union. To overcome that crisis, long-cherished principles of public finance had to be abandoned, and the scope of the national government had to be considerably enlarged in ways that Polk would have found unacceptable. Out of that deep crisis emerged an American state that was different but also far stronger than the national government that had conquered Mexico.

CHAPTER SIX

A Rank among the Very First of Military Powers: Mr. Lincoln's War

The attack on Fort Sumter on April 12–13, 1861, forced upon the United States "the distinct issue, 'Immediate dissolution or blood.'" In words reminiscent of his later and more famous address at Gettysburg Military Cemetery, President Abraham Lincoln announced that Fort Sumter placed before the American nation the question "whether a constitutional republic, or democracy—a government of the people by the same people—can or can not maintain its territorial integrity against its own domestic foes." Lincoln's own answer was clear. Undecided on many issues throughout the Civil War, he never wavered on the need to preserve the Union and the nation's integrity at all costs.[1]

To do so required four years of war at an enormous cost in lives and money. Like most people at the time, Lincoln initially thought the contest would be "a short and decisive one." His address to the special session of the Thirty-Seventh Congress nonetheless called for an unprecedented demonstration of strength. The president asked for an army of four hundred thousand men and a war chest of $400 million. This was mobilization for war on a giant scale. Even before the first engagement at Bull Run, it was clear that the Civil War would be a conflict of a magnitude that the nation had not experienced since the War of Independence—another civil war. Admittedly, half a million men served in the War of 1812, but the vast majority for less than six months. Far fewer, around one hundred thousand regulars and volunteers, saw some form of service, although not always military action, over the course of the Mexican War. The amount of money that the president asked for was also extraordinary. Four hundred million dollars would have paid the direct cost of four Wars of 1812 and five Mexican Wars. Nevertheless, Lincoln's request for men and money proved to be woefully inadequate. Before the Confederacy had been vanquished, some two million men had enlisted in the Union armies. More than 360,000 of them lost their lives. The national debt shot up from $90 million in the summer of 1861 to more than $2.7 billion five years later. In the five years before the war, the Treasury collected $267 million. In the five years after the war the figure was $2.2 billion. Not until the Second World War would the economy and population of the United States be taxed to a similar extent in time of war. Never again would the nation suffer such appalling loss of human life.[2]

In the American historical memory the Civil War is remembered primarily as an epic struggle over the future of slavery in the United States, the moment in time when the nation took a giant step toward the realization of the ideals of universal liberty and equality expressed in the Declaration of Independence. Without question, the eradication of slavery was the most important outcome of the war. Yet for contemporaries in the North, the Civil War began as a war to preserve the Union and its "territorial integrity," as Lincoln put it, and not as a crusade against slavery. Like the abolition of slavery, the successful defense of the Union was also of immense importance to the future of the country. To nineteenth-century Americans the preservation of the Union seemed a prerequisite for the continuation of the United States as a federal union of state-republics, a polity in which a limited central government imposed only the lightest of burdens on the citizenry. A dis-United States, in contrast, would turn the North American continent into a world of competing nation-states jockeying for advantage and keeping each other in check by means of war preparations, balance-of-power diplomacy, and foreign alliances. Standing armies and navies would be created and employed in frequent wars. Like their unfortunate European brethren, the peoples of North America would see their property diminished and their liberty undermined by the constant and growing demands of the state. This dystopian vision of disunion is the reason Lincoln believed that only by crushing the southern bid for nationhood could the American people ensure that "government of the people, by the people, for the people, shall not perish from the earth."[3]

Across the Atlantic Ocean, European observers were well aware that the war between the Union and the Confederacy would determine the future course of the North American continent. Not since the Revolution had Europeans paid as much attention to American affairs. When the war began, many members of the governing elite in Britain thought that the conflict would rend the American union apart or, at the very least, permanently change the nature of the federal republic. The disintegration of the Union into two, or even as many as "half a dozen moderate sized republics," was widely welcomed in conservative circles. By 1861 the United States was fast on its way to dominating North America and the vital commercial routes that cut through the Central American isthmus and the Gulf of Mexico. Most European rulers had little love for American democracy, but regardless of such aversion it was plain to see that it was not in Europe's best interest for the United States to achieve hegemony in North America. "Why should the Continent of America be bound into a single State and nation" when Europe was subdivided into several different powers, one British journal asked. "Why, in a word, should the dream of 'universal dominion,' long since banished from one hemisphere, be permitted to take refuge in another?"[4]

A war that to Americans was a struggle to preserve the Union seemed to Britain's political leadership a war for continental domination or empire. As Sherman marched through the Carolinas in the final stages of the Civil War, Britain's foreign secretary, Lord Russell, told the House of Lords that "I have always thought, and I stated the opinion at the commencement of the civil war, that on the part of the North it was a contest for empire; just as I believe our contest in 1776, which we continued till 1783, was a contest for empire and for nothing else." But whereas Americans and Europeans saw the nature of the conflict in strikingly different terms, their analysis of the stakes involved was nevertheless surprisingly similar. The outcome of the Civil War would determine whether North America would remain under the direct and indirect domination of one power or would be governed by several states whose interactions would be regulated by a balance-of-power system akin to European international relations.[5]

Europeans commonly explained the anticipated breakdown of the Union as a result of its past expansion. It was difficult to keep nations the size of the United States together. This was even more true of republics, which were considered inherently unstable systems of government, too weak to prevent dissolution. It was a long-established truth in political science that republics possessed less executive power than monarchies and were therefore ill-equipped to deal with crises and conflicts. Few Europeans believed that the national government had either the will or the resources necessary to suppress an insurrection on the scale of the southern secession. Americans' experience with war was obviously limited. Surveying the nation's history, one member of Britain's House of Commons acknowledged US involvement in only two wars, both against Britain. Tellingly, he passed over the Mexican War and the many conflicts with Native American nations in silence. To the London-based journal the *Economist*, American victory in the first of the wars against Britain owed more to the "imbecility" of the North ministry than to the valor of the Continental army. Admittedly, the

Americans had done better in the War of 1812, but this had been a short and limited conflict. "All their other contests have been against naked Indians and degenerate and undisciplined Mexicans," the journal said. They had been "raids rather than wars." Although the Union side expressed confidence about its ability to defeat the South, the truth was that the American nation had "never been tested by any great difficulty, any great danger, any great calamity; they have never been called upon for any sustained effort, any serious sacrifice, any prolonged endurance." In 1861, Americans were still "*a wholly untried people.*"[6]

The Civil War served as Americans' first great trial as a people, and in important respects the war represents the United States' rite of passage to great-power status. After Lee had surrendered at Appomattox Courthouse, Europeans still thought that the war had altered the course of American history. With peace the national government faced a large and hostile population in a vast conquered domain. Subduing the vanquished would require a centralization of power and the creation of a "strong Government" with "an army at command." Peace therefore did not return the country to the antebellum status quo. Instead Union victory would effect "a very great difference in the condition of the United States." A stronger American state was a power that European nations now would have to reckon with. "I think," Benjamin Disraeli remarked in the winter of 1865, that "when you have to consider the balance of power in future, you will have to take into consideration States and influences which cannot be counted among European Powers." Such changing perceptions of US power were deeply colored by the enormous mobilization that had taken place during the war. "Four years ago," J. B. Smith noted in the House of Commons in 1865, "the army of the United States was less than 20,000 men, and her navy was composed of a few frigates. Now she is become one of the greatest military and naval powers in the world." For the most part, Britain's political leaders and literati grudgingly came to acknowledge that a state that had never much impressed them had now become a military power second to none. On learning the news of Lee's surrender, the London *Times*, whose sympathies had all along remained with the Confederacy, noted that if the Union had not earned the South's "reputation for desperate valour," it had nevertheless won something far more tangible. Northerners had "shown a patience, a fortitude, and an energy which entitles them to rank among the very first of military powers."[7]

Money played an important part in the Union victory and the subsequent elevated status of the United States. "The North raised army after army," wrote the *Times* in its postwar commentary, "and was always prepared with undiminished forces for a fresh campaign." The Confederacy, in contrast, "could not afford to offer a thousand dollars a man" in the manner of the Union. The US secretary of the Treasury, the *Economist* had remarked a year earlier, had "worked a miracle in finance" by managing "to find supplies for the most costly war ever known. He has not, to use Napoleon's phrase, 'organized victory;' even now the Federal arms are far indeed from having attained their end;—but he has organized *persistence*, he has enabled his countrymen to continue a struggle which, whatever we may say of the object, is in its scale mighty and gigantic."[8]

As the American postwar debate made clear, the organization of persistence came at a price. If the United States was now ranked among the great powers of the world, it was in no small part because it had a national debt in excess of almost all other countries. In his controversial pamphlet *How Our National Debt May Be a National Blessing*, Samuel Wilkeson observed that "the five great Powers of the World have each a Permanent National Debt," and he hinted that this institution was "incidental to the growth and development of States." Statistical tables compared the debts of Great Britain, France, Russia, and Austria to that of the United States, showing that the United States now had the world's second-largest debt, trailing only Britain, and the highest annual interest liability. Wilkeson's view that the American debt should be perpetuated was universally rejected, but his belief that the government's ability to finance the Civil War had contributed to the nation's rise in international status was widely shared. The war, one newspaper editorial said, "demonstrated our national strength—and all the world over, national strength is but another word for national credit." "The greatest war of modern history has ended in triumph," another newspaper noted. "The country has demonstrated the vastness of its power. *We* knew that it was great; now all the world knows it." The United States had won the respect of Europe's great powers because "a young nation that can raise two millions of fighting men and two thousand millions of money, just for the asking is worthy of being considered." According to the *Baltimore Sun*, "The history of the civilized world records no parallel in its finances and national strength to compare with the United States." The *Sun* continued, "We behold ourselves standing up in just pride before all the powers of the civilized earth, the architects and masters of our own greatness. Princes and potentates and kingdoms and empires of the old world are looking upon us this very day with awe and admiration."[9]

The ability of the federal government to borrow such enormous sums to finance the conquest of the South is all the more remarkable when one recalls that in 1861 the American people really was "wholly untried" in the

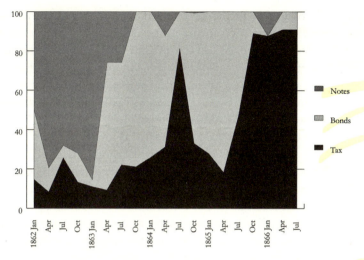

Fig. 6.1. Relative importance of government income, 1862–1866. The diagram shows the sources of government income per quarter. January 1862 represents the third quarter of fiscal year 1862, or January to March 1862, and so on. In tables 6.3 and 6.4, some types of government revenue are given a negative number to represent repayments of debt. In this figure, repayments have been treated as no income rather than negative income. "Notes" refers to demand notes, legal-tender notes, and various short-term loans. "Bonds" refers to both long-term bonds and Treasury notes. *Sources*: See tables 6.2 through 6.4.

management of a major war. Mastering this art was not an easy process. According to one historian, "The Treasury and Congress had to resort in hit-or-miss fashion to every conceivable method of raising money." The long and expensive war forced the government to experiment with a range of different securities. The result was a debt whose complexity is second only to the financial tangle left by the War of Independence. As a classic textbook on United States financial history puts it, "Loans followed each other with great rapidity, and with a perplexing variation in terms and conditions, which embarrass an orderly presentation of the government financiering. And when to the loans are added the issue of treasury notes and certificates of deposit the disorder becomes still more bewildering."[10]

Some semblance of order can be reached by subdividing the financial history of the Civil War into four periods corresponding to four different methods of war finance (see figure 6.1). Treasury secretary Salmon P. Chase's original war finance plan, which rested on precedents from Albert Gallatin's funding of the War of 1812, did not survive the first six months of the conflict. It was replaced with a desperate measure adopted by Congress much against the inclinations of Chase: the issue of an irredeemable federal fiat currency. At this point the government appeared set to journey down the route traveled by the Continental Congress during the War of Independence, when the printing press had churned out Continentals by the bucketful until the notes finally became worthless. But for reasons that have to do with Congress's greater fiscal and financial powers under the Constitution, this time the outcome of the experiment was vastly different. Greenbacks successfully paid for the war until the spring of 1863, when the Treasury's loan agent Jay Cooke—"our modern Midas," as one admiring newspaperman referred to him—embarked on a large-scale campaign to sell long-term war bonds. Cooke's bonds kept the Treasury in funds until the end of the year. Hard months then followed before fiscal legislation originally passed in the summer of 1862 began to pay dividends. For the remainder of the war, from mid-1864 onward, the Treasury financed the war through a combination of tax revenue and yet another successful mass sale of government securities, again under the directorship of Jay Cooke.[11]

The funding of the Civil War forced Congress to transcend the fiscal system and financial principles that had been in place since 1789. Needs could not be met by existing policies and institutions, and the demise of the first American fiscal regime can be dated to July 1862. During the War of 1812 and the Mexican War the government had floated loans for $10 million or $20 million. During the Civil War it borrowed several million dollars per day. Initially the securities' market could not provide such sums. It was only when more money had been created by government note emissions that bond sales began to proceed smoothly. Hundreds of millions of legal-tender notes, or greenbacks, were emitted, a policy that would have been unthinkable to Alexander Hamilton, Albert Gallatin, and Robert Walker. Both bonds and notes were backed by a major reform of the tax system. The structure of federal taxation was broadened to include internal taxes, and a large internal revenue administration became part of the federal bureaucracy. To ensure that home industries would be protected from foreign competition, customs duties were increased to record levels. The result was a very productive revenue regime. In fiscal year 1866, the federal government collected $558 million from taxes. In the entire prewar period, the government had never collected more than $74 million in any single year.[12]

But not everything changed. The ideal of a nation unencumbered by public debt remained, and debt retrenchment in the decades after the Civil War was as spectacular as wartime borrowing had been. As it had always done before, the government recognized the face value of its debt and paid the interest in specie. Nor were the ideals of light and nonintrusive taxation abandoned. Civil War taxes were rapidly scaled back in the late 1860s, and even though an internal revenue service remained, its duties fell on tobacco, spirits, and fermented liquors, articles that American political economists had for generations designated "luxuries," if not "pernicious" luxuries. It is true that the Civil War caused a considerable ratchet effect in government spending. Annual costs settled at about four or five times prewar levels. Yet government expansion stopped after the war, and the strong army and navy that British statesmen had come to fear were not retained. The American Hercules had flexed his muscles, but for the time being rested content as the unchallenged master of the North American continent.

I

Salmon Portland Chase's appointment to head the Treasury was politically motivated. A United States senator and former governor of Ohio, Chase had been one of the contenders for the Republican presidential nomination along with William Seward and Edward Bates. To secure broad support from the fledgling Republican Party, Lincoln co-opted his rivals into his administration. Seward became secretary of state, Bates attorney general, and Chase was offered the Treasury. A lawyer by training, Chase knew no more about public finance than his chief did. Proud, humorless, and self-conscious, he found the president's personality and leadership style difficult. In 1864 Chase made a grasp for the presidential nomination from inside the cabinet, a move that has tainted his historical reputation with disloyalty ever since. Even his biographer admits that Chase was a difficult man who walked through life "a majestic figure with an air of conscious superiority that many found repellent." Chase was a good man with an unsound theology, a contemporary said. "He thinks there is a fourth person in the Trinity."[13]

Chase thought Lincoln a weak war leader but was not himself an effective leader in financial matters. During the war he became obsessed with his national banking scheme when he should have sought means to address the pressing difficulties of the Treasury. Instead many of the new and radical features of the financing of the Civil War originated in Congress. In the House of Representatives Thaddeus Stephens, Justin S. Morrill, and Elbridge G. Spaulding chaired the Ways and Means Committee and its subcommittees. In the Senate, William P. Fessenden, who would replace Chase as secretary of the Treasury in June 1864, was chair of the Finance Committee. Most financial historians have found Secretary Chase wanting in the management of his department. They all note his inexperience and "mediocre knowledge of monetary and financial history, theory, and practice." He often made the wrong choices, and he treated the nation's bankers and capitalists in a haughty and overbearing manner. In the cabinet he was "a troubler," in the Treasury "a misfortune."[14]

Chase's first report to Congress revealed a man wedded to past practice of American public finance. He hoped to raise $318 million to subdue the southern rebellion "with the least possible inconvenience" to the people. As his predecessors had in the past, he turned to loans to achieve this. Taxation nevertheless played a part in the secretary's plans. A "sound system of finance" required "adequate provision by taxation for the prompt discharge of all ordinary demands, for the punctual payment of the interest on loans, and for the creation of a gradually increasing fund for the redemption of the principal." To those who knew the nation's financial history, it was clear that Chase meant to dust off the Gallatin war finance plan from 1807. The updated formula called for $80 million in taxes and $240 million in loans.[15]

The Treasury secretary's traditionalism was evident also in his recommendations for fiscal legislation. Having noted that the people and their government had always been partial to customs duties as the principal source of national government revenue and had contemplated alternative taxation only "on occasions of special exigency," Chase declared that "no departure is proposed by the Secretary from the line of policy thus sanctioned." To increase the yield from the impost, he proposed the reintroduction of import duties on coffee, tea, and sugar, the very articles that Robert Walker had in vain asked Congress to tax during the Mexican War. Even with these new duties the Treasury would fall $20 million short. To fill this gap Chase appealed to "the superior wisdom of Congress" and made only vague suggestions about a property tax and an excise on "articles of luxury" like distilled spirits, beer, and tobacco, which, as all informed Americans knew, was a major source of revenue in Britain at the time. Congress responded with higher duties, a direct tax apportioned between the states, and a federal income tax, the first of its kind in the United States. Hoping to avoid the creation of a costly internal revenue service and "the introduction into the States of federal agencies for the assessment and collection of taxes," Chase trusted to the state governments to assess and collect the direct tax and forward the money to the Treasury. He was also critical of the income tax, which would require a new and expensive bureaucracy. The secretary therefore put off action. When the Thirty-Seventh Congress assembled for its second session in December 1861, he had done very little to increase the tax revenue.[16]

The other pillar of Chase's war finance plan called for $240 million in loans. An inconsequential sum in the twenty-first century, this was substantially more than the government had borrowed in the past. Three separate loans were proposed. Long-term bonds would be marketed to domestic and foreign capitalists, and Chase considered making interest payments in London to accommodate investors. Very likely drawing on French precedence under Napoleon III, a popular "national loan" would be marketed broadly toward the citizenry at large, thereby extending "the circle of contribution" to the war effort. This loan would take the form of three-year "treasury notes, or exchequer bills" bearing 7.3 percent interest. At this rate a fifty-dollar treasury note would earn a penny a day in interest, making it easier to calculate the value of the note and thereby facilitating their circulation. By making the minimal subscription fifty dollars and considering appointing the nation's numerous postmasters as loan agents, Chase signaled his intention to sell the loan broadly. The third and final loan consisted of one-year Treasury notes to pay for procurements and salaries to government employees. It would be all too easy for the government to turn these into an irredeemable paper currency in the hope of avoiding difficult bond sales and tax reforms, and Chase took great care to avoid this. A loan act incorporating the secretary's proposals with only minor alterations was rushed through Congress and signed into law on July 17. Additional legislation followed three weeks later.[17]

Very few of Chase's original war finance measures went according to plan. A European loan never materialized. August Belmont, who as the American agent of the House of Rothschild was in the know, told Chase in late October that "any direct or indirect attempt on the part of the government" to sell a loan in Europe "would be worse than useless and you will have to look for all your wants to our home market." Months earlier, the *Economist* had predicted that "Mr. Chase will obtain no money in Europe or next to none." A federal state struggling to prevent its southern half from seceding was a serious credit risk. Today's "respectable aggregate" might be "scattered atoms tomorrow," and what would then happen to the bondholders? "If the fragmentary parts of a once integral State decline to pay the debts of that State, we, the lenders, shall go without our money." A few years into the war, the inability of the government to borrow abroad was turned into a sign of strength. "We don't want to be the debtor of the old world," one Philadelphia newspaper said in the spring of 1863. "Americans have money enough to pay American armies, and they have a Government which deserves their confidence, and which they will maintain with the dollar as well as the bayonet." But in the fall of 1861 the lack of interest from foreign investors must have been cause for considerable anxiety to Secretary Chase.[18]

On the domestic market Chase entered into negotiations with banking houses in Boston, New York, and Philadelphia. A consortium of banks agreed to advance three $50 million installments in exchange for Treasury notes or bonds taken at par for resale. Treasury notes would also be sold by the Treasury and specially appointed loan agents. According to the plan, these sales would rapidly repay to the banks the money they had advanced to the government. The first $50 million was paid in August, the second installment in October, and the third in December. But the plan was not well executed. Altogether, the banks and government loan agents sold $45 million of the first emission of 7-30 Treasury notes, so called because of the 7.3 percent interest rate. But by the time of the second installment, security prices had depreciated, and it was impossible to sell the Treasury notes at par. The Civil War's most serious foreign policy crisis was partly to blame. In November Captain Charles Wilkes of the *USS San Jacinto* boarded the British steamer *Trent* in international waters and arrested and removed Confederate emissaries James Mason and John Slidell. War with Great Britain threatened, and the stock market plummeted. When Chase came knocking for the third $50 million payment, the banks refused to take more Treasury notes. Instead the Treasury sold the banks 6 percent twenty-year bonds at a discount of 8.4 percent, which equaled a par price for 7 percent bonds.[19]

Although the annual Treasury report for 1862 struck an optimistic note, the banks and, by extension, the government were in a precarious situation. The bankers had believed that the Treasury would deposit its loans with the lending banks and draw on them by check. But Chase was a hard-money advocate who considered himself bound to abide by the regulations of the Independent Treasury. In the secretary's opinion this prevented the Treasury from having accounts with the banks. Instead he made them pay cash and deposited the money in the subtreasuries located in the nation's major cities. As a result, the banks were drained of their specie reserves, and when Treasury notes and bonds could not be sold, they were unable to rebuild their reserves. By December, gold reserves in New York banks were running dangerously low, and calls for specie suspension began to be aired in the banking sector.[20]

When Congress met in December, the war appeared to have stalled. No major engagements had followed Bull Run in August. The public finances were troubled. Chase's July estimate for expenditures had been revised upward from $318 million to $532 million, and the revenue estimates had been revised downward from $80 million to $55 million. There was a deficit of more than $200 million for the remainder of fiscal year 1862 (i.e., to

June 30) alone. Chase hoped that the war would be over by midsummer and did not offer any concrete proposals for new taxes beyond the vague remark that "a more absolute reliance, under God, upon American labor, American skill, and American soil" was in order. He also refrained "from making any recommendation concerning the authorities with which it may be expedient to invest him in respect to future loans" but referred this question "to the better judgment of Congress." Much of the report was devoted to the national banking scheme, which would become a favorite of the secretary. In brief, the plan was that the government should appropriate the note issues of state-chartered banks by taxing their notes out of circulation and substituting US notes issued by nationally chartered banks on the security of federal government bonds. With one stroke this scheme promised to create a demand for war bonds and limit the government's ability to inflate the note issue to dangerous levels. But regardless of the potential benefits, the Treasury secretary himself admitted that the scheme was not a quick fix for the government's financial troubles. The national banking scheme would eventually be realized, and its long-term significance for the nation's economic and political development was very significant. Both the federal reserve system and the national currency of the modern United States have roots stretching back to Chase's banking scheme. But its contribution to the financing of the Civil War was marginal.[21]

Worried by the Treasury's lack of vision, hearing nothing about military progress, and still fearful of war with Britain, the banks of New York City decided to end specie conversion on December 30. The rest of the country and the government followed the next day. Borrowing was now impossible other than at ruinous terms, and Chase's war finance plan lay in ruins. The vagueness of the secretary's Treasury report caused the policy initiative to pass to Congress and in particular to the House Ways and Means Committee. Congress rose to the challenge posed by specie suspension with two measures that would be crucial to the financing of the Civil War. The first was a stopgap measure intended to see the government through the spring and summer of 1862, but which would in fact last longer: the introduction of the "greenbacks," or legal-tender notes. The second was H.R. 312, a far-reaching reform of the fiscal system that created an internal revenue service responsible for the collection of a very extensive range of excise and stamp duties. It took considerable time before this legislation started to generate any real revenue. But Congress's readiness to pass new fiscal laws was instrumental in maintaining government credit, which made possible the large-scale bond sales that began in 1863.[22]

II

Specie suspension made bond sales impossible, as potential investors could not acquire the gold or silver coin they needed to pay for government securities. A discount in the region of 40 percent was needed to attract buyers. The alternative was to accept payment in banknotes, bound to depreciate as an effect of specie suspension. This had happened during "the last English war" fifty years earlier, and Congress was not in the mood to repeat the experience. Both houses realized that the only way out of the conundrum was to tax and to do so "speedily, strongly, vigorously." But a comprehensive fiscal bill would take time to write and longer to put into effect. Meanwhile the gap between income and expenditure was wide and growing in the first three months of 1862. Customs duties brought in around $160,000 per day, but the army and navy spent around $1.5 million to $2 million. By February government payments were in arrears by $45 million. Something had to be done quickly or the continuation of the war effort was in danger.[23]

The House of Representatives responded with a bill authorizing the issue of $150 million in non-interest-bearing notes, receivable for all payments owed by the government and "for all salaries, debts, and demands owing by the United States to individuals, corporations, and associations within the United States." Of utmost importance was the section that made the notes "lawful money and a legal tender in payment of all debts, public and private." Redeemed notes could be reissued by the government at will. To redeem the notes and maintain their value, the bill also authorized the "funding" of the notes by exchange for 6 percent twenty-year bonds. A Senate amendment made these bonds callable in five and payable in twenty years, and they quickly became known as "5-20 bonds" or "5-20 sixes." With time they would become a major source of government funds.[24]

The legal-tender notes, which became known as "greenbacks," held several attractions to the government. Most obviously, they would provide immediate funds for the Treasury. But other and more long-term consequences were just as important. Once the banks stopped paying out coin, banknotes became the only available form of money. In the absence of national banknotes, these had "only a local character and credit." During the War of 1812, the Treasury had been forced to accept payment in such banknotes, something that caused considerable difficulties. Treasury collections could not be used at the points of Treasury dispersions without a cumbersome and expensive exchange of currency. The greenbacks, in contrast, would circulate nationally. They would also inject a large dose of money into the economy, filling "the purse of the capitalist" and "the stocking of the poor but patriotic citizens," whence it would find its way back to the Treasury in return for bond sales. Although inflation was inevitable, at least there would be money with which to purchase securities. Lawmakers pointed out that there were important precedents for the measure. Great Britain would never have been able to borrow the money that defeated Napoleon "had she not adopted a national currency of paper money" and "used this currency as a medium of exchange with which she facilitated the payment of taxes and the negotiation of loans."[25]

In 1787 the Constitutional Convention had struck from the draft Constitution Congress's right to emit bills of credit. Nevertheless, ever since Gallatin first issued Treasury notes, the national government had made frequent use of this proscribed power. But the real issue was not the emission of notes but the decision to make government bills legal tender. All creditors, public *and* private, would be forced to accept greenbacks. In contrast, Treasury notes had only ever been receivable "at the option of the receiver." Chase explained that he had always felt "a great aversion to making anything but coin a legal-tender in payment of debts," and Fessenden confessed that the legal-tender clause was "opposed to all my views of right and expediency. It shocks all my notions of political, moral, and national honor." In the Senate he supported the move to strike it out because the clause "propose[d] something utterly unknown in this Government from its foundation" and represented a measure that had "always been denounced as ruinous to the credit of any Government which has recourse to it." Fessenden noted that legal-tender notes were "of doubtful constitutionality," and the next speaker argued at length that the notes were "a new feature, never before attempted in any extremities of our Government, at any period of its history, since the formation of the present Constitution" and clearly unconstitutional.[26]

The legal-tender clause could "only be justified on the grounds of necessity" in order to safeguard the circulation of the notes. Had everyone accepted greenbacks, the clause would have been unnecessary. But the old demand notes had not been universally accepted, and this created "discriminations in business, against those who, in this matter, give a cordial support to the Government, and in favor of those who do not." Banks could not accept notes on deposit unless they could be certain that the notes could be used to pay their creditors. Without the legal-tender provision, public creditors, government providers, and soldiers who received payments in US notes would be unable to pay their debts or support their families should the greenbacks be refused in payment.[27]

A divisive measure, the legal-tender bill caused considerable debate in both houses. Before it became law on February 25, the bill was amended in two important respects. To prevent the hoarding of greenbacks, the Treasury and assistant treasurers were granted the right to receive notes on deposit at 5 percent interest. Creditors were issued certificates of deposit that could be cashed after ten days notice. At first restricted to $25 million, the limit on deposits was gradually increased to $150 million, and in some periods of the Civil War this form of short-term loan would contribute substantially to government revenue. The second amendment to the bill prevented the use of greenbacks in two financial transactions. Interest on government bonds and Treasury notes would not be paid in notes but in coin only. Fessenden explained that the object was to safeguard the public credit by adhering to long-established practices of debt management. The federal government had always paid interest on its debt obligations punctually and in specie, and many considered this practice essential to the government's credit. Interest payment in coin proved "the good faith of the Government" and saved public creditors from being caught in "a circle of paper." To guarantee that there would be enough hard money in the Treasury to meet interest payments, the legal-tender act prohibited the payment of import duties in anything but specie. The downside of these two measures was that they introduced a distinction between money in the form of legal-tender notes and in the form of gold and silver coin that opened for the depreciation of the greenbacks. In effect, Congress undermined the value of its own currency.[28]

The immediate consequence of the legal-tender act was to bring much-needed relief to the Treasury. In late March Chase reported that "just now things are looking very well" and that "the credit of the Government is wonderfully sustained considering all disadvantages." By July 1 "not a single requisition from any department upon the Treasury remained unanswered." In his annual report of December 1862, Chase claimed that the measures of an "enlightened" Congress, whose members had risen admirably to the challenge of specie suspension, had "worked well" and that "their results have more than fulfilled the anticipations of the Secretary." In reality the public finances were far from healthy, however. Despite repeated pledges in January and February not to print more than $150 million greenbacks, another $150 million was approved in July 1862. In September Chase reported that the Treasury was $36 million in arrears and that "the 5-20s cannot be negotiated." The annual report for 1863 noted that close to $280 million had to be borrowed for the remainder of the fiscal year. Chase advised against more legal-tender notes, because further emissions would turn the greenbacks "into a positive calamity," leading to "inflation of prices, increase of expenditures, augmentation of debt, and, ultimately, disastrous defeat of the very purposes sought to be attained by it." Nevertheless, another $100 million emission followed in mid-January 1863 and a final emission of $50 million in March the same year.[29]

Chase was right to fear price inflation and currency depreciation. Specie suspension led to the opening of a gold exchange in New York City, and as table 6.1 demonstrates, there was considerable depreciation of the greenbacks. By the time of the second emission, they had lost over a tenth of their face value. They were down by a quarter of their value when the third emission was made, and when the fourth and final authorization passed, greenbacks were worth only two-thirds of their nominal value relative to gold. The notes hit rock bottom in the summer of 1864. Nevertheless, the critics were wrong to think that currency emissions would go on endlessly and that the greenbacks, like the Continentals of the American and the *assignats* of the French Revolution, to which they were frequently compared, would become worthless. Defenders of the original legal-tender act were adamant that no more than $150 million would be issued and insisted that this limitation was essential to the measure's success. If the "revolutionary scrip" of the War of Independence and the French *assignats* "had been confined to a small sum in proportion to the wealth of the country," such as "one tenth of the annual production," then "there would have been no dan-

TABLE 6.1. Price of gold in currency in New York City ($)

Month	1862	1863	1864	1865
Jan.	98	69	64	46
Feb.	97	62	63	49
Mar.	98	65	61	57
Apr.	98	66	58	67
May	97	67	57	74
June	94	69	47	71
July	87	77	39	70
Aug.	87	79	39	70
Sept.	84	74	45	69
Oct.	78	68	48	69
Nov.	76	68	43	68
Dec.	76	66	44	68

Source: Davis Rich Dewey, *Financial History of the United States*, 12th ed. (1934; repr., New York: Augustus Kelley, 1968), 293.

ger." Even though this promise was broken, the supporters of the greenbacks were right in thinking that the economy had the capacity to absorb the currency. They were also right that currency emission would not go on forever. After the last authorization in March 1863, emission stopped. The crucial difference between the greenbacks and the Continentals was that during the Civil War, Congress was able to turn to alternative sources of funds. This was also the major difference between Union and Confederate war finance. In the South, the government relied almost exclusively on paper money, which eventually lost all value. In the North, legal-tender notes were "a mere temporary expedient." As John Sherman pointed out, "It is manifest that we must rely upon some other source of obtaining money."[30]

As table 6.2 shows, currency finance saw the government through the war from spring 1862 to spring 1863. But it is important to note that in this period more sustainable forms of war finance were in the making. When the *Economist* tried to make sense of Union war finance from across the Atlantic, its editors repeatedly shook their heads at the "ignorant contempt of economical laws" openly flaunted by "Brother Jonathan," a popular name for the United States in the nineteenth-century. Although the journal's reports on American public finance were seldom insightful, they are interesting for clearly spelling out the reigning principles of war finance in Britain, at the time the most advanced economy of the world. These principles had hardly changed since the days of the Glorious Revolution. Unless equipped with a mature domestic money market, governments going to war should raise tax revenue in order to secure foreign loans:

> If a heavy income tax had been imposed at the outset of the war, the Federal Government would probably have been able to borrow largely in Europe. Their credit was excellent when the civil struggle commenced, and their bonds were favourite securities with many opulent and careful persons whose judgment was good, and who had real money to lend if they decided favourably. . . . Under proper management this vast wealth would have been a source of vast military strength, but Mr. Chase has so managed as to throw it away.

An annual tax income of £30 million, or roughly $130 million, would have given Chase access to "the hoarded capital of Europe." According to the *Economist*, however, the American form of government made ambitious fiscal measures impossible. Whereas the executive power was "expressly forbidden to tax, the cumbrous machinery of Senate and representatives, unguided by a Parliamentary Cabinet, will not tax, cannot tax,—is an inca-

TABLE 6.2. Major sources of government revenue January 1, 1862, to June 30, 1863, by quarter ($ million)

Revenue source	1862				1863	
	Jan.–Mar.	Apr.–June	July–Sept.	Oct.–Dec.	Jan.–Mar.	Apr.–June
	US notes and temporary loans					
Old demand notes	25.9	—	−27.7	−16.2	−10.8	−1.6
Legal-tender notes	—	98.6	72.4	53.8	106.7	58.3
Treasury deposits	18.9	39.1	12.9	12.2	9.2	13.4
Certificates of indebtedness	5.6	44.2	6.2	53.4	56.7	−9.3
Fractional currency	—	—	0.8	6.1	12.1	1.3
Total	50.4	181.9	64.6	109.3	173.9	62.1
	Long-term bonds and Treasury notes					
7-30 Treasury notes, 1861	11.2	14.0	3.6	13.7	—	—
Loan of 1861	24.3	—	—	—	—	—
5-20 bonds	—	13.8	2.5	8.7	7.2	156.6
Total	35.5	27.8	6.1	22.4	7.2	156.6
	Taxation					
Customs	14.6	18.9	23.0	12.4	15.4	17.2
Internal revenue	—	—	0.5	7.0	15.3	15.3
Miscellaneous	0.2	0.2	0.8	0.8	0.8	0.8
Total	14.8	19.1	24.3	20.2	31.5	33.3

Source: Rafael A. Bayley, *History of the National Loans of the United States from July 4, 1776, to June 30, 1880*, in *Report on Valuation, Taxation, and Public Indebtedness in the United States, as Returned at the Tenth Census (June 1, 1880)* (Washington, DC: Government Printing Office, 1884), 446–54; Report of the Secretary of the Treasury for the Year Ending June 30, 1862, Sen. Ex. Doc. 1, 37th Cong., 3d sess., 37; Report of the Secretary of the Treasury on the State of the Finances for the Year Ending June 30, 1863, , H.R. Ex. Doc. 3, 38th Cong., 1st sess., 34–35, 43, 241.

Note: Figures for loan income are issues minus redemptions. No quarterly breakdown of internal revenue is available for fiscal year 1863. There is a statement for the first quarter and one for the first two quarters. No quarterly breakdown of miscellaneous revenue is available for fiscal years 1862 and 1863. Total figure for these year are $0.93 million and $3.04 million.

pable machine, without real power of its own, but standing in the path of those who would exercise real power."³¹

These sweeping judgments, typical of the period's contempt for republican governments in Britain, were made around the time when Lincoln had signed a major new tax bill into law and are thus suggestive also of the degree of ignorance of American affairs in the editorial office of the *Economist*. Congressmen knew well that Europeans thought their government, like other popular republics, weak and likely to fold in a crisis. When Justin Morrill introduced his tax bill in the House, he did so with a challenge to the Old World. "Observers living under other forms of government, proclaim that our weak point is incapacity for taxation, and our securities therefore have no solidity abroad," he said. "Representative democracy is now on trial. Let us see to it that the Republic suffers no shame at our hands." In fact, the tax bill was part of a plan that was just as orthodox as any offered by America's European critics. In future, at least $200 million of the money spent on the war would be raised from taxation every year. An equal amount would be raised from the sale of bonds. This, Sherman said in the Senate, amounted to a proper "financial system in this country." As the lawmakers of the Thirty-Seventh Congress made clear, the greenbacks did not signify a return to the financial methods that had brought such disaster in the War of Independence but a temporary respite that would buy the time necessary to create a "financial system" based on taxation and the sale of long-term war bonds.³²

III

The legal-tender act authorized the Treasury to sell up to $500 million in 5-20 bonds. These could be bought at par for US notes but earned interest in coin. With currency depreciation, the return on investments increased, making the notes more attractive to investors. Initially there was little interest in converting greenbacks to bonds, however, and by early December 1862 no more than $24 million had been sold. Chase was also pessimistic about future sales and thought no more than $35 million in bonds would be sold before the end of the fiscal year on June 30, 1863. Chase had sounded the market in search of takers for another $50 million loan. The response had been cool, and the secretary was led to believe that $97 to $98 was the best price that could be had for a $100 bond. On a $50 million loan this equaled a loss of $1 million to $1.5 million. Current expenditures meant that Chase would have to negotiate a $50 million loan every other month, and as long as the war continued, the rate of each successive loan was destined to deteriorate. The only alternative to such sales was selling bonds to the public in the manner of the 7-30 "popular loan" of the previous fall. In October Chase turned to the government's most successful loan agent, the Philadelphia-based private banker Jay Cooke. The Treasury needed conversions from greenbacks to bonds to rise to $1 million per day. "Can this be done?" Chase asked Cooke. "Are you willing to undertake it?"[33]

Like Chase's, Cooke's father was a New England man transplanted to Ohio, and the two families had close personal and political ties. But it was not family friendship but Cooke's demonstrated record as a successful broker of government bonds that led Chase to approach him. Cooke's experience went all the way back to the 1840s, when he had worked for E. W. Clark & Co., a broker that had sold both Republic of Texas and Mexican War bonds. In the summer of 1861, Cooke became the agent for a $3 million Commonwealth of Pennsylvania loan. He sold it at par despite widespread belief that the commonwealth's tarnished reputation warranted a price of no more than seventy-five cents on the dollar. In light of what was to come, it was a modest operation, but Cooke now for the first time employed methods that would turn the sale of 5-20 bonds and 7-30 notes into such remarkable successes: he marketed the bonds widely, reaching rural areas and new social groups; he used the press extensively; and he appealed to the people's patriotism as well as their pocketbooks. The banker also gained further experience and boosted his reputation by selling Chase's 7-30 Treasury notes in the fall of 1861 as one of 148 specially appointed loan agents. Cooke's results were impressive. Of the $25 million sold by non-Treasury personnel, his share was $5.2 million, and this made him the most successful agent by far. He was both more energetic and more innovative than other agents. Whereas the Treasury expected agents to spend $150 on advertising, Cooke spent twenty times that sum. The following year he continued as "Agent for Conversions into 5-20s," and according to Chase, he "succeeded better than any other Officer of the Government." The sums involved remained relatively small, however. By late October, Cooke had sold around $3 million in 5-20 bonds.[34]

When Chase asked Cooke to take charge of the 5-20 campaign in October 1862, the banker eagerly accepted the chance to serve his country in a role he saw as similar to that of Robert Morris during the struggle for independence. Nevertheless, it took about five months from Cooke's appointment until the yield from bond sales began to reach the Treasury. There were several reasons for this delay. Cooke needed time to set up his sales organization, which would come to employ some twenty-five hundred subagents nationwide. New legislation in the winter of 1863 created incentives for investors. In March the right to convert greenbacks to bonds at par was limited to July 1. In January and March Congress also authorized further emissions of $150 million in US notes. Despite fear of depreciation, the greenbacks had been popular, and the hoarding of notes had made them scarce. When more notes became available, investors found it easier to acquire the money needed to buy bonds. The legal-tender act therefore led to the "restoration from depression and doubt of all governmental securities, to active demand and full credit." More greenbacks also meant that the notes depreciated further in value relative to gold. By March 1863, one gold dollar cost $1.50 in notes, and the current yield on a nominal 6 percent bond was therefore 9 percent. With compound interest, and assuming that the government would repay the bond in specie, the value of an investment of one dollar in gold would more than double in five years.[35]

Bond sales picked up in the second quarter of 1863 and then rose rapidly. In his report from December that year Chase noted that "success quite beyond anticipation crowned the efforts of the Secretary to distribute the five-twenty loan in all parts of the country." On January 21, 1864, the loan closed after being oversubscribed by $11 million. Of the total $511 million sold, Cooke and his agents were responsible for the sale of $362 million. The balance was sold by the subtreasuries, whose personnel benefited from Cooke's energetic sales campaign. As tables 6.2 and 6.3 show, bonds replaced greenbacks as the mainstay of war finance from the spring of 1863. Once again the Treasury was flush. By mid-May there was not "a single unsatisfied requisition from the Naval, Military, or Civil Service." A European loan, which had only recently seemed desirable, was no longer wanted. The bonds had been distributed widely, and the Treasury secretary believed that the "history of the world may be searched in vain for a parallel case of popular financial support to a national government." He felt reassured about the future and was intent on continuing the productive partnership with Cooke.[36]

A couple of blunders soon dimmed future prospects. Accused of favoritism, Chase terminated the contract with Cooke and tried to sell bonds directly through the Treasury. He also reduced the interest rate on the bonds to 5 percent, which caused the greenbacks to depreciate. Meanwhile the war had stalled, and peace seemed distant. These factors combined to make the spring and summer of 1864 a trying time for the Treasury. After a quarrel with the president over a Treasury appointment in late June, Chase resigned and was replaced by William Fessenden, the chairman of the Senate Finance Committee. Although Chase advised his successor to resume the services of Cooke, it was not until January 28, 1865, that Fessenden approached the financier.[37]

TABLE 6.3. Major sources of government revenue July 1, 1863, to December 31, 1864, by quarter ($ million)

Revenue source	1863		1864			
	July–Sept.	Oct.–Dec.	Jan.–Mar.	Apr.–June	July–Sept.	Oct.–Dec.
US notes and temporary loans						
Old demand notes	25.9	—	-27.7	-16.2	-10.8	-1.6
Legal-tender notes	15.1	48.4	-8.5	-11.2	2.3	-0.8
Treasury deposits	5.5	-67.8	7.8	26.5	-25.3	9.2
Certificates of indebtedness	2.5	-24.7	-5.2	31.5	70.3	-4.6
Fractional currency	-1.3	-1.3	2.0	3.3	-2.5	-0.6
Total	47.7	-45.4	-32.3	33.9	-72.3	1.6
Long-term bonds and Treasury notes						
7-30 Treasury notes, 1861	—	—	-0.7	—	-106.3	-2.8
5-20 bonds	84.6	161.5	75.5	—	—	—
10-40 bonds, 1863	—	—	—	42.1	31.8	0.2
10-40 bonds, 1864	—	—	—	73.3	6.9	36.5
5-20 bonds, 1864	—	—	—	—	—	77.1
Treasury notes, 1863	11.7	34.6	118.9	26.8	-59.0	-28.5
Compound interest notes	—	—	—	15.0	87.3	19.8
7-30 Treasury notes, 1864	—	—	—	—	56.5	54.4
Total	96.3	196.1.8	193.7	157.2.4	17.2	159.5
Taxation						
Customs	22.6	23.2	27.4	29.1	19.3	15.1
Internal revenue	17.6	27.3	27.7	37.2	46.6	55.1
Miscellaneous	0.6	1.9	12.5	32.4	9.0	9.3
Total	40.8	52.4	67.6	86.9	74.9	79.5

Source: Rafael A. Bayley, History of the National Loans of the United States from July 4, 1776, to June 30, 1880, in Report on Valuation, Taxation, and Public Indebtedness in the United States, as Returned at the Tenth Census (June 1, 1880) (Washington, DC: Government Printing Office, 1884), 446–60; Report of the Secretary of the Treasury on the State of the Finances for the Year Ending June 30, 1864, H.R. Ex. Doc. 3, 38th Cong., 2nd sess., 31; Report of the Secretary of the Treasury on the State of the Finances for the Year 1865, H.R. Ex. Doc. 3, 39th Cong., 1st sess., 43.

The timing was fortuitous. In December, Sherman had captured Savannah, and Thomas had destroyed Hood's army at Nashville. Union victory now seemed certain, and confidence in the government and its securities returned. With his usual skill and energy, Cooke took charge of what would become the war's greatest bond sale in the winter of 1865. Since the previous summer Fessenden had sold 7-30 Treasury notes through the Treasury and the nation's banks. These notes were three-year securities that could be converted into 5-20 bonds on maturity. In contrast to the 5-20s, interest was paid in currency rather than coin, a consequence of the fact that interest charges on the public debt were getting dangerously close to the government's specie income from customs duties. Sales had been considerable, netting around $1.5 million per day, but Cooke would boost sales far beyond that figure.[38]

Despite criticism from some of his competitors, Cooke knew that he now had a reputation for working magic in the securities market, and he spread the word of his appointment widely. The press greeted Fessenden's decision with relief. The *Washington Daily Chronicle* noted that in appointing Cooke the Treasury had reverted to "its original policy": "Individual enterprise is found more effective than Government machinery." Newspaper editors went out of their way to support the campaign and ensure that it would become a resounding success. To bring the war to a close, the government needed not only soldiers but money to feed and clothe its troops, one Philadelphia editor wrote. "As we thus contribute, we give force and power at home and command respect and confidence abroad; and, since money is the great lever that moves the world, its contribution in a time like this reflects in the most marked degree the patriotism and devotion of the citizens for the land of his love. Let us rally then for the 'seven-thirties' and absorb the loan at once."[39]

Within a few weeks of his appointment Cooke doubled sales, and by the last week of February he sold $5 million a day. When the loan closed on July 26, $830 million had been issued. The following day the *Washington Daily Chronicle* wrote that "yesterday the last of the $830,000,000 loan authorized by the last Congress was taken by the people—all within the current year—a fact unparalleled in the financial history of the world. Among all the wonderful achievements which the loyal people have accomplished during the last four years in the science of war on land and sea . . . there have been effected no such remarkable results as have grown out of our financial struggle."[40]

Together the 5-20s and the 7-30s raised $1.3 billion for the Treasury. In the context of the nation's history of war finance, this was an enormous achievement. Marketing hundreds of millions of bonds posed both a logistic and a pedagogic challenge. There were no nationwide institutions dedicated to the sale of government securities, and there was limited knowledge about war bonds among the general population. Cooke addressed the logistical problem of bond sales by recruiting bankers, insurance men, brokers, and community leaders in a nationwide network of subagents. He also accepted subscriptions by mail. Traveling agents and government postmasters advertised the loan in the more isolated parts of the Union. In the cities, night offices took subscriptions from people who could not visit banks during the day. Advertisements were nailed to trees, posted in tramways, distributed on trains, and left in public places. Some of the rich material used in the campaign is still preserved among the Jay Cooke papers at the Historical Society of Pennsylvania. Here can be found printed forms used daily to communicate sales figures to the Associated Press; instructions for traveling agents and 7-30 agents; printed leaflets of "Interesting Questions and Answers" about the 5-20 bonds in English and, curiously, in French; a highly popular and much reprinted broadside entitled "Seven-Thirty Facts and Figures"; the telegraph key used to relay bond orders to Cooke's South Third Street office in Philadelphia from across the country; and a cardboard sign to be put up in the shop windows of subagents announcing that 7-30 Treasury notes were "for sale here." More than anything else, the key to Cooke's success was his active use of the press. He advertised the government loans in newspapers all across the land and used his patronage to persuade editors to print material and editorials promoting his bond drives.[41]

There was nothing subtle about Cooke's use of the press. The advertising agent Peasle & Co. had been hired by Cooke to place advertisements for the 7-30 loan. The firm accompanied requests for advertising space with a printed letter addressed "To the Editor" and marked "private and confidential." The letter "respectfully suggest[ed]" that the newspapers "call Editorial attention to Mr. Cooke's appointment as General Subscription Agent" and asked them to keep the loan "prominently before the public." The advertising agent also included "a brief summary of *facts*, and beg[ged] that you will present them to your readers with such improvements as may occur to you in your better editorial style." The frequent reprinting of the article "Facts About the 7-30s—The Advantages they Offer" is testimony to the success of the strategy. In similar manner Cooke supplied the press with information and opinions about the government loans and thereby made sure that the nation's newspapers spoke with one voice.[42]

Many if not most Americans knew little about the securities market in general and war bonds in particular in the 1860s. The press printed humorous stories about "German Hans" asking loan agents "how much Seven-Tirty will you gif me for vun hunerd thalers?" and about "Patrick," an Irishman, who was disappointed to find that his fifty dollars in greenbacks would only buy him a fifty-dollar bond. "Troth, I thought I could get it chaper." Such anecdotes show awareness that Americans, with or without amusing accents, found government bonds something of a mystery. In one of his most reprinted newspaper items, Cooke engaged in a fictive correspondence with a patriotic but suspicious farmer from Berks County, Pennsylvania. Their exchange of questions and answers dealt with practical matters such as how to buy bonds, the interest paid, and the security offered by the government, all in plain language free of technical jargon. Although the appeal to patriotism is a prominent feature of Cooke's campaigns, he was always careful to stress that war bonds were both a safe and a profitable investment. Depreciation meant that the true interest rate was high. The proscription against local and state taxation of federal securities meant that the income they generated was tax free. Finally, the pledge of the government to pay interest and principal meant that government bonds were the safest possible investment: "The investment is certainly the best that an American citizen can make for it is endowed by the whole credit of the nation, and if the United States is not 'good,'—what bank, what corporation is good?"[43]

Cooke's marketing machine worked hard to make a nation out of a federal union of republics. In carefully crafted newspapers reports he declared his preference for the small investors who retained their bonds and "weave themselves into the very life and interests of the government." Brandishing a fistful of subscription telegrams, Cooke on another occasion exclaimed: "I hold in this fist the guarantee of permanent union between the east and west and the center and the extremes." His was a democratic version of Alexander Hamilton's alleged attempt to use the Revolutionary debt to tie the interests of bondholders to the fate of the national government. Selling bonds to a black regiment, Cooke noted that "it is not altogether a white man's war, is it? I am glad to have black soldiers take the government loan. The subscription should run like a cord through the whole country, tying it together, making one interest, removing prejudices and solidifying the nation." A Philadelphia newspaper called it a "sublime" spectacle when "men of all classes, all polities, all professions, unite in the determination to make the Government strong with the wealth of a nation. The earnest, hard working Cabinet officer, the earnest hard working mechanic stand side by side in their firm devotion to the country. The millionaire invests his hundreds of thousands, the laboring man his fifty to hundred dollars." The

New York Times reported that "the loyal masses are freely and wisely investing the funds of their industry" in government securities and the New York Tribune reported that "all sorts of people—all varieties of race and character" gathered to subscribe at the 7-30 night offices, also known as "The Working Men's Savings Bank." Of the 157 buyers present at a Bleecker Street office one July night,

> 27 were shop-keepers; 19 were machinists, boiler-makers, foundry men, etc. all workers in iron; 17 returned soldiers and sailors; 12 clerks and store-tenders; 10 saloon-keepers; nine steamboat men, engineers, etc.; five bartenders; four hotel servants; five hatters; four saddlers; four car-drivers; two cabmen; two farmers; three stall-keepers; five shoemakers; four tailors; five bookbinders; six store and working women; six barbers; four cigarmakers; one was a telegrapher; one an actor; one a journalist; one a peddler. Of this congregation 10 were colored men; two were boys; 13 were Irishmen; 16 Germans, and Portuguese, Chinese, and one Moor, were part of the curiosity of nationality. These facts give only a glimpse of a world-wide democratic phase of the 7-30.[44]

Such lists presented the image of a patriotic people coming out in force in support of their government. An early advertisement spoke of the people's "solemn duty to perform to your Government and to posterity!" and one of the most popular broadsheets for the 7-30 loan carried the slogan "Your Sons and your Money on your Country's altar." Because money was "the great power in war," it followed that "he who contributes his money to aid his country in its hour of danger evince as much patriotism as he who marches in the battlefield." The contribution of service and savings were portrayed as the expression of the same patriotic sentiment, and their connection was frequently underlined by the use of martial terms and metaphors to describe the sales campaign. "All day long that line of citizen soldiery constantly forming in the rear as it melted away in the front marched up single file to do the nation service" by investing in war bonds, one 1865 report from Jay Cooke's office read. Others noted that money was just as important as manpower to the outcome of the war. In 1861, the Philadelphia Inquirer compared eight hundred subscribers to a regiment of infantry: "Their charge of money bags is quite as efficient as a charge of bayonets."[45]

In addition to appeals to patriotism and self-interest as well as practical advice on how and why to invest in government bonds, Cooke also skillfully kept up the momentum of his campaigns by the daily publication of bond sales. Sales reports drove home the message that subscribers to the loans came from all walks of life and all corners of the Union. They also reminded potential investors that the bonds would eventually sell out and that procrastinators might miss out on a golden opportunity. Typically, reports followed the preprinted form handed to the Associated Press at the end of each day of sales and then relayed to the rest of the nation by telegraph. Total subscriptions along with the largest single eastern and western subscription were listed, as were the "numbers of individual subscriptions by working men and women" and the number of fifty- and one-hundred-dollar subscriptions. In May 1865, when the 7-30 campaign reached its peak, record sales figures were announced in bold type: "$15,165,300! Something Wonderful in National Finance" on May 10 was followed three days later by "$13,762,300! Another Great Day for the Popular Loan." The widespread knowledge about and interest in Cooke's campaign is revealed in the *New York Times*'s use of Cooke's telegraph key in its headline "One Banking House Alone Sends for Five Choctaws." "Choctaw," as the public must have known, was code for one million dollars, just as "Gipsy" meant half a million and "Belle" $1,000.[46]

"In his department," the *New York Times* remarked of Cooke toward the close of the 7-30 campaign, "he has been as useful to the country as Grant on the land, or Farragut on the sea." Certainly no one knew better the role of money to modern warfare than Cooke, and his associates and the financier took pride in his contribution to Union victory. When news of the fall of Richmond reached Washington, Cooke's branch office in the city displayed three large inscriptions on the building. Over the two doors were signs saying "5-20" and "7-30," and in between was a larger banner bearing the words

> The Bravery of Our Army
> The Valor of Our Navy
> Sustained by Our Treasury
> upon the Faith and
> Substance of
> A Patriotic People.[47]

IV

The London journal the *Economist* had accused American policy makers of not understanding that the "critical element of the soundness or unsoundness of finance is *taxation*." Nothing could be further from the truth. Ever since the 1790s, the national government had taken care to pay interest to bondholders punctually from the proceeds from customs duties, thereby keeping the public credit inviolate. When the Civil War broke out, the initial plan had been to borrow to pay for the war effort but to tax to pay for the interest on the war loans. Heavy borrowing meant that even this plan, had it been adhered to, would have required new fiscal legislation. But the crisis caused by specie suspension in late 1861 forced both the Treasury and Congress to accept that in the long term the funding of the war would only be sustainable if a substantial share of the direct costs of the war were paid for by taxation. Reforming the fiscal system took time, but in the last year of the war fiscal revenue accounted for around a quarter of total government income. And once the Civil War was over, a productive revenue system would prove instrumental to the restructuring of the war debt.[48]

Congress rather than the Treasury secretary took the lead in fiscal legislation. The special session of the Thirty-Seventh Congress increased customs duties, imposed an income tax, and introduced a direct tax apportioned among the states. Much later the federal income tax would become controversial, but when it was first introduced in 1861 as an "income duty," there was little opposition despite the fact that it had scant constitutional support and interfered with the privacy of the citizens. The lack of protests over the income tax reflects the fact that congressmen were much less concerned with the rights of individuals than with the rights of states. This priority also left its mark on the direct tax, which was designed to be assessed and collected by the states without involvement from the national government, thus representing a step back from direct rule by the national government in fiscal matters. The direct tax was no success, however. The states could offset their spending on the war effort against their quota payments to the Treasury, and they paid no more than $5 million to the Treasury throughout the war.[49]

In his annual report for 1862, the Treasury secretary asked for a total tax revenue of $87 million. Faced with the slump in the securities market that followed after specie suspension, the Ways and Means Committee chose to go considerably further than the Treasury secretary. On January 15, Erastus Corning introduced a resolution calling for internal taxes that together with customs would secure an annual revenue of $150 million "in order to pay the ordinary expenses of the Government, the interest on the national loans, and have an ample sinking fund for the ultimate liquidation of the public debt." It was a statement of intent meant to reassure public creditors that the government would have the money to both service its debt and destroy the Confederacy. Yet the committee realized that a major tax reform would mean entering uncharted territory and that a bill could not be brought in on the spur of the moment.[50]

Two months later Justin Morrill introduced H.R. 312, which heralded the demise of the fiscal regime created by the Impost and Tonnage Acts of the First Congress in 1789. Quite fittingly Morrill presented the bill as the end of America's age of innocence. The southern rebellion had driven the nation "from our untaxed garden," and the size of the war debt ensured that no return was possible. New needs required that federal taxation expand beyond the customary impost. But with a tradition of minimal fiscal imposition, the past offered legislators little guidance. With a quote from Milton's *Paradise Lost,* Morrill noted that like Adam exiled from the Garden of Eden, Congress now had "all the world before us where to choose." Nevertheless, H.R. 312 was significantly shaped by established fiscal principles. The new system would tax manufactures by means of excises and leave agriculture alone by avoiding property taxes. Rather than impose high duties on a few items, like Britain did, the Ways and Means Committee opted for low duties on a wide range of manufactures. The exception to this rule was alcohol, but Morrill maintained that even a high tax would make it "possible for any man or brute to get drunk in our land on cheaper terms than in any other I know of." The result of the committee's labors was a tax bill running hundreds of pages that introduced excises on virtually all manufactured items and on receipts of railroads, steamships, toll bridges, and advertisements and a long list of stamp duties on financial transactions, telegrams, and products such as playing cards and medicines. The bill also increased the income tax and introduced an inheritance tax. As the *New York Times* pithily remarked, "Nearly every class will probably find something to complain of."[51]

In contrast to Chase's implementation of the direct tax, the Ways and Means Committee proposed a return to direct fiscal administration and came down strongly in favor of federal assessment and collection of internal taxes. "In this emergency," Morrill said, "we cannot afford to return to the pusillanimity of the old Confederation, and request the States to make their contributions, and shiver in the wind if any should fail to do so, or declare war upon them for delinquency." The committee also adhered to tradition by recognizing the fiscal needs of the states. Despite the expansion of federal taxation, the ambition to separate the fiscal spheres of the Union and the states remained. Property, principally land, was left alone because the "orbit of the United States and the States must be different and not conflicting." Although many states levied excises, the Ways and Means Committee imposed federal duties on "new objects of taxation" and items that could bear double taxation, such as alcohol. A final nod to tradition was the attempt to distribute the incidence of taxation equally among the members of the Union. This was easier said than done, however, as "what could be easily sustained in one quarter of the country might sink another in hopeless dishonor and repudiation."[52]

The founders of the Union had often argued that unlimited powers of taxation were needed to defend the nation against foreign aggression and domestic insurrection, and congressmen now quoted from *The Federalist* to bring this point home. Nevertheless, heavy taxes imposed to service a perpetual public debt had always been viewed as a danger to a republican system of government in America. H.R. 312 would make the United States resemble the European nations it had consciously distanced itself from in the past. As a result of the war, the government's expenses were now on par with "those of a first-class Power." In 1820, in a review of Adam Seybert's *Statistical Annals of the United States of America*, the cleric, man of letters, and cofounder of the *Edinburgh Review* Sydney Smith had warned of the consequences that were sure to follow if the United States tried to emulate the Old World. Smith's humorous account of Britain's fiscal system became a classic all over the Anglophone world. Four decades later it came instantly to the mind of commentators on the American tax bill on both sides of the Atlantic:

> We can inform Jonathan what are the inevitable consequences of being too fond of glory;—Taxes upon every article which enters into the mouth, or covers the back, or is placed under the foot—taxes upon everything which it is pleasant to see, hear, feel, smell, or taste—taxes upon warmth, light, and locomotion—taxes on everything on earth, and the waters under the earth—on everything that comes from abroad, or is grown at home—taxes on the raw material—taxes on every fresh value that is added to it by the industry of man—taxes on the sauce which pampers a man's appetite, and the drug that restores him to health—on the ermine which decorates the judge, and the rope which hangs the criminal—on the poor man's salt, and the rich man's spice—on the brass nails of the coffin, and the ribands of the bride—at bed or board, couchant or levant, we must pay.—The schoolboy whips his taxed top—the beardless youth manages his taxed horse, with a taxed bridle, on a taxed road:—and the dying Englishman, pouring his medicine, which has paid 7 per cent., into a spoon that has paid 15 per cent.—flings himself back upon his chintz bed, which has paid 22 per cent.—and expires in the arms of an apothecary who has paid a license of a hundred pounds for the privilege of putting him to death. His whole property is then immediately taxed from 2 to 10 per cent. Besides the probate, large fees are

demanded for burying him in the chancel; his virtues are handed over to posterity on taxed marble; and then he is gathered to his father—to be taxed no more.[53]

As a description of the new tax bill it was not far off the mark, and John Law, who quoted it in the House of Representatives, remarked that "it does appear to me that we are getting along pretty well towards that state." What had taken well over a century to develop in Britain happened overnight in the United States. Never before, commented the *Economist*, had a government told its people: "Hitherto all your industry has been free; now all of it shall be fettered. Hitherto all your enjoyments have been unburdened; now all of them shall be hampered. Hitherto any one might choose what calling he liked; now he shall ask a license for every pursuit and trade, and pay for it. Hitherto you have been taxed on nothing; now you shall be taxed on everything." The American press had come to a similar conclusion. "We are called upon, in a day, to provide a revenue which, with other nations has been the work of generations, if not centuries," the *New York Times* remarked.[54]

Protests against such a sweeping reform were inevitable. And given the federal structure of the United States, it was equally inevitable that protests would revolve around state interests. "We are not a homogenous people in any sense of the word," William Fessenden admitted. "Our territory is very broad. The pursuits in which we are interested are exceedingly diverse." It was next to impossible, therefore, to frame legislation "as to prevent marked inequalities, and to operate in such a manner as to be satisfactory to the whole people." Fessenden could only urge congressmen "to look with an eye single to the whole country, and to divest themselves so far as possible of local feelings and local interests." Like previous debates about fiscal measures, the debate over H.R. 312 would pit a states' rights idiom against Unionist sentiment. Even so, the debates in Congress are noteworthy most of all for the willingness of the lawmakers to support the war.[55]

A general support for the war did not stop representatives from disagreeing about specific taxes. Their deeply ingrained instinct to shift the burdens of taxation away from their own constituencies influenced the debate as always. The duty on alcohol, for instance, drew resistance from representatives of corn-producing areas. At twenty cents per gallon, the tax amounted to 100 percent of the value of distilled spirits. Because the principal ingredient was corn produced in the Midwest, the tax on alcohol fell disproportionally on the production of one region. To William Kellogg of Illinois the whisky tax meant that corn was taxed more than "any other production of the country," and he asked for a reduction of five cents. An Ohio Democrat went further by suggesting the substitution of a 10 percent ad valorem duty that would have slashed nine-tenths of the tax. Such demands were met by counterproposals for an increase of the duty to fifty cents or a dollar per gallon. It surprised nobody that representatives from dry states, who obviously had little to lose from the tax, were prominent in the counterattack. But as Morrill pointed out, alcohol already paid thirty to forty times more than most other products. The balance between a productive revenue system and the specific interests of the Midwest therefore called for a relatively moderate tax. "The West is largely engaged in the raising of corn, and if there be any addition to this tax, then we will cripple to some extent the ordinary business of the agriculturalists of that region." In the end, all amendments were rejected and the duty was left to stand.[56]

Attempts to add duties on iron and coal met with the same fate. These were valuable raw materials produced almost exclusively in Pennsylvania. The Ways and Means Committee had left them untaxed on the principle that manufactured items rather than raw material should bear the new duties. But Indiana's John Law wished to tax pig iron because "we are to be taxed to death in the West, and I want to provide, if I can, that other sections of the country shall also bear a proportion of the burdens of the Government." When his amendment was voted down, another midwestern congressmen immediately proposed a duty on coal, which caused Pennsylvania representatives to rally to the defense of their commonwealth. A coal duty was unfair on Pennsylvania as long as no one contemplated "to tax wheat, corn, or wood." Coal was also a "necessary" of life, and a tax on coal would in practice be "a tax on the poor." Such arguments had a long pedigree. But the most interesting rebuttal came from William Davis, who argued that coal and iron were "sources of power." There did not exist a people "that has prospered and grown to power and consideration among the nations of the earth who ever dreamed of levying a tax upon the foundations on which their productive industry was based," Davis claimed. Steam power multiplied the productive capacity of a people far beyond population numbers, and in Britain it allowed a hundred thousand workers to do the work of six hundred million. For this reason Britain viewed coal and iron as "the right and left hands of her domination" and left these products untaxed. Davis was not interested in justice for Pennsylvania but in the prosperity and international standing of the United States. This required leaving coal well alone as "the source of national prosperity and national independence and power." Whether or not his argument had any effect, the House of Representatives voted against the amendment.[57]

It took almost six months before the original resolution to increase the tax revenue to $150 million became law on July 1, 1862. Two weeks later followed a general increase of customs duties. Imports were now taxed on average 37 percent. It was a direct consequence of the new excise duties on American manufactures, which would make it difficult for domestic producers to compete with imported goods. Needless to say, if domestic industries folded, the new tax regime would be a failure. Initially it seemed to be one anyway. Rather than the estimated income of $85.5 million, the tax raised no more than $37.6 million. But it took time to build an internal revenue service, and the government could at least take heart from the fact that there had been virtually no opposition to the new taxes. According to the commissioner of internal revenue, the duties had not "been merely endured, but welcomed by the people in a manner, it is believed, elsewhere unparalleled." And if the tax law had not yet delivered on its promises, it had raised enough money "to improve largely the credit of the government, and to demonstrate the immense resources which it possesses yet untouched in the loyalty and growing wealth of the people." When the Thirty-Seventh Congress met for its final session in December 1862, the duties had not been in place long enough to determine their effectiveness. Chase therefore refrained from recommending further fiscal legislation. This task would be left to the next Congress.[58]

By December 1863 the internal revenue had started to contribute substantial income although it again fell short of the estimates. In his final annual report, Chase pressed Congress to increase the tax revenue further. He foresaw no problems negotiating loans—the successful 5-20 campaign was still ongoing—but it was "an object of patriotic solicitude" to keep down the public debt. Somewhat belatedly he also declared that it was time to abandon the Gallatin plan that had guided his early policy. A prolonged and expensive war required a different approach to war finance. In late February 1864, Chase for the first time expressed an expectation that taxes should finance "at least one half of our whole expenses." When the sale of 5 percent 10-40 bonds failed in the spring, Chase became more insistent. By mid-May he had concluded that "we must pay as we go or very nearly that; if we want to maintain credit at its highest point." He grew increasingly critical of Congress's tardiness and failure to grasp that tax income had to be boosted to prevent the debt from reaching unsustainable levels. In his very last letter to Lincoln as Treasury secretary, written the day after his offer of resignation, Chase urged the president to pressure congressmen to adopt more stringent measures than the pending tax bill, which would fall $100 million short of Treasury needs. Instead Lincoln fired Chase and signed the bill. A fortnight into his retirement, Chase had mellowed somewhat. Although the legislation "was not adequate to the support of the highest degree of credit" it could always be improved in the next session. At least it "afforded ground on which an appeal might be made with probable success for the loans necessary for the service until next winter."[59]

The revenue act of 1864 built on the act of 1862 by increasing most rates. Duties on manufactures were doubled and the income tax considerably increased. The duties on alcohol and tobacco, the items that would form the backbone of the internal revenue system in the decades after the war, saw the greatest increase. The tax on cigars was quadrupled, and the duty on distilled alcohol was increased to 60 cents per gallon by a separate act in March and to $1.50 by the June 30 act. The following March it reached $2.00 per gallon. This rate amounted to 1,000 percent of the production cost, which was very close to the rate in Britain.[60]

As can be seen in tables 6.3 and 6.4, the income from internal revenue rose steadily from the fall of 1863. The Treasury had estimated an income of $60 million for the nine months between October 1 and June 30, but actual income exceeded that sum by $32 million. In fiscal year 1865, the final year of the war, the income continued to grow, reaching a total of $209 million. In the same period customs duties generated no more than $85 million. This development represented a fundamental shift in the structure of American taxation. It also represented a shift in war finance. In the final year of the Civil War taxes contributed close of 28 percent to overall government income (see figure 6.1). Given the inexperience of internal taxation and the role of popular protests against central government impositions at the founding of the nation, it was a significant achievement to build a highly productive revenue system so rapidly and with so little friction. Among the reasons for the success were that the new duties targeted manufacturers rather than farmers and that the government relied on indirect taxes in the form of excise duties rather than direct taxes on land. There was an obvious parallel between the excise duty that fell on the manufacturer and the customs duty that fell on the merchant. Collection was made easier and protests less likely when the taxman could turn to businessmen with ready access to money and credit instead of going door to door throughout the country. Another reason behind the success was that the war justified extraordinary measures. Impositions considered illegitimate or dangerous in ordinary times became acceptable during a war for national existence. Despite their republican convictions, most Americans accepted that high taxes, at least temporarily, were a price worth paying for the preservation of their federal union.

TABLE 6.4. Major sources of government revenue January 1, 1865, to June 30, 1866, by quarter ($ million)

Revenue source	1865 Jan.–Mar.	1865 Apr.–June	1865 July–Sept.	1865 Oct.–Dec.	1866 Jan.–Mar.	1866 Apr.–June
	US notes and temporary loans					
Old demand notes	-0.4	-0.3	-0.2	-0.1	—	—
7-30 Treasury notes, 1861	—	-29.3	-0.1	-0.1	-0.1	-0.5
Legal-tender notes	-0.8	-1.6	-4.1	-1.3	-3.4	-21.6
Treasury deposits	-10.9	39.9	16.3	-5.2	14.2	-4.5
Certificates of indebtedness	-53.2	-56.3	-54.0	-5.3	4.6	-34.5
Fractional currency	0.1	1.2	1.0	-0.5	2.3	-1.1
Total	-65.2	-46.4	-41.1	-12.5	17.6	-62.2
	Long-term bonds and Treasury notes					
7-30 Treasury notes, 1861	—	-29.3	-0.1	-0.1	-0.1	-0.5
5-20 bonds, 1862	—	—	4.0	—	—	—
10-40 bonds, 1863	—	0.1	0.1	—	—	—
10-40 bonds, 1864	56.2	—	—	0.2	-1.6	—
5-20 bonds, 1864	—	13.6	9.2	—	3.7	0.2
Treasury notes, 1863	-15.1	-54.6	-12.0	-24.0	—	-5.5
Compound interest notes	5.7	65.9	24.3	-36.2	-9.6	-13.0
Coin certificates	—	—	—	18.7	-8.0	—
7-30 Treasury notes	185.1	375.2	158.1	0.4	—	-16.2
5-20 bonds, 1865	—	—	—	58.3	2.9	47.9
Total	231.9	370.9	183.6	17.3	-12.7	12.9
	Taxation					
Customs	20.5	30.0	47.0	39.2	46.6	46.2
Internal revenue	65.2	42.5	96.6	82.6	66.2	63.9
Miscellaneous	4.1	10.5	18.8	17.9	11.7	18.6
Total	89.8	83.0	162.4	139.7	124.5	128.7

Source: Rafael A. Bayley, *History of the National Loans of the United States from July 4, 1776, to June 30, 1880*, in *Report on Valuation, Taxation, and Public Indebtedness in the United States, as Returned at the Tenth Census (June 1, 1880)* (Washington, DC: Government Printing Office, 1884), 446–61; Report of the Secretary of the Treasury on the State of the Finances for the Year 1865, H.R. Ex. Doc. 3, 39th Cong., 1st sess., 43; Report of the Secretary of the Treasury on the State of the Finances for the Year 1866, H.R. Ex. Doc. 4, 39th Cong., 2d sess., 31.

If a productive revenue system was instrumental in upholding the government's credit and in contributing to the war effort, it was no less important to the public finances in the postwar period. After the War of Independence, it took several years of political turbulence and governmental reforms before the new national government could begin to put the public debt in order. In 1865, by contrast, Congress and the Treasury could rely on both well-established practices of debt management and very substantial tax returns. But the situation was nonetheless new. "Until a few years ago, we were the most lightly taxed nation on earth," one representative of the Thirty-Ninth Congress said. "Now we are amongst the most heavily burdened of them all." The public debt, too, had reached new proportions. At its peak on September 1, 1865, it stood at $2,846,000,000. This was more than twenty-two times the size of the public debt after the War of 1812, its previous high point.[61]

In the months after Appomattox, the future of the debt began to be debated in earnest. Schemes to liquidate the debt by subscription were aired, but others thought repayment ought to be postponed. As the nation grew in wealth and population, the burden of the public debt would become lighter. A final liquidation date as distant as the 1950s was mentioned. The most controversial intervention in this debate was a pamphlet written by Samuel Wilkeson but endorsed by Jay Cooke. *How Our National Debt May Be a National Blessing* advanced the claim that the national debt represented an addition of wealth to the nation. Government bonds were as good as cash capital, and "to extinguish this capital and lose this wealth would be an inconceivably great national misfortune." Wilkeson's tract was widely reprinted but found few followers. The overwhelmingly hostile response made it clear that Cooke had made a major mistake in backing Wilkeson, and it spurred Peasle & Co. to attempt damage limitation. The *New York Herald* in particular engaged in a vicious attack on Cooke, who was called "a financial charlatan, a perfect quack." Wilkeson got off more easily, being dismissed as "some literary Bohemian" hardly worth taking seriously. The idea that "our national debt, made permanent and rightly managed, will be a national blessing" was clearly a nonstarter in 1865. Everyone except Wilkeson accepted that the debt had to be paid off, even if there was no agreement on how soon the debt should be redeemed.[62]

The government does not appear to have seriously reconsidered the place of a national debt in a federal republic any more than the nation's newspapers. When Fessenden's replacement at the Treasury, Hugh McCulloch, presented his first annual report in December 1865, he used words that could just as well have been spoken by Thomas Jefferson, James Polk, or almost any other statesman of the antebellum period. The influence of a public debt was "anti-republican," he said. "It adds to the power of the Executive by increasing federal patronage. It must be distasteful to the people because it fills the country with informers and tax-gatherers." The following year, McCulloch remarked that "the idea that a national debt can be anything else than a burden . . . a mortgage upon the property and industry of the people—is fortunately not an American idea." In other countries "public debts may be regarded as public blessings; but no such fallacy will ever be countenanced by the free and intelligent people of the United States." To the Treasury secretary it remained a fundamental principle that a debt should "be paid by the generation that created it." Fortunately for the Civil War generation, debt retrenchment could be combined with tax reduction. A rapid demobilization drastically cut expenditures and created large surpluses despite the repeal of most wartime taxes. Within three years of the surrender of the Confederacy, the excises on manufactures were repealed. After four more years, stamp taxes were abolished too. The income tax was reduced in 1867 and abolished in 1872. Still the revenue system remained extraordinarily productive. From 1866 to 1893 the public finances showed a yearly surplus. The total for the period came to $1.8 billion, which provided ample means for the reconstruction and reduction of the public debt.[63]

Although the figures were inflated, the principles of debt reconstruction remained what they had always been. During every major war in the long eighteenth century, Britain had seen its floating, or short-term, debt grow, and the funding of that debt after the return of peace had always been a top priority to governments. The same development took place in the United States after the War of 1812 and again, on a much larger scale, after the Civil War. On the last day of August 1865, the outstanding short-term debt was $1.7 billion, compared to a funded long-term debt of $1.1 billion. In the next few years, $830 million in 7-30 Treasury notes and some $440 million in short-term loans were exchanged for 6 percent long-term bonds. By the end of fiscal year 1870, the short-term debt had been absorbed. Contrary to expectations, the greenbacks, which had been intended as a temporary measure, remained in place. In the postwar years the currency became an inflamed issue. Hard-money advocates wished to see the notes withdrawn, but the American people had become fond of the greenbacks and feared the consequences of too rapid a contraction of the money stock. In the first three years after the war the outstanding amount was gradually retired from $430 million to around $350 million. Here the reduction stopped, and greenbacks continued to serve the United States as a circulating medium.[64]

The funded debt also developed in accordance with past practice. Chase had been anxious to make war bonds callable after five years in order to take advantage of falling interest rates to refinance the debt after the war. The legislation passed in 1870 and 1871 did precisely this. Five percent bonds were refinanced at 4, 4.5, or 5 percent interest. In 1870, $1.8 billion in 6 percent bonds were outstanding. Ten years later, that figure had fallen to $240 million. Now the funded debt of the United States consisted of $740 million in 4 percent bonds, $250 million in 4.5 percent bonds, and $480 million in 5 percent bonds. Refinancing reduced the average interest rate on the funded debt from 5.9 percent to 4.6 percent and thereby cut expenditures drastically. In a departure from established practice, the Treasury at this point issued bonds redeemable only after ten, fifteen, or thirty years. When the market interest fell further, this action proved to be premature and costly. Yet surpluses allowed the government not only to restructure but also to reduce the debt. Repayments brought it down to $961 million in 1893, when an economic downturn turned the surplus into deficits for the remainder of the 1890s. With the Spanish-American War the debt increased to $1.4 billion. It then hovered around $1.2 billion until the First World War once more took borrowing to a new level.

In 1865, McCulloch had claimed that the "strength of the government" had been proved by its ability to pay for "the greatest war of modern times." It now remained "to be demonstrated that a republican government can not only carry on a war on the most gigantic scale, and create a debt of immense magnitude, but can place this debt on a satisfactory basis, and meet every engagement with fidelity." Although the United States would never again realize the Jeffersonian dream of a debt-free existence, the statesmen of the post–Civil War era remained true to age-old ideals about the need for retrenchment of expenditures, reduction of taxation, and the repayment of the public debt. On a much greater scale than in previous wars, American statesmen once again demonstrated that a central state capacity second to none could be combined with republican ideals. It was a demonstration also meant to make an impact on the other side of the Atlantic.[65]

V

Prior to the Civil War, the United States had fought its conflicts in the nation's borderlands, on the high seas, or in foreign lands. This time the war was fought in the heart of the country. Primarily an internal contest over the future of the federal union, the Civil War nevertheless had important international dimensions. The cotton famine and the slaughter of thousands of men on American battlefields brought the United States to the attention of European governments to a degree not witnessed since the American Revolution. On several occasions, most dramatically during the Trent crisis, the Civil War threatened to spill over into an international war with Britain. Up to the Battle of Antietam there was also a very real possibility of British or French intervention through mediation or recognition of the Confederacy. In the South, the leadership was well aware that nationhood depended on international recognition and support. In the North, Lincoln and Seward worked to prevent foreign involvement from the same conviction. In the end, it would be the North's and not the South's diplomacy that would prove successful. But the international history of the Civil War is not exhausted by the non-events of intervention and international war, however. Closer to home the war also brought about a lasting geopolitical reconfiguration on the continent of North America.[66]

From the very start Britain and its remaining American colonies watched the progress of the Civil War with an anxious eye to the consequences for Britain's future on the continent. When the war first broke out, it was seen as the herald of an expected implosion of the United States. Alexander Beresford Hope, Conservative MP and founder of the *Saturday Review*, expressed a typical sentiment when he argued that an "impartial" view of the United States demonstrated that "the country should be divided into at least four great commonwealths," the North East, the Midland, the South, and the Pacific. Every one of these new nations would "be a check upon the others," and every one of them would become entangled in a European alliance. To British opinion this represented a coming of age. In this scenario the disunited American states would grow to resemble the nations of Europe: "Each would have to maintain its frontier, to keep up a standing army, to have a watchful Foreign Office. . . . Every country in the world does the like, and it is time that our bumptious cousins, now that they have become men and acquired bone and sinew, should assume the responsibilities of life and no longer display the childish petulance which may have been excusable in the young days of the Republic." Foreign observers less sympathetic to the interests of the British Empire had no problem seeing through Beresford Hope's "impartial" views. To them it seemed that the British government had always desired the separation of the federal union into two or more states, "which will watch over each other jealously and counterbalance one another," as the Russian ambassador to Britain remarked. "Then England, on terms of peace and commerce with both, would have nothing to fear from either; for she would dominate them, restraining them by their rival ambitions."[67]

In the long term, Britain's future as a North American power was predicated on the maintenance of a continental balance of power. United States growth and expansionism made such a continental order increasingly difficult to uphold as the nineteenth century progressed. Against this background, the Civil War also held out the hope that disunion would improve the prospects of Britain's American colonies. The chances that US domination would be replaced by a multipolar state system in North America increased when France intervened in Mexico to create an empire under the Habsburg archduke Maximilian. Union success in the war, by contrast, would make any attempt to break the American grip on the continent futile. While battling the armies of the Confederacy, Union mobilization had also altered the international balance of power in America.

The rapid expansion of the navy and the construction of coastal fortifications along the Atlantic seaboard upset Britain's long-standing strategic plans for an American war. Previously the military weakness of the federal union had made Britain's American colonies relatively safe from conquest. When mobilization for the Civil War turned the United States into a first-rate military power, this was no longer the case. As the war progressed and Union victory appeared more likely, the question of Canadian defense grew increasingly important. These concerns had begun with the war scare over the Trent affair but came to the fore in the winter and early spring of 1865 when the House of Commons debated the question of Canadian defense, debates that reveal just how much the Civil War had changed British perceptions of its major North American rival.[68]

By 1864, the scornful views that British political and military observers had long entertained about the United States had turned to a reluctant recognition that the Union's military capacity was now "formidable"—apparently a favorite turn of phrase. In April, Britain's minister to Washington, Lord Lyons, forwarded to the Foreign Office a report by Captain James Goodenough, which argued that the Lincoln administration was "steadily making preparations to enable it to engage with advantage in foreign war." The United States capacity for naval warfare was "becoming everyday more formidable." Lyons feared that naval strength would invite an attack on Canada because it made the United States immune from retaliation by the Royal Navy. An extensive fortification program had made most Atlantic seaports unassailable, and new ships gave the United States the means to harass British merchant shipping in the event of war. This was a serious blow to British strategy, which rested on the premise that in a war with the United States, Canada would be defended while the navy went on the offensive from its bases in Halifax and Bermuda against American seaports and commercial shipping. With the tables turned, Lyons admitted in November 1863 that "the relative positions of the United States and its adversary would be nearly the reverse of what they would have been if a war had broken out three or even two years ago. Of the two Powers the United States would now be the better prepared for the struggle." Shortly thereafter, the comptroller of the Royal Navy, Admiral Robert Spencer Robinson, put it even more succinctly: "It is clear that what was in 1861 is no longer so in 1865."[69]

The immediate context of the Commons debate in 1865 was a report by Colonel Drummond Jervois of the Royal Engineers on Canadian defense, which was laid before the Commons together with an appropriation of £50,000, or roughly $220,000, for the improvement of the Imperial Fortress at Quebec City. The appropriation passed easily, but the report gave rise to debate. Members of Parliament still had the cost of reinforcing Canada during the Trent crisis in fresh memory, and there was a growing feeling that the colonists did not assume their fair share of defense costs. In March 1862, the House of Commons had adopted a resolution that "colonies exercising the right of self-government ought to undertake the main responsibility of providing for their own internal order and security, and ought to assist in their own external defence." A vocal minority had even begun to argue that it was in Britain's best interest to withdraw militarily from Upper and Lower Canada altogether. The troops that Britain could hope to maintain on a permanent basis in Canada, some sixteen thousand men at most, could not realistically hope to stop an American invasion. To the contrary, a small British army in Canada would be "a glittering bait" to American ambition and constitute a source of weakness rather than strength. Nor could British sea power be relied on to even the scales in an American war. The United States was now unassailable from the sea. Portland's works were of granite, Boston was guarded by "the most formidable artillery," and, according to the best naval expertise, New York City was "infinitely more formidable" than either Kronstadt or Sebastopol, Russian fortresses made famous by the recent Crimean War, and "equal to any fleet that can be brought against them."[70]

Colonel Jervois assumed that with proper defensive works, Montreal and Quebec could be held even against overwhelming odds until relieved from across the sea, but critics found his understanding of the military situation in North America hopelessly outmoded. Technological developments such as the railroad together with the enormous expansion of United States military power meant that North America was no longer what it had been in the days of James Wolfe, Guy Carleton, and Isaac Brock, British commanders in the Seven Years' War, the War of Independence, and the War of 1812 and famous for their exploits in Canada. "Old things have passed away," J. B. Smith remarked; "everything is become new." There was now an "enormous disproportion between the power and resources of Canada and those of the United States." The Union had become possibly "the greatest military and naval Power in the world." The United States had several population centers close to the borders that were well served by railroads operational year-round. From such staging points an army several hundred thousand men strong and supported by "an unparalleled artillery" could sweep over Canada. One member of Parliament pointed out that the United States could command "trained, disciplined, veteran troops, ten times the number that we could bring into the field." On the Great Lakes the Americans would also have overwhelming superiority because, whereas gunboats could easily be transported from the American seaboard, they could not from faraway Britain. The only reasonable conclusion from this new strategic situation was military disengagement. A stubborn refusal to see the effects of the newfound strength of the United States could only make Canada "the grave either of the honour or the power of England."[71]

The skeptics did not get their way in 1865, but they soon would. A reorganization of imperial defense had first been broached in the late 1840s and early 1850s. It picked up speed in the late 1850s, and in 1868 a new government had made the redeployment of the army a central issue of defense policy. A combination of economic and security concerns drove this development. The Concert of Europe, which had maintained peace on the continent since the end of the Napoleonic Wars, was sounding increasingly disharmonious. The proclamation of the Second Empire ushered in a period of more ambitious French foreign policy. Although British leaders for the most part distrusted Napoleon III, Britain and France went to war against Russia in the Crimean War of 1854–1856. In the 1850s and 1860s, Italian and German unification further upset the balance of power. When Britain failed to mediate the conflict between Prussia and Denmark in the Second Schleswig War in 1864, it was clear that the future of Europe was unlikely to be peaceful. In this new environment, the British government chose to redeploy both its army and its navy to be better prepared for home defense. This meant pulling troops out of the colonies and posting them in Britain. Finances were an added incentive because the colonies contributed very little to imperial defense costs.

This shift in policy led the imperial government to support a union of the British North American colonies. Military withdrawal meant a loss of prestige, and British statesmen did not underestimate the symbolic importance of imperial retreat. Canadian confederation promised to create a nation that had sufficient population and wealth to be able to sustain a defensive force on its own, and this would allow for the ordered retreat of the British Empire from the continent. The Civil War brought these concerns to a head. From July 1863, when the Battle of Gettysburg and the capture of Vicksburg suggested that the cause of the Confederacy was doomed, the need to solve the defense of British America became pressing. In 1864, Canadian politicians had embarked on a movement for union, and the imperial government gave the project its strongest endorsement. Three years later the former colonies were given dominion status. Although the Canadians could count on British assistance in the event of war with their neighbor to the south, their defensive arrangements were from now on their own responsibility.[72]

On November 11, 1871, the First Battalion of the Sixtieth Rifle Corps marched out of the Imperial Fortress at Quebec, the last troops to leave the former colony. It was deeply symbolic that the Sixtieth Rifle Corps formed the rearguard of the imperial retreat. Formed as the Royal Americans in the French and Indian Wars, it had fought with Wolfe on the Plains of Abraham to wrest Quebec from the French. In the ensuing five decades the battalion served at many locations in Canada and the West Indies before leaving for Europe and the Napoleonic War in 1810. It only returned to garrison Quebec in 1867. With the recall of the Sixtieth Rifles first to Halifax and then to England and Ireland, Britain's era as a military power in North America, begun well over a century ago, had come to an end.

When the London *Times* commented on the withdrawal of troops from Canada, it pointed to the Civil War as the event that had forced this decision on the British government. Once the war was over, politicians of both parties had accepted that the colony, "exposed throughout its whole length to the attack of a powerful neighbour, could not be defended with success, by British arms in the event of a war." Canada could only become secure through "the organization of a national force in the Colony" itself. As long as the British army retained a foothold, the colonists had been reluctant to assume this responsibility, and the withdrawal of the empire's direct military presence would leave the Canadians no choice but to address the issue. For this reason, the paper concluded, the "withdrawal of the last Battalion of the British Army marks the commencement for the Canadian dominion of a new career."[73]

If the *Times*, the organ of Britain's ruling elite, hoped that a Canadian nationality would arise to build a state possessing the military capacity to resurrect the North American balance of power, history would prove disappointing. Although the United States showed little interest in conquering its defenseless new neighbor, its economic and cultural domination of the North American continent would continue to grow. As a dominion and later an independent nation, Canada would never be either a military threat or a monarchical alternative to American republicanism. The *New York Times* sensed as much when it reported that it was not only the Sixtieth Rifles who left Quebec in 1871 but also increasing numbers of emigrants, heading not for Halifax but for the United States. In this context the paper noted that "it is safe to assume that there is a strong feeling among the young men of Canada in favor of our more progressive civilization, and which may eventually take the shape of a popular movement in favor of annexation." Formal annexation never happened, but it is difficult not to conclude that in other respects the *New York Times* came closer than the London *Times* to capturing the future relationship between Britain's North American successor states.[74]

CONCLUSION

The Ideology, Structure, and Significance of the First American Fiscal Regime

In the popular imagination the American founding represents the realization of political ideals of liberty and equality. The Revolution is the moment in time when the American people rejected the ways of the Old World in favor of a system of government where the happiness of the citizens replaced the glory of the monarch as the central aim of the state. Flawed in important respects, this view of the origins of the American nation nevertheless embodies considerable truth. But it is far from the full story. Aside from the crucial problem of the exclusive and narrow definition of the political nation, the founding was also a process whereby the newly created United States rejected much but also adopted certain important elements of the contemporary European state. Indeed, the revolutionaries had little choice but to do so if they were to defend their nation's newly won independence and promote its interests against international competitors.

Independence came about only after a long and costly war. Although the War of Independence gave rise to considerable friction among the American states over the distribution of the burdens of the war, the need to pool resources to fight the mother country nevertheless worked to keep their union together. Once independence was formally recognized in the Peace of Paris in 1783, external pressures and common commitments arising out of the recent war served as the rationale for continued union. When it became clear that these pressures and commitments could not be effectively addressed within the existing institutional framework of the Articles of Confederation, the American union was thoroughly overhauled in the summer of 1787. The first federal Congress, which met in New York City in April 1789, successfully turned the edicts of the new Constitution into the institutions and policies of a functioning national government. Among its numerous important achievements were the creation of a stable fiscal regime and the reform of the Revolutionary debt that made possible the restoration of public credit. Treasury Secretary Alexander Hamilton meanwhile formulated the basic principles that would guide the nation's public finances. This work, carried out in the short span of a few years, set up a system of public finance that would last for more than seven decades.

Thanks to the Constitution and the First Congress, the United States acquired a capacity to raise money through taxation and loans by means similar to the most advanced European states at the time. The productive fiscal system of the national government and its restored capacity to borrow enabled federal spending on wars, on territorial expansion, and on efforts to neutralize domestic challenges to central authority ranging from the expedition that put down the Whiskey Rebellion in 1794 to the pacification of hostile Indian nations and recalcitrant Mormons and the much larger effort that crushed the southern rebellion in the Civil War. But even though government coercion was sometimes directed against renegade members of the body politic, far more often the nation's military power was projected on states and peoples outside its pale. By means both peaceful and violent, the independence and territorial integrity of the United States was upheld, new federal territories were incorporated into the Union, and the national domain grew.

The threat of international war and the need to be able to mobilize and employ coercive power to defend national independence and interests served both as the primary rationale behind the creation of a national government after independence and the principal force driving its development and expansion in the nineteenth century. An efficient central state in charge of international relations and defense was necessary for national survival and success in a competitive international state system. In this respect the origins and development of central state power in the United States are no different from the origins and development of state power in other parts of the world. It is true that a fortunate geographical location meant that security costs were considerably lower in North America than in Europe. Comparative analysis of government expenditure, always notoriously difficult, suggests that US security costs were about a third of such costs for Britain and France in the decades between the Napoleonic Wars in Europe and the American Civil War. Nevertheless, because North America remained a theater of European great-power politics and because all states, colonies, and peoples on the continent were involved, to a greater or lesser extent, in exchange on competitive Atlantic and global markets, no polity intent on mastering its own fate could dispense with military power. Decades ago, the historical sociologist Charles Tilly concluded a broad survey of European state formation in the sixteenth to eighteenth centuries with the observation that "war made the state, and the state made war." His maxim holds true also for North America.[1]

I

Although the duties of the national government in the United States were similar to those of the central governments of Europe, war making and state expansion remained deeply problematical in the American political tradition. Despite its rendering great services to the core constituency of the American federal union, there was little love for the national government among the citizenry. The people identified with their states rather than with a congress and executive that were designed not to realize the popular will but to protect and advance the interests of the states. In such a polity few saw the national government as anything more than an extension of the state governments or, alternatively, as a threat to their integrity. Rather than identifying with the national government, the citizenry approached it with considerable wariness. The American Revolution was a reaction to perceived abuses of Britain's authority over the imperial periphery, and a strong and persistent antietatism survived the independence struggle in the form of republican and antimonarchical convictions that were embraced by both the citizens and the leaders of the new nation. To an extent not always recognized, such sentiments were rooted in an analysis of the dangers posed to personal liberty by war-making governments.

At the time of the Revolution, radical writers such as Thomas Paine sometimes put forward the proposition that war was an affliction peculiar to monarchies. If the existing world of monarchies could be replaced by a world of republics, wars would end and peace would reign. But such notions never became common in the United States. War was accepted as an instrument of statecraft useful to both republics and monarchies. American statesmen saw the solution to the problem of war not in the republican form of government but in the formation of a union between the state-republics that had declared their independence from Britain. Such union would allow for the peaceful negotiation of conflicts of interest and make intermember warfare redundant. In the struggle over ratification the Federalists consistently presented the dissolution of the Union as the inevitable consequence of a refusal to adopt the Constitution. The dissolution of the Union, in turn, would lead to war between the member states. If the confederation fell apart, state interests would be given free vent, and the unbridled pursuit of state interests would eventually lead to armed conflict.

From the moment of disunion, James Madison remarked in *The Federalist*, "the face of America will be but a copy of that of the Continent of Europe. It will present liberty every where crushed between standing armies and perpetual taxes." This coupling of disunion and war retained a central place in American political thought long after the Constitution's adoption. Half a century later Andrew Jackson echoed Madison's concerns when he warned that union alone could preserve peace on the continent of North America:

> If the Union is once severed, the line of separation will grow wider and wider, and the controversies which are now debated and settled in the halls of legislation will then be tried in the fields of battle and determined by the sword.... The first line of separation would not last for a single generation; new fragments would be torn off, new leaders would spring up, and this great and glorious Republic would soon be broken into a multitude of petty States, without commerce, without credit, jealous of one another, armed for mutual aggression, loaded with taxes to pay armies and leaders, seeking aid against each other from foreign powers, insulted and trampled upon by the nations of Europe, until, harassed with conflicts and humbled and debased in spirit, they would be ready to submit to the absolute dominion of any military adventurer and to surrender their liberty for the sake of repose.[2]

To both Madison and Jackson the horrors of war took the shape not so much of death and destruction as of heavy and inordinate taxation. In part this was because eighteenth- and nineteenth-century armies were made up of elements thought to be dispensable and marginal to the political nation, whose loss of either life or limb there was little reason to mourn. But more fundamental than the aversion to standing armies and professional soldiers was the threat posed by war and the state to the material foundation of republican government. Jackson's and Madison's fear made sense in the light of a long tradition of critique against the exploitative fiscal-military state that had first appeared in European political thought in the seventeenth century. Writers in this tradition claimed that modern governments weighed so heavily on their subjects that they caused widespread poverty and even depopulation. When the people lost their property, they also lost their ability to stand up to kings and aristocrats, whose power was increased by the mobilization and centralization of resources that took place in war. "Of all the enemies to public liberty war is, perhaps, the most to be dreaded because it comprises and develops the germ of every other," Madison once remarked. "War is the parent of armies; from these proceed debts and taxes;

and armies, debts, and taxes are the known instruments for bringing the many under the domination of the few."³

No one expressed the dread of the evil trinity of public debts, heavy taxation and standing armies more forcefully than Madison's close friend Thomas Jefferson. In a letter written soon after the War of 1812, he warned of the dangers of public debts run up by unnecessary wars. It does of course ad an important dimension to his republican convictions that the letter was written at Monticello, where Jefferson's intellectual pursuits and civic engagement were made possible by slave labor. He wrote:

> We must not let our rulers load us with perpetual debt. We must make our election between *economy and liberty*, or *profusion and servitude*. If we run into such debts, as that we must be taxed in our meat and in our drink, in our necessaries and our comforts, in our labors and our amusements, for our callings, and our creeds, as the people of England are, our people, like them, must come to labor sixteen hours in the twenty-four, give the earnings of fifteen of these to the government for their debts and daily expenses; and the sixteenth being insufficient to afford us bread, we must live, as they now do, on oatmeal and potatoes, have no time to think, no means of calling the mismanagers to account; but be glad to obtain subsistence by hiring ourselves to rivet their chains on the necks of our fellow sufferers.⁴

Jefferson wrote this letter in 1816, by which time the Federalists, whom he liked to describe as "crypto-monarchists," had long lost their hold on government. The incumbent president was Jefferson's lieutenant Madison, and Republican congressmen had nominated Jefferson's friend and neighbor James Monroe as Madison's successor. Eight year later, when the nation had been ruled and the government shaped by Jeffersonian statesmen for a quarter of a century, Jefferson still believed "that we have more machinery of government than is necessary, too many parasites living on the labor of the industrious." No matter who ruled, it seemed, the state would always remain dangerous.⁵

Just like the fear of disunion, so the concern that an expanding national government would undermine the social order necessary to sustain a republican system of government, and thereby turn the United States into another England, survived the founding and remained an important element of American political culture at least up to the Civil War. In 1848, when the United States had recently conquered Mexico and its army of occupation stood in the enemy's capital, the fear of an expansive and ambitious national government could still be distinctly heard in an eclectic list of American decline drawn up by the *New York Herald*. "The United States," the paper said, "in their population, habits, increasing power, growing influence, military tastes, public spirit, increasing taxes, relish for Italian opera, increasing public debt, delight in naked dancers, great ambition, and the glory of a costly government, is fast, very fast, assimilating to the greatest, proudest, and most luxurious nation of the Old World."[6]

In a country that held war and the governments that waged it to be dangerous threats to republican liberty, there is little wonder that a national government designed to deal with foreign affairs and defense was treated with distrust and often held at arm's length. No matter how necessary such a government might be in a troubled and often hostile world, it could never aspire to the people's affection. Nor is it surprising that frugality became a leading principle among the people's representatives in Congress. Protecting the citizenry from excessive taxation meant protecting their property, the material basis for the economic and political power that was needed to secure their liberty. Statesman after statesman, Treasury secretary after Treasury secretary subscribed to the idea that small and frugal government was necessary to maintain a republican social order and that the exploitative state was a principal threat to republican liberty.

Alongside, and sometimes in conflict with, the general principle of frugality was the conviction that congressmen and senators had the right and the duty to protect and promote the specific interests of their states and constituents. This conviction also made its mark on the nation's fiscal arrangements. In a vast and diverse country like the United States, no tax would affect all sections and states in precisely the same way. From the duty on molasses, the object of the special ire of the representatives from Massachusetts in the First Congress, to the income tax during the Civil War—three-fifths of which was paid by Massachusetts, New York, and Pennsylvania alone—it was impossible to find a tax that imposed the same burden on all members of the Union. States' rights sentiments shaped the nation's fiscal institutions by forcefully directing the national government toward sources of funds that would not trigger resistance centered in state assemblies or provoke sectional feelings. By default rather than design this meant that customs duties became the backbone of the federal fiscal regime.

The notion that the central government had the right to levy and collect duties on trade had a long pedigree; therefore the assumption of this power by the national government after 1789 was relatively uncontroversial. In the colonial period, the imperial government had the right to regulate trade within and without the British Empire. After independence, proposals to amend the Articles of Confederation made clear that the impost was considered a safe and proper tax to place in the hands of Congress. When the Constitution was debated in Philadelphia, and later in the great struggle over ratification, the Federalists argued that the new national government would be funded from international duties on trade because this was the most acceptable type of tax to the American taxpayers. Thus, when the First Congress assembled in New York City to reform the fiscal system, the outcome was a foregone conclusion.

Every Treasury secretary from Hamilton to Salmon P. Chase subscribed to the idea that the impost was the most proper tax to be levied by the national government: the impost rested lightly on the people, fell roughly equally on the different sections of the country, required no central government tax assessors or collectors in the interior of the states, and left ample resources for running state governments. In reality, the second of these assumptions had been contested from the beginning and would become increasingly controversial from the late 1820s onward. Yet to the men in charge of the nation's finances, customs duties always remained preferable to every other alternative, and there was no serious attempt to radically reform the fiscal regime. As late as 1861, Chase noted that "the advantages of indirect taxation, by means of duties on imports, are found in economy of collection, in facility of payment, in adaptability to the encouragement of industry, and, above all, in the avoidance of federal interference with the finances of the States, whose main reliance for revenue for all objects of State administration must, necessarily, be upon levies on property."[7]

Restricting federal taxation to the impost had serious consequences because it made the national government extremely vulnerable to fluctuations in foreign trade. Well into the nineteenth century international commerce was competitive and restricted, and the government in effect became dependent for its income on the vagaries of foreign nations rather than on contributions from its own citizens. This shortcoming was plain for all to see, and complaints about the state of affairs transcended party differences. As early as December 1790, Hamilton told Congress that a "diversification of the nature of the funds" was "desirable." It was too dangerous to rely on "the vicissitude of the continuance, or interruption of foreign intercourse." Despite abolishing Hamilton's internal duties, Albert Gallatin knew that customs duties alone would not see the government through a European war. "In time of peace, it is almost sufficient to defray the expenses of a war," Gallatin noted about the federal fiscal regime. But "in time of war, it is hardly competent to support the expense of a peace establishment." In his first report after the War of 1812, the new Treasury secretary, Alexander

Dallas, asked Congress to consider "the establishment of a revenue system, which shall not be exclusively dependent upon the supplies of foreign commerce." And as late as 1828, Richard Rush, who headed the Treasury under John Quincy Adams, remarked that manufactures should "ultimately unfold the means of providing revenue for the public wants, when war, or other external events, not to be controlled, may abridge foreign commerce." Yet Congress never acted. In part this inaction is explained by the productiveness of the impost, which made the search for additional income unnecessary. But it was also a result of the belief that any attempt to radically alter the existing fiscal arrangements risked provoking considerable resistance from the state governments and the people.[8]

The combination of the pressure to create and maintain efficient central government institutions to protect and promote the national interest, on the one hand, and the counterbalancing influence of a benign geopolitical location, republican antietatism and states' rights ideology, on the other hand, goes a long way to explain the structure of the fiscal institutions and financial policies of the federal government between 1789 and 1861. Whereas the absence of powerful neighbors and immediate threats made it possible to keep down the cost of government, the fear of overbearing government and protection of state interests made it imperative to do so. The nineteenth-century United States was a rich country, yet the share of society's wealth expropriated as taxes was low. The antebellum period saw the economy grow and diversify, yet there was very little fiscal innovation before the Civil War. The compromises reached in the aftermath of the War of Independence, which crystallized in the Constitution and the policies and institutions of the new national government, proved remarkably resilient. No administration deviated significantly from the core principles that were hammered out by the Constitutional Convention, the First Congress, and the Washington administration. In ordinary times the national government would be financed from the income from customs duties. In extraordinary times of crisis, this income would be supplemented by loans. As soon as a state of normalcy returned, loans would be repaid in order to ready the American union for a new round of borrowing when the need arose. Given these basic principles of public finance, it became a principal task of every Treasury secretary to carefully guard the public credit, and no one dared to neglect the government's loan obligations.

In the end, it would take another conflict on the scope of the War of Independence to transform the federal fiscal regime. The enormous Civil War debt, which could not possibly be liquidated in the short span of a decade or two, and the acceptance of a greater role for the national government altered the fiscal system of the United States. Yet despite far-ranging change, the legacy of the 1789–1861 regime would continue to shape the policies and principles of American public finance at least up to the expansion of the federal government that grew out of the Great Depression.

II

The Revolutionary debt was a major impetus behind the drafting of the Constitution in 1787. When the new Congress assembled in 1789, the debt was perhaps the most pressing issue on the political agenda. Because the numerous accounts from the War of Independence were still being audited, no one yet knew the full extent or composition of the public debt. Nor did anyone know if and to what extent the government would honor the claims of its creditors. Suggestions for full and partial repudiation were aired and supported in many corners of the Union. Eventually, Congress chose to accept and implement a proposal from Treasury Secretary Alexander Hamilton. The claims of creditors were met almost in full, and the federal government also assumed the major share of the very substantial debts run up by the states.

In addition to being thus nationalized or federalized, the debt was also funded on the model of Britain's public debt. The government pledged to use specified tax incomes from customs duties to pay interest on the debt, but it made no stipulation for the repayment of the principal. The US government even restricted its right to make repayments. This decision was based on the recognition that, in the words of one of Hamilton's successors, "the public creditor regards it, individually, as a hardship to be paid off. His reliance upon the faith and resources of the nation is so unbounded, that he prefers to let his capital stock remain in its hands, subject only to his call for the interest." Public creditors, in other words, were content as long as interest payments were punctual, and they did not ask for the return of their capital. If they needed to liquidate their assets, the creditors could always do so by selling their claims on the government to a third party. Even so, the contract with the creditors allowed for fairly rapid redemption, should the government develop the wish and the means to pay off its debt. An awkwardly worded passage of the Funding Act—often misconstrued or overlooked by political opponents and latter-day commentators—gave the government the right to pay a maximum of $8 on every $100 of debt originally contracted in any given year. With compound interest taken into account, at a fixed interest rate of 6 percent, such payment would retire the debt in twenty-four years. In addition to funding and nationalizing the do-

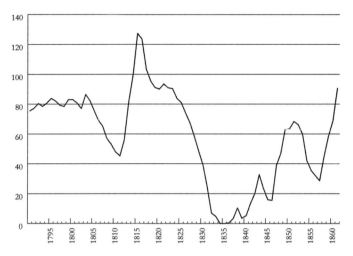

Fig. C.1. US Public Debt, 1791–1861 ($ million). *Source*: Susan B. Carter et al., eds., *Historical Statistics of the United States: Millennial Edition*, 5 vols., (New York: Cambridge University Press, 2006), 5:80, table Ea587, "Federal Government Finances—Revenue, Expenditure, and Debt: 1789–1939."

mestic debt in this manner, Congress also followed Hamilton's proposal to restructure the foreign debt by transferring most of the nation's obligations to Amsterdam.[9]

With Hamilton's reforms completed, it was possible to take stock of the public debt. In 1791, the total debt stood at $75 million. Its development to 1861 is shown in figure C.1. Despite the fact that the reforms had reduced interest rates considerably, debt charges were heavy and constituted the major expenditure item in the federal budget up to the 1830s. With limited incomes, there was no room for repayments of the principal in the early years of the national government. Before he left the Treasury in 1795, however, Hamilton engineered an amortization plan that would retire the foreign debt from the War of Independence together with the two principal domestic revolutionary loans (i.e., the "six percent" and "deferred six percent" bonds) by 1818 and 1824, respectively. Although the plan was adopted and followed, the War of 1812 added a significant new debt. This in turn was rapidly retired starting in the mid-1820s. By 1835 the United States was for the first, and so far only, time completely free from debt. But it was not long before budget deficits in the wake of the Panic of 1837 forced the national government to borrow again. When President James K. Polk led the nation to war against neighboring Mexico in 1846, another $49 million was added to the public debt. The government reduced this debt through large open-market purchases in the early and mid-1850s, and when the Civil War broke out, no more than $18.3 million was still outstanding. Toward the end of the 1850s, however, very substantial budget deficits again forced the government to borrow money to make ends meet.[10]

Figure C.1 depicts the aggregate public debt of the United States and therefore conceals the fact that there was continual borrowing and repayment of loans in the period 1789–1861. Although there was one public debt, it was formed from many separate loans. In the seven decades after 1789 many old loans were liquidated and many new ones contracted. As table C.1 reveals, the national government made frequent use of its credit in this period. The Washington administration was an avid borrower but mainly in order to reform and restructure the debt inherited from the Revolution. Contrary to what might have been expected, it was the critics of the public debt, statesmen in the Jeffersonian and Jacksonian tradition, who resorted most to borrowing. Thomas Jefferson financed the Louisiana Purchase with a loan sold in London, James Madison went to war against Britain on credit, and Polk conquered Mexico with the help of $49 million in long-term bonds. There were five reasons why the national government borrowed: to finance wars (items 6, 11, 20, and 25 in table C.1); to finance territorial expansion (items 7, 12, 17, and 21); to refinance existing debt (items 1, 2, 3, 5, 8, 10, 13, 18, and 23); to cover budget deficits (items 9, 15, 16, 19, 22, and 24); and to buy stock in the central bank (items 4 and 14). All but one of the loans in the third category refinanced war loans. In the fifth category, both the First and the Second Bank of the United States were institutions created in part to sink outstanding war bonds. War and territorial expansion were unquestionably the dominant causes of federal government borrowing.

The importance of war and territorial expansion can also be seen in patterns of government spending. In the seventy years between George Washington's first administration and the administration of James Buchanan, expenditures grew nineteenfold, from an annual average of $4.1 million to an average of $78.5 million. The trend was unaffected by the ideology of the incumbent president. George Washington, John Adams, and John Quincy Adams are often associated with expansive government, whereas the Virginia dynasty of Thomas Jefferson, James Madison, and James Monroe, as well as Andrew Jackson and James Polk, are traditionally associated with government retrenchment. But as figure C.2 reveals, time is a much more important determinant of expenditure levels than ideology. The most significant shift in expenditure levels appears with the War of 1812. Given the cost of war, this is hardly surprising. But spending levels remained high after the war. This was due in part to the cost of new loans, but the Monroe

TABLE C.1. Major long-term loans, 1789–1861

Loan	Authorized	Liquidated	Amount ($ million)	Purpose
1. Dutch loans	1790	1809	9.4	Nine loans raised in Amsterdam and Antwerp to refinance the foreign debt from the War of Independence
2. Six percent stock of 1790	1790	1824	44.7	Funding of the domestic debt from the War of Independence
3. Three percent stock of 1790	1790	1832	19.7	Funding of outstanding interest on the domestic debt from the War of Independence
4. Subscription loan	1791	1801	2.0	Payment for $2 million of stock in the first Bank of the United States
5. Loans of 1795	1795	1808	2.0	Two loans raised to refinance part of the foreign debt from the War of Independence owed to France
6. Quasi War loans	1798/1800	1809	7.2	Three loans raised in 1798 and 1800 to finance military and naval build-up during the Quasi War
7. Louisiana 6 percent	1803	1821	11.2	Payment to France for cession of Louisiana
8. Exchange loan of 1807	1807	1813	1.9	Partial refinancing of the three percent stock of 1790
9. Six percent loan of 1810	1810	1811	2.8	Raised to cover budget deficit
10. Exchange loan of 1812	1812	1825	3.0	Partial refinancing of six percent stock of 1790
11. War of 1812 loans	1812–1815	1830	63.3	Eight loans raised to finance the War of 1812
12. Mississippi stock	1814	1821	4.3	Compensation to claimants of public lands in Mississippi territory

(continued)

TABLE C.1. *continued*

Loan	Authorized	Liquidated	Amount ($ million)	Purpose
13. Converted stock of 1815	1815	1825	10.6	Two loans converting the floating debt from the War of 1812 to long-term debt
14. Subscription loan of 1816	1816	1831	7.0	Payment for $7 million of stock in the second Bank of the United States
15. Five and 6 percent of 1820	1820	1822/1833	3.0	Two loans raised to cover budget deficit
16. Five percent of 1821	1821	1835	4.7	Loan raised to cover budget deficit
17. Loan of 1824	1824	1832	5.0	Assumption of claims against Spain as compensation for Spanish cessions according to the treaty of 1819
18. Exchange loans of 1824, and 1825	1824/1825	1834	11.0	Three loans that partially refinanced the debt from the War of 1812
19. Loan of 1841, 1842, and 1843	1841/1842/1843	1845/1866/1854	21.0	Three loans raised to cover budget deficits
20. Mexican War loans	1846–1848	1869	49.2	Three loans raised to finance the Mexican War
21. Texas indemnity stock	1850	1867	5.0	Compensation to Texas for claims arising from Texas annexation
22. Loan of 1858	1858	1874	20.0	Loan raised to cover budget deficit
23. Loan of 1860	1860	1871	7.0	Loan converting outstanding short-term debt to long-term debt
24. Loan of 1861	1861		18.4	Loan raised to cover budget deficit
25. Oregon War loan	1861		1.1	Loan raised to cover costs of the Oregon War (1855–1856)

Source: Rafael A. Bayley, *History of the National Loans of the United States from July 4, 1776, to June 30, 1880,* in *Report on Valuation, Taxation, and Public Indebtedness in the United States, as Returned at the Tenth Census (June 1, 1880)* (Washington, DC: Government Printing Office, 1884); Franklin Noll, *Chronological Inventory of United States Public Debt Issues, 1775–1976,* http://eh.net/databases/uspublicdebt, accessed April 21, 2010.

THE FIRST AMERICAN FISCAL REGIME   235

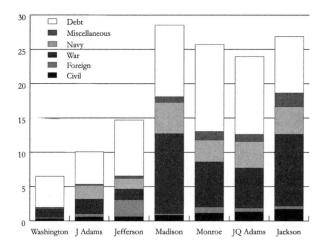

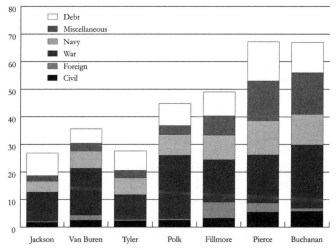

Fig. C.2. Average annual expenditure per administration ($ million). Expenditures on the national debt include debt repayments. *Source*: Report of the Secretary of the Treasury on the State of the Finances for the Year 1866, H.R. Ex. Doc. 4, 39th Cong., 2d sess., 308–9.

and John Quincy Adams administrations also spent two and a half times as much as Jefferson did on the civil administration, the military, and the navy. Under Jackson and Martin Van Buren large sums were spent on Indian removal, fortification projects, and military pensions. Another rise in expenditure occurred with the Mexican War, which, like the War of 1812, also caused a noticeable ratchet effect. Thus in the first decade of the nineteenth century, average annual expenditure was $13.1 million, in the 1820s and 1830s $26.9 million, and in the 1850s $67.8 million.

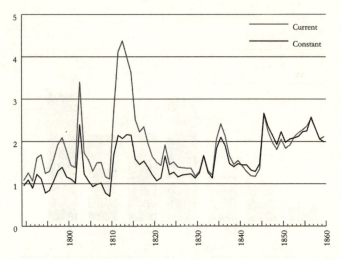

Fig. C.3. Per capita expenditures, 1792–1861 ($, current and constant 1860 prices). Expenditure does not include repayments on the public debt. *Sources*: Report of the Secretary of the Treasury on the State of the Finances for the Year 1866, H.R. Ex. Doc. 4, 39th Cong., 2d sess., 306–7. Population: *Historical Statistics of the United States, Colonial Times to 1970*, Bicentennial ed., 2 vols. (Washington, DC: Bureau of the Census, 1975), vol. 1, series A7. GDP: Susan B. Carter et al., eds., *Historical Statistics of the United States: Millennial Edition*, 5 vols. (New York: Cambridge University Press, 2006), 5:671, table Eg 217–22.

The rise in expenditure levels is less dramatic when the growth of the nation is entered into the equation. Between 1790 and 1860, the population increased from roughly four million to thirty-two million, and the national domain was extended from the Mississippi to the Pacific. Figure C.3 shows that in constant prices, per capita expenditures varied relatively little between 1792 and 1861, with the major exceptions of the War of 1812 and the Mexican War. The magnitude of the War of 1812 is even more pronounced if expressed in current prices. The other spikes can also be explained by extraordinary exertions of government power. In 1804, the foreign relations budget item jumped to $12.4 million because of the Louisiana Purchase. In 1824, $5 million were paid to Spain as compensation for the Florida Cession. The spike in 1832 is due to increased expenditure that was only partly related to war, in the form of increased payments of pensions, and territorial expansion, in the shape of Indian removal. In per capita terms there is a ratchet effect after the wars against Britain and Mexico, although not nearly as marked as the change in absolute administration spending traced in figure C.2. In the decade between 1801 and 1810, the national government spent on average $1.17 per capita per year in 1860 prices. The corresponding figure for the 1820s and 1830s is $1.38, and for the 1850s $2.19. In per capita terms, the overall picture of national government spending is thus one of only modest growth.

An analysis of early US public finance has to address not only how much the federal government spent but also where the money went. Here, too, continuity is the rule. To every administration between 1789 and 1860 except one, the major items of expenditure were the public debt on the one hand and the military on the other hand. The Louisiana Purchase and military and naval retrenchment meant that Jefferson spent roughly equal amounts on foreign relations and the military. Yet under Jefferson debt charges were greater than these items combined. Because the public debt was almost exclusively contracted to pay for the cost of war, close to four-fifths of all federal spending between 1789 and 1860 inclusively was related to war or preparation for war. Not all of this money was spent on soldiers, sailors, equipment, and warships, however. The federal government financed an extensive system of coastal fortifications and spent increasing sums on the construction of roads and canals. Substantial sums were also paid in compensation for territorial acquisitions from France, Spain, Mexico, Texas, and various Indian nations. Beginning in 1850 the "miscellaneous" category of expenditure grew very rapidly. In part this is explained by an alteration in the government accounts. After 1849, the cost of the Customs Service, approximately $2 million per year, was charged to miscellaneous expenditures. But in the 1850s the national government also invested $15 million in public buildings and stepped up its spending on internal improvements. Nevertheless, for the period as a whole, spending patterns support the conclusion that in contrast to what the founding fathers claimed and modern historians have often repeated, the early federal government was designed for war, not peace.[11]

III

The powers granted by the Constitution to the national government made possible a wholesale reform of the American fiscal system. This process began as soon as the new Congress met in 1789, and a new fiscal regime was created within the span of merely a few years. The reform consisted in three moves: first, a change from indirect to direct rule in the administration of taxation; second, an inversion of the fiscal structure by which customs duties were substituted for direct taxes as the main source of fiscal revenue; and third, a considerable increase in the productivity of the impost, and thereby a considerable increase in the overall tax income.

The supporters of the Constitution as well as the Federalists in the First Congress strongly denounced the requisition system that had been in effect during the War of Independence and the immediate postwar period. It was a method they believed had neither worked in the past nor ever would in the future. In the interest of efficient administration, the Constitution instead introduced a dual sovereignty in the fiscal sphere. Congress was granted very broad powers over taxation. Article I, section 8, of the Constitution gave Congress the power to "lay and collect Taxes, Duties, Imposts and Excises, to pay the Debts and provide for the common Defense and general Welfare of the United States." The state governments meanwhile retained their right of taxation. Much as the debate in the Philadelphia convention had suggested would happen, the First Congress used its powers under the Constitution to replace the indirect administration of taxation in the shape of the requisition system with direct fiscal rule administered by the US Customs Service. Direct rule would remain an essential feature of the national fiscal administration of the American union forever after.

In the heated debate over the Constitution, the Federalists had often argued that taxes administered by the national government rather than the states would ease the burden of taxation on the people. When the national government began to levy customs duties to pay the public debt, it would be possible for the state governments to reduce or abolish taxes on property and persons. If correct, this would amount to an important change. State taxation had generated considerable hardship and popular protest in the 1780s and had brought the very future of the Union into doubt. A comparison of tax levels before and after the adoption of the Constitution shows that the Federalists did in fact deliver on their promise to reduce direct taxation. By the early 1790s, direct taxes had fallen by at least 75 percent compared to the mid-1780s. As far as direct taxation is concerned, this was one of the greatest tax breaks in the nation's history.

The combined tax intake of state and federal governments did not decline, however. Total state tax levies between 1785 and 1788 were around $10 million. In contrast, the national government alone collected $19 million between 1792 and 1795. Because many states were still levying some form of tax, combined state and federal taxation from 1792 to 1795 probably amounted to at least twice the sum raised by the states from 1785 to 1788. But whereas the states had enormous difficulty raising money in the 1780s, the federal government did so rather effortlessly in the 1790s. The reason for this difference can be found in the shift from direct taxes to customs duties. Approximately two-thirds of total tax levies in the 1780s were levied on property and polls. Around 25 percent of the total was levied on imports and exports. In the early 1790s, the tax structure had been completely reversed. Around 90 percent of total tax revenue now came from the impost, while the remainder came from direct taxes and excises. Indirect taxes were easier than direct taxes to collect because they targeted merchants and manufacturers, who typically had liquid assets, rather than cash-starved farmers and planters, who had their assets tied up in land, livestock, slaves, buildings, and implements.

The third and final move of the fiscal reform was the substantial increase in the yield from customs duties. Hamilton's promise in *The Federalist* that the impost could be "prudently improved to a much greater extent under foederal than under State regulation" turned out to be correct. Figures from New York, Philadelphia, Baltimore, and Charleston suggest that income from customs duties was six times greater in the 1790s than in the 1780s. Nor is this increase explained by increasing imports, as the income from customs duties grew much faster than foreign trade. The major reason for the increased productivity of customs duties instead lies in higher tariff rates and more efficient customs collection.[12]

Nothing comparable to the fiscal regime change brought about by the First Congress took place again until the Civil War. Instead, the federal fiscal system was characterized by institutional continuity and growing returns. As figure C.4 shows, federal revenue grew steadily up to the War of 1812. During the war itself and its immediate aftermath, revenue levels

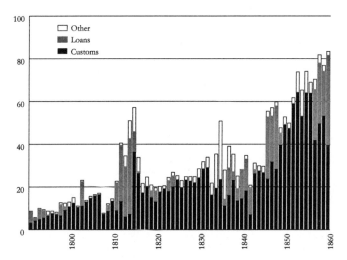

Fig. C.4. Total revenue, customs revenue, and loan revenue, 1792–1861 ($ million).
Source: Report of the Secretary of the Treasury on the State of the Finances for the Year 1866, H.R. Ex. Doc. 4, 39th Cong., 2d sess., 306–7.

were five times higher than before the war. On the return of peace, the revenue level settled at about twice the prewar level. Another spike appeared in 1835 and 1836 as a result of record sales of public lands. Revenue also increased during the Mexican War, and after the war it continued to grow very rapidly. This was the effect of the Walker tariff adopted in 1846 and of growing volumes of trade. Table C.2 shows the development of the tax revenue as five-year averages in constant prices. From the early 1790s to the 1850s, federal revenue grew more than fortyfold. Yet, just like expenditure levels, this growth mainly mirrors the rapid growth of the popu-

TABLE C.2. Total tax revenue, per capita tax revenue, and tax revenue as share of GDP, 1789–1861 (1860 prices)

Year	Total revenue ($ million)	Per capita revenue ($)	Revenue as share of GDP (%)
1790	1.6	0.34	0.4
1795	4.6	1.00	1.9
1800	7.5	1.40	2.1
1805	9.7	1.54	2.1
1810	7.6	1.06	1.5
1815	14.0	1.64	2.9
1820	13.6	1.41	2.3
1825	18.3	1.63	2.3
1830	24.9	1.92	2.4
1835	31.1	2.07	2.4
1840	21.4	1.25	1.4
1845	26.8	1.32	1.2
1850	45.2	1.92	1.6
1855	68.1	2.49	1.7
1860	49.9	1.58	1.1

Sources: Revenue: Report of the Secretary of the Treasury on the State of the Finances for the Year 1866, H.R. Ex. Doc. 4, 39th Cong., 2d sess., 306–7.Population: *Historical Statistics of the United States, Colonial Times to 1970*, Bicentennial ed. (Washington, DC: Bureau of the Census, 1975), vol. 1, series A7. GDP: Susan B. Carter et al., eds., *Historical Statistics of the United States: Millennial Edition* (New York: Cambridge University Press, 2006), 5:671, table Eg217–22, "Gross Domestic Product: 1650–1800"; John J. McCusker, "Estimating Early American Gross Domestic Product," *Historical Methods* 33, no. 3 (2000): 155–62.

Notes: Figures are five-year averages centered on the stated year except 1790, which states the average for 1789–1792, and 1860, which states the average for 1858–1861. Figures are recalculated to constant prices on the basis of the commodity price index provided by John J McCusker, *How Much Is That In Real Money? A Historical Commodity Price Index for Use as a Deflator of Money Values in the Economy of the United States*, 2d ed. (Worcester, MA: American Antiquarian Society 2001), 41–60. Because GDP figures for the period are only crude estimates, the figures for revenue as percentage of GDP are estimates only.

lation and the economy. In per capita terms, the revenue level was fairly constant, fluctuating for most of the period between $1.00 and $1.60 per person per year in constant prices. Between the 1790s and the peak years in the 1850s, per capita revenue grew approximately two and a half times. Although estimates of national economic output for this period are highly uncertain, available figures suggest that in terms of the share of the gross domestic product appropriated as taxes, the income of the federal government was also relatively constant over time. Up to the late 1830s, federal revenue was between 2.0 and 2.5 percent of GDP except for the mid-1810s, when the figure was higher because of the War of 1812. Beginning in the late 1830s the government's revenue as a share of GDP declined to around 1.5 percent, a trend that was not offset even by the Mexican War.

An analysis of the structure of the federal revenue again reveals the strong continuities in the American fiscal system. Figure C.4 charts the income from customs duties and loans together with total revenue. The importance of the tariff to the first American fiscal regime is clearly demonstrated. This is further confirmed by table C.3, which shows the relative contribution of different types of revenue to total government income. During the period 1789 to 1861, customs duties provided the government with 69 percent of its total income. The other main source of income was loans, which were significant in five periods: during the initial years of the new federal government, when Hamilton refinanced the debt and dared not impose higher taxes; during the War of 1812; after the Panic of 1837, when the government ran a deficit; during the Mexican War; and just before the Civil War, when the government again ran a very substantial deficit (see table C.1). It should be remembered that loans were secured on the income from customs duties and that without an efficient Customs Service the federal government would have looked in vain for investors in government bonds. Hence, there is no doubt that customs duties formed the backbone of the first fiscal regime of the United States. As table C.3 makes clear, only rarely did other forms of taxation contribute significant sums to the federal treasury. Not even in the years 1814 and 1815, when taxation reached its highest point in the entire pre–Civil War period, did internal duties and direct taxes combined yield more than the duties on international trade. In the mid-1830s, land sales reached record levels, generating significant federal income. With tariffs reduced, land sales raised more money than customs duties during fiscal year 1836. But this was highly exceptional. When the government stopped selling land on credit, the income from the sale of public lands immediately dropped off. The reliance on one type of taxation contrasted with the more diverse fiscal system of Britain. In Britain, cus-

TABLE C.3. Structure of federal revenue, 1789–1861 (%)

Year	Customs	Internal duties	Direct taxes	Land sales	Loans	Other
1790	41.2	1.2	—	—	57.4	0.2
1795	68.6	4.8	—	—	20.1	5.3
1800	75.6	6.6	2.3	0.5	11.4	3.8
1805	85.6	0.5	0.3	3.1	10.0	0.5
1810	78.5	—	—	5.1	15.9	0.4
1815	41.1	6.2	4.7	3.4	44.0	0.6
1820	77.4	1.3	0.4	9.7	8.0	3.2
1825	83.9	0.1	—	5.0	7.8	3.3
1830	89.5	—	—	7.8	—	2.7
1835	60.1	—	—	29.9	2.1	8.0
1840	52.4	—	—	9.9	30.1	7.4
1845	68.5	—	—	6.3	23.7	1.5
1850	74.8	—	—	4.2	19.7	1.2
1855	88.5	—	—	9.9	—	1.7
1860	59.2	—	—	2.6	36.4	1.8

Source: Report of the Secretary of the Treasury on the State of the Finances for the Year 1866, H.R. Ex. Doc. 4, 39th Cong., 2d sess., 306–7.

Notes: Figures are five-year averages centered on the stated year except 1790, which states the average for 1789–1792, and 1860, which states the average for 1858–1861. Percentages may not add up to 100 because of rounding.

toms duties overtook excises as the principal form of tax income only in the 1830s, but even then it accounted for no more than a third of total tax income. Meanwhile excise duties remained an important form of revenue and contributed 25 to 30 percent of total income, with the reminder made up by income from property and income taxes and stamp duties.[13]

Conflicts over the tariff provide some of the most dramatic moments in the political history of the antebellum United States, pitting North against South and Whigs against Democrats. South Carolina's opposition to the "Tariff of Abominations" of 1828 was an important step on the road to southern secession, and the debate over Henry Clay's "American System" economic plan saw the development of radically different visions of the future of the American union. It is all too easy to think that these dramatic clashes over the tariff meant that the federal fiscal regime was highly contested. But this conclusion would be a gross exaggeration. Conflict took place in the context of a broad agreement over the basic structure of the national tax regime. The rates of import duties and the policy objectives behind them could be questioned, but there were no serious proposals for radical transformation of the American fiscal regime away from customs duties toward income and property taxes or even internal duties. Heated rhetoric and secessionist threats led to changes in the tariff but not to structural reform of the fiscal system.[14]

Protectionists and free traders took turns in implementing seven major tariff reforms between 1816 and 1861. Table C.4 shows the effects of these

TABLE C.4. Customs, imports, and GDP, 1789–1861

Year	Customs as share of imports (%)	Imports as share of GDP (%)
1790	6.7	10.5
1795	13.7	12.5
1800	21.0	8.8
1805	20.7	9.6
1810	23.9	6.2
1815	36.7	8.4
1820	25.6	8.1
1825	35.4	5.9
1830	37.4	6.8
1835	18.8	8.1
1840	16.7	6.2
1845	24.3	4.9
1850	23.3	6.4
1855	22.1	7.0
1860	15.8	6.7

Sources: Customs revenue: Report of the Secretary of the Treasury on the State of the Finances for the Year 1866, H.R. Ex. Doc. 4, 39th Cong., 2d sess., 306. Imports: *Historical Statistics of the United States, Colonial Times to 1970*, Bicentennial ed. (Washington DC: Bureau of the Census, 1975), vol. 2, series U193 and U192. GDP: Susan B. Carter et al., eds., *Historical Statistics of the United States: Millennial Edition* (New York: Cambridge University Press, 2006), 5:671, table Eg217–22, "Gross Domestic Product: 1650–1800"; John J. McCusker, "Estimating Early American Gross Domestic Product," *Historical Methods* 23, no. 3 (2000): 155–62.

Notes: All figures are five-year averages centered on the stated year except 1790, which is for 1790–1792. Imports are retained imports (i.e., reexports have been subtracted from total imports). Because GDP figures for the period are only crude estimates, the figures for imports as percentage of GDP are estimates only. Based on other sources, Robert E. Lipsey provides slightly different figures for imports as percentage of GDP: 1790–1800: 15–20, 1800: 8.4, 1810: 5.6, 1820: 8.0, 1830: 6.1, 1840: 6.1, 1850: 6.6, 1860: 6.7. See Lipsey, "U.S. Foreign Trade and the Balance of Payments, 1800–1913," in Stanley L. Engerman and Robert E. Gallman, eds. *The Cambridge Economic History of the United States*, vol. 2, *The Long Nineteenth Century* (New York: Cambridge University Press, 2000), table 15.3.

reforms. In the late 1820s and early 1830s, at the peak of the protectionists' control over commercial policy, the government expropriated approximately 37 percent of the total value of the nation's imports. When power passed to their opponents, the result was not a free-trade regime. Imports still carried an average duty of more than 20 percent. As long as the fiscal regime rested on the Customs Service, neither an extreme protectionist nor an extreme free-trade option was viable. The former endangered the volume of trade and the latter the government's revenue. Only if the national government was willing to diversify the tax system to rely more on internal duties or property taxes would it be possible to fully pursue a policy of either protectionism or free trade. This was not an option any major political figure was ready to advocate.

The War of 1812 introduced a higher tariff, and this war measure remained in place to pay for the war loans. The first protectionist tariff proper was passed in 1824, and duties were increased with the "Tariff of Abominations" of 1828. A backlash produced the tariff of 1832, which reduced duties significantly. The following year saw the adoption of the so-called Compromise Tariff, which reduced duties even further. It is no coincidence that these reduced tariffs were adopted when the government was about to liquidate the public debt. In the early 1830s the government faced the prospect of running a very large surplus, which proved to be more of a curse than a blessing. An overflowing national treasury inevitably invited demands for federal spending, which in turn gave rise to political and constitutional conflicts over the proper and legitimate scope of the national government. It was far safer to avoid growth of the national government by shrinking its revenue.[15]

For obvious reasons the design of the American fiscal system tied the government closely to the commercial sector of the economy. Although international commerce grew in absolute terms between 1789 and 1861, it declined relative to other sectors. As table C.4 demonstrates, up to the time of Jefferson's embargo in 1807, imports amounted to between 9 and 12.5 percent of GDP. After the embargo and the War of 1812, this figure fluctuated between 6 and 8 percent up to the mid-1830s and then between 5 and 7 percent up to the Civil War. Despite the fact that international trade declined relative to the home market, the federal government did not attempt to tap into alternative sources of income but continued to rely almost exclusively on duties on commerce. When the federal government began operations, customs duties amounted to about 14 percent of the total value of imports. In the mid-1820s and early 1830s, this share had grown to more than 35 percent. When a reaction followed and tariff rates were reduced in the mid-1830s, the share of the value of imports expropriated as federal taxes returned to the levels of the pre–War of 1812 period.

It was not tariff battles or secession threats but war that ended the first federal regime. In American history three wars stand out for the extraordinary level of resource mobilization engendered by the war effort and the severe strains they imposed on the economy: the War of Independence, the Civil War, and the Second World War. All three brought about far-reaching change in the organization of the central state apparatus. The War of Independence generated the debt that forced the creation of the first fiscal regime. During the Civil War the need for resources exceeded what the existing fiscal and financial system could generate. To support public credit and fund the war, Congress therefore introduced an ambitious and productive program of internal taxation. Borrowed money paid the greatest share of the war effort, but the costs of the enormous debt this policy created meant that war taxes had to become permanent. In a nation with a persistent record of tax resistance, the achievements of the Thirty-Seventh and Thirty-Eighth Congresses are both surprising and impressive. Faced with the choice between preserving the Union and protecting states' rights, Congressmen overwhelmingly chose the former, even at the cost of central government expansion and infringement on state interests. In an important sense, therefore, the Civil War does not mark the eclipse of Unionist sentiment but its high point. In the loyal states the conviction that a republican future hinged on the preservation of the Union trumped states' rights and mobilized the means to crush secession. At the moment of its deepest crisis the federal union proved to be much sturdier than either friends or foes had expected.

A $2.8 billion debt that could not possibly be liquidated for decades and an expansion of the fiscal regime beyond customs duties to include a broad range of internal taxes were two significant changes to American public finances bequeathed by the Civil War. But not everything changed. There were in fact important continuities between the pre- and the postwar systems. The public debt continued to be regarded as an evil institution alien to republican rule. "The idea of perpetual debt is not of American nativity, and should not be naturalized," Treasury Secretary Salmon Chase had said in 1861. When Jay Cooke, the great financier of the Civil War, after the war floated the idea that the debt could be made a national blessing, he was met by a storm of protests and ridicule. Despite its bloated size, the popular expectation was that the public debt would be paid off as soon as possible. Fifteen years after the peace, it had been reduced by over 25 percent, or $725 million. Thanks to continued population growth, the per capita debt had been halved. Although the United States would never again be free from debt, periods of peace saw significant debt reduction right up to the New Deal, after which the policy of sustained debt reduction in peacetime was abandoned.[16]

In the fiscal sphere, customs duties did not go away. Because of high tariffs, customs revenue exceeded the income from internal revenue up to 1897 and again in the early years of the twentieth century. The decisive shift to a reliance on internal revenue happened only with the income tax legislation of 1917 that was adopted to finance US entry into the First World War. Nor did post–Civil War Congresses abandon age-old principles that taxes should rest lightly on the people or that Congress should tax "luxuries" rather than "necessaries." After the war the income tax was rapidly scaled down and finally repealed in 1872. The general duty on manufactures went the same way. By 1869, it contributed only a token sum to the Treasury. Although internal revenue became a permanent feature of the postwar fiscal regime, nearly all the money came from duties on tobacco, distilled spirits, and beer, items that Justin Morrill, echoing the words of Alexander Hamilton, had called not only "luxuries" but "deleterious, if not vicious" luxuries.[17]

IV

The limitations of the first federal fiscal regime are in plain view. Compared to modern times and to the fiscal regimes of nineteenth-century European governments, the sums raised were small. This is true in absolute terms but even more so in per capita terms or relative to the size of the economy. As a point of comparison, the central governments of Britain and France spent around five to seven times as much as the national government in the United States. It was a serious matter that a fiscal system designed to allow the national government to go to war could not deliver in the event of a conflict with a major maritime power, something that happened in the War of 1812. Yet such limitations should not detract from the fact that throughout the period under review the sums generated managed to meet the government's needs and that, outside the War of 1812 and the Civil War, these sums were raised relatively effortlessly. Furthermore, and in contrast to what some European observers claimed, Congress had the willpower to transcend the limitations of the fiscal system whenever it became necessary. During the War of 1812, the attempt was late in coming and never completed. But during the Civil War decisive reforms came early and proved productive. The overall verdict on the federal financial institutions and policies of the early republic and antebellum era must be a positive one. Whatever flaws there were in the national government of the United States, an inability to secure funds was not among them.[18]

Efficient governmental institutions allowed for resource mobilization that could be translated into financial and military power. Between 1789 and 1867 the United States employed such power to expand the national domain from 820,000 square miles to 3.5 million square miles. The original thirteen states grew to thirty-four by 1861 in a process whereby federal territories were transformed into states as European American settlers spread across the land. In contrast to the frontier myth, the regions into which the United States extended its domain were not empty wastelands but the territorial domains of other states and peoples, and the transfer of sovereignty could only be secured through state action. Annexation, purchase, conquest, and negotiation transferred title to territory from sovereign states and Indian nations to the national government. To make way for American citizens, hostile American Indians were pacified and often cleared off the land altogether in forced migrations, sometimes involving thousands or tens of thousands of people moving over long distances. War making, policing, and forced migrations demanded advanced institutions and considerable administrative skill. In the US Army, Indian Department, land offices, territorial governments, and State Department, the national government created the governmental institutions that oversaw the process whereby foreign domains became federal territories that became state-republics. Whatever we may think of the way in which the national domain was expanded and organized, it is impossible to deny that the process was rapid and the results spectacular. It was hardly the work of a weak and inefficient government.[19]

The expansion across the North American continent was mirrored in a much less dramatic but nonetheless significant maritime expansion. United States consuls appeared in seaports all over the world. The national government concluded treaties not only with European and Latin American nations but also with principalities in South and East Asia. By the 1830s, the United States had a naval presence in all of the world's oceans.

Resource mobilization also permitted the national government to go to war. The international wars fought in the first half of the nineteenth century—the Quasi War with France in 1798, the War of 1812 against Britain, and the Mexican War in 1846–1848—showed European powers that the United States had considerable military resources and skill, even if the nation did not as yet inspire fear. This changed with the Civil War. Despite much severe criticism directed against the inefficiency and waste of the Union war effort, it was recognized in European courts and parliaments that the Civil War had turned the United States into a military power of rank.

There is a world of difference between Lord Sheffield's remark in his *Observations on the Commerce of the American States* in 1783 that "it will not be an easy matter to bring the American States to act as a nation; they are not to be feared as such by us" and the admission by the Marquess of Hartington in the House of Lords in 1865 that the United States had grown into "a great military nation."[20]

The territorial, demographic, and economic growth of the United States forced European powers to take note of the federal union in their strategic considerations for North America. In 1861, the secession of the southern states appeared to have derailed the continent's manifest destiny and opened alternative futures. A disunited United States organized into two or more nations would have meant that instead of directing their ambitions outward, Americans would have to keep careful guard on each other. The future of North America became still more open when Napoleon III took advantage of the United States' preoccupation with the Confederacy to intervene in Mexico. His attempt to turn Mexico from a weak and conflict-ridden federal republic into a strong and stable empire under a Habsburg prince promised to further alter the continent's political landscape. If only the provinces of British North America could be molded into a confederation, the geopolitical realignment would be complete and the international state system of the New World would mirror the Old World. A continental balance of power would replace US domination.

American statesmen had always feared such a development. Eighteen months into the Civil War, an article in the London *Economist* tried to define the American "idea of the Union." As always highly critical of the United States, the journal nonetheless captured what Americans feared they were now about to lose from disunion. In the United States, union meant "that undivided and illimitable Republic, whose magnitude and prosperity would enable it to dictate to all the world, which should have no rival and no neighbour, which should be co-extensive with a continent, which should have no army, no navy, and no taxes, and yet bully all nations without those instruments." The Civil War threatened to destroy this world. To Americans the preservation of republican rule—"government of the people, by the people, and for the people"—depended on the preservation of a union that could prevent a competitive state system, and its ensuing wars, from arising in North America. In contrast, Britain's future as an American power hinged on maintaining a balance between the United States and the other nations on the continent. Growing American strength in the nineteenth century gradually undermined that balance until southern secession gave it a new life. In the same manner, Napoleon III's chances of establishing a foothold on the southern tip of the continent from which to develop his dream of an *Amérique latine* to counterbalance the Anglo-Saxon offshoots to the north depended even more on the disintegration of the United States into two or more rival nations. The international and geopolitical stakes of the Civil War were therefore extraordinarily high.[21]

If the attack on Fort Sumter seemed to derail North American history, Lee's surrender at Appomattox Courthouse put it back on track. The American people knew their nation's strength, and some thought the time had come to take action against both Britain to the north and France to the south. In New York City, the famous banjoist James Gaynor performed Edward Burke's "There's a Heap of Work to Do" to an enthusiastic audience at Tony Pastor's Opera House, a song in which "Max," that is, Maximilian, would be sent packing and "John," that is, John Bull, was warned that "the hour of retribution's drawing nigh." Meanwhile, Massachusetts Civil War veteran Andrew Jackson Wilcox offered helpful advice to President Andrew Johnson in a letter entitled "The Annexation of Mexico the means of paying the National Debt," which Wilcox subsequently printed. But shocked by the assassination of Abraham Lincoln and faced with the monumental task of reconstructing the South, the government never brought any of its considerable power to bear on either France or Britain. An army was ordered to the Mexican border, aid was given to the forces under Juarez who were fighting Maximilian, and a demand was sent to Napoleon III to withdraw French troops forthwith. But no troops crossed the border of either Mexico or Canada. There was little need for them to do so. Both France and Britain understood that the outcome of the Civil War would force them to once again reconsider their position in North America.[22]

The outcome of that reconsideration was retreat. The Union's wartime mobilization and victory was by no means the sole cause of this. Other factors were also at work. While North and South fought, Europe went through a period of turbulence. The 1850s and 1860s saw Italian and German unification and the rise of a powerful and ambitious Prussia in the middle of Europe, developments that drastically altered the strategic situation of both Britain and France. When Britain failed to prevent the combined Prussian and Austrian attack on Denmark in the Second Schleswig War in 1864, it became clear that the era of European peace was drawing to an end. This conclusion was further confirmed by the Franco-Prussian War of 1871 and the subsequent proclamation of the Second German Empire. Britain's response was to reorganize its defenses. Rather than spreading its resources thin over imperial outliers, the army and navy were concentrated in the home islands to better guard European developments.

Canada was one victim of this reorientation of imperial defense. Once the matter of prestige was overcome, it was evident that Britain's military position would be strengthened by a disengagement from North America. With all chances of maintaining a balance of power in America gone, British troops stationed in Canada would merely serve as hostages to Britain's good behavior without any realistic possibility of withstanding an attack from the United States. The political development that led to the formation of the Confederation of British North America, granted dominion status in 1867, was mirrored in a military development whereby Britain's garrisons were withdrawn from Canada and the Maritime Provinces. The last of the imperial troops left the fortress at Quebec in 1871. Henceforth Britain restricted its military presence in North America to naval bases in Halifax, the Bermudas, and Esquimalt. Yet retreat did not mean that the United States was no longer a factor in British foreign policy. In military terms, withdrawal from Canada made the British Empire better equipped to deal with threats posed by the United States. But in geopolitical terms it was nonetheless a significant move. From 1867 on, Britain would no longer be a North American power.[23]

The year 1867 also saw two other important geopolitical developments. This was the year Maximilian was captured and executed, and the inglorious Second Mexican Empire came to an end. Napoleon III never meant the French presence to be indefinite. Even more than British leaders, he had reason to feel concern about developments in Germany, and he was deeply involved in the Italian unification process. But the outcome of the Civil War was an added incentive to leave Mexico. In 1865, Secretary of State William Seward demanded that French troops withdraw from the country. An army of fifty thousand troops was sent to the Mexican border to give added weight to the request. Napoleon chose to comply, and by 1866 all French forces had left. Increasingly isolated, Maximilian's regime came crashing down the following year. Soon engulfed in a rivalry with Germany that would not be finally resolved until 1945, France abandoned its trans-Atlantic ambitions. Never again would the French attempt to establish a significant presence in the Americas.[24]

It was in 1867, too, that Russia surrendered its aspirations to remain an American power. In contrast to Britain and France, Russia was openly supportive of the Union in the Civil War. Relations with Britain were strained because of Russian ambitions in Central Asia that threatened India. In the mid-1850s, concern over Russian actions against a disintegrating Ottoman Empire had led to the Crimean War, when Russia was attacked by an Anglo-French-Ottoman alliance. The Russian empire therefore stood opposed to

Britain in the European balance of power and any British rival was a potential friend. In America, meanwhile, Russia's grasp was slipping. The activities of the Russian America Company were no longer profitable, and American and British settlement on the Pacific Coast made the absorption of Russian America by either of these powers only a question of time. In this situation it made sense to sign over the colony to the United States. This move would further cement Russo-American friendship, and US possession of Alaska invited Anglo-American competition over British Columbia and the possibility that Britain would lose its Pacific foothold. When Russia agreed to cede the colony for $7.2 million, the Stars and Stripes were raised above Castle Hill in New Archangel on October 18, 1867.[25]

Within less than three years of the end of the Civil War, the last of the major geopolitical realignments on the North American continent had run its course. It was only fitting that the United States was the driving force and the major beneficiary of this great shift. Ever since the nation's birth, American ambition and expansion had been the principal engine behind all such previous realignments. And in all of the many corrections made to the political map of North America between 1783 and 1867, the United States had stood to gain. Now, four score and four years after the signing of the Peace of Paris, the United States stood as the undoubted master over the continent of North America. Yet in the remarkable history of this young nation it was no more than the beginning. After a few short decades devoted to consolidating its hold over its western conquests, the United States would begin to exert its influence and power on a global scale. The rapid territorial expansion and the institutional machinery and political experience developed in the century after independence would stand the young nation in good stead as dawn broke over the American Century.

NOTES

ABBREVIATIONS

ASP: Finance — *American State Papers: Documents, Legislative and Executive, of the Congress of the United States; Selected and Edited under the Authority of Congress*, 38 vols., Class III, *Finance*, 5 vols. (Washington, DC: Gales and Seaton, 1832–1861)

DHFFC — *Documentary History of the First Federal Congress of the United States of America, March 4, 1789–March 3, 1791*, ed. Linda Grant DePauw, 20 vols. (Baltimore: Johns Hopkins University Press, 1972–2012)

DHRC — *The Documentary History of the Ratification of the Constitution*, ed. Merrill Jensen, John P. Kaminski, and Gaspare J. Saladino, 26 vols. to date (Madison: Wisconsin Historical Society Press, 1976–)

Federalist — *The Federalist*, ed. Jacob E. Cooke (Middletown, CT: Wesleyan University Press, 1961)

JAH — *Journal of American History*

Messages and Papers — *A Compilation of the Messages and Papers of the Presidents, 1789–1897*, ed. James D. Richardson, 10 vols. (Washington, DC: Government Printing Office, 1897)

PAH — *The Papers of Alexander Hamilton*, ed. Harold C. Syrett, 27 vols. (New York: Columbia University Press, 1961–1987)

PJM — *The Papers of James Madison*, ed. William T. Hutchinson and William M. E. Rachal, 17 vols. (Chicago: University of Chicago Press, 1962–1991)

PJM: Presidential Series	The Papers of James Madison: Presidential Series, ed. Robert A. Rutland et al., 7 vols. to date (Charlottesville: University of Virginia Press, 1984–)
PTJ	Papers of Thomas Jefferson, ed. Julian P. Boyd, 40 vols. to date (Princeton, NJ: Princeton University Press, 1950–)
Records of the Federal Convention	The Records of the Federal Convention of 1787, ed. Max Farrand, 4 vols. (New Haven, CT: Yale University Press, 1966)
Scrapbook, Jay Cooke Papers	Scrapbook, Jay Cooke Manuscript Papers, Historical Society of Pennsylvania
SPCP	The Salmon P. Chase Papers, ed. John Niven, 5 vols. (Kent, OH: Kent State University Press, 1993–1998)
WAG	The Writings of Albert Gallatin, ed. Henry Adams, 3 vols. (Philadelphia: J. B. Lippincott, 1879)
WMQ	William and Mary Quarterly

INTRODUCTION

1. Nils Collin, "Relation om Förenta Staterna, 1791–1792," n.p., Collin Papers, Royal Academy of Science, Stockholm.

2. Frank H. Sommer, "Emblem and Device: The Origin of the Great Seal of the United States," *Art Quarterly* 24 (1961), 57–76; Franklin and Abbé André Morellet, "Explanation of a Medal Struck by the Americans in 1783," in Leonard W. Labaree, ed., *Papers of Benjamin Franklin*, 40 vols. to date (New Haven, CT: Yale University Press, 1959–) 39:549–55; Alexander Hamilton to George Washington, April 14, 1794, *PAH*, 26:272; *Made in America: Printmaking 1760–1860. An Exhibition of Original Prints, Library Company of Philadelphia and Historical Society of Pennsylvania, April–June 1973* (Philadelphia: Library Company of Philadelphia, 1973), 19–20; Joan Elliot Price, "Robert Sully's Nineteenth-Century Paintings of Sauk and Winnebago Indians," *Wisconsin Academy Review* 65, no. 1 (Winter 1988–1989): 26; Albert C. Ramsey, trans. and ed., *The Other Side; or, Notes for the History of the War between Mexico and the United States, Written in Mexico* (New York: John Wiley, 1850), 2. Hercules was also a popular icon in the French Revolution; see Lynn Hunt, "Hercules and the Radical Image in the French Revolution," *Representations* 1, no. 2 (Spring 1983): 95–117.

3. Arthur P. Whitaker, "The Pseudo-Aranda Memoir of 1783," *Hispanic American Historical Review* 17, no. 3 (August 1937): 287–313; *Other Side*, 3–4.

4. P. B. Waite, ed., *The Confederation Debates in the Province of Canada, 1865: A Selection*, 2d ed. (Montreal: McGill-Queen's University Press, 2006), 56.

5. George Washington, Farewell Address, in *Messages and Papers*, 1: 221; Thomas Jefferson, Inaugural Address, in ibid., 1:323; Andrew Jackson, Farewell Address, in ibid., 3:294; James K. Polk, Inaugural Address, ibid., 5:2230; Henry Adams, *History of the United States of America*, 9 vols. (New York: C. Scribner's Sons, 1890), 4:136; John Fiske,

The Critical Period of American History, 1783–1789 (1888; repr., Boston: Houghton Mifflin, 1899), vi–vii; Daniel H. Deudney, "The Philadelphian System: Sovereignty, Arms Control, and Balance of Power in the American States-Union, circa 1787–1861," *International Organization* 49 (Spring 1995): 191–228; David C. Hendrickson, *Peace Pact: The Lost World of the American Founding* (Lawrence: University Press of Kansas, 2003).

    6. Fred Anderson and Andrew Cayton, *The Dominion of War: Empire and Liberty in North America, 1500–2000* (New York: Viking, 2005), xv.

    7. Anderson and Cayton, *Dominion of War*, xiii ("imperial ambitions"). Gordon S. Wood, *Radicalism of the American Revolution* (New York: Knopf, 1992), and Sean Wilentz, *Rise of American Democracy: Jefferson to Lincoln* (New York: Norton, 2005), are two grand syntheses of the early republic's political development that hardly make any mention of international affairs. But see Wood's recent *Empire of Liberty: A History of the Early Republic, 1789–1815* (New York: Oxford University Press, 2009) for an overview that pays much greater attention to foreign affairs. An important attempt to give greater weight to external factors in early American political history comes from the discipline of political science. See Ira Katznelson, "Rewriting the Epic of America," in Katznelson and Martin Shefter, eds., *Shaped by War and Trade: International Influences on American Political Development* (Princeton, NJ: Princeton University Press, 2002), 3–23; Katznelson, "Flexible Capacity: The Military and Early American Statebuilding," in ibid., 82–110; and Aristide R. Zolberg, "International Engagement and American Democracy: A Comparative Perspective," in ibid., 24–54. A recent work on discussions of the American Revolution in France is Philipp Ziesche, *Cosmopolitan Patriots: Americans in Paris in the Age of Revolution* (Charlottesville: University of Virginia Press, 2010). On Atlantic history, see Bernard Bailyn, *Atlantic History: Concept and Contours* (Cambridge, MA: Harvard University Press, 2005). On world history, see Thomas Bender, *A Nation among Nations: America's Place in World History* (New York: Hill and Wang, 2006), and for a call for a global approach to the antebellum United States, see Rosemarie Zagarri, "The Significance of the 'Global Turn' for the Early American Republic," *Journal of the Early Republic* 31, no. 1 (Spring 2011): 1–37. On the United States as the heir of Britain's imperial ambitions, see Alan Taylor, *American Colonies* (New York: Viking, 2001), xv–xvii, 477; Linda Colley, "The Difficulties of Empire: Present, Past and Future," *Historical Research* 79, no. 205 (August 2006): 367–82. Imperialism is also central to the magisterial work of Donald Meinig; see Meinig, *The Shaping of America: A Geographical Perspective on 500 Years of History*, vol. 1, *Atlantic America, 1492–1800* (New Haven, CT: Yale University Press, 1986), xviii–xix.

    8. Peter S. Onuf and Nicholas G. Onuf, *Federal Union, Modern World: The Law of Nations in an Age of Revolutions, 1776–1814* (Madison, WI: Madison House, 1993); James R. Sofka, "The Jeffersonian Idea of National Security: Commerce, the Atlantic Balance of Power, and the Barbary War, 1786–1805," *Diplomatic History* 21, no. 4 (Fall 1997): 519–44; Peter S. Onuf, "A Declaration of Independence for Diplomatic Historians," *Diplomatic History* 22, no. 1 (Winter 1998): 71–83; Peter S. Onuf, *Jefferson's Empire: The Language of American Nationhood* (Charlottesville: University Press of Virginia, 2000); Peter S. Onuf and Leonard J. Sadosky, *Jeffersonian America* (Malden, MA: Wiley, 2002), 172–221; Hendrickson, *Peace Pact*; Eliga H. Gould, "The Making of an Atlantic State System: Britain and the United States, 1795–1825," in Julie Flavell and Stephen Conway,

eds., *Britain and America Go to War: The Impact of War and Warfare in Anglo-America, 1754–1815* (Gainesville: University Press of Florida, 2004), 241–65; Peter S. Onuf, "Nations, Revolutions, and the End of History," in Michael A. Morrison and Melinda Zook, eds., *Revolutionary Currents: Nation Building in the Transatlantic World* (Lanham, MD: Rowman and Littlefield, 2004), 173–88; Anderson and Cayton, *Dominion of War*; Leonard J. Sadosky, *Revolutionary Negotiations: Indians, Empires, and Diplomats in the Founding of America* (Charlottesville: University of Virginia Press, 2009); James R. Sofka, "'A Commerce Which Must Be Protected': Thomas Jefferson and the Atlantic International System," paper presented at The Old World and the New: Exchanges between America and Europe in the Age of Jefferson international conference, arranged by the Robert H. Smith International Center for Jefferson Studies, at Schloss Leopoldskron, Salzburg, Austria, October 12–16, 2005. On new directions in the study of the early republic, see the special forum in the *Journal of the Early Republic* 24, no. 2 (Summer 2004).

9. These works include William H. Bergmann, *The American State and the Early West* (New York: Cambridge University Press, 2012); Stefan Heumann, "The Tutelary Empire: State- and Nation-Building in the 19th-Century United States" (PhD diss., University of Pennsylvania, 2009); Richard R. John, *Spreading the News: The American Postal System from Franklin to Morse* (Cambridge, MA: Harvard University Press, 1995); Katznelson and Shefter, *Shaped by War and Trade*; Gautham Rao, "The Creation of the American State: Customhouses, Law, and Commerce in the Age of Revolution" (PhD diss., University of Chicago, 2008); Stephen J. Rockwell, *Indian Affairs and the Administrative State in the Nineteenth Century* (New York: Cambridge University Press, 2010); and the forthcoming work of Peter Kastor on the creation of the federal government from 1789 to 1829.

10. Paul W. Gates, *History of Public Land Law Development* (Washington, DC: Zenger, 1968), 86. Figures provided are as follows: Original domain 821,020 square miles, Louisiana Purchase 817,885 square miles, Florida 67,725 square miles, Texas Annexation 386,032 square miles, Oregon Compromise 282,527 square miles, Mexican Cession 522,624 square miles, Gadsden Purchase 29,628 square miles, Alaska Purchase, 571,065 square miles. On the European powers see David S. Heidler and Jeanne T. Heidler, *Old Hickory's War: Andrew Jackson and the Quest for Empire* (Baton Rouge: Louisiana State University Press, 2003); J. C. A. Stagg, *Borderlines in Borderlands: James Madison and the Spanish-American Frontier, 1776–1821* (New Haven, CT: Yale University Press, 2009); David M. Pletcher, *The Diplomacy of Annexation: Texas, Oregon, and the Mexican War* (Columbia: University of Missouri Press, 1973). On the legal aspects of taking possession of American territory, see Anthony Pagden, "Law, Colonization, Legitimation, and the European Background," in Michael Grossberg and Christopher Tomlins, eds., *Cambridge History of Law in America*, 3 vols. (New York: Cambridge University Press, 2008), 1:1–31; Lauren Benton and Benjamin Straumann, "Acquiring Empire by Law: From Roman Doctrine to Early Modern European Practice," *Law and History Review* 28, no. 1 (February 2010): 1–38. On Native American territoriality, see Juliana Barr, "Geographies of Power: Mapping Indian Borders in the 'Borderlands' of the Early Southwest," *WMQ*, 3d ser., 68, no. 1 (2011): 5–46; and Barr, "Second Thoughts on Colonial Historians and American Indians," *WMQ*, 3d ser., 64, no. 3 (July 2012): 477–84. On the transformation of the land from territory to private property, see Gates, *History of Public Land Law*;

Peter Onuf, *Statehood and Union: A History of the Northwest Ordinance* (Bloomington: Indiana University Press, 1987); Malcolm J. Rohrbough, *The Land Office Business: The Settlement and Administration of American Public Lands, 1789–1837* (New York: Oxford University Press, 1968); Richard White, *"Its Your Misfortune and None of My Own": A New History of the West* (Norman: University of Oklahoma Press, 1991), 135–54. Indian treaties are reprinted in *Eighteenth Annual Report of the Bureau of American Ethnology to the Secretary of the Smithsonian Institution 1896–97*, part 2, *Indian Land Cessions in the United States 1784–1894*, , H.R. Doc. No. 736/3, 56th Cong., 1st sess., and discussed in Francis Paul Prucha, *American Indian Treaties: The History of a Political Anomaly* (Berkeley: University of California Press, 1994).

11. Letter from Major General Scott, November 3, 1849, List of Documents Accompanying the Report of the Secretary of War to the President, November 30, 1849, 30th Cong., 1st sess., Sen. Ex. Doc. 549, 98–103. I have found Durwood Ball, *Army Regulars on the Western Frontier 1848–1861* (Norman: University of Oklahoma Press, 2001), the most insightful treatment of the antebellum peacetime army in the West. I have also drawn on Francis Paul Prucha, *The Sword of the Republic: The United States Army on the Frontier* (New York: Macmillan, 1968); Robert Wooster, *American Military Frontiers: The United States Army in the West, 1783–1900* (Albuquerque: University of New Mexico Press, 2009); and Robert M. Utley, *The Indian Frontier of the American West 1846–1890* (Albuquerque: University of New Mexico Press, 1984). On the Trade and Intercourse Act and the Indian frontier, see Francis Paul Prucha, *American Indian Policy in Formative Years: The Indian Trade and Intercourse Acts, 1790–1834* (Cambridge, MA: Harvard University Press, 1962). For the list of armed encounters, see the United States Adjutant General's Office, *Chronological List of Actions, &c., with Indians from January 15, 1837 to January, 1891* (Washington, DC, 1891), supplemented by George W. Webb, *Chronological List of Engagements between the Regular Army of the United States and Various Tribes of Hostile Indians Which Occurred during the Years 1790–1898, Inclusive* (1939; repr., New York: AMS, 1976).

12. On Indian removal, see Prucha, *American Indian Policy*, 213–49; Prucha, *American Indian Treaties*, 156–207; Prucha, *The Great Father: The United States Government and the American Indians* (Lincoln: University of Nebraska Press, 1984), 179–69; Anthony F. Wallace, *Jefferson and the Indians: The Tragic Fate of the First Americans* (Cambridge, MA: Harvard University Press, 1999); and Wallace, *The Long Bitter Trail: Andrew Jackson and the Indians* (New York: Hill and Wang, 1993).

13. I have found John H. Schroeder, *Shaping a Maritime Empire: The Commercial and Diplomatic Role of the American Navy, 1829–1861* (Westport, CT: Greenwood, 1985), invaluable to an understanding of the many functions of the antebellum navy. The diplomatic activities of the nineteenth-century navy are given extensive treatment in David F. Long, *Gold Braid and Foreign Relations: Diplomatic Activities of Naval Officers, 1789–1883* (Annapolis, MD: Naval Institute Press, 1988). On the nineteenth-century navy generally, see also K. Jack Bauer, "Naval Shipbuilding Programs 1794–1860," *Military Affairs* 29, no. 1 (Spring 1965): 29–40; Howard P. Nash Jr., *The Forgotten Wars: The Role of the U.S. Navy in the Quasi War with France and the Barbary Wars 1798–1805* (South Brunswick, NJ: A. S. Barnes, 1968); Kenneth J. Hagan, *This People's Navy: The Making of American Sea Power* (New York: Free Press, 1991), 21–160;

Harold Sprout and Margaret Sprout, *The Rise of American Naval Power, 1776–1918* (Princeton, NJ Princeton University Press, 1939). On navy activities, see the essays in Clayton R. Barrow Jr., ed., *America Spreads Her Sails: U.S. Seapower in the 19th Century* (Annapolis, MD: Naval Institute Press, 1973); and Craig L. Symonds, ed., *New Aspects of Naval History* (Annapolis, MD: Naval Institute Press, 1981). On the naval squadrons and their actions, see Gardner Allen, *Our Navy and the West Indian Pirates* (Salem, MA: Essex Institute, 1929); Francis B. Bradlee, *Piracy in the West Indies and Its Suppression* (Salem, MA: Essex Institute, 1923); and Raymond L. Shoemaker, "Diplomacy from the Quarterdeck: The U.S. Navy in the Caribbean, 1815–1830," in Robert W. Lowe, ed., *Changing Interpretations and New Sources in Naval History* (New York: Garland, 1980), 169–79, for the West Indies; James A. Field Jr., *America and the Mediterranean World, 1776–1882* (Princeton, NJ: Princeton University Press, 1969), for the Mediterranean; Donald W. Griffin, "The American Navy at Work on Brazil Station, 1827–1860," *American Neptune* 19 (1959): 239–56, for the South Atlantic; Robert Erwin Johnson, *Thence Round Cape Horn: The Story of United States Naval Forces on Pacific Station, 1818–1923*.(Annapolis, MD: United States Naval Institute, 1963), and T. Ray Schurbett, "Chile, Peru, and the U.S. Pacific Squadron, 1823–1850," in Symonds, *New Aspects of Naval History*, 201–20, for the Pacific Station; Curtis T. Henson Jr., *Commissioners and Commodores: The East India Squadron and American Diplomacy in China* (Tuscaloosa: University of Alabama Press, 1982), Robert Erwin Johnson, *The Far China Station: The U.S. Navy in Asian Waters, 1800–1898* (Annapolis, MD: United States Naval Institute, 1979), and James M. Merrill, "The Asiatic Squadron: 1835–1907," *American Neptune* 29 (1969): 106–17, for the East India Squadron; and George M. Brooke, "The Role of the United States Navy in the Suppression of the African Slave Trade," *American Neptune* 21 (1961): 28–41, Judd Scott Harmon, "Marriage of Convenience: The United States Navy in Africa, 1820–1843," *American Neptune* 32 (1972): 264–76, Harmon, "The United States Navy and the Suppression of the Illegal Slave Trade, 1830–1850," in Symonds, *New Aspects of Naval History*, 211–19, and Spencer J. Tucker, "Lieutenant Andrew H. Foote and the African Slave Trade," *American Neptune* 60 (2000): 31–48, for Africa.

    14. Andrew Cayton, "'Separate Interests' and the Nation-State: The Washington Administration and the Origins of Regionalism in the Trans-Appalachian West," *JAH* 79, no. 1 (June 1992): 39–67; François Furstenberg, "The Significance of the Trans-Appalachian Frontier in Atlantic History," *American Historical Review* 113, no. 3 (June 2008): 647–77; Collin G. Galloway, "The End of an Era: British-Indian Relations in the Great Lakes Region after the War of 1812," *Michigan Historical Review* 12, no. 2 (Fall 1986): 1–20; Patrick Griffin, *American Leviathan: Empire, Nation, and Revolutionary Frontier* (New York: Hill and Wang, 2007), 183–277; Eric Hinderaker, *Elusive Empires: Constructing Colonialism in the Ohio Valley, 1673–1800* (New York: Cambridge University Press, 1997), 187–270; Leonard J. Sadosky, *Revolutionary Negotiations: Indians, Empires, and Diplomats in the Founding of America* (Charlottesville: University of Virginia Press, 2009), 176–205; Richard White, *The Middle Ground: Indians, Empires, and the Republic in the Great Lakes Region, 1650–1815* (New York: Cambridge University Press, 1991), 413–532.

    15. Ball, *Army Regulars*; Pekka Hämäläinen, *Comanche Empire* (New Haven, CT:

Yale University Press, 2009), 292–362; Utley, *Indian Frontier*, 1–64; White, *"Your Misfortune,"* 61–118; Wooster, *American Military Frontiers*, 96–237.

16. Lord Lyons to Lord Russell, November 3, 1863, in James J. Barnes and Patience P. Barnes, eds., *The American Civil War through British Eyes: Dispatches from British Diplomats*, 3 vols. (Kent, OH: Kent State University Press, 2005), 3:106; James Gibson, "The Colonial Office View of Canadian Confederation, 1856–1868," *Canadian Historical Review* 35 (1954): 308; Michele Cunningham, *Mexico and the Foreign Policy of Napoleon III* (Basingstoke, UK: Palgrave, 2001).

17. Theda Skocpol, *Bringing the State Back In* (Cambridge: Cambridge University Press, 1985), 16–18, cited in Martin J. Daunton, *Trusting Leviathan: The Politics of Taxation in Britain, 1799–1914* (Cambridge: Cambridge University Press, 2001), 1; "The Building of Twelve Seventy-Fours, and Estimates of Expense," December 29, 1798, in *American State Papers: Documents, Legislative and Executive, of the Congress of the United States; Selected and Edited under the Authority of Congress*, 38 vols., Class VI, *Naval Affairs*, 5 vols. (Washington, DC: Gales and Seaton, 1832–1861), 1:67–68; "Additional Military Force," January 31, 1812, ibid., Class V, *Military Affairs*, 7 vols., 1:316.

18. Chase to William P. Fessenden, February 10, 1862, *SPCP*, 3:132.

CHAPTER 1

1. Alexander Hamilton, "Federalist 30," in *Federalist*, 188.

2. Gordon Wood, "Interest and Disinterestedness in the Making of the Constitution," in Richard Beeman, Stephen Botein, and Edward C. Carter II, eds., *Beyond Confederation: Origins of the Constitution and American National Identity* (Chapel Hill: University of North Carolina Press, 1987), 69–109, quotation at 70; John Brooke, "Cultures of Nationalism, Movements of Reform, and the Composite-Federal Polity: From Revolutionary Settlement to Antebellum Crisis," *Journal of the Early Republic* 39, no. 1 (Spring 2009): 6–7; John M. Murrin, "The Great Inversion, or Court versus Country: A Comparison of the Revolutionary Settlements in England (1688–1721) and America (1776–1816)," in J. G. A. Pocock, ed., *Three British Revolutions: 1641, 1688, 1776* (Princeton, NJ: Princeton University Press, 1980), 368–425, quotation at 425.

3. On the international turn in the history of the founding, see David Armitage, *The Declaration of Independence: A Global History* (Cambridge, MA: Harvard University Press, 2007); David M. Golove and Daniel J. Hulsebosch, "A Civilized Nation: The Early American Constitution, the Law of Nations, and the Pursuit of International Recognition," *New York University Law Review* 85, no. 4 (October 2010): 932–1066; David C. Hendrickson, *Peace Pact: The Lost World of the American Founding* (Lawrence: Kansas University Press, 2003); Martin Öhman, "The American Union in an Age of Revolutions: Federal Politics, Political Economy, and the Geopolitical Origins of Interstate Cooperation and Conflict, 1783–1821" (PhD diss., University of Virginia, 2010); Peter S. Onuf, "A Declaration of Independence for Diplomatic Historians," *Diplomatic History* 22, no. 1 (Winter 1998): 71–83; Leonard J. Sadosky, *Revolutionary Negotiations: Indians, Empires, and Diplomats in the Founding of America* (Charlottesville: University of Virginia Press, 2009); Robbie J. Totten, "Security, Two Diplomacies, and the Formation of the U.S. Constitution: Review, Interpretation, and New Directions for the Study of the Early American

Period," *Diplomatic History* 36, no. 1 (Winter 2012): 77–117. Four decades ago, Gerald Stourzh pointed out that our understanding of the founding suffered from our artificial separation of international from domestic politics, a separation that the founders themselves would scarcely have understood. See Stourzh, *Alexander Hamilton and the Idea of Republican Government* (Stanford, CA: Stanford University Press, 1970), 127–28. Despite the excellent works cited here, the full reincorporation of international relations into our understanding of the political theory of the founding remains before us.

    4. Roger Sherman to ——, December 8, 1787, in James H. Hutson, ed., *Supplement to Max Farrand's The Record of the Federal Convention of 1787* (New Haven, CT: Yale University Press, 1987), 288.

    5. Madison, "Federalist 45," in *Federalist*, 314.

    6. Declaration of Independence, *DHRC*, 1:73–75; Committee Report on Carrying the Confederation into Effect and on Additional Powers Needed by Congress, *DHRC*, 1:145; Journals of Congress, June 7, 1776, in Worthington C. Ford et al., eds., *Journals of the Continental Congress*, 34 vols. (Washington, DC: Government Printing Office, 1904–1937), 5:425; Act of Confederation of the United States of America, *DHRC*, 1:86; introduction to the Articles of Confederation, *DHRC*, 1:78; Armitage, *Declaration of Independence*; Onuf, "Declaration of Independence"; Jack N. Rakove, *The Beginnings of National Politics: An Interpretative History of the Continental Congress* (New York: Knopf, 1979), 135–191; Sadosky, *Revolutionary Negotiations*, 59–89.

    7. Declaration of Independence, *DHRC*, 1:75; Act of Confederation of the United States of America, *DHRC*, 1:86, 88–91; Rakove, *Beginnings of National Politics*, 157–58, 162, 172, 276; John M. Murrin, "1787: The Invention of American Federalism," in David E. Narrett and Joyce S. Goldberg, eds., *Essays on Liberty and Federalism: The Shaping of the U.S. Constitution* (College Station: Texas A&M University Press, 1988), 20–47, quotation at 32; Hendrickson, *Peace Pact*, 136. The first draft of the Articles made specific use of the term "internal police" in the third article: "Each colony shall retain and enjoy as much of its present Laws, Rights, and Customs, as it may think fit, and reserves to itself the sole and exclusive Regulation of Government of its internal police, in all matters that shall not interfere with the Articles of this Confederation." Draft of Articles of Confederation, *DHRC*, 1:79. There was a Court of Appeals that heard admiralty appeals from state trial courts during the Confederation. See Henry J. Bourguignon, *The First Federal Court: The Federal Appellate Prize Court of the American Revolution, 1775–1787* (Philadelphia: American Philosophical Society, 1977). Executive departments also developed toward the close of the War of Independence. A post office was set up already in 1775, and departments for foreign affairs, war, and finance were created in 1781. The Continental army can of course be seen as a field service of Congress, and there were diplomatic agents and collectors of revenue. See Jennings B. Sanders, *Evolution of Executive Departments of the Continental Congress, 1774–1789* (Chapel Hill: University of North Carolina Press, 1935).

    8. John Locke, *Two Treatises of Government*, ed. Peter Laslett (Cambridge: Cambridge University Press, 1988), 365; Montesquieu, *The Spirit of the Laws*, trans. and ed. Anne M. Cohler, Basia Carolyn Miller, and Harold Samuel Stone (Cambridge: Cambridge University Press, 1989), 156–57; "The Essex Results," in Philip P. Kurland and Ralph Lerner, eds., *The Founders' Constitution*, 5 vols. (Chicago: University of Chicago Press,

1986), 1:117; Sadosky, *Revolutionary Negotiations*, 85; Peter S. Onuf, *Origins of the Federal Republic: Jurisdictional Controversies in the United States, 1775–1787* (Philadelphia: University of Pennsylvania Press, 1983); Rakove, *Beginnings of National Politics*, 163–215.

9. Adams and Braxton quoted in Rakove, *Beginnings of National Politics*, 148–49; Burke quoted in Hendrickson, *Peace Pact*, 135; Murrin, "Invention of American Federalism," 32; Onuf, "First Federal Constitution," 89; Hendrickson, *Peace Pact*, 135–37.

10. A Citizen of New-York [John Jay], "An Address to the People of the State of New York," April 15, 1788, *DHRC*, 17:108–9; Andrew C. McLaughlin, *The Confederation and the Constitution, 1783–1789* (New York: J. and J. Harper, 1905), 45–46. There is an enormous literature on the political ideology of the American Whigs; see principally Bernard Bailyn, *Ideological Origins of the American Revolution* (Cambridge, MA: Harvard University Press, 1967); Gordon S. Wood, *The Creation of the American Republic, 1776–1787* (Chapel Hill: University of North Carolina Press, 1969); and Lance Banning, *The Jeffersonian Persuasion: Evolution of a Party Ideology* (Ithaca, NY: Cornell University Press, 1978). On the military aspects of the War of Independence, see Robert Middlekauff, *The Glorious Cause: The American Revolution, 1763–1789*, rev. and ext. ed. (New York: Oxford University Press, 2005). Financial weakness led to logistical problems in supplying the Continental army; see E. Wayne Carp, *To Starve the Army at Pleasure: Continental Army Administration and American Political Culture, 1775–1783* (Chapel Hill: University of North Carolina Press, 1984); and James A. Huston, *Logistics of Liberty: American Services of Supply in the Revolutionary War and After* (Newark: University of Delaware Press, 1991).

11. Ford, *Journals of the Continental Congress*, 2:103 (quotation), 105–6, 221–22, 3:390, 475–78; Farley Grubb, "The Continental Dollar: How Much Was Really Issued?," *Journal of Economic History* 68 (2008): 283–91; E. James Ferguson, "Currency Finance: An Interpretation of Colonial Monetary Practices," *WMQ*, 3d ser., 10, no. 2 (April 1953): 153–83; Edwin J. Perkins, *American Public Finance and Public Services, 1700–1815* (Columbus: Ohio State University Press, 1994), 85–95; Robert Morris to Jacques Necker, June 15, 1781 (never sent), in E. James Ferguson, ed., *The Papers of Robert Morris*, 9 vols. (Pittsburgh: University of Pittsburgh Press, 1973–1999), 1:150; Nils Collin, "Relation of Förenta Staterna," n.p., Collin Papers, Royal Academy of Science, Stockholm. The depreciation of the Continental currency is traced in John J. McCusker, *How Much is That in Real Money? A Historical Commodity Price Index for Use as a Deflator of Money Values in the Economy of the United States* (Worcester, MA: American Antiquarian Society, 2001), 76–77, table C-1. A contemporary estimate of the colonial money stock placed it at $30 million, whereas modern estimates have been $11–12 million; see John J. McCusker and Russel R. Menard, *The Economy of British America, 1607–1789*, 2d ed. (Chapel Hill: University of North Carolina Press, 1991), 337–41; Perkins, *American Public Finance*, 55. The standard account of the funding of the War of Independence remains E. James Ferguson, *The Power of the Purse: A History of American Public Finance, 1776–1790* (Chapel Hill: University of North Carolina Press, 1961), 25–47.

12. Ferguson, *Power of the Purse*, 25–69; Perkins, *American Public Finance*, 85–105. On the depreciation of state currency during the revolution, see McCusker, *How Much*, 76–79, tables C-1 and C-2.

13. E. James Ferguson, "Political Economy, Public Liberty, and the Formation of the Constitution," *WMQ*, 3d ser., 40, no. 3 (July 1983), 389–412; Ferguson, *Power of the Purse*, 40–46, 55–56, 124–76; Perkins, *American Public Finance*, 104–35; William Graham Sumner, *The Financier and the Finances of the American Revolution* (New York: Dodd, Mead, 1891).

14. Noah Webster, *Sketches of American Policy* (Hartford: Hudson and Goodwin, 1785), 22. Webster also wrote that "a law without penalty is mere *advice*; a magistrate without the power of punishment is a *cypher*." See also Pelatiah Webster, *A Dissertation on the Political Union and Constitution of the Thirteen United States, of North America* (Philadelphia: T. Bradford, 1783), 7–8; Alexander Hamilton, "Continental Congress: Unsubmitted Resolution Calling for a Convention to Amend the Articles of Confederation," July 1783, *PAH*, 3:420–26; A Citizen of New York [John Jay], *DHRC*, 17:109; Hamilton, "Federalist 22," in *Federalist*, 21, 129–30.

15. François Furstenberg, "The Significance of the Trans-Appalachian Frontier in Atlantic History," *American Historical Review* 113, no. 3 (June 2008): 647–77; Marie-Jeanne Rossignol, *The Nationalist Ferment: The Origins of U.S. Foreign Policy, 1792–1812* (Columbus: Ohio State University Press, 2004), 3–11.

16. Frederick W. Marks III, *Independence on Trial: Foreign Affairs and the Making of the Constitution* (Baton Rouge: Louisiana State University Press, 1973); Drew R. McCoy, "The Virginia Port Bill of 1784," *Virginia Magazine of History and Biography* 84, no. 3 (July 1975): 288–303; Onuf, *Origins of the Federal Republic*; Sadosky, *Revolutionary Negotiations*, 119–40; Golove and Hulsebosch, "A Civilized Nation," 953–57, Sheffield quote at 957; Hamilton, "Federalist 15," in *Federalist*, 91.

17. Webster, *Dissertation on Political Union*, 40, 42.

18. Merrill Jensen, introduction to *DHRC*, 1:52–68. On the western question, see Peter S. Onuf, *Statehood and Union: A History of the Northwest Ordinance* (Bloomington: Indiana University Press, 1987).

19. Grant of temporary power to regulate commerce, April 30, 1784, *DHRC*, 1:154; Amendment to grant commercial powers to Congress, March 28, 1785, ibid., 1:155; Amendments to the Articles of Confederation proposed by a Grand Committee of Congress, August 7, 1786, ibid., 1:164.

20. Amendment to give Congress coercive power over the states and their citizens, *DHRC*, 1:142–43.

21. Grant of power to collect import duties, *DHRC*, 1:140–41; Grant of temporary power to collect import duties and request for supplementary funds, April 18, 1783, ibid., 1:146–48; Roger H. Brown, *Redeeming the Republic: Federalists, Taxation, and the Origins of the Constitution* (Baltimore: Johns Hopkins University Press, 1993); Robin Einhorn, *American Taxation, American Slavery* (Chicago: University of Chicago Press, 2006), 132–38; Ferguson, *Power of the Purse*, 145–76; Rakove, *Beginning of National Politics*, 297–329.

22. "Proceedings and Report of the Commissioners at Annapolis, Maryland," September 11–14, 1786, *DHRC*, 1:184; "Confederation Congress Calls the Constitutional Convention," February 21, 1787, *DHRC*, 1:187.

23. There is a large literature on the convention. Standard scholarly accounts are Max Farrand, *The Framing of the Constitution of the United States* (New Haven, CT:

Yale University Press, 1913); Charles Warren, *The Making of the Constitution* (Boston: Little, Brown, 1928); and Clinton Rossiter, *1787: The Grand Convention* (New York: Macmillan, 1966). The most recent narrative history is Richard Beeman, *Plain, Honest Men: The Making of the American Constitution* (New York: Random House, 2009). The best analytical works are Lance Banning, *The Sacred Fire of Liberty: James Madison and the Founding of the Federal Republic* (Ithaca, NY: Cornell University Press, 1995), 1–191; Jack N. Rakove, *Original Meanings: Politics and Ideas in the Making of the Constitution* (New York: Knopf, 1996); and Michael P. Zuckert, "A System without Precedent: Federalism in the American Constitution," in Leonard W. Levy and Denis J. Mahoney, eds., *The Framing and Ratification of the Constitution* (New York: Macmillan, 1987), 132–50.

24. Pelatiah Webster, *Dissertation on Political Union*, 17–47; Noah Webster, *Sketches of American Policy*, 44; James Madison to Thomas Jefferson, March 19, 1787, *PJM*, 9:317–22; Madison to Edmund Randolph, April 8, 1787, ibid., 9:368–71; Madison to George Washington, April 16, 1787, ibid., 9:382–87, quotation at 369; "The Virginia Resolutions," *DHRC*, 1:243–45; *Records of the Federal Convention*, 1:33 (quotation); Rakove, *Original Meanings*, 35–56; Banning, *Sacred Fire*, 111–37.

25. Madison to George Washington, April 16, 1787, *PJM*, 9:383; *Records of the Federal Convention*, 1:21, 53; Banning, *Sacred Fire*, 159.

26. *Records of the Federal Convention*, 1:18–19, 20.

27. *Records of the Federal Convention*, 1:34, 133, 243.

28. *Records of the Federal Convention*, 2:158–59. The original of the Pinckney Plan is not extant, and scholars have had to reconstruct his proposal; see Beeman, *Plain, Honest Men*, 96–97; J. Franklin Jameson, "Portions of Charles Pinckney's Plans for a Constitution, 1787," *American Historical Review* 9, no. 3 (April 1903): 117–20; Andrew C. McLaughlin, "Sketch of Charles Pinckney's Plan for a Constitution, 1787," *American Historical Review* 9, no. 4 (July 1904): 735–47.

29. *Records of the Federal Convention*, 1:124. On the Connecticut Compromise and the convention's debate about representation, see Beeman, *Plain, Honest Men*, 200–25; and Rakove, *Original Meanings*, 57–70.

30. *Records of the Federal Convention*, 1:21, 164–68, 2:27–28, 390–92; Madison to George Washington, April 16, 1787, *PJM*, 9:383–84; Charles F. Hobson, "The Negative on State Laws: James Madison, the Constitution, and the Crisis of Republican Government," *WMQ*, 3d ser., 36, no. 2 (April 1979): 215–35; Banning, *Sacred Fire*, 117–21; Rakove, *Original Meanings*, 50–52.

31. *Records of the Federal Convention*, 2:27–28.

32. Hobson, "Negative on State Laws," 226, 228–29.

33. *Records of the Federal Convention*, 1:21, 34, 54. In a letter to Thomas Jefferson, Madison remarked that an administration of the laws relying on coercion of delinquent states resembled "much more a civil war, than the administration of a regular Government." Madison to Thomas Jefferson, October 24, 1787, *PJM*, 10:207.

34. *Records of the Federal Convention*, 1:243, 256, 339–40. See also Hamilton, "Federalist 15," in *Federalist*, 95–96.

35. *Records of the Federal Convention*, 1:286, 2:26, 181, 354, 359, 569.

36. *Records of the Federal Convention*, 2:182.

37. *Records of the Federal Convention*, 2:182–83; George William Van Cleve, *A*

Slaveholder's Union: Slavery, Politics, and the Constitution in the Early American Republic (Chicago: University of Chicago Press, 2010), 130; David Waldstreicher, *Slavery's Constitution: From Revolution to Ratification* (New York: Hill and Wang, 2009), 90–93.

38. *Records of the Federal Convention*, 2:307–8, 449, 450. See also Madison, in *Records of the Federal Convention*, 2:306–7, 451–52; and Hamilton, "Federalist 13," in *Federalist*, 81–82.

39. *Records of the Federal Convention*, 2:307, 360, 363–64; Rakove, *Original Meanings*, 84–88.

40. *Records of the Federal Convention*, 2:305–8, 359–65, 369–75, quotations at 364, 374; Waldstreicher, *Slavery's Constitution*, 93–97.

41. *Records of the Federal Convention*, 2:400, 414–17, 449–53, quotations at 449–50, 453; Van Cleve, *Slaveholders' Union*, 144–53; Waldstreicher, *Slavery's Constitution*, 97–101.

42. *Records of the Federal Convention*, 1:20; "Amendment to Share Expenses According to Population," April 18, 1783, *DHRC*, 1:150; Einhorn, *American Taxation, American Slavery*, 120–32, 138–49.

43. *Records of the Federal Convention*, 2:223, 307. The process whereby the convention adopted the three-fifths rule can be traced in *Records of the Federal Convention*, 1:201, 243, 592–93, 595, 597, 2:178, 219, 357. See also Einhorn, *American Taxation, American Slavery*, 162–73; Howard A. Ohline, "Republicanism and Slavery: Origins of the Three-Fifths Clause in the United States Constitution," *WMQ*, 3d ser., 26, no. 4 (October 1971): 563–84; Van Cleve, *Slaveholder's Union*, 115–30; Waldstreicher, *Slavery's Constitution*, 72–87.

44. *Records of the Federal Convention*, 2:308–10.

45. *Records of the Federal Convention*, 2:325–27, 392, 413.

46. *Records of the Federal Convention*, 2:327–28, 355–56, 377, 392, 412–14.

47. "The President of the Convention to the President of Congress," September 17, 1787, *DHRC*, 1:305–6.

48. "Cumberland County Petition to the Pennsylvania Convention, 28 November, 1787," *DHRC*, 2:299.

49. The history of ratification is masterfully told in Pauline Maier, *Ratification: The People Debate the Constitution, 1787–1788* (New York: Simon and Schuster, 2010). For the ratification debate, see Max M. Edling, *A Revolution in Favor of Government: Origins of the U.S. Constitution and the Making of the American State* (New York: Oxford University Press, 2003).

50. Hamilton, "Federalist 34," in *Federalist*, 213–15.

51. Hamilton, "Federalist 30" and "Federalist 34," in *Federalist*, 192–93, 210–13. Hamilton's political theory is spelled out in essays 6–9 and 11. It places war and international competition at the center of political life.

52. Hamilton, "Federalist 31" and "Federalist 34," in *Federalist*, 195–96, 214.

53. Hamilton, "Federalist 12," "Federalist 15," and "Federalist 30," in *Federalist*, 78–79, 93, 189–90. See also "Federalist 23" and "Federalist 31," in ibid., 147–48, 195–96.

54. Hamilton, "Federalist 12," in *Federalist*, 75–76.

55. Hamilton, "Federalist 12" and "Federalist 36," in *Federalist*, 75–79, 227–29.

56. Hamilton, "Federalist 21," "Federalist 35," and "Federalist 36," in *Federalist*, 133–34, 221–22, 228–29.

CHAPTER 2

1. *DHFFC*, 10:1.
2. Fisher Ames, *DHFFC*, 10:550.
3. Robert A. Becker, *Revolution, Reform, and the Politics of American Taxation, 1763–1783* (Baton Rouge: Louisiana State University Press, 1980), 219–29; Becker, "Salus Populi Suprema Lex: Public Peace and South Carolina Debtor Relief Laws," *South Carolina Historical Magazine* 80 (1979): 65–75; Roger H. Brown, *Redeeming the Republic: Federalists, Taxation, and the Origins of the Constitution* (Baltimore: Johns Hopkins University Press, 1993), 32–138; Richard Buel Jr., *Dear Liberty: Connecticut's Mobilization for the Revolutionary War* (Middletown, CT: Wesleyan University Press, 1980), 326–27, 330; John P. Kaminski, "Democracy Run Rampant: Rhode Island in the Confederation," in James Kirby Martin, ed., *The Human Dimensions of Nation Making: Essays on Colonial and Revolutionary America* (Madison: State Historical Society of Wisconsin, 1976), 243–69; Edwin J. Perkins, *American Public Finance and Financial Services, 1700–1815* (Columbus: Ohio State University Press, 1994), 137–96.
4. Oliver Wolcott, "Direct Taxes," *ASP: Finance*, 1:437; Alexander Hamilton, "The Defence of the Funding System," *PAH*, 19:17–18. For contemporary reactions to Shays's Rebellion, see Forrest McDonald and Ellen Shapiro McDonald, *Requiem: Variations on Eighteenth-Century Themes* (Lawrence: University Press of Kansas, 1988), 72–76.
5. Hamilton, "Defence of the Funding System," *PAH* XIX, 35.
6. *DHFFC*, 10:2–3.
7. The standard account of the public finances of the War of Independence and the postwar period makes only a passing reference to tax reductions in Connecticut, Massachusetts, New York, Pennsylvania, and Maryland and says nothing about their scope; see E. James Ferguson, *The Power of the Purse: A History of American Political Finance, 1776–1790* (Chapel Hill: University of North Carolina Press, 1961), 332. The funding and assumption plans are treated in Stanley Elkins and Eric McKitrick, *The Age of Federalism* (New York: Oxford University Press, 1993), 114–23, which takes no note of changes in the fiscal system resulting from the reforms. Two important neoprogressive interpretations of the origins of the Federalists' financial program, which are also silent on tax reductions, are Terry Bouton, *Taming Democracy: "The People," the Founders, and the Troubled Ending of the American Revolution* (New York: Oxford University Press, 2007); and Woody Holton, *Unruly Americas and the Origins of the Constitution* (New York: Hill and Wang, 2007).
8. Becker, *Revolution*, 48, 70, 79–80; Paul B Trescott, "Federal-State Financial Relations, 1790–1860," *Journal of Economic History* 15 (1955): 227, 232 (investments and loans); Don C. Sowers, *The Financial History of New York State from 1789 to 1912* (New York, 1914), appendix 2, "Classified Receipts," 324–25 (land); Perkins, *American Public Finance*, 138 (loyalist property). There are many accounts of paper money issues. See, for instance, E. James Ferguson, "Currency Finance: An Interpretation of Colonial Monetary Practices," *WMQ*, 3d ser., 10, no. 2 (April 1953), 153–80; Merrill Jensen, *The New Nation:*

A History of the United States during the Confederation, 1781–1789 (1950; repr., Boston: Northeastern University Press, 1981), 313–26; Forrest McDonald, *E Pluribus Unum: The Formation of the American Republic 1776–1790*, 2d ed. (Indianapolis: Liberty, 1979), 80, 97–99, 111–13, 146–48, 179–81; Perkins, *American Public Finance*, 137–72; *Votes and Proceedings of the House of Delegates of the State of Maryland, November Session, 1785* (November 14, 1785–March 12, 1786) (Annapolis, 1786), 12–18; *Votes and Proceedings of the House of Delegates of the State of Maryland, November Session, 1786* (Annapolis, 1787), 39–40; *Votes and Proceedings of the House of Delegates of the State of Maryland, November Session, 1787* (Annapolis, 1788), 26–27.

9. See sources cited in tables 2.2 and 2.4. For secondary accounts of taxation in the period, see Becker, *Revolution*; Edwin J. Perkins, *Economy of Colonial America*, 2d ed. (New York: Columbia University Press, 1988), 123–44; and Robin L. Einhorn, *American Taxation, American Slavery* (Chicago: University of Chicago Press, 2006), 25–199.

10. A reading of the session laws of the period shows that most states experimented with a wide range of fees as well as excise and impost duties. See also Becker, *Revolution*, 46; Perkins, *Economy of Colonial America*, table 7.1.

11. See Patrick K. O'Brien, "The Political Economy of British Taxation, 1660–1815," *Economic History Review*, 2d ser., 41, no. 1 (1988): 1–32, for the structure of the British tax revenue.

12. Brown, *Redeeming the Republic*, 98, 118; Richard Buel Jr., "The Public Creditor Interest in Massachusetts, 1780–1786," in Robert A. Gross, ed., *In Debt to Shays: The Bicentennial of an Agrarian Rebellion* (Charlottesville: University Press of Virginia, 1993), 50; Max M. Edling, *A Revolution in Favor of Government: Origins of the U.S. Constitution and the Making of the American State* (New York: Oxford University Press, 2003), 180–83; Jackson Turner Main, *The Antifederalists: Critics of the Constitution, 1781–1788* (Chapel Hill: University of North Carolina Press, 1961), 143–46; "South Carolina House Journal, 7 January 1790," in Michael E. Stevens, ed., *The State Records of South Carolina: Journals of the House of Representatives 1789–1790* (Columbia: University of South Carolina Press, 1984), 302.

13. Becker, *Revolution*, 38.

14. For the Massachusetts estimate, see McDonald and McDonald, *Requiem*, 70.

15. Becker, *Revolution*, 38–39, 72–74, 109–10; Brown, *Redeeming the Republic*, tables 7 and 11.

16. For two examples of a tax laws see [Delaware, Session Laws (Wilmington)], June 4, 1785; [New Jersey, Session Laws (Trenton)], December 20, 1783. For state fiscal policy and its consequences, see Terry Bouton, "A Road Closed: Rural Insurgency in Post-Independence Pennsylvania," *JAH* 87, no. 3 (December 2000): 859; and Buel, *Dear Liberty*, 320, 322–24. On Massachusetts and Shays's Rebellion, see Brown, *Redeeming the Republic*, 97–121; Buel, "Public Creditor Interest," 47–56; McDonald and McDonald, *Requiem*, 59–83; Perkins, *American Public Finance*, 173–86. For British taxes and population, see O'Brien, "Political Economy," table 2; and Edward A. Wrigley and Roger S. Schofield, *The Population History of England, 1541–1871* (London: Arnold, 1981), table 7.8. Conversion of Massachusetts and Sterling pounds to dollar values is based on John J. McCusker, *How Much Is That in Real Money? A Historical Commodity Price Index for Use as a Deflator of Money Values in the Economy of the United States*, 2d ed. (Worces-

ter, MA: American Antiquarian Society, 2001), 34, table 1. According to McDonald and McDonald, current and overdue taxes amounted to thirty-three dollars per adult male in the three western counties that took part in the rebellion. *Requiem*, 69.

17. Brown, *Redeeming the Republic*, 236, tables 7 and 11; *State of the Accounts of David Rittenhouse, Esq., Treasurer of Pennsylvania; from 1st of January till 1st November, 1787; Including His Continental and State Money Accounts for the Year 1786* (Philadelphia: Aitken, 1790), 6–40; North Carolina House Journal, Dec. 2, 1788, in William L. Saunders and Walter Clark, eds., *State Records of North Carolina*, 26 vols. (Goldsboro, NC: Nash Brothers, 1886–1907), 21:142; *Proceedings of the House of Delegates of the State of Maryland, November Session, 1790* (Annapolis, 1791), 78–79; *Journal of the House of Delegates of the Commonwealth of Virginia* (December 4, 1797–January 19, 1798) (Richmond: Davis, 1798), 53.

18. Ferguson, *Power of the Purse*; McCusker, *How Much*, 61–88; Robert E. Wright, *Hamilton Unbound: Finance and the Creation of the American Republic* (Westport, CT: Greenwood, 2002), 9–57; Ronald Michener and Robert E. Wright, "State 'Currencies' and the Transition to the U.S. Dollar: Clarifying Some Confusions," *American Economic Review* 95, no. 3 (June 2005): 682–703.

19. Ferguson, *Power of the Purse*, 220–50; Brown, *Redeeming the Republic*, 53–138.

20. Robert E. Wright, *The Wealth of Nations Rediscovered: Integration and Expansion in American Financial Markets, 1780–1850* (New York: Cambridge University Press, 2002), 64; Mathew M'Connell, *An Essay on the Domestic Debts of the United States of America* (Philadelphia: Robert Aitken, 1787), iii, quoted in ibid., 65.

21. As economic historians explore the role of the financial sector in economic growth and especially in the coming of the industrial revolution, we are likely to learn more about the securities market in the 1780s, but at present this is unmapped territory. See Richard Sylla, "Shaping the U.S. Financial System," in Sylla, Richard Tilly, and Gabriel Tortella, eds., *The State, the Financial System, and Economic Modernization* (New York: Cambridge University Press, 1999), 249–70; Wright, *The Wealth of Nations Rediscovered*. The state and federal public debt are discussed and a number of securities and indents illustrated in William G. Anderson, *The Price of Liberty: The Public Debt of the American Revolution* (Charlottesville: University Press of Virginia, 1983).

22. Woody Holton, "'From the Labor of Others': The War Bonds Controversy and the Origins of the Constitution in New England," *WMQ*, 3d ser., 61, no. 2 (April 2004): 308–11, tables I, II; Ferguson, *Power of the Purse*, 220–50; Perkins, *American Public Finance*, 137–72.

23. The emissions of the 1780s are treated in Perkins, *American Public Finance*, 142–65. The emission of Rhode Island is treated in Ferguson, *Power of the Purse*, 243–44; Brown, *Redeeming the Republic*, 83–96; Kaminski, "Democracy Run Rampant" ; and Kaminski, *George Clinton: Yeoman Politician of the New Republic* (Madison, WI: Madison House, 1993), 98–104.

24. For bills of credit, see Perkins, *American Public Finance*, 142–65; Brown, *Redeeming the Republic*, 69–82, 123–31, 137–38; W. Robert Higgins, "A Financial History of the American Revolution in South Carolina" (PhD diss., Duke University, 1969), 243–67; and *Charleston Evening Gazette*, February 9, 1786.

25. Comparisons between colonial and British tax rates are found in Perkins,

Economy of Colonial America, 125; and H. James Henderson, "Taxation and Political Culture: Massachusetts and Virginia, 1760-1800," *WMQ*, 3d ser., vol. 47, no. 1 (January 1990): 94n4. Massachusetts taxes are from Joseph B. Felt, "Statistics of Taxation in Massachusetts, Including Valuation and Population," American Statistical Association, *Collections* 1, no. 3 (1847), 410; all others from Becker, *Revolution*, 34, 70–72. On colonial taxation generally, see Alvin Rabushka, *Taxation in Colonial America* (Princeton, NJ: Princeton University Press, 2008).

26. Felt, "Statistics of Taxation," 543.

27. Nor did the Pennsylvania bills of credit circulate widely. Michener and Wright argue that because of depreciation the bills became an object of speculative investment rather than a circulating medium. "State 'Currencies' and the Transition to the US Dollar," 682–703.

28. New Jersey raised £10,000 annually to finance the running costs of the government and £43,750 to pay debt charges. In other words, about 80 percent of total taxes were intended for debt payments. In 1784, it was estimated that payments on the public debt in Virginia also amounted to about 80 percent of total expenses. Expenses in Massachusetts were $352,400 in 1786. Of this sum, interest payments accounted for $278,700, or 79 percent of the total. New Jersey sources are listed in table 2.2. See Jensen, *New Nation*, 304; Paul Studenski and Herman E. Krooss, *Financial History of the United States: Fiscal, Monetary, Banking, and Tariff, Including Financial Administration and State and Local Finance*, 2d ed. (New York: McGraw-Hill, 1963), 58n19; B. U. Ratchford, *American State Debts* (Durham, NC: Duke University Press, 1941), 46. Jensen also notes that in the early 1780s, 50 to 90 percent of state expenditures went to interest payments on the state debts, whereas Ratchford gives the same figures for the later half of the 1780s.

29. Perkins, *American Public Finance*, 142–43, 213.

30. Ferguson, *Power of the Purse*, 289–343; McDonald, *Alexander Hamilton: A Biography* (New York: Norton, 1979), 143–88; Perkins, *American Public Finance*, 199–234.

31. Jensen, *New Nation*, 425, 348; Brown, *Redeeming the Republic*, 3, 242. See also Bouton, "A Road Closed," 877; Bouton, "'No Wonder the Times Were Troublesome': The Origins of Fries's Rebellion, 1783–1799," *Pennsylvania History* 67 (Winter 2000): 37.

32. Brown, *Redeeming the Republic*, 236. See also Merrill Jensen, *The Making of the American Constitution* (Princeton, NJ: D. Van Nostrand, 1964), 81, which notes that the federal government used its fiscal power sparingly after the adoption of the Constitution.

33. Pelatiah Webster, "Strictures on the Net Produce of the Taxes of Great Britain," in *Political Essays on the Nature and Operation of Money, Public Finances and Other Subjects* (Philadelphia, 1791), 468. For the views of some of the leading political theorists and economists of the time, see William Blackstone, *Commentaries on the Laws of England*, 4 vols. (Oxford, 1765–1769) 1:316–71; David Hume, "Of Taxes," in *Political Essays*, ed. Knud Haakonssen (Cambridge: Cambridge University Press, 1994), 162–63; Charles de Secondat, Baron de Montesquieu, *Spirit of the Laws*, ed. and trans. Anne M. Cohler, Basia Carolyn Miller, and Harold Samuel Stone (Cambridge: Cambridge University Press, 1989), 217; Adam Smith, *An Inquiry into the Nature and Causes of the Wealth of Nations*, ed. R. H. Campbell, A. S. Skinner, and W. B. Todd, 2 vols. (Oxford: Oxford University Press, 1976), 2:826, 895.

34. The relevant revenue acts are An Act for Laying a Duty on Goods, Wares, and Merchandises Imported into the United States, July 4, 1789, and An Act Imposing Duties on Tonnage, July 20, 1789, ch. 2 and ch. 3, *US Statutes at Large*, 1:24–27, 27–28. These rates were increased by subsequent legislation. See Webster, "Strictures on the Taxes of Great-Britain," 468; and Hamilton, "Federalist 21," in *Federalist*, 134.

35. *DHFFC*, 10:2–6 (Madison, Boudinot).

36. *DHFFC*, 10:11, 29, 53, 193.

37. *DHFFC*, 10:374, 553 (Madison), 555 (White). For the opposition to Fitzsimons, see *DHFFC*, 10:31–39 (White, Tucker, Hartley, Madison, and Boudinot). For Madison's commercial policy recommendations, see ibid., 10:313–14.

38. *DHFFC*, 11:1087 (Sedgwick), 10:418 (Madison).

39. *DHFFC*, 10:20 (Tucker), 22 (Madison), 127–30 (Tucker and Fitzsimons), 517 (Smith).

40. For the debate, see *DHFFC*, 10:334–38, 367–80, 623–28, quotations at 627 (Gerry) and 369 (Thatcher).

41. On molasses, see *DHFFC*, 5:964, 974n, 940. On the slave impost, see ibid., 10:644–45 (Jackson), 645 (Tucker), 646 (Sherman), 647–49, and 651.

42. Alexander Hamilton to James Madison, October 12, 1789, *PAH*, 5:439.

43. Stephen Higginson to Alexander Hamilton, November 11, *PAH*, 5:511; William Bingham to Alexander Hamilton, November 25, 1789, ibid., 5:549–50; James Madison to Alexander Hamilton, November 19, 1789, *PJM*, 12:449–50.

44. *Report on Public Credit*, *PAH*, 6:102; *Report on Funds for the Payment of the Interest on the States' Debts*, ibid., 6:287–89. Philadelphia collector of the customs Sharp Delaney suggested a duty on sales at auction in January 1790; see Sharp Delaney to Alexander Hamilton, January 8, 1790, ibid., 6:185.

45. *Report on Public Credit*, *PAH*, 6:99; *Report on Funds for the Payment of the Interest on the States' Debts*, ibid., 6:286–89; *First Report on the Further Provision Necessary for Establishing Public Credit*, ibid., 7:231.

46. An Act Laying Duties upon Carriages for the Conveyance of Persons, June 5, 1794, ch. 45, *US Statutes at Large*, 1:373–75; An Act Laying Duties on Licenses for Selling Wines and Foreign Distilled Spirituous Liquors by Retail, June 5, 1794, ibid., ch. 48, 1:376–78; An Act Laying Certain Duties upon Snuff and Refined Sugar, June 5, 1794, ibid., ch. 51, 1:384–90; An Act Laying Duties on Property Sold at Auction, June 9, 1794, ibid., ch. 55, 1:397–400.

47. *Historical Statistics of the United States, Colonial Times to 1970*, 2 vols. (Washington, DC: Bureau of the Census, 1975) vol. 2, series Y, 352–53; Felt, "Statistics of Taxation," 438; "Statement of Receipts at the Treasury from the Collectors of the Customs, from the Commencement of the Present Government to the Close of the Year 1799," *ASP: Finance*, 5:666.

48. John J. McCusker, "Estimating Early American Gross Domestic Product," *Historical Methods* 33, no. 3 (2000): 155–62, quotation at 159; Brown, *Redeeming the Republic*, 235–36.

49. *Historical Statistics of the United States, Colonial Times to 1970*, vol. 2, series U, 9. Because most of the states imposed duties according to weight and measure and the federal government according to value, it is necessary to know the value of goods—for

instance a pound of tea or a gallon of Madeira—in order to compare customs duties. A comparison between federal legislation of 1789 and ad valorem rates on some items in New York legislation from 1784 and 1787 suggests that customs rates were doubled. See An Act for Laying a Duty on Goods, Wares, and Merchandises Imported into the United States, July 4, 1789, ch. 2, *US Statutes at Large*, 1:24–27; William F. Zornow, "New York Tariff Polices, 1775–1789," *New York History* 37 (1956): 44–47. On the Federalists, the Customs Service, and the merchants, see Frederick Dalzell, "Prudence and the Golden Egg: Establishing the Federal Government in Providence, Rhode Island," *New England Quarterly* 65, no. 3 (September 1992): 355–88; Dalzell, "Taxation with Representation: Federal Revenue in the Early Republic" (PhD diss., Harvard University, 1993), 84–106; and Carl E. Prince and Mollie Keller, *The U.S. Customs Service: A Bicentennial History* (Washington, DC: Dept. of the Treasury, US Customs Service, 1989), 35–67.

50. Norman K. Risjord, *Chesapeake Politics, 1781–1800* (New York: Columbia University Press, 1978), 472; Van Beck Hall, *Politics without Parties: Massachusetts, 1780–1791* (Pittsburgh: University of Pittsburgh Press, 1972), 296–97; Brown, *Redeeming the Republic*, 236.

51. For the Jeffersonian opposition, see Lance Banning, *The Jeffersonian Persuasion: Evolution of Party Ideology* (Ithaca, NY: Cornell University Press, 1978). On the Whiskey and Fries's Rebellions, see Thomas P. Slaughter, *The Whiskey Rebellion: Frontier Epilogue to the American Revolution* (New York: Oxford University Press, 1986); and Paul Douglas Newman, *Fries's Rebellion: The Enduring Struggle for the American Revolution* (Philadelphia: University of Pennsylvania Press, 2004); and the special issue on Fries's Rebellion in *Pennsylvania History* 67 (Winter 2000).

52. "Estimates of Receipts and Expenditures for 1791–2," *ASP: Finance*, 1:145; "Sinking Fund," ibid., 1:238; Wolcott, "Direct Taxes," 1:418–36.

CHAPTER 3

1. On the visions of Hamilton and Jefferson, compare Dumas Malone, *Jefferson and the Rights of Man*, vol. 2, *Jefferson and His Time* (Boston: Little, Brown, 1951), 286, with Forrest McDonald, *Alexander Hamilton: A Biography* (New York: Norton, 1979), 361–62.

2. "Report Relative to a Provision for the Support of Public Credit," *PAH*, 6:66n99 (quotation). Historians who have claimed that Hamilton wished to perpetuate the debt include Curtis P. Nettles, *The Emergence of a National Economy, 1775–1815* (New York: Holt, Rinehart and Winston, 1962), 116–17; Stanley Elkins and Eric McKitrick, *The Age of Federalism* (New York: Oxford University Press, 1993), 112–13; Lance Banning, *Jefferson and Madison: Three Conversations from the Founding* (Madison, WI: Madison House, 1995), 44; Cathy Matson, "The Revolution, the Constitution, and the New Nation," in Stanley L. Engerman and Robert E. Gallman, eds., *The Cambridge Economic History of the United States*, vol. 1, *The Colonial Era* (New York: Cambridge University Press, 1996), 390; Herbert E. Sloan, *Principle and Interest: Thomas Jefferson and the Problem of Debt* (1995; repr., Charlottesville: University of Virginia Press, 2001), 126. Authoritative accounts of the funding and assumption proposals include E. James Ferguson, *The Power of the Purse: A History of American Public Finance, 1776–1790* (Chapel Hill: University of North Carolina Press, 1961), 289–343; McDonald, *Alexander*

Hamilton, 163–88; Elkins and McKitrick, *Age of Federalism*, 114–23; Edwin J. Perkins, *American Public Finance and Financial Services, 1700–1815* (Columbus: Ohio State University Press, 1994), 199–234.

3. Saul Cornell, *The Other Founders: Anti-Federalism and the Dissenting Tradition in America, 1788–1828* (Chapel Hill: University of North Carolina Press, 1999), 174 (quotation). On Madison's opposition, see Irving Brant, *James Madison: Father of the Constitution, 1787–1800* (Indianapolis: Bobbs-Merrill, 1950), 290–305; Lance Banning, *The Sacred Fire of Liberty: James Madison and the Founding of the Federal Republic* (Ithaca, NY: Cornell University Press, 1995), 309–25. Historians who have argued that funding and assumption created undeserved profits for speculators include John M. Murrin, "The Great Inversion; or, Court versus Country: A Comparison of the Revolutionary Settlements in England (1688–1721) and America (1776–1816)," in J. G. A. Pocock, ed., *Three British Revolutions: 1641, 1688, 1776* (Princeton, NJ: Princeton University Press, 1980), 407; Banning, *Jefferson and Madison*, 41–43. This view is challenged by Edwin J. Perkins, "Madison's Debt Discrimination Proposal Revisited: The Application of Present Value Financial Analysis," in Perkins, *Perkins on U.S. Financial History and Related Topics* (Lanham, MD: University Press of America, 2009), 55–60.

4. Madison's proposal was to give the present holders the equivalent of the highest market price for securities and to give the difference between the market price and the par value to the original holder. Contemporaries debated to what extent it was even possible to determine who the original owners were. Whereas this would most likely have been feasible, it would no doubt have been a time-consuming process; see Brant, *James Madison*, 293–99; and Perkins, *American Public Finance*, 222–23. On the dinner-table bargain, see Brant, *James Madison*, 306–18; Malone, *Jefferson and the Rights of Man*, 286–306; Jacob E. Cooke, "The Compromise of 1790," *WMQ*, 3d ser., 27, no. 4 (October 1970): 523–45; Kenneth R. Bowling with a rebuttal by Jacob E. Cooke, "Dinner at Jefferson's: A Note on Jacob E. Cooke's 'The Compromise of 1790,(closes}" *WMQ*, 3d ser., 28, no. 4 (October 1971): 629–48; McDonald, *Alexander Hamilton*, 181–87; Elkins and McKitrick, *Age of Federalism*, 155–61; and Joseph J. Ellis, *Founding Brothers: The Revolutionary Generation* (New York: Knopf, 2002), 48–80. Jefferson's own account is found in the preface to the *Anas*, in Franklin B. Sawvel, ed., *The Complete Anas of Thomas Jefferson* (New York: Round Table, 1903), 30–34.

5. Thomas Jefferson wrote two important letters to George Washington in which he denounced Alexander Hamilton and the funding and assumption of the public debt in traditional Country Whig terms. He also explained that his own role in securing adoption of the Funding Act was due to his failure to perceive Hamilton's ulterior motives. See Jefferson to Washington, Philadelphia, May 23, 1792, *PTJ*, 23:535–41, quotation at 537; Jefferson to Washington, September 9, 1792, ibid., 24:351–60, quotations at 352, 355. For more on Jefferson's views on public debt, see Sloan, *Principle and Interest*, 44–48, 132, 148–49, 182–83; and McDonald, *Alexander Hamilton*, 184.

6. For the Virginia protest, see "State Debts," *ASP: Finance*, 1:90–91; Sloan, *Principle and Interest*, 169–70. The principal works on the role and influence of the Country Whig tradition in America are Bernard Bailyn, *The Ideological Origins of the American Revolution* (Cambridge, MA: Harvard University Press, 1967); Gordon S. Wood, *The Creation of the American Republic, 1776–1787* (Chapel Hill: University of North Carolina Press,

1969); J. G. A. Pocock, *The Machiavellian Moment: Florentine Political Thought and the Atlantic Republican Tradition* (Princeton, NJ: Princeton University Press, 1975); and Lance Banning, *The Jeffersonian Persuasion: Evolution of a Party Ideology* (Ithaca, NY: Cornell University Press, 1978).

7. Malone, *Jefferson and the Rights of Man*, 305 ("dictator"); Paul Douglas Newman, "The Federalists' Cold War: The Fries Rebellion, National Security, and the State, 1787–1800," *Pennsylvania History* 67, no. 1 (Winter 2000): 64 ("true Machiavellian"). The idea that Hamilton aimed to use the debt to interest the elite in the government's fate can be found in Brant, *James Madison*, 291–92; Banning, *Jeffersonian Persuasion*, 134–40; Murrin, "Great Inversion," 407; E. James Ferguson, "Political Economy, Public Liberty, and the Formation of the Constitution," *WMQ*, 3d ser., 40, no. 3 (July 1983): 389–412; Richard K. Mathews, *The Radical Politics of Thomas Jefferson: A Revisionist View* (Lawrence: University Press of Kansas, 1984), 114; John R. Nelson, *Liberty and Property: Political Economy and Policymaking in the New Nation, 1789–1812* (Baltimore: Johns Hopkins University Press, 1987), 28–32; Gordon S. Wood, *The Radicalism of the American Revolution* (New York: Knopf, 1992), 262–64; James Roger Sharp, *American Politics in the Early Republic: The New Nation in Crisis* (New Haven, CT: Yale University Press, 1993), 40; Banning, *Sacred Fire*, 311. Hamilton's reputation is traced in Stephen F. Knott, *Alexander Hamilton and the Persistence of Myth* (Lawrence, KA: University Press of Kansas, 2002).

8. "The Defence of the Funding System," *PAH*, 19:40–42. Hamilton apparently shared the view of Malachy Postlethwayt, a British writer with whom he was familiar, that "the throne of that prince, in a free nation, must be most firmly established, whose affairs will permit him to ask, and who desires to collect, the fewest taxes from his people." See Postlethwayt, *The Universal Dictionary of Trade and Commerce*, 4th ed. (London, 1774), 1, s.v. "funds".

9. John C. Miller, *Alexander Hamilton: Portrait in Paradox* (New York: Harper, 1959), 229–37, 252–55; Nettles, *Emergence of a National Economy*, 113; McDonald, *Alexander Hamilton*, 165–66; Elkins and McKitrick, *Age of Federalism*, 115; Perkins, *American Public Finance*, 214; Banning, *Sacred Fire*, 310; Richard Sylla, "Shaping the US Financial System, 1690–1913: The Dominant Role of Public Finance," in Sylla, Richard Tilly, and Gabriel Tortella, eds., *The State, the Financial System, and Economic Modernization* (New York: Cambridge University Press, 1999), 262; Ellis, *Founding Brothers*, 64; Sean Wilentz, *The Rise of American Democracy: Jefferson to Lincoln* (New York: Norton, 2005), 43–45.

10. Elkins and McKitrick, *Age of Federalism*, 112; McDonald, *Alexander Hamilton*, 161; Sylla, "Shaping the US Financial System," 258.

11. "Defence of the Funding System," *PAH*, 19:57, 60; Alexander Hamilton to Robert Morris, April 30, 1781, ibid., 2:604–35, quotation at 606; "The Continentalist No. IV," ibid., 2:669–74 quotation at 672; "Report on a Plan for the Further Support of Public Credit," ibid., 18:106, 125. Hamilton's early thoughts on public credit before his appointment as Treasury secretary can be traced in the letter to Morris; "The Continentalist No. IV"; and "Federalist 30," in *Federalist*, 187–93.

12. James R. Sofka, "The Jeffersonian Idea of National Security: Commerce, the Atlantic Balance of Power, and the Barbary War, 1786–1805," *Diplomatic History* 21, no. 4 (Fall 1997): 519–44; Peter S. Onuf and Leonard J. Sadosky, *Jeffersonian America* (Malden,

MA: Blackwell, 2002), 172–221; Leonard J. Sadosky, *Revolutionary Negotiations: Indians, Empires, and Diplomats in the Founding of America* (Charlottesville: University of Virginia Press, 2009); Sofka, "'A Commerce Which Must Be Protected': Thomas Jefferson and the Atlantic International System," paper presented at The Old World and the New: Exchanges Between America and Europe in the Age of Jefferson international conference, arranged by the Robert H. Smith International Center for Jefferson Studies, at Schloss Leopoldskron, Salzburg, Austria, October 12–16, 2005.

13. "Report Relative to a Provision for the Support of Public Credit," *PAH*, 6:67 (quotations). See also Elias Boudinot, *DHFFC*, 12:191, 229. For Hamilton's ideas about international relations and foreign policy, see Gerald Stourzh, *Alexander Hamilton and the Idea of Representative Government* (Stanford, CA: Stanford University Press, 1970); Karl-Friedrich Walling, *Republican Empire: Alexander Hamilton on War and Free Government* (Lawrence: University Press of Kansas, 1999); Lawrence S. Kaplan, *Alexander Hamilton: Ambivalent Anglophile* (Wilmington, DE: Scholarly Resources Books, 2002). For the Jeffersonians, see Onuf and Sadosky, *Jeffersonian America*, 172–221, 253–61.

14. "Defence of the Funding System," *PAH*, 19:54–55; Michael Jenifer Stone, *DHFFC*, 12:262. Stone's remark drew on a long tradition of thought that criticized funding systems for encouraging wars, which is excellently covered in Sloan, *Principle and Interest*, 86–124. Hamilton mentioned the importance of credit to frontier defense and the expedition against the Whiskey Rebellion in "Report on a Plan for the Further Support of Public Credit," *PAH*, 28:125.

15. Jasper Wilson, *A Letter, Commercial and Political, Addressed to the Rt. Honble. William Pitt, In Which the Real Interests of Britain, in the Present Crisis are Considered, and Some Observations are Offered on the General State of Europe*, 3d ed. (London, 1793), 2; Adam Smith, *An Inquiry into the Nature and Causes of the Wealth of Nations*, ed. R. H. Campbell, A. S. Skinner, and W. B. Todd, 2 vols. (Oxford: Oxford University Press, 1976), 2:919–20. The concerns of another prominent critic of Britain's public debt, David Hume, are treated at length in Istvan Hont, "The Rhapsody of Public Debt: David Hume and Voluntary State Bankruptcy," in Nicholas Phillipson and Quentin Skinner, eds., *Political Discourse in Early Modern Britain* (Cambridge: Cambridge University Press, 1993), 321–48.

16. Gabriel Ardant, "Financial Policy and Economic Infrastructure of Modern States and Nations," in Charles Tilly, ed., *The Formation of National States in Western Europe* (Princeton, NJ: Princeton University Press, 1975), 164–242; James C. Riley, *International Government Finance and the Amsterdam Capital Market, 1740–1815* (Cambridge: Cambridge University Press, 1980), 101–8, 195–216; Patrick K. O'Brien, "The Political Economy of British Taxation, 1660–1815," *Economic History Review*, 2d ser., 41, no. 1 (February 1988): 1–32.

17. P. G. M. Dickson, *The Financial Revolution in England: A Study in the Development of Public Credit, 1688–1756* (London: Macmillan, 1967); Riley, *International Government Finance*; Henry Roseveare, *The Financial Revolution, 1660–1760* (London: Longman, 1991).

18. Dickson, *Financial Revolution in England*, 457–520; Robert E. Wright, *The Wealth of Nations Rediscovered: Integration and Expansion in American Financial Markets, 1780–1850* (New York: Cambridge University Press, 2002), 10–16.

19. Fisher Ames, *DHFFC*, 12:220. Intellectual influences on Hamilton's thoughts on public credit are discussed in the introductory note to "Report Relative to a Provision for the Support of Public Credit," *PAH*, 6:51–65; and McDonald, *Alexander Hamilton*, 160–61.

20. Pelatiah Webster, *An Essay on Credit* (Philadelphia: Eleazer Oswald, 1886), quoted in Jennifer J. Baker, *Securing the Commonwealth: Debt, Speculation, and Writing in the Making of Early America* (Baltimore: Johns Hopkins University Press, 2005), 105; Elias Boudinot, *DHFFC*, 12:398; "Report on a Plan for the Further Support of Public Credit," *PAH*, 18:118; "Report Relative to a Provision for the Support of Public Credit," ibid., 6:68. Hamilton's view that public credit depended on the government's ability to honor its promise to creditors was perhaps best expressed in his rejection of proposals that the government levy a tax on securities and sequester investments in the public debt held by subjects of an enemy nation. This discussion makes up the final part of "Report on a Plan for the Further Support of Public Credit," ibid., 18:115–29.

21. "Report Relative to a Provision for the Support of Public Credit," *PAH*, 6:76; Elias Boudinot, *DHFFC*, 12:216, 229 (quotation), 394–410. See also ibid., 324 (John Laurance), 336, 338 (Theodore Sedgwick), 369 (Benjamin Goodhue), 220–21, 339–45 (Fisher Ames), 367, 373 (Thomas Hartley), 451–59 (Elbridge Gerry), 328 (William Smith, SC).

22. "Report Relative to a Provision for the Support of Public Credit," *PAH*, 6:86–87, 137; Ferguson, "Political Economy" ; Frederick Arthur Dalzell, "Taxation with Representation: Federal Revenue in the Early Republic" (PhD diss., Harvard University, 1993); Max M. Edling, *A Revolution in Favor of Government: Origins of the U.S. Constitution and the Making of the American State* (New York: Oxford University Press, 2003), 149–218.

23. Hugh Williamson, *DHFFC*, 13:960.

24. Alexander Hamilton to James Madison, October 12, 1789, *PAH*, 5:439; "Report on a Plan for the Further Support of Public Credit," ibid., 18:102. In September 1790 Hamilton cautioned President Washington that the American people would not be willing to pay even for war except in the most pressing of circumstances: "Our national government is in its infancy," he wrote. "The habits and dispositions of our people are ill suited to those liberal contributions to the treasury, which a war would necessarily exact." Hamilton to Washington, September 15, 1790, ibid., 7:50.

25. "Report Relative to a Provision for the Support of Public Credit," *PAH*, 6:87 (quotation). Edwin J. Perkins points out that Hamilton merely continued a policy of gradual and slow debt redemption that had begun in the states in the mid-1780s after their failure to redeem the Revolutionary debt rapidly through high taxes; see Perkins, *American Public Finance*, 199–234. In the debate on funding and assumption, it was rare for delegates to argue in favor of high taxes. One who did was James Jackson, *DHFFC*, 12: 206, 261.

26. "Defence of the Funding System," *PAH*, 19:23, 30; "Report Relative to a Provision for the Support of Public Credit," ibid., 6:80. Hamilton's argument was often repeated in Congress. See *DHFFC*, 12:504–6, 901 (John Laurance), 506–7, 583 (Fisher Ames), 516–17, 880 (Benjamin Goodhue), 522, 560 (Elbridge Gerry), 539–40 (Theodore Sedgwick), 574, 911–12 (William Smith, SC), 13:1115 (Elbridge Gerry). I am grateful to Richard Buel for stressing Hamilton's belief that the state creditor interest had to be attached to the federal government to facilitate taxation.

27. Elbridge Gerry, *DHFFC*, 13:951, 1117. See also ibid., 12:602, 911–12 (William Smith, SC), 13:1106 (Gerry), 1121–22 (William Smith, SC). Not much work has been done on fiscal administration at the ground level, but see Frederick Dalzell, "Prudence and the Golden Egg: Establishing the Federal Government in Providence, Rhode Island," *New England Quarterly* 45, no. 3 (September 1992): 355–88; Dalzell, "Taxation with Representation," 140–281. This neglect will be corrected by Gautham Rao's forthcoming *At the Water's Edge: Commerce, Governance, and the Origins of the American State* (Chicago: University of Chicago Press, forthcoming). The 1790s tax rebellions are treated by Thomas P. Slaughter, *The Whiskey Rebellion: Frontier Epilogue to the American Revolution* (New York: Oxford University Press, 1986); and Paul Douglas Newman, *Fries's Rebellion: The Enduring Struggle for the American Revolution* (Philadelphia: University of Pennsylvania Press, 2004).

28. Jefferson quoted in Sloan, *Principle and Interest*, 183. For British indebtedness and tax income, see Brian R. Mitchell, *British Historical Statistics* (Cambridge: Cambridge University Press, 1988), 600–601; O'Brien, "Political Economy," table 2. I have set the sterling and dollar exchange rate to 0.225 (4s. 6d. equals $1). See John J. McCusker, *How Much Is That in Real Money? A Commodity Price Index for Use as a Deflator of Money Values in the Economy of the United States*, 2d ed. (Worcester, MA: American Antiquarian Society, 2001), 84.

29. "Report Relative to a Provision for the Support of Public Credit," *PAH*, 6:84–85 (quotations). In Congress Fisher Ames discussed British renegotiations of loan terms after the Jacobite Rebellion in 1715 and after the War of the Austrian Succession. He also said that a "reloan" such as was suggested by Hamilton did not seem "strange and visionary in Europe. In this transaction government is to accommodate its proposals to the ideas which experience has established in other countries," see Ames, *DHFFC*, 12:685, 690.

30. "Report Relative to a Provision for the Support of Public Credit," *PAH*, 6:64, 68, 73–74, 76; Postlethwayt, *Universal Dictionary of Trade and Commerce*, 1, s.v. "action"; David Hume, "Of Public Credit," in *Political Essays*, ed. Knud Haakonssen (Cambridge: Cambridge University Press, 1994), 168. To Hamilton it was evident that "all restraints upon alienanation by fettering the free use and circulation of an article of property naturally lessen its value." "Defence of the Funding System," *PAH*, 19:64. He would also oppose a tax on the alienation of securities with the argument that the "stock in its *creation is made transferrable*. This quality constitutes a material part of its value." "Report on a Plan for the Further Support of Public Credit," ibid., 28:120. According to Fisher Ames, "The best condition of the paper is, when it has a *fixed exchangeable* value, and at the highest rate. For then the holder can dispose of it at pleasure, and without loss. He has no occasion to desire the public to pay off the loan, as he can get his money more conveniently at the time, and in the place he may chuse by selling at market." Ames, *DHFFC*, 12:683. See also Theodore Sedgwick, ibid., 12:336. Elbridge Gerry made it clear that failure to uphold the right to transfer securities would affect the government's future chances to borrow in times of crisis. Gerry, ibid., 12:457 See also Ames, ibid., 12:343–44.

31. "Report Relative to a Provision for the Support of Public Credit," *PAH*, 6:84–85; An Act for Making Provision for the Debt of the United States, August 4, 1790, ch. 34, *US Statutes at Large*, 1:138–44.

32. "Report Relative to a Provision for the Support of Public Credit," *PAH*, 6:88.

In the House debates, this message was often repeated. See *DHFFC*, 12:216, 228 (Elias Boudinot), 257 (Theodore Sedgwick), 326 (John Laurance), 373 (Thomas Hartley), 682–90 (Fisher Ames). According to Hartley, the federal government was party to a contract with its creditors and one party "had no right to change a contract without the consent of the other." The interest rates and terms of repayment might be changed, "but before either of these measures can take effect, the consent of the other party must be obtained." Hartley, ibid., 12:255. For some critical arguments, see "Public Creditors," in *ASP: Finance*, 1:76–81; Ferguson, *Power of the Purse*, 303–4; and *DHFFC*, 12:365 (Alexander White), 422 (James Madison), 656 (Thomas Tudor Tucker), 702–4 (Elbridge Gerry).

33. "Report Relative to a Provision for the Support of Public Credit," *PAH*, 6:68, 87; "Address to the Public Creditors," ibid., 7:2–3.

34. "Report Relative to a Provision for the Support of Public Credit," *PAH*, 6:88–90, quotation at 88; "Report on a Plan for the Further Support of Public Credit," ibid., 18:93–94, 96; An Act for Making Provision for the Debt of the United States, August 4, 1790, ch. 34, *US Statutes at Large*, 1:140. Securities of the new emission are illustrated in William G. Anderson, *The Price of Liberty: The Public Debt of the American Revolution* (Charlottesville: University Press of Virginia, 1983), 104–5.

35. "Address to the Public Creditors," *PAH*, 7:2; "Report on a Plan for the Further Support of Public Credit," ibid., 18:94. Hamilton defined funded debts as debts that were "*bottomed on certain specifyed revenues pledged* or *hypothecated* for the payment of the *Interest* upon them." Ibid., 18:78. For Hamilton's fear that the debt might be repudiated, see "Defence of the Funding System," *PAH*, 19:47. On British developments, see Dickson, *Financial Revolution in England*; John Brewer, *The Sinews of Power: War, Money, and the British State, 1688–1783* (Boston: Unwin Hyman, 1989); Roseveare, *Financial Revolution*.

36. "Defence of the Funding System," *PAH*, 19:61. The remark made in Congress is from a summary reported by the *Gazette of the United States* of speeches made by Theodore Sedgwick, Elias Boudinot, Michael Jenifer Stone, and Elbridge Gerry, *DHFFC*, 13:1359. See also Gerry, ibid., 13:1346.

37. "Address to the Public Creditors," *PAH*, 7:2; "Report on a Plan for the Further Support of Public Credit," ibid., 18:95.

38. "Report Relative to a Provision for the Support of Public Credit," *PAH*, 6:106; "Report on a Plan for the Further Support of Public Credit," ibid., 18:59.

39. George Washington, Sixth Annual Address, in *Messages and Papers*, 1:167.

40. Fisher Ames, in *Annals of Congress*, 3d Cong., 2d sess., 1106. On the growth of the money stock, see Peter L. Rousseau and Richard Sylla, "Emerging Financial Markets and Early US Growth," *Explorations in Economic History*, 42, no. 1 (January 2005): 1–26.

41. "Report Relative to a Provision for the Support of Public Credit," *PAH*, 6:106; "Report on a Plan for the Further Support of Public Credit," ibid., 18:102; Fisher Ames, in *Annals of Congress*, 3d Cong., 2d sess., 1106. For a positive comment from 1790 on the debt's ability to benefit the economy, see William Smith (SC), *DHFFC*, 12:263.

42. William Playfair, *For the Use of the Enemies of England: A Real Statement of the Finances and Resources of Great Britain . . .* (London, 1796), 6–8, quotation at 23; Thomas Paine, *The Decline and Fall of the English System of Finance* (London, 1796), 1; *Reflections on the Present State of the Resources of the Country* (London, 1796),

6–7, 22, quotation at 7; Ralph Broome, *Observations on Mr. Paine's Pamphlet, Entitled the Decline and Fall of the English System of Finance; in a Letter to a Friend, June 4, 1796* (London, [1796]), 36–37, 48; Nicholas Vansittart, *An Inquiry into the State of the Finances of Great Britain; in Answer to Mr Morgan's Facts* (London, 1796), 58–75. On the reaction of Playfair and like-minded Scottish writers to the French Revolution and its British defenders, see Paul Tonks, "Scottish Historical Discourse and Arguments for Metropolitan Authority in the Eighteenth-Century British Atlantic Empire" (PhD diss., Johns Hopkins University, 2004), chap. 5. For Blackstone's, Hume's, and Smith's views on the British debt, see William Blackstone, *Commentaries on the Laws of England*, 7th ed. (Oxford, 1775), 1:335; Hume, "Of Public Credit," 173–77; Smith, *Wealth of Nations*, 2:928.

43. Playfair, *For the Use of the Enemies*, 5, 32 (quotations); Broome, *Observations on Mr. Paine's Pamphlet*, 41; [Baron Auckland, William Eden], *The Substance of a Speech made by Lord Auckland on Monday the Second Day of May, 1796, on the Occasion of a Motion Made by the Marquis of Lansdown* (London, 1796), 34–35; Vansittart, *Inquiry into the State of Finances*, 36–40. Part of the debate on Pitt's sinking fund concerned his failure to credit Price as the source of his proposal. See for instance William Morgan, *A Review of Dr. Price's Writings on the Finances of Great Britain. To Which are Added, the Three Plans, Communicated by Him to Mr Pitt in the Year 1786, for Redeeming the National Debt . . .* , 2d ed. (London, 1795), 16–48; Morgan, *Additional Facts, Addressed to the Serious Attention of the People of Great Britain, Respecting the Expences of the War, and the State of the National Debt* (London, 1796), 32–37; and Vansittart, *Inquiry into the State of Finances*, 27–30.

44. Robert Goodloe Harper, in *Annals of Congress*, 4th Cong., 1st sess., 851. Hamilton took credit for the economic development in "Defence of the Funding System," *PAH*, 19:65.

45. Hume, "Of Public Credit," 176; "Report on a Plan for the Further Support of Public Credit," *PAH*, 18:108–9. Hamilton also used the phrase "rendering public credit immortal" in "Report Relative to a Provision for the Support of Public Credit," ibid., 6:106; Fisher Ames, in *Annals of Congress*, 3d Cong., 2d sess., 1106.

46. An Act Making Further Provision for the Support of Public Credit, and for the Redemption of the Public Debt, Mar. 3, 1795, ch. 45, *US Statutes at Large*, 1:433–38; An Act in Addition to an Act Intituled "An Act Making Further Provision for the Support of Public Credit, and for the Redemption of the Public Debt," April 28, 1796, ch. 16, *US Statutes at Large*, 1:458–59; Oliver Wolcott, "Public Debt," *ASP: Finance*, 1:371–83. See also the correspondence between Hamilton and Wolcott in the spring and summer of 1795, much of which, unfortunately, is missing: Hamilton to Wolcott, April 10, 1795, *PAH*, 18:316–28; Wolcott to Hamilton, June 18, 1795, ibid., 18:379–82; Hamilton to Wolcott, June 22, 1795, ibid., 18:384–86; Wolcott to Hamilton, July 28, 1795, ibid., 18:509–12. Hamilton's biographers generally review the "Report on a Plan for the Further Support of Public Credit" but pay only limited attention to it. Broadus Mitchell, Forrest McDonald, Jacob E. Cooke, and Ron Chernow mention that the report led to legislation, yet none of them investigate whether the report and the legislation led to any debt redemption. See Mitchell, *Alexander Hamilton: The National Adventure, 1788–1804* (New York: Macmillan, 1962), 360–65; McDonald, *Alexander Hamilton*, 303–5; Jacob E. Cooke, *Alex-

ander Hamilton (New York: Scribners, 1982), 154–55; and Chernow, *Alexander Hamilton* (New York: Penguin, 2004), 480. John C. Miller implies that the report did not do so. Miller, *Alexander Hamilton*, 438–39. Donald F. Swanson and Andrew P. Trout analyze the original amortization plan in the "Report Relative to a Provision for the Support of Public Credit." They also note that Hamilton proposed the realization of this plan in the "Report on a Plan for the Further Support of Public Credit" in 1795 but make no specific statement about actual debt redemption. The effect of compound interest on the debt is explained by tables supplied by Oliver Wolcott in his report to Congress; see "Public Debt," *ASP: Finance*, 1:383. See also Swanson and Trout, "Alexander Hamilton's Hidden Sinking Fund," *WMQ*, 3d ser., 49, no. 1 (January 1992): 113, table 1.

47. Wolcott, "Public Debt," *ASP: Finance*, 1:381.

48. "Report on a Plan for the Further Support of Public Credit," *PAH*, 18:113; Rafael A. Bayley, *History of the National Loans of the United States from July 4, 1776, to June 30, 1880*, in *Report on Valuation, Taxation, and Public Indebtedness in the United States, as Returned at the Tenth Census (June 1, 1880)* (Washington, DC: Government Printing Office, 1884), 469–70.

49. See, for instance, Joyce Appleby, *Capitalism and a New Social Order: The Republican Vision of the 1790s* (New York: New York University Press, 1984), 103; Swanson and Trout, "Hamilton's Sinking Fund," 116; Banning, *Jefferson and Madison*, 46.

50. More than six decades ago, Leonard D. White pointed to the great degree of continuity between the administrations of the Federalists and the Republicans in *The Jeffersonians: A Study in Administrative History, 1801–1829* (New York: Macmillan, 1951), 546–47, 558–59.

51. Thomas Jefferson, First Inaugural Address, in *Messages and Papers*,1:323; Alexander Hamilton to Harry Gray Otis, December 23, 1800, in the Gilder Lehrman Collection on deposit at the New-York Historical Society, GLC00496.028; Hamilton to Gouverneur Morris, December 24, 1800, *PAH*, 25:273. See also Hamilton to James Ross, December 29, 1800, ibid., 25:281.

52. Brant, *James Madison*, 258–61. Edwin J. Perkins has pointed to the strong element of continuity in American public finances during the transitions from British dependencies to independent nation and from Federalists to Republicans. See Perkins, *American Public Finance*; Perkins, "Jeffersonian Principles and the Shaping of American Financial Services, 1790–1815," in *Perkins on U.S. Financial History*, 61–65.

CHAPTER 4

1. Thomas Jefferson to Spencer Roane, September 6, 1819, in Andrew A. Lipscomb et al., eds., *Writings of Thomas Jefferson*, 20 vols. (Washington, DC: Thomas Jefferson Memorial Association, 1905), 15:212; Jefferson, First Inaugural Address, March 4, 1801, *PTJ*, 33:150.

2. For the dominant interpretation, see, for example, the Society for Historians of the Early American Republic presidential addresses by John Murrin, "The Jeffersonian Triumph and American Exceptionalism," *Journal of the Early Republic*20, no. 1 (Spring 2000): 1–25; and John L. Brooke, "Cultures of Nationalism, Movements of Reform, and the Composite-Federal Polity: From Revolutionary Settlement to Antebellum Crisis,"

Journal of the Early Republic 29, no. 1 (Spring, 2009), especially 5–8. Another recent statement by an influential historian is Gordon S. Wood, *Empire of Liberty: A History of the Early Republic, 1789–1815* (New York: Oxford University Press, 2009).

    3. *The Diary of James Gallatin, Secretary to Albert Gallatin, A Great Peace Maker, 1813–1827*, ed. Count Gallatin (1916; repr., New York: Charles Scribner's Sons, 1924), 50; Edwin G. Burrows, *Albert Gallatin and the Political Economy of Republicanism* (New York: Garland, 1986), 435–44. The veracity of the *Diary of James Gallatin* is questionable, and this work should be treated with caution. Gallatin still awaits his modern biographer. The classic is Henry Adams, *The Life of Albert Gallatin* (Philadelphia: J. P. Lippincott, 1879). A recent brief and popular biography is Nicholas Dungan, *Gallatin: America's Swiss Founding Father* (New York: New York University Press, 2010).

    4. Albert Gallatin, *A Sketch of the Finances of the United States*, WAG, 3:144–50, quotation at 149–50; Burrows, *Gallatin*, 444–46.

    5. Gallatin, *Sketch of the Finances*, WAG, 3:122, 127–28, 135, 144, 148; Gallatin to Jefferson, 13 December 1803, WAG, 1:171; Gallatin to Jefferson, received June 18, 1802, ibid., 1:80; Gallatin to Jefferson, August 11, 1803, ibid., 1:136.

    6. Gallatin, *Sketch of the Finances*, WAG, 3:132–33; Burrows, *Gallatin*, 444–46.

    7. Gallatin to Jefferson, November 8, 1809, WAG, 1:465; Gallatin to A. C. Flagg, December 31, 1841, in ibid., 2:572.

    8. Gallatin to Gales and Seaton, February 5, 1835, WAG, 2:502; Gallatin to A. C. Flagg, December 31, 1841, ibid., 571; Gallatin to Madame de Staël, October 4, 1814, in *Diary of James Gallatin*, 42–43.

    9. Gallatin, *Sketch of the Finances*, WAG, 3:149–50.

    10. Gallatin, *Sketch of the Finances*, WAG, 3:143; Gallatin, *Expenses of the War* (Washington, DC: Towers, 1848), 1–2; Gallatin to Edward Everett, December 16, 1847, in WAG, 2:658–59; Burrows, *Gallatin*, 444–46.

    11. Gallatin to James Monroe, October 26, 1814, in WAG, 1:642; Gallatin to Secretary of the Treasury, December 24, 1814, in ibid., 1:644; Jefferson to Elbridge Gerry, January 26, 1799, PTJ, 30:646–47; Jefferson, First Inaugural Address, ibid, 33:151.

    12. Jefferson, First Annual Address, PTJ, 36:60; Alexander Hamilton, "The Examination," no. 2, PAH, 25:462–63.

    13. Gallatin, *Sketch of the Finances*, WAG, 3:143; Jefferson, First Annual Address, PTJ, 36:61.

    14. Jefferson, First Annual Address, PTJ, 36:60; Gallatin to Jefferson, on or before November 16, 1801, ibid., 35:627–28.

    15. Ch. 19, *US Statutes at Large*, 2:148–50; Act of March 3, 1807, ch. 30, *US Statutes at Large* 2:436–37.

    16. Albert Gallatin's Remarks on the Draft Message, PTJ, 35:633; Gallatin to Jefferson, January 18, 1803, WAG, 1:117–18; Gallatin to Jefferson, May 30, 1805, ibid., 1:234; Gallatin to Jefferson, November 21, 1805, ibid., 1:262–63; Hugh McCulloch, *Annual Report of the Secretary of the Treasury, December 3, 1866*, H.R. Ex. Doc. 4, 39th Cong., 2d sess., 308.

    17. Hamilton, "The Examination," no. 18, PAH, 25:595–97; Alexander Balinky, *Albert Gallatin: Fiscal Theories and Policies* (New Brunswick, NJ: Rutgers University Press, 1958), 97–116.

18. Hamilton, "The Examination," no. 3, *PAH*, 25:468.

19. For the modern view, see Balinky, *Albert Gallatin*, 229–32.

20. Gallatin to Joseph H. Nicholson, July 17, 1807, *WAG*, 1:339; Gallatin to Mathew Lyon, May 7, 1816, ibid. 1:700.

21. Gallatin to Matthew Lyon, May 7, 1816, *WAG*, 1:700; Gallatin, *Expenses of the War*, 1–2; Gallatin to Garrett Davis, February 16, 1848, *WAG*, 2:661; Gallatin to Jefferson, March 10, 1812, ibid., 1:517.

22. Donald R. Hickey, *The War of 1812: A Forgotten Conflict* (Urbana: University of Illinois Press, 1989), 301 ("negligent," "weakest"); Reginald Horsman, *The War of 1812* (New York: Knopf, 1969), 166 ("unsound"); Paul Studenski and Herman E. Krooss, *Financial History of the United States: Fiscal, Monetary, Banking, and Tariff, Including Financial Administration and State and Local Finance* (New York: McGraw-Hill, 1952), 75 ("bungled"). The harsh verdict on the administration's financial policy is old, consistent, and universal and shared by financial and political historians alike. See, for instance, Henry C. Adams, "American War-Financiering," *Political Science Quarterly* 1, no. 3 (September 1886): 355–69; Charles J. Bullock, "Financing the War," *Quarterly Journal of Economics* 31, no. 3 (May 1917): 359–60; Davis Rich Dewey, *Financial History of the United States*, 12th ed. (1934; repr., New York: A. M. Kelley, 1968), 128–42; Curtis P. Nettels, *The Emergence of a National Economy, 1775–1815* (New York: Holt, Rinehart and Winston, 1962), 331–34.

23. The plan can be found in the annual Treasury report of 1807. In details it was subsequently modified in 1811 and 1812 before the outbreak of war. Albert Gallatin, "State of the Finances," November 7, 1807, *ASP: Finance*, 2:247–49. On Gallatin's prewar thoughts on war finance, see Balinky, *Albert Gallatin*, 164–83; Balinky, "Gallatin's Theory of War Finance," *WMQ*, 3d ser., 16, no. 1 (January 1959): 73–82; Dewey, *Financial History*, 128–30; Gallatin to Jefferson, July 25, 1807, *WAG*, 1:353. The $10 million estimate was made in Gallatin to Joseph H. Nicholson, July 17, 1807, *WAG*, 1:339; Gallatin, "State of the Finances," November 25, 1811, *ASP: Finance*, 2:497;, and Gallatin to Ezekiel Bacon, January 10, 1812, *WAG*, 1:515.

24. Albert Gallatin, "State of the Finances," *ASP: Finance*, 2:248; William Jones, "State of the Finances," June 3, 1813, *ASP: Finance*, 2:624. Jefferson, too, supported loans as the means to avoid placing undue burdens on the taxpayers. Such a policy amounted to "throwing a part of the burden of war on times of peace and commerce." Thomas Jefferson to James Monroe, October 16, 1814, in Lipscomb et al., *Writings of Thomas Jefferson*, 14:208–9.

25. Gallatin to Joseph H. Nicholson, July 17, 1807, *WAG*, 1:339.

26. On the Bank of the United States, see Bray Hammond, *Banks and Politics in America from the Revolution to the Civil War* (Princeton, NJ: Princeton University Press, 1957), 114–43, 197–226; and Edwin J. Perkins, *American Public Finance and Financial Services, 1700–1815* (Columbus: Ohio State University Press, 1994), 235–65. On Gallatin's views on the bank, see *Sketch of the Finances*, *WAG*, 3:135; Gallatin to Jefferson, received June 18, 1802, *WAG*, 1:80; Gallatin to Jefferson, August 11, 1803, ibid., 1:136; Gallatin to Jefferson, December 13, 1803, ibid., 1:171.

27. Perkins, *American Public Finance*, 238–39; Hew V. Bowen, "The Bank of England during the Long Eighteenth Century, 1694–1820," in Richard Roberts and David

Kynaston, eds., *The Bank of England: Money, Power, and Influence, 1694–1994* (Oxford: Clarendon Press, 1995), 1–18; John Clapham, *The Bank of England: A History* (Cambridge: Cambridge University Press, 1944), 1–104, 173–223; P. G. M. Dickson, *The Financial Revolution in England: A Study in the Development of Public Credit, 1688–1756* (London: Macmillan, 1967), 39–245.

28. Alexander Dallas to John W. Eppes, October 17, 1814, in George Mifflin Dallas, ed., *Life and Writings of Alexander James Dallas* (Philadelphia: J. P. Lippincott, 1871), 236; Alexander Dallas to John W. Eppes, February 20, 1815, in ibid., 272–79, quotation at 273; Hickey, *War of 1812*, 224–25; Gallatin to the Secretary of the Treasury, December 24, 1814, *WAG*, 1:644; Hammond, *Banks and Politics in America*, 227–33.

29. Gallatin to Ezekiel Bacon, Committee of Ways and Means, January 10, 1812, *WAG*, 1:504–5.

30. Gallatin to Bates Cooke, March 2, 1839, *WAG*, 2:541; Gallatin, "State of the Finances," November 7, 1807, *ASP: Finance*, 2:248. In his annual message to Congress in 1811, Madison asked the legislature to consider "the propriety of insuring a sufficiency of annual revenue at least to defray the ordinary expenses of Government, and to pay the interest on the public debt, including that on new loans which may be authorized." Madison, Third Annual Message, November 5, 1811, in *Messages and Papers*, 1:496. These words were quoted in the Treasury report of the same year; see Gallatin, "State of the Finances," November 25, 1811, *ASP: Finance*, 2:497. On the Ways and Means Committee, see "Plan for Increasing the Revenue," February 17, 1812, *ASP: Finance*, 2:540. Gallatin's formula was repeated in William Jones, "State of the Finances," June 3, 1813, ibid., 2:623; Jones, "State of the Finances," January 10, 1814, ibid., 2:652; George Campbell, "State of the Finances," September 26, 1814, ibid., 2:842.

31. Gallatin, "State of the Finances," November 25, 1811, *ASP: Finance*, 2:497; Gallatin, "State of the Finances," November 7, 1807, *ASP: Finance*, 2:248 ("cheerfully"); Gallatin to Ezekiel Bacon, Chairman of the Ways and Means Committee, January 10, 1812, *WAG*, 1:501–10, 517, quotations at 505, 508–9. On taxation, see Gallatin, "State of the Finances," November 25, 1811, *ASP: Finance*, 2:495–97; House Committee of Ways and Means report, "Plan for Increasing the Revenue," February 17, 1812, ibid., 2:539–41; Gallatin, "State of the Finances," December 7, 1812, ibid., 2:580–81; Jones, "State of the Finances," ibid., 2:622–24; House Committee of Ways and Means report, "Increase of Revenue," ibid., 2:627–28; Jones, "State of the Finances," Jan. 10, 1814, ibid., 2:651–53; George W. Campbell, "State of the Finances," *ASP: Finance*, 2:840–842; Alexander J. Dallas, "State of the Finances," ibid., 2:854–55; Dallas, "State of the Treasury," January 21, 1815, ibid., 2:885–89; Dallas, "State of the Finances," Dec. 8, 1815, ibid., 3:1–19. The "cheerful taxpayers" made repeated appearances in Madison's rhetoric; see Madison, Special Session Message, May 25, 1813, in *Messages and Papers*, 1:529–30; and Madison, Sixth Annual Message, September 20, 1814, in ibid., 1:550. Not everyone responded "cheerfully" to the idea of new taxes, however. One Federalist newspaper believed that a war would lead to heavy taxes and would make the taxpayer ask, "'Why this load of taxes to be laid upon us?'" *Alexandria Daily Gazette, Commercial & Political*, March 5, 1812. Another argued that the conquest of Canada would impose further expenses on American taxpayers. This "cold inhospitable country" was populated by a people who *"never has paid any tax to any government*, and never will."

The government of Canada would therefore be financed by Americans; see *Trenton Federalist*, October 5, 1812. For secondary accounts of the period leading up to the outbreak of war, see Hickey, *War of 1812*, 20–21, 165–67; Nettels, *Emergence of a National Economy*, 331–32; Donald R. Stabile, *The Origins of American Public Finance: Debates over Money, Debt, and Taxes in the Constitutional Era, 1776–1836* (Westport, CT: Greenwood, 1998), 85–154; J. C. A. Stagg, *Mr. Madison's War: Politics, Diplomacy, and Warfare in the Early American Republic, 1783–1830* (Princeton, NJ: Princeton University Press, 1983), 154, 314–16.

32. Gallatin to John W. Eppes, Ways and Means Committee, *WAG*, 1:468; Gallatin, "State of the Finances," November 7, 1807, *ASP: Finance*, 2:248; Gallatin to Thomas Jefferson, March 10, 1812, *WAG*, 1:517; Gallatin to Ezekiel Bacon, January 10, 1812, ibid., 1:505. In this letter to Bacon, the chairman of the Ways and Means Committee, Gallatin argued that complete repayment of war loans together with what remained of the Revolutionary War debt, but excepting the 3 percent securities, would "probably be effected within fifteen years after the restoration of peace"; see ibid., 1:516.

33. Gallatin to James Monroe, London June 13, 1814, *WAG*, 1:643; Gallatin to Robert Walsh, April 17, 1830, ibid., 2:426–27; Gallatin to G. C. Verplanck, May 22, 1830, ibid., 2:428.

34. Gallatin, "War Expenses," *WAG*, 3:543 ("transcript"); Gallatin to Ezekiel Bacon, Committee of Ways and Means, January 10, 1812, ibid., 1:514; Gallatin to Caleb Cushing, January 7, 1842, ibid., 2:572. On Exchequer bills, see Mortimer, *Every Man His Own Broker; Or, a Guide to the Stock Exchange* (London: W. J. and J. Richardson, 1807), 177–78, 218–19. A good sense of how Treasury notes worked can be gained from Gallatin to William Whann [President of the Bank of Columbia], November 20, 1812, in *The Papers of Albert Gallatin* [microform] (Philadelphia: Rhistoric Publications, 1969); and *Niles' Baltimore Weekly Register*, reprinted in *Hudson (NY) Bee*, July 14, 1812. See also Dewey, *Financial History*, 136–37, and Nettels, *Emergence of a National Economy*, 332–33. Perkins suggest that the Treasury notes were modeled on bills issued from the 1750s onward by the colonial government of Massachusetts; see Perkins, *American Public Finance*, 330, 337. Studenski and Krooss call Treasury notes "only a step removed from the paper currency issued during the Revolutionary War." *Financial History*, 76–77. Some of the newspapers that equated Treasury notes with Exchequer bills were the *Republican Star or Eastern Shore General Advertiser*, February 18, 1812; and *Providence Rhode-Island American, and General Advertiser*, June 23, 1812. The *Providence Gazette*, August 22, 1812, and *Trenton Federalist*, October 5, 1812, called them "Continentals." Republican papers commented that "attempts are making (what will not the *onery* attempt?) to depreciate the value of this intended emission, by comparing it with the old 'continental money,' etc." *Niles' Baltimore Weekly Register*, reprinted in *Hudson (NY) Bee*, July 14, 1812, and *New Jersey Journal*, July 14, 1812.

35. An Act Authorizing a Loan for a Sum Not Exceeding Eleven Millions of Dollars, March 14, 1812, ch. 41, *US Statutes at Large*, 2:694–95; An Act Authorizing a Loan for a Sum Not Exceeding Sixteen Millions of Dollars, February 8, 1813, ch. 12 *US Statutes at Large*, 2:798–99; An Act Authorizing a Loan for a Sum Not Exceeding Seven Millions Five Hundred Thousand Dollars, August 2, 1813, ch. 51, *US Statutes at Large*, 3:75–77; An Act to Authorize a Loan for a Sum Not Exceeding Twenty-Five Millions of Dollars,

March 24, 1814, ch. 29, *US Statutes at Large*, 3:111–12; An Act to Authorize a Loan for a Sum Not Exceeding Eighteen Millions Four Hundred and Fifty-Two Thousand Eight Hundred Dollars, March 3, 1815, ch. 87, *US Statutes at Large*, 3:227–28.

36. Gallatin to Ezekiel Bacon, Committee of Ways and Means, January 10, 1812, *WAG*, 1:512–13. The advertisement for the loan can be found in, for instance, *New York Columbian*, April 25 and 28, 1812; and *New York Gazette*, April 29, 1812. It is reprinted in Albert Gallatin, "Subscription to the Loan of Eleven Million Dollars," May 18, 1812, *ASP: Finance*, 2:565–66. On the subscription process see "Circular to Certain Commissioners of Loans," Treasury Department Comptroller's Office, May 24, 1812, in Anthony M. Brescia, ed., *The Letters and Papers of Richard Rush* [microform], (Wilmington, DE: Scholarly Resources, 1980). On British loan subscriptions, where eight monthly installments were also the norm during the French Revolutionary and Napoleonic Wars, see Dickson, *Financial Revolution in England*, 220–28; and for a contemporary account see Mortimer, *Every Man His Own Broker*, 164–70.

37. For some newspaper reports on the $11 million loan, see *Poulson's Philadelphia American Daily Advertiser*, May 4, 1812; *National Intelligencer and Washington Advertiser*, May 5, 1814 (quotation); *Alexandria Daily Gazette, Commercial & Political*, May 6, 1814; *Richmond Enquirer*, May 8, 1814; *Goshen (NY) Orange County Patriot; or, the Spirit of Seventy-Six*, May 12 and 19, 1814; *Pittsfield (MA) Sun, or, Republican Monitor*, May 16, 1812; *Greenfield (MA) Franklin Herald*, May 19, 1812. On Federalist sabotage see *Philadelphia Democratic Press*, May 4, 1812, reprinted in *Pittsfield (MA) Sun, or, Republican Monitor*, May 16, 1812. For Gallatin's comments on the loan, see Gallatin, "Subscription to the Loan of Eleven Millions of Dollars," communicated to the House of Representatives May 18, 1812, *ASP: Finance*, 2:564–65; Gallatin to Ezekiel Bacon, June 24, 1812, *Papers of Albert Gallatin*. For secondary accounts of this loan, see Perkins, *American Public Finance*, 326–27, 329–30; Stagg, *Mr. Madison's War*, 151–52.

38. Gallatin to James Madison, *WAG*, 1:528; Gallatin, "Memo on Stephen Girard's Loan to U.S.," n.d., 1812, *Papers of Albert Gallatin*; Stephen Girard to George Simpson, August 6, 1812, *Papers of Albert Gallatin*; John Jacob Astor to Gallatin, February 6, 1813, *Papers of Albert Gallatin*; John Jacob Astor to Gallatin, February 14, 1813, *Papers of Albert Gallatin*; Gallatin to James Madison, ca. February 17, 1813, *PJM: Presidential Series*, 6:34; Gallatin to Madison, March 5, 1813, ibid., 6:90–91. The advertisement for the $16 million loan is reprinted in *ASP: Finance*, 2:625–26. It can be found in the *Portsmouth New Hampshire Gazette*, March 9, 1813; *Charleston City Gazette*, March 5, 6, and 11, 1813; *Salem Gazette*, March 9 and 12, 1813; *Boston Independent Chronicle*, March 11, 1813; *Boston Yankee*, March 12, 1813; and *Salem Essex Register*, March 13, 1813.

39. *New York Gazette*, March 17, 1813 (quotation). Newspaper reports on the subscription can be found in *Poulson's Philadelphia American Daily Advertiser*, March 15, 1813; *Albany Argus*, March 16, 1813; *Salem Essex Register*, March 17, 1813; *Boston Independent Chronicle*, March 18, 1813; and *Charleston City Gazette and Commercial Daily Advertiser*, March 22, 1813. Many of these reports were widely reprinted in other newspapers. The advertisement inviting subscriptions and proposals is reprinted in *ASP: Finance*, 2: 626. It can also be found in *Richmond Enquirer*, March 23, 1813, and *New York Statesman*, March 27, 1813. On the result of the first loan, see William Jones, "State

of the Finances," *ASP: Finance*, 2:624; and Jones, "Terms of the Loan of Sixteen Millions of Dollars," ibid., 2:646–47. On Britain, see Mortimer, *Every Man His Own Broker*, 163.

40. Newspapers reports on the second round of subscriptions and the invitation of proposals can be found in *Boston Daily Advertiser*, March 26, 1813; *Plattsburgh (NY) Republican*, March 26, 1813; *Newark Centinel of Freedom*, April 13, 1813 (quotation); *Elizabethtown New Jersey Journal*, April 13, 1813; *Newport Mercury*, April 17, 1813; and *Halifax (MD) Hagers-Town Gazette*, April 27, 1813. On the proposals and their reception, see David Parish and Stephen Girard to Gallatin, April 5, 1813, *ASP: Finance*, 2:647; John Jacob Astor to Gallatin, April 5, 1813, ibid., 2:647; Gallatin to Parish and Girard, April 7, 1813, ibid., 2:647; and Gallatin to Madison, April 19, 1816, *WAG*, 1:696. On the terms of the loan, see Gallatin, "United States Loan," April 15, 1813, *ASP: Finance*, 2:626; Jones, "Terms of the Loan of Sixteen Millions of Dollars," July 29, 1813, ibid., 2:646–47; James Madison, "Special Session Message," May 25, 1813, in *Messages and Papers*, 1:529. Donald R. Adams Jr., *Finance and Enterprise in Early America: A Study of Stephen Girard's Bank 1812–1831* (Philadelphia: University of Pennsylvania Press, 1978), 30–33; Hickey, *War of 1812*, 122; Perkins, *American Public Finance*, 330–33; Stagg, *Mr. Madison's War*, 297–300.

41. William Jones to James Madison, September 18, 1813, *PJM: Presidential Series*, 6:639; Jones to Madison, September 25, 1813, ibid., 6:657; Jones, "State of the Finances," January 10, 1814, *ASP: Finance*, 2:651; "Loan of Seven Millions Five Hundred Thousand Dollars," ibid., 6:661. The advertisement for the $7.5 million loan is reprinted in ibid., 6:662. See also Jonathan Smith to Jones, September 25, 1813, ibid., 6:662; Jones to Jonathan Smith, September 25, 1813, ibid., 6:662; James Madison, Fifth Annual Message, December 7, 1813, in *Messages and Papers*, 1:538. Hickey, *War of 1812*, 123; and Perkins, *American Public Finance*, 333–34.

42. Jones, "State of the Finances," January 10, 1814, *ASP: Finance*, 2:651–53; *New York Evening Post*, February 25, 1814 ("distinct ideas"); Jones to James Madison, March 9, 1814, *PJM: Presidential Series*, 7:355–57; Hickey, *War of 1812*, 159–60, 284–87; George Campbell to James Madison, May 4, 1814, *PJM: Presidential Series*, 7:454–55; William Jones to James Madison, May 6, 1814, ibid., 7:457–59; James Madison to George Campbell, May 7, 1814, ibid., 7:460–61. Newspaper reports on the $10 million loan can be found in *Newburyport (MA)–Herald*, March 25 and May 13, 1814; *Georgetown (DC) Federal Republican*, April 16 and May 3, 1814; *Albany Gazette*, April 18, 1814; *Providence Rhode-Island American, and General Advertiser*, April 19, 1814; *Cooperstown (NY) Otsego Herald*, April 23, 1814; and *Boston New-England Palladium*, April 26, 1814. The advertisement inviting proposals to the loan is reprinted in *ASP: Finance*, 2:845. The list of bids is in "State of the Finances," September 26, 1814, appendix Bb, *ASP: Finance*, 2:846. On Barker, see Jacob Barker to George Campbell, April 30, 1814, *ASP: Finance*, 2:845; George Campbell to Jacob Barker, May 2, 1814, *ASP: Finance*, 2:845–46; *New York Mercantile Advertiser*, May 26, 1814; *Boston Repertory*, June 3, 1814; *Washington Daily National Intelligencer*, June 4, 1814; *Georgetown (DC) Federal Republican*, June 10, 1814; Alexander J. Dallas to James Madison, November 15, 1814, transcript in James Madison Papers project at the University of Virginia (from National Archives and Records Administration, RG 217, Records of the First Comptroller, Correspondence, Letters Received from the Secretary of the Treasury, 1801–1856); *Alexandria Gazette, Commer-*

cial & Political, December 15, 1814; Alexander Dallas to James Madison, "Memorandum in Jacob Barker's Case," March 19, 1816, in Dallas, *Life and Writings of Alexander James Dallas*, 450–51; Jacob Barker to James Madison, December 26, 1815, transcript in James Madison Paper project at the University of Virginia (from Library of Congress). Barker's own account of his services offered during the war can be found in Jacob Barker, *Incidents in the Life of Jacob Barker, of New Orleans, Louisiana; With Historical Facts, His Financial Transactions With the Government, and His Course on Important Political Questions, from 1800 to 1855* (Washington, DC, 1855), 46–106. For secondary accounts of this loan, see Hickey, *War of 1812*, 167; Perkins, *American Public Finance*, 334; and Stagg, *Mr. Madison's War*, 378–79.

43. Gallatin to W. H. Crawford, April 21, 1814, *WAG*, 1:602–5, quotations at 602; Gallatin to James Monroe, June 13, 1814, ibid., 1:627. The British campaign of 1814 and the burning of Washington are treated in Irving Brant, *James Madison: Commander in Chief* (Indianapolis: Bobbs-Merrill, 1961), 298–308; Hickey, *War of 1812*, 182–220; Horsman, *War of 1812*, 194–214; and Stagg, *Mr. Madison's War*, 410–18.

44. Advertisement for the $6 million loan appeared in the newspapers in July and August 1814; see *Washington Daily National Intelligencer*, July 25 and 30, August 15, 1814; *Boston Independent Chronicle*, August 8, 1814; *Salem Essex Register*, August 13, 1814. The advertisement is reprinted in *ASP: Finance*, 2:846–47. See also D. A. Smith to George Campbell, August 22, 1814, ibid., 2:847; and Campbell to ——, August 31, 1814, ibid., 2:847. Newspaper reports can be found in *New Haven Connecticut Journal*, August 22, 1814; *Boston New-England Palladium*, August 26, 1814; *Portland Gazette, and Maine Advertiser*, September 5, 1814. For secondary accounts, see Hickey, *War of 1812*, 167; Perkins, *American Public Finance*, 334.

45. George Campbell, "State of the Finances," *ASP: Finance*, 2:840–43, quotation at 843.

46. Alexander Dallas to John W. Eppes, October 17, 1814, in Dallas, *Life and Writings of Alexander James Dallas*, 234–43, quotation at 237; "Plan for Increasing the Revenue," February 17, 1812, *ASP: Finance*, 2:539.

47. Alexander Dallas to John W. Eppes, October 17, 1814, in Dallas, *Life and Writings of Alexander James Dallas*, 234–42; Alexander Dallas to William Lowndes, November 27, 1814, in ibid., 244–48; Alexander Dallas to John W. Eppes, December 2, 1814, in ibid., 248–56; Alexander Dallas, "State of the Treasury," January 17, 1815, *ASP: Finance*, 2:885–89. James Madison, January 12, 1815, in *Messages and Papers*, 1:558; Hickey, *War of 1812*, 247–48.

48. Hickey, *War of 1812*, 297–98; Howe, *What Hath God Wrought: The Transformation of America, 1815–1848* (New York: Oxford University Press, 2007), 63; *New York Evening Post* notice reprinted in *Washington Daily National Intelligencer*, February 22, May 31, 1815; Alexander Dallas, "Public Debt," February 24, 1815, *ASP: Finance*, 2:918.

49. Balinky, *Albert Gallatin*, 183.

50. Gallatin to Ezekiel Bacon, Committee of Ways and Means, January 10, 1812, *WAG*, 1:504–5; Gallatin, "State of the Finances," December 25, 1811, *ASP: Finance*, 2:497.

51. "Bank of the United States," April 13, 1830, *U.S. Serial Set*, 21st Cong., 1st sess., Rep. No. 358. The figure is repeated in Dewey, *Financial History*, 134; Nettels, *Emer-*

gence of a National Economy, 332; Hammond, *Banks and Politics in America*, 229; and Hickey, *War of 1812*, 303. Studenski and Krooss claim that the loan, with a face value of $55 million, represented a real value of $28 million (51 percent of par). *Financial History*, 76. Their figure is repeated in Stabile, *Origins of American Public Finance*, 162. Reginald Horsman claims that up to the end of 1814 $40 million in securities were sold for $28 million in cash (70 percent of par). *War of 1812*, 167. Raymond Walters Jr., is a lone voice in describing the $16 million loan of 1813 as "excellent" and the true yield as "not too high." The basis for his claims is left unstated, however. Walters, *Albert Gallatin: Jeffersonian Financier and Diplomat* (New York: Macmillan, 1957), 258.

52. Gallatin to G. C. Verplanck, May 22, 1830, *WAG*, 2:429. For estimates of banknote depreciation, see Hammond, *Banks and Politics in America*, 228–29; and Perkins, *American Public Finance*, 403n14.

53. Gallatin, *Expenses of the War*, 10; Bernard Cohen, *Compendium of Finance* (London, 1822), 228; Jonathan Elliot, *The Funding System of the United States and of Great Britain* (Washington, DC, 1845), 1202; Mortimer, *Every Man His Own Broker*, 31–35, quotation at 34–35.

54. Worthington C. Ford et al., eds., *Journals of the Continental Congress*, 34 vols. (Washington, DC, 1904–1937), 2:103, 105–6, 221–22, 3:, 390, 475–78. The depreciation of the Continental currency is traced in John J. McCusker, *How Much Is That in Real Money? A Historical Commodity Price Index for Use as a Deflator of Money Values in the Economy of the United States*, 2d ed. (Worcester, MA: American Antiquarian Society, 2001), 76–77, table C-1. The standard account of the funding of the War of Independence remains E. James Ferguson, *The Power of the Purse: A History of American Public Finance, 1776–1790* (Chapel Hill: University of North Carolina Press, 1961), 25–47.

55. Gallatin to James Madison, June 7, 1816, *WAG*, 1:707; William Crawford to Gallatin, April 23, 1817, ibid., 2:37.

56. Dallas, "State of the Finances," *ASP: Finance*, 3:7–8; William Crawford, "State of the Finances," December 8, 1817, *ASP: Finance*, 3:222. Repayments necessitated limited new borrowing, in effect refinancing the war loans at lower interest. But these loans were limited and the loan period only a few years. Five million dollars was borrowed at 4 percent in 1824 and repaid by 1832. Another $1.5 million was borrowed at 4.5 percent in 1825 and repaid by 1831. Secretary of the Treasury Levi Woodbury quoted in Stabile, *Origins of American Public Finance*, 181.

57. Madison, Seventh Annual Message, December 5, 1815, in *Messages and Papers*, 1:568; Gallatin to James Monroe, December 25, 1814, *WAG*, 1:645. Gallatin retained this view; see Gallatin to Edward Everett, January 1835, *WAG*, 2:500.

CHAPTER 5

1. Robert J. Walker, "Report on the Finances," December 9, 1846, Cong. Globe, 29th Cong., 2d sess., appendix, 12; Walker, "Report on the Finances," December 11, 1848, 30th Cong., 2d sess., appendix, 14–15.

2. Albert C. Ramsey, trans. and ed., *The Other Side; or, Notes for the History of the War Between Mexico and the United States. Written in Mexico* (New York: John Wiley, 1850), 1–32, quotations at 2, 32.

3. Paul H. Bergeron, *The Presidency of James K. Polk* (Lawrence: University Press of Kansas, 1987), 64; K. Jack Bauer, *The Mexican War, 1846–1848* (1974; repr., Lincoln: University of Nebraska Press, 1992), xxv, 4; Josefina Zoraida Vásquez, "Causes of the War with the United States," in Richard V. Francaviglia and Douglas W. Richmond, eds., *Dueling Eagles: Reinterpreting the U.S.-Mexican War, 1846–1848* (Fort Worth: Texas Christian University Press, 2000), 59; Orlando Martinez, *The Great Landgrab: The Mexican-American War, 1846–1848* (London: Quartet Books, 1975), 5–6.

4. On "manifest destiny" see Albert K. Weinberg, *Manifest Destiny: A Study of Nationalist Expansionism in American History* (Baltimore: Johns Hopkins University Press, 1935); Bernard DeVoto, *The Year of Decision, 1846* (Boston: Houghton Mifflin, 1943); Norman Graebner, *Empire on the Pacific: A Study in American Continental Expansion* (New York: Ronald, 1955); Frederick Merk, *Manifest Destiny and Mission in American History: A Reinterpretation* (New York: Knopf, 1963); Reginald Horsman, *Race and Manifest Destiny: The Origins of American Racial Anglo-Saxonism* (Cambridge, MA: Harvard University Press, 1981); Thomas Hietala, *Manifest Design: Anxious Aggrandizement in Jacksonian America* (Ithaca, NY: Cornell University Press, 1985). On the most powerful Indian nation of the Southwest, see Pekka Hämäläinen, *The Comanche Empire* (New Haven, CT: Yale University Press, 2008).

5. Daniel W. Howe, *What Hath God Wrought: The Transformation of America, 1815–1848* (New York: Oxford University Press, 2007), 707.

6. *Economist* 19, no. 947 (October 19, 1861): 1151.

7. Bancroft quoted in Charles Grier Sellers, *James K. Polk: Continentalist* (Princeton, NJ: Princeton University Press, 1966), 213.

8. James K. Polk, First Annual Message, December 2, 1845, in *Messages and Papers*, 4:403, 406–8; "Report on the Finances," Cong. Globe, 29th Cong., 2d sess., appendix, 8–12; An Act Reducing the Duty on Imports and for Other Purposes, July 20, 1846, ch. 74, *US Statutes at Large*, 9:42–49; An Act to Provide for the Better Organization of the Treasury, and for the Collection, Safekeeping, Transfer, and Disbursement of the Public Revenue, August 6, 1846, ch. 90, *US Statutes at Large*, 9:59–66; Bergeron, *Presidency of James K. Polk*, 185–93; James P. Shenton, *Robert J. Walker: A Politician from Jackson to Lincoln* (New York: Columbia University Press, 1961), 74–76, 79–89. On banks, see Bray Hammond, *Banks and Politics in America from the Revolution to the Civil War* (Princeton, NJ: Princeton University Press, 1957); and Howard Bodenhorn, *A History of Banking in Antebellum America: Financial Markets and Economic Development in an Era of Nation-Building* (New York: Cambridge University Press, 2000).

9. James Buchanan to John Sliddel, November 10, 1845, in William J. Manning, ed., *Diplomatic Correspondence of the United States: Inter-American Affairs, 1831–1860*, 12 vols. (Washington, DC: Carnegie Endowment for International Peace, 1932–1939), 8:180; Bergeron, *Presidency of James K. Polk*, 69–72; Kinley J. Brauer, "The United States and British Imperial Expansion, 1815–1860," *Diplomatic History* 12, no. 1 (Winter 1988): 19–37; Sam W. Haynes, "Anglophobia and the Annexation of Texas: The Quest for National Security," in Sam W. Haynes and Christopher Morris, eds., *Manifest Destiny and Empire: American Antebellum Expansionism* (College Station: Texas A&M University Press, 1997), 115–45; Sam W. Haynes, "'But What Will England Say?'—Great Britain, the United States, and the War with Mexico," in Francaviglia and Richmond, *Dueling Eagles*, 25, 34.

10. James Buchanan to William S. Parrot, March 28, 1845, in Manning, *Diplomatic Correspondence*, 8:164–66; Buchanan to Slidell, in ibid., 172–82, quotation at 176–77; Bergeron, *Presidency of James K. Polk*, 60–62; Bauer, *Mexican War*, 1–45; John S. D. Eisenhower, *So Far from God: The U.S. War with Mexico, 1846–1848* (1989; repr., Norman: University of Oklahoma Press, 2000), 3–48; Thomas M. Leonard, *James K. Polk: A Clear and Unquestionable Destiny* (Wilmington, DE: S. R. Books, 2001), 147–57.

11. Message from the President to the Senate and House of Representatives, May 11, 1846, in *Messages and Papers*, 4:442; *New York Herald* quoted in Howe, *What Hath God Wrought*, 720; Cong. Globe, 29th Cong., 1st sess., 783–88, 791–804, 810; Bergeron, *Presidency of James K. Polk*, 76–78, 113–35; Bauer, *Mexican War*, 46–80; Eisenhower, *So Far from God*, 49–68; Howe, *What Hath God Wrought*, 701–22; Leonard, *James K. Polk*, 157–60; Frederick Merk, *The Oregon Question: Essays in Anglo-American Diplomacy and Politics* (Cambridge, MA: Harvard University Press, 1967). Rather than signing the treaty with Britain over Oregon and then submitting it to Congress for ratification, Polk submitted it to the Senate for approval before signing it. In this manner it would appear as if the president had carried out the will of the Senate and had not in fact backed down from his more extreme demand that Britain give up all of Oregon. When the treaty reached the Senate, war had been declared against Mexico, which helped mute opposition to it.

12. "Message from the President of the United States, In answer to a resolution of the Senate of June 3, 1846, calling for information relative to the mode of raising funds for carrying on the war with Mexico," June 16, 1846, Sen. Doc. No. 392, 29th Cong., 1st sess., vol. 8, Serial 477, 1–18, quotation at 3.

13. "Letter to General Taylor on peace from George Beckwith, Secretary of the American Peace Society," *Boston Emancipator and Republican*, December 22, 1848; *American Cottage Library; or, Useful Facts, Figures, and Hints, for Everybody* (New York: Burgess, Stringer, 1848), 1, 172; *The American Almanac and Repository of Useful Knowledge for the Year 1847* (Boston: James Munroe, 1846), 159; *The Whig Almanac and United States Register for 1852* (New York: Greeley and McElrath, 1851), 46. See also *Dissertation on the Subject of a Congress of Nations, for the Adjustment of International Disputes without Recourse to Arms* (New York: E. Collier, 1837).

14. Thomas Cooper, *A Manual of Political Economy* (Washington, DC: Duff Green, 1834), 66–67; Cooper, *Lectures on the Elements of Political Economy* (Columbia, SC: D. E. Sweeney, 1826), 215.

15. Friedrich List, *Outlines of Political Economy. On the Plan of the Rev. David Blair. Adapted for the Use of Schools in the United States of America* (Boston: S. G. Goodrich, 1828), 267; List, *National System of Political Economy* (Philadelphia: J. B. Lippincott, 1856), 127.

16. Albert Gallatin to Lafayette, May 12, 1833, *WAG*, 2:471; Gallatin to A. C. Flagg, December 31, 1841, ibid., 2:572. See also Gallatin to Edward Everett, December 16, 1847, ibid., 2:658–59; Gallatin, *Expenses of the War* (Washington, DC: J. T. Towers, 1848), 1–2; *American Almanac and Repository of Useful Knowledge for the Year 1847*, 159.

17. Polk, Inaugural Address, in *Messages and Papers*, 4:377.

18. William Jay, *A Review of the Causes and Consequences of the Mexican War* (Boston: Benjamin B. Mussey, 1849), 332; *American Cottage Library*, 172.

19. Cong. Globe, 29th Cong., 1st sess., 1094–95, 1098–1100, 1103, 1109–10, 114–15;

An Act to Authorize an Issue of Treasury Notes and a Loan," July 22, 1846, ch. 64, *US Statutes at Large*, 9:39–40; Sen. Doc. No. 392, 29th Cong., 1st sess., vol. 8, Serial 477, 4; James William Cummings, "Financing the Mexican War" (PhD diss., Oklahoma State University, 2003), 80.

20. Cong. Globe, 29th Cong., 1st. sess., 1094–95, 1109–10, 1114. On the Whigs and the war see Howe, *What Hath God Wrought*, 762–64; and Michael F. Holt, *The Rise and Fall of the American Whig Party: Jacksonian Politics and the Onset of the Civil War* (New York: Oxford University Press, 1999), 231–38, 248–57.

21. Milton Quaife, ed., *Diary of James K. Polk during His Presidency, 1845 to 1849*, 4 vols. (Chicago: A. C. McClurg, 1910), 2:164, 166–67, 192, 194–95, 200–201, 205, 213; "Report on the State of the Finances," H.R. Ex. Doc. 6, 30th Cong., 1st sess., Serial 514, 116; Cummings, "Financing the Mexican War," 85–86, 88–89, 292; Shenton, *Robert J. Walker*, 92–93.

22. Quaife, *Diary of James K. Polk*, 2:213; "Report . . . on the States of the Finances," S. Doc. No. 2, 29th Cong., 2d sess., Serial 493, appendix FF, 28–29; *Washington Daily National Intelligencer*, November 9, 1846; Cummings, "Financing the Mexican War," 91–100, 103, 145, 260, 299; Shenton, *Robert J. Walker*, 91–93.

23. Polk, Second Annual Message, in *Messages and Papers*, 4:494; Bauer, *Mexican War*, 81–200; Bergeron, *Presidency of James K. Polk*, 91–94; Eisenhower, *So Far from God*, 71–165; Leonard, *James K. Polk*, 173–74.

24. Second Annual Message to Congress, in *Messages and Papers*, 4:497–98.

25. William Marcy to Zachary Taylor, September 22, 1846, H.R. Ex. Doc. 60, 30th Cong., 1st sess., , Serial 520, 341–42; John Y. Mason to Winfield Scott, September 1, 1847, ibid., 1005–1006; Quaife, *Diary of James K. Polk*, 3:156–57; Polk Third Annual Message, in *Messages and Papers*, 4:541; "Report on the Finances," December 8, 1847, Cong. Globe, 30th Cong., 1st sess., appendix 9; Cummings, "Financing the Mexican War," 172–73. In fairness to Marcy and Polk, it should be mentioned that this analysis of the situation was repeated by some Mexicans who argued that decades of misrule had killed all national feeling among the Mexican people. See José Fernando Ramirez, "Mexico during the War With the United States," trans. Elliot B. Scherr, ed. Walter V. Scholes, *University of Missouri Studies* 23, no. 1 (1950): 124; and Mariano Otero, "Considerations Relating to the Political and Social Situation of the Mexican Republic in the Year 1847," in Cecil Robinson, ed. and trans., *The View from Chapultepec: Mexican Writers on the Mexican-American War* (Tucson: University of Arizona Press, 1989), 17.

26. Quaife, *Diary of James K. Polk*, 2:145, 422, 425–26, 437–38, 442–43, 446–47, 450, 451, 3:222–23; "Executive Order to the Secretary of the Treasury," March 23, 1847, in *Messages and Papers*, 4:523–24; "Report on the Finances," December 8, 1847, Cong. Globe, 30th Cong., 1st sess., appendix, 9; Cummings, "Financing the Mexican War," 171–89.

27. "Report on the Finances," December 9, 1846, Cong. Globe, 29th Cong., 2d sess., appendix, 9; "Report on the Finances," December 8, 1847, Cong. Globe, 30th Cong., 1st sess., appendix, 10.

28. Cong. Globe, 30th Cong., 1st sess., 370; ibid., appendix, 323; *Cleveland Express*, June 17, 1846; *Boston Emancipator*, September 16, 1846.

29. Cong. Globe, 29th Cong., 2d sess., 102–3, 129–30, 226–31, 247–62, quotations at 130 (John Milton Niles) and 238 (Johnson).

30. Cong. Globe, 29th Cong., 2d sess., 250 (Evans and Huntington).

31. Cong. Globe, 29th Cong., 2d sess., 249, 256, 258, 268.

32. Cong. Globe, 30th Cong., 1st sess., appendix, 292; Holt, *Rise and Fall of the Whig Party*, 246–47.

33. "Report on the Finances," December 9, 1846, Cong. Globe, 29th Cong., 2d sess., appendix, 9; Cong. Globe, 29th Cong., 2d sess., 225–31, 247–51, 256–62, 267; An Act Authorizing the Issue of Treasury Notes, a Loan, and for Other Purposes, January 28, 1847, ch. 5, *US Statutes at Large*, 9:118–22.

34. "Report on the State of the Finances," H.R. Ex. Doc. 6, 30th Cong., 1st sess., Serial 514, 107–10, 116; *Washington Daily National Intelligencer*, February 15, April 22 and 28, 1847; *New York Herald*, March 10, 1848; *Cleveland Herald* March 15, 1848; *Milwaukee Daily Sentinel and Gazette*, April 11, 1848; Cummings, "Financing the Mexican War," 120, 127–28, 147; Shenton, *Robert J. Walker*, 95–98.

35. Bauer, *Mexican War*, 232–325; Cummings, "Financing the Mexican War," 115–17, 121, 127–28, 141, 147; Eisenhower, *So Far from God*, 253–342; Shenton, *Robert J. Walker*, 95–98.

36. Polk, Third Annual Message, in *Messages and Papers*, 4:545; Quaife, *Diary of James K. Polk*, 3:270.

37. Polk, Third Annual Message, in *Messages and Papers*, 4:545; Quaife, *Diary of James K. Polk*, 3:350–51.

38. Quaife, *Diary of James K. Polk*, 2:50–51, 56–58, 76–77, 291; Howe, *What Hath God Wrought*, 766–68.

39. Polk, Third Annual Message, in *Messages and Papers*, 4:533–49, quotations at 533, 541, 542.

40. Ibid., 4:533–49; "Report on the Finances," Cong. Globe, 30th Cong., 1st sess., appendix, 9–16; Quaife, *Diary of James K. Polk*, 3:322; Holt, *Rise and Fall of the Whig Party*, 328; Howe, *What Hath God Wrought*, 770.

41. *Philadelphia North American and United States Gazette*, January 19, 1848; Cong. Globe, 30th Cong., 1st sess., 312–19, 322–26, 331–48, 351–60, 363, 368–74, 530–35, 549, quotation at 347, and appendix, 289–302, 316–41, 410–15, 472–77, quotations at 302, 313–14, 342, and 372. Outright denouncement of the war remained a minority position among the Whigs. See Holt, *Rise and Fall of the Whig Party*, 249.

42. An Act to Authorize a Loan Not to Exceed the Sum of Sixteen Millions of Dollars, March 31, 1847, ch.26, *US Statutes at Large*, 9:217–19; *New York Herald*, February 21, 1848; Cummings, "Financing the Mexican War," 224.

43. H.R. Ex. Doc. 7, 30th Cong., 2d sess., Serial 538, appendix M, 56–63, appendix S, 70–71; *Washington Daily National Intelligencer*, April 18 and June 19, 1848; *Concord New Hampshire Patriot and State Gazette*, April 27, 1848; *New York Herald*, June 18, 1848; *Mississippian*, June 30, 1848; Cummings, "Financing the Mexican War," 220–63; Shenton, *Robert J. Walker*, 114–16.

44. Cong. Globe, 30th Cong., 2d sess., appendix, 11–20, quotation at 11; *Boston Daily Atlas*, September 27, 1848; *Little Rock Arkansas State Democrat*, October 27, 1848; Cummings, "Financing the Mexican War," 245–63.

45. Susan B. Carter et al., eds., *Historical Statistics of the United States: Millennial Edition*, 5 vols. (New York. Cambridge University Press, 2006), 5:370, table Ed172. On

banks, see Hammond, *Banks and Politics in America*; and Bodenhorn, *History of Banking in Antebellum America*.

46. *Historical Statistics of the United States, Colonial Times to 1970*, 2 vols. (Washington, DC: Bureau of the Census, 1975), vol. 2, series Y, 904, 1142. The total cost of the war is difficult to determine but has been estimated at $73 million, exclusive of veterans' benefits and interest on the war loans. Carter et al., *Historical Statistics of the United States: Millennial Edition*, 5:82–83, 91, 97, 370, tables Ea589, Ea636–641, Ea 650–651, Ed168, Ed172.

47. Timothy J. Henderson, *A Glorious Defeat: Mexico and Its War with the United States* (New York: Hill and Wang, 2007), 188; Ramirez, "Mexico during the War with the United States," 122.

48. Mariano Otero, "Considerations Relating to the Political and Social Situation of the Mexican Republic in the Year 1847," in Robinson, *View from Chapultepec*, 31; Pletcher, *Diplomacy of Annexation*, 32–33; Jaime E. Rodriguez O., introduction to Rodriguez O., ed., *The Independence of Mexico and the Creation of the New Nation* (Los Angeles: UCLA Latin American Center Publications, 1989), 2–10; John H. Coatsworth, "Obstacles to Economic Growth in Nineteenth-Century Mexico," *American Historical Review* 83, no. 1 (February 1978): 80–100; Robert McCaa, "The Peopling of Mexico from Origins to Revolution," in Michael R. Haines and Richard H. Steckel, eds., *A Population History of North America* (Cambridge: Cambridge University Press, 2000), 279, table 7.4; *Historical Statistics of the United States, Colonial Times to the Present*, series A7, 8.

49. Barbara A. Tenenbaum, *The Politics of Penury: Debts and Taxes in Mexico, 1821–1856* (Albuquerque: University of New Mexico Press, 1986), 2–5; John Jay TePaske, "The Financial Disintegration of the Royal Government of Mexico during the Epoch of Independence," in Rodriguez O., *Independence of Mexico*, 64–65, 68–69, 79; Carlos Marichal, *Bankruptcy of Empire: Mexican Power and the Wars between Spain, Britain, and France, 1760–1810* (New York: Cambridge University Press, 2007); Carter et al., *Historical Statistics of the United States: Millennial Edition*, 5:707, table Eg420, 5:369, table Ea584.

50. TePaske, "Financial Disintegration," 67–68, 73.

51. Barbara A. Tenenbaum, "Taxation and Tyranny: Public Finance during the Iturbide Regime, 1821–1823," in Rodriguez O., *Independence of Mexico*, 201–13; Jaime E. Rodriguez O., "Mexico's First Foreign Loans," in ibid., 219.

52. Rodriguez O., *Independence of Mexico*, 215–35.

53. *Enciclopedia de México* (Mexico City: Seretaría de Educación Pública, 1987–1988), . 6:3353–62, s.v. "Gobernantes." For general information about the political development of postindependence Mexico, I have relied principally on Timothy E. Anna, *Forging Mexico, 1821–1835* (Lincoln: University of Nebraska Press, 1998); Stanley C. Green, *The Mexican Republic: The First Decade, 1823–1832* (Pittsburgh: University of Pittsburgh Press, 1987); Pedro Santoni, *Mexicans at Arms: Puro Federalists and the Politics of War, 1845–1848* (Forth Worth: Texas Christian University Press, 1996); and Donald Fithian Stevens, *Origins of Instability in Early Republican Mexico* (Durham, NC: Duke University Press, 1991).

54. Michael P. Costeloe, "The Extraordinary Case of Mr. Falconnet and 2,500,000 Silver Dollars: London and Mexico, 1850–1853," *Mexican Studies/Estudios Mexicanos* 15, no. 2 (Summer 1999): 261–89; Howe, *What Hath God Wrought*, 741; John M.

Belohlavek, *"Let the Eagle Soar!": The Foreign Policy of Andrew Jackson* (Lincoln: University of Nebraska Press, 1985), 238; Michele Cunningham, *Mexico and the Foreign Policy of Napoleon III* (Basingstoke, UK: Palgrave, 2001), quotation at 215. On the primitive nature of the Mexican credit market in the early nineteenth century, see Michael P. Costeloe, "Guadalupe Victoria and a Personal Loan from the Church in Independent Mexico," *Americas* 25, no. 3 (January 1969): 223–46.

55. Gene M. Brack, *Mexico Views Manifest Destiny, 1821–1846: An Essay on the Origins of the Mexican War* (Albuquerque: University of New Mexico Press, 1975), 153–57, 160–62, 172–73, 178; William A. Depalo Jr., *The Mexican National Army, 1822–1852* (College Station: Texas A&M University Press, 1997); Brian R. Hamnett, *A Concise History of Mexico*, 2d ed. (Cambridge: Cambridge University Press, 2006), 205.

56. Ramirez, "Mexico during the War with the United States," 124; David J. Weber, *The Mexican Frontier, 1821–1846: The American Southwest under Mexico* (Albuquerque: University of New Mexico Press, 1982), 81–121; Miguel A. González Quiroga, "The War between the United States and Mexico," in Francaviglia and Richmond, *Dueling Eagles*, 91–102; Douglas W. Richmond, "A View from the Periphery: Regional Factors and Collaboration during the U.S.-Mexico Conflict, 1845–1848," ibid., 127–54; Brian DeLay, "Independent Indians and the U.S.-Mexican War," *American Historical Review* 112, no. 1 (February 2007): 35–68; DeLay, *War of a Thousand Deserts: Indian Raids and the U.S.-Mexican War* (New Haven, CT: Yale University Press, 2008).

57. *Enciclopedia de México*, 6:3353–62, s.v. "Gobernantes."

58. Cummings, "Financing the Mexican War," 155–58; Santoni, *Mexicans at Arms*, 166; Tenenbaum, *The Politics of Penury*, 77–78.

59. Cummings, "Financing the Mexican War," 159–60; Santoni, *Mexicans at Arms*, 169–73; Tenenbaum, *The Politics of Penury*, 78–82; Ramirez, "Mexico during the War with the United States," 133–34. On the *Polkos* revolt, see Michael P. Costeloe, "The Mexican Church and the Rebellion of the Polkos," *Hispanic American Historical Review* 46, no. 2 (May 1966): 170–78; Santoni, *Mexicans at Arms*, 175–97; Cummings, "Financing the Mexican War," 162–67.

60. Charles A. Hale, "The War with the United States and the Crisis in Mexican Thought," *Americas* 15, no. 2 (Oct. 1957): 153–73.

61. James Buchanan to the Minister of Foreign Affairs of Mexico, January 18, 1847, in Manning, *Diplomatic Correspondence*, 7:197.

62. Polk, "To the Senate and House of Representatives," July 6, 1848, in *Messages and Papers*, 4:587–88; Polk, Third Annual Message, ibid., 534; Walker, "Report on the Finances," December 11, 1848, Walker, "Report on the Finances," 30th Cong., 2d sess., appendix, 15; *The Rough and Ready Almanac, for 1848* (Philadelphia: R. Wilson Desilver, 1847), 9; Polk, Fourth Annual Message, December 5, 1848, in *Messages and Papers*, 4:632, 634. For Anglo-American relations after the war, see Sam W. Haynes, *Unfinished Revolution: The Early American Republic in a British World* (Charlottesville: University of Virginia Press, 2010), 274–96.

63. Polk, "Inaugural Address," in *Messages and Papers*, 4:377; Polk, "To the Senate and House of Representatives, July 6, 1848," in ibid., 4:591; Polk, Fourth Annual Message, in ibid., 4:650.

64. Polk, "To the Senate and House of Representatives, July 6, 1848," in *Messages and Papers*, 4:592–93; Polk, Fourth Annual Message, in ibid., 644, 650.

CHAPTER 6

1. "Special Session Message," July 4, 1861, in *Messages and Papers*, 6:23.
2. War of 1812: "Letter from the President of the United States, Communicating Information in Relation to the Number of Troops Engaged in the Service of the United States in the Late War with Great Britain," House Ex. Doc. 72, 35th Cong., 1st sess. Serial 956, 2. Mexican War: "Letter from the Secretary of War, Transmitting a Report Showing the Number of Regulars and Volunteers Employed during the War with Mexico, and the Casualties Incident to Each Description of Force," House Ex. Doc. 118, 43d Cong., 2d sess., Serial 1648, 2. Of the militia serving in the War of 1812, 383,000 served for six months and 145,000 for less than six months. The figures are for enlistments, and a given person may have enlisted more than once. The figures for the Mexican War are aggregates of forces employed and mustered into service during the war. Average length of service was ten months. Civil War: "Soldiers Furnished by Each State. Letter from the Secretary of War, in Answer to a Resolution of the House of December 18, Transmitting a Statement of the Number of Soldiers Furnished by Each State since April 1, 1861," House Ex. Doc. 15, 39th Cong., 1st sess., Serial 1255, 2; "Letter from the Secretary of War, addressed to Chairman of the Committee on Military Affairs, Relative to Equalizing the Bounties of All Soldiers Who served during the War," House Misc. Doc. 22, 39th Cong., 2d sess., p. 3. The majority of Civil War volunteers enlisted for three years. The average period of enlistment was a little less than 2.5 years. Susan B. Carter et al., eds., *Historical Statistics of the United States: Millennial Edition*, 5 vols. (New York: Cambridge University Press, 2006), 5:80, table Ea587. Figures for enlistment are uncertain because many soldiers enlisted more than once. The official figure of enlistment is 2,778,304, but most historians estimate the number of individuals to have served to be between 1.5 and 2.2 million. See Herman H. Hattaway, "The Civil War Armies: Creation, Mobilization, and Development," in Stig Förster and Jörg Nagler, eds., *On the Road to Total War: The American Civil War and the German Wars of Unification, 1861–1871* (Washington, DC: German Historical Institute; New York: Cambridge University Press, 1997), 179. For more on mobilization, see James W. Geary, *We Need Men: The Union Draft in the Civil War* (DeKalb: Northern Illinois University Press, 1991). Nor is there a certain figure for the number of deaths in the Civil War. The most recent attempt to estimate the number of lives lost, which investigated age cohorts, concluded that the death tally for both sides together was probably in the region of 750,000. See J. David Hacker, "A Census-Based Count of the Civil War Dead," *Civil War History* 57, no. 4 (December 2011): 307–48.
3. The Gettysburg Address, in *Abraham Lincoln Speaks: A Selection of the Writings and Sayings of a Great American* (Washington DC: United States Information Service, 1959), 49–50.
4. *Economist* 20, no. 993 (September 6, 1862): 982.
5. Earl Russell, Speech to the House of Lords, February 20, 1865, *Parl. Deb.*, Lords, 3d ser., vol. 177 (1865), cols. 437–38; *Economist* 19, no. 949, (November 2, 1861): 1209. See

also *John Bull*, March 22, 1862. On perceptions of the Civil War abroad, see Ephraim Douglass Adams, *Great Britain and the American Civil War*, 2 vols. (London: Longmans, Green, 1925); Lynn M. Case and Warren F. Spencer, *The United States and France: Civil War Diplomacy* (Philadelphia: University of Pennsylvania Press, 1970); D. P. Crook, *The North, the South, and the Powers, 1861–1865* (New York: Wiley, 1974); Harold Hyman, ed., *Heard Round the World: The Impact Abroad of the Civil War* (New York: Knopf, 1969); Brian Jenkins, *Britain and the War for the Union*, 2 vols. (Montreal: McGill-Queen's University Press, 1980); Donaldson Jordan and Edwin J. Pratt, *Europe and the American Civil War* (Boston: Houghton Mifflin, 1931); Belle Becker Sideman and Lillian Friedman, eds., *Europe Looks at the Civil War* (New York: Orion, 1960); Warren R. West, *Contemporary French Opinion on the American Civil War* (Baltimore: Johns Hopkins University Press, 1924).

6. Charles Buxton, Speech to the House of Commons, April 6, 1865, *Parl. Deb.*, Commons, 3d ser., vol. 178 (1865), col. 809; *Economist* 19, no. 938 (August 17, 1861): 897.

7. Benjamin Disraeli, Speech to the House of Commons, March 13, 1865, *Parl. Deb.*, Commons, 3d ser., vol. 177 (1865), col. 1575; J. B. Smith, Speech to the House of Commons, April 6, 1865, *Parl. Deb.*, Commons, 3d ser., vol. 178 (1865), col. 809; London *Times*, April 24, 1865.

8. London *Times*, April 17 and 18, 1865; *Economist*, 22, no. 1063 (January 9, 1864): 33.

9. Samuel Wilkeson, *How Our National Debt May Be a National Blessing: The Debt Is Public Wealth, Political Union, Protection of Industry, Secure Basis for National Currency, the Orphans' and Widows' Savings Fund* (Philadelphia: M'Laughlin Brothers, 1865); *Wooster Republican*, May 18, 1865; *Union Flag*, May 16, 1865; *Baltimore Sun*, May 26, 1865, all in Scrapbook, Jay Cooke Papers. The Jay Cooke Papers at the Historical Society of Pennsylvania contain several scrapbooks with newspaper clippings and other material related to the sales campaigns of Civil War bonds directed by Jay Cooke.

10. Paul Studenski and Herman E. Krooss, *Financial History of the United States: Fiscal, Monetary, Banking, and Tariff, Including Financial Administration and State and Local Finance* (New York: McGraw-Hill, 1952), 138; Davis Rich Dewey, *Financial History of the United States*, 12th ed. (1934; repr., New York: Augustus Kelley, 1968), 306.

11. *Constitutional Union*, February 15, 1865, in Scrapbook, Jay Cooke Papers.

12. Carter et al., *Historical Statistics of the United States: Millennial Edition*, 5:80, table Ea587.

13. David Herbert Donald, *Lincoln* (New York: Simon and Schuster, 1995), 257–94; John Niven, *Salmon P. Chase: A Biography* (New York: Oxford University Press, 1995), vii ("majestic), 222–38, 355–62; James M. McPherson, *Battle Cry of Freedom: The Civil War Era* (New York: Oxford University Press, 1988), 259–61, 713–15 ("Trinity"). A more positive assessment of Chase's personality is Frederick J. Blue, "The Moral Journey of a Political Abolitionist: Salmon P. Chase and His Critics," *Civil War History* 57, no. 3 (September 2011): 210–33.

14. Dewey, *Financial History*, 274; Bray Hammond, *Sovereignty and an Empty Purse: Banks and Politics in the Civil War* (Princeton, NJ: Princeton University Press, 1970), 33, 34 ("troubler"), 349 ("misfortune"); Studenski and Krooss, *Financial History*, 139 ("mediocre"). One of the major gaps in American historiography is a solid monograph on the financing of the Civil War. Hammond is good on the first part of the war, especially on the events leading to the suspension of specie conversion and on the legislative history

of the greenbacks. Heather Cox Richardson, *The Greatest Nation of the Earth: Republican Economic Policies during the Civil War* (Cambridge, MA: Harvard University Press, 1997), has chapters on the legislation on war bonds, greenbacks, and fiscal measures. Two well-documented but older biographies of Jay Cooke provide much information about bond sales: Ellis Paxson Oberholtzer, *Jay Cooke: Financier of the Civil War*, 2 vols. (Philadelphia: George W. Jacobs, 1907); and Henrietta M. Larson, *Jay Cooke, Private Banker* (Cambridge, MA: Harvard University Press, 1936). Civil War taxation is treated in Jane Flaherty, *The Revenue Imperative* (London: Pickering and Chatto, 2009). Although valuable, this study lacks real empirical depth.

    15. Report of the Secretary of the Treasury on the Finances, July 5, 1861, Sen. Ex. Doc. No. 2, 37th. Cong., 1st sess., 5–6. In light of the criticism that Chase's measures drew from a hostile British press, it is interesting to note that the *New York Times*, July 8, 1861, believed that the war finance plan not only adhered to American traditions but also to British practice, averring, "Financial doctrines like these, duly manifested by acts, safely carried England through her giant struggle of twenty years with the first Napoleon. They will assuredly carry the credit of the American Union, without any spot or blemish, to the end of the present Rebellion."

    16. Report of the Secretary of the Treasury on the Finances, July 5, 1861, Sen. Ex. Doc. 2, 37th Cong., 1st sess., 7–10; Report of the Secretary of the Treasury on the State of the Finances for the Year Ending June 30, 1862, Sen. Ex. Doc. 2, 37th Cong., 2d sess., 13–15; Act of August 5, 1861, ch. 46, *US Statutes at Large*, 12:313–14. For the passage of this bill through the House, see Cong. Globe, 37th Cong., 1st sess., 152, 171–77, 202–5, 354, 365, 415–16, 428; for the Senate, ibid., 208, 253–55, 278–79, 313–23, 335–36, 344, 395–400. Act of July 5, 1861, ch. 46, *US Statutes at Large*, 12:313–14.

    17. Report of the Secretary of the Treasury on the Finances, July 5, 1861, Senate Ex. Doc. 2, 37th. Cong., 1st sess., 12–14; Chase to John Austin Stevens, June 26, 1861, SPCP, 3:69–70; An Act to Authorize a National Loan, July 17, 1861, ch. 5, *US Statutes at Large*, 12:259; An Act Supplementary to an Act Entitled "An Act to Authorize a National Loan," August 5, 1862, ch. 46, *US Statutes at Large*, 12:313; Cong. Globe, 37th Cong., 1st sess., 109–10, 128. That the French popular loans of 1854, 1855, and 1859 were well known in America is evident from the scattered references to them in the press. See *Imlay and Bricknell's Bank Note Reporter*, December 5, 1862, in Scrapbook, Jay Cooke Papers; *Indiana Weekly Register*, March 31, 1863, in ibid.; *Union County Herald*, May 20, 1865, in Scrapbook, Jay Cooke Papers, in ibid.; *New York Times*, April 9, 1864.

    18. Belmont quoted in Larson, *Jay Cooke*, 117; *Economist* 19, no. 939 (August 24, 1861): 927; *Economist* 20, no. 989 (August 2, 1862): 870; *Fitzgerald City Stern*, April 18, 1863, in Scrapbook, Jay Cooke Papers; Jay Sexton, *Debtor Diplomacy: Finance and American Foreign Relations in the Civil War Era, 1837–1873* (Oxford: Oxford University Press, 2005), 82–133.

    19. Report of the Secretary of the Treasury on the State of the Finances for the Year Ending June 30, 1862, Sen. Ex. Doc. 2, 37th Cong., 2d sess., 8–10; *New York Times*, July 12, 1861; Hammond, *Sovereignty and an Empty Purse*, 73–128; Larson, *Jay Cooke*, 110–11; Studenski and Krooss, *Financial History*, 142.

    20. Chase's treatment of the banks has been severely criticized by Hammond, *Sovereignty and an Empty Purse*, 71–163.

21. Report of the Secretary of the Treasury on the State of the Finances for the Year Ending June 30, 1862, Sen. Ex. Doc. 2, 37th Cong., 2d sess., 13, 23; *New York Times*, December 2, 1861. On the military situation, see McPherson, *Battle Cry of Freedom*, 339–68. On the national banking scheme, see Bray Hammond, *Banks and Politics in America from the Revolution to the Civil War* (Princeton, NJ: Princeton University Press, 1957), 718–39; Hammond, *Sovereignty and an Empty Purse*, 283–351.

22. Report of the Secretary of the Treasury on the State of the Finances for the Year Ending June 30, 1863, Sen. Ex. Doc. 1, 37th Cong., 3d sess. 7–9; Hammond, *Sovereignty and an Empty Purse*, 129–63; McPherson, *Battle Cry of Freedom*, 444–45. It was only in the very last stages of the war that the National Banking Act was finally realized; see Jeremy Atack and Peter Passell, *A New Economic View of American History from Colonial Times to 1940*, 2d ed. (New York: Norton, 1994), 502–5.

23. Cong. Globe, 37th Cong., 2d sess., February 6, 1862, 687 (Stevens), February 12, 1862, 766 (Fessenden), February 13, 1862, 789–90 (Sherman); Chase to Thaddeus Stevens, February 25, 1862, *SPCP*, 3:141–42.

24. H.R. 240, 37th Cong. (1862); Chase to Stevens, January 29, 1861, *SPCP*, 3:126–28; Cong. Globe, 37th Cong, 2d sess., 774; Elbridge G. Spaulding, *A Resource of War—The Credit of the Government Made Immediately Available: History of the Legal Tender Paper Money Issued during the Great Rebellion. Being a Loan without Interest and a National Currency* (Buffalo: Express Printing House, 1869), 13–28, presents the recollections of the chairman of the Ways and Means subcommittee responsible for originating the bill together with contemporary documents. Spaulding first intended to append the right to issue US notes to the national bank bill he was preparing. Realizing that the money was needed urgently, he introduced a separate bill authorizing demand Treasury notes on January 7. The bill was recommitted to the Ways and Means Committee and reintroduced as H.R. 240 on January 22, 1862.

25. Spaulding, *Resource of War*, 14; Report of the Secretary of the Treasury on the State of the Finances for the Year Ending June 30, 1863, Sen. Ex. Doc. 1, 37th Cong., 3d sess., 7–8; Cong. Globe, 37th Cong., 2d sess., February 13, 1862, 789–91. The politicians' comparison of greenbacks to Bank of England notes were echoed in the press, where references to Britain's funding of the Napoleonic Wars were frequently made throughout the Civil War. "Any American of common reading knows that no long wars have ever been carried on with paper money," the *New York Times* remarked on July 8, 1864. The "course of this country in preserving its national life, has a sufficiently exact parallel, financially, in the course of England, when seeking to ruin Napoleon." See also ibid., February 22, 1863, and "Seven-Thirty Facts and Figures," broadsheet issued by Jay Cooke, n.d. [1865], in Scrapbook, Jay Cooke Papers.

26. Chase to Stevens, January 29, 1861, *SPCP*, 3:126; Francis Fessenden, *Life and Public Services of William Pitt Fessenden*, 2 vols. (Boston: Houghton Mifflin, 1907), 1:194; Cong. Globe, 37th Cong., 2d sess., February 12, 1862, 763, 766–67 (Fessenden), 767–69 (Jacob Collamer).

27. Chase to Stevens, January 29, 1861, *SPCP*, 3:127; Cong. Globe, 37th Cong., 2d sess., February 13, 1862, 789; *New York Times*, December 28, 1861, and February 7, 1862.

28. An Act to Authorize the Issue of United States Notes, and for the Redemption or Funding Thereof, and for Funding the Floating Debt of the United States, February 25,

1862, ch. 33, *US Statutes at Large*, 12:345; Cong. Globe, 37th Cong., 2d sess., February 12, 1862, 763–64; Hammond, *Sovereignty and an Empty Purse*, 211–25. For passage of the bill through Congress, see Cong. Globe, 37th Cong., 2d sess., 435, 522–27, 549–52, 593–94, 614–18, 629–42, 655–54, 679–95, 696, 707, 719, 762–75, 787–804, 827–28, 874, 881–91, 898–902, 909, 911, 929, 938–40, 946–48, 953, 954.

29. Chase to Bradford R. Wood, March 28, 1862, *SPCP*, 3:153; Chase to Benjamin Butler, September 23, 1862, ibid., 3:283; Report of the Secretary of the Treasury on the State of the Finances for the Year Ending June 30, 1863, Sen. Ex. Doc. 1, 37th Cong., 3d sess., 7–11; Hammond, *Sovereignty and an Empty Purse*, 244–54.

30. Cong. Globe, 37th Cong., 2d sess., February 12, 1862, 770, 791.

31. *Economist*, 20, no 983 (June 28, 1862): 702 ("expressly forbidden"); *Economist* 20, no. 986 (July 19, 1862): 787; *Economist*, 20, no. 998 (October 11, 1862): 1123 ("a heavy income tax"); *Economist*, 20, no. 999 (October 18, 1862): 1154 ("ignorant"); *Economist* 20, no. 1008 (December 20, 1862): 1403 ("hoarded").

32. Cong. Globe, 37th Cong., 2d sess., February 13, 1862, 791; ibid., March 12, 1862, 1195.

33. Report of the Secretary of the Treasury on the State of the Finances for the Year Ending June 30, 1862, Sen. Ex. Doc. 1, 37th Cong., 3d sess., 12; Report of the Secretary of the Treasury on the State of the Finances for the Year Ending June 30, 1863, H.R. Ex. Doc. 3, 38th Cong., 1st sess., 1, 14; Chase to John Bigelow, October 7, 1862, *SPCP*, 3:291–92; Chase to Jay Cooke, October 23, 1862, ibid., 299–300; Letter from the Secretary of the Treasury, in Answer to a Resolution of the House of Representatives Relative to the Services of Jay Cooke & Company in the Sale of United States Securities, H.R. Ex. Doc. 66, 38th Cong., 1st sess. 2–3.

34. Chase to Jay Cooke, October 23, 1862, *SPCP*, 3:300; Letter from the Secretary of the Treasury, in Answer to a Resolution of the House of Representatives Relative to the Services of Jay Cooke & Company in the Sale of United States Securities, H.R. Ex. Doc. 66, 38th Cong., 1st sess., 2; *New York Times*, January 14, 1863; *United States Journal*, April 18, 1863, in Scrapbook, Jay Cooke Papers ("restoration"); "The National Banking Scheme," letter to the editor signed "S," *New York Times*, January 31, 1863; Larson, *Jay Cooke*, 67–72, 105–18; Oberholtzer, *Jay Cooke*, 1:103–212, 217.

35. Letter from the Secretary of the Treasury, in Answer to a Resolution of the House of Representatives Relative to the Services of Jay Cooke & Company in the Sale of United States Securities, H.R. Ex. Doc. 66, 38th Cong., 1st sess., 2–3; Report of the Secretary of the Treasury on the State of the Finances for the Year Ending June 30, 1862, Sen. Ex. Doc. 1, 37th Cong., 3d sess., 14; *Philadelphia Bulletin*, April 8, 1863, in Scrapbook, Jay Cooke Papers. The calculation was based on the assumption that the government would redeem the bond in specie after five years according to contract: "One thousand dollars in gold, if kept hoarded forever will be only $1,000. Now if this amount of gold is sold at 50 per cent. premium you will have $1,500 to invest in 5-20 six per cent bonds. These will pay annually $90 in gold, making in five years $450 besides the compound interest; and at the end of five years, if then paid, the holder will receive the $1,500 in gold. Thus the $1,000 will produce over $2,000." It was common for 5-20 advertisements to calculate the yield of government bonds paid for in depreciated greenbacks; several examples can be found in the Jay Cooke Papers, e.g., *Imlay and Bicknell's Bank Note Reporter*, December 5, 1862;

"The New Twenty Year 6 Per. Cent Bonds," n.d., and "United States Five-Twenties," n.d., leaflets issued by Jay Cooke, in ibid. A London correspondent to the *Economist* also pointed out that the journal had failed to take note depreciation into account when discussing the American debt. The writer claimed that he could buy notes for gold at 65 cents gold to a dollar bill. On a $1,000 bond the "interest is 60 gold dollars and the return about 8.5 percent after turning dollars into pounds," *Economist* 22, no. 1067 (February 6, 1863): 167.

36. Letter from the Secretary of the Treasury, in Answer to a Resolution of the House of Representatives Relative to the Services of Jay Cooke & Company in the Sale of United States Securities, H.R. Ex. Doc. 66, 38th Cong., 1st sess., 3; Report of the Secretary of the Treasury on the State of the Finances for the Year Ending June 30, 1863, H.R. Ex. Doc. 3, 38th Cong., 1st sess., 2, 14; Chase to William H. Aspinwall and John Murray Forbes, May 14, 1863, *SPCP*, 4:30–31; Chase to George Harrington, November 19, 1863, ibid., 4:195; Larson, *Jay Cooke*, 119–51; Oberholtzer, *Jay Cooke*, 1:212–325.

37. Report of the Secretary of the Treasury on the State of the Finances for the Year Ending June 30, 1863, H.R. Ex. Doc. 3, 38th Cong., 1st sess., 14; Letter from the Secretary of the Treasury, in Answer to a Resolution of the House of Representatives Relative to the Services of Jay Cooke & Company in the Sale of United States Securities, H.R. Ex. Doc. 66, 38th Cong., 1st sess., 1–4; Chase to Abraham Lincoln, June 29, 1864, *SPCP*, 4:409–10; Lincoln to Chase, June 30, 1864, ibid., 4:411; Chase to William P. Fessenden, August 27, 1864, ibid., 4:426; Larson, *Jay Cooke*, 160–62.

38. Fessenden, *Life and Public Services*, 1:313–74. On Fessenden, see Robert Cook, " 'The Grave of All My Comforts': William Pitt Fessenden as Secretary of the Treasury, 1864–65," *Civil War History* 41, no. 3 (September 1995), 208–26; and Cook, *Civil War Senator: William Pitt Fessenden and the Fight to Save the American Republic* (Baton Rouge: Louisiana State University Press, 2011).

39. *Washington Daily Chronicle*, January 31, 1865; *Philadelphia Inquirer*, February 1, 1865 ("force and power"), in Scrapbook, Jay Cooke Papers. Newspapers that carried the news of Cooke's appointment include *Constitutional Union*, January 31, 1865; *North American*, February 1, 1865; *Free Press*, February 1, 1865; *Philadelphia Daily News*, February 1, 1865; *New York Times*, February 1, 1865; *New York Tribune*, February 1, 1865; *Commercial List*, February 1, 1865; *Lehigh Valley Express*, February 4, 1865, all in Scrapbook, Jay Cooke Papers.

40. *Washington Daily Chronicle*, July 27, 1865, in Scrapbook, Jay Cooke Papers. The *New York Times* editorial for July 28, 1865, spoke of the "eminent fitness" of Cooke to launch the 7-30 bond drive. "Never in the history of nations, was such an enormous amount of money raised for public use, with such extraordinary rapidity and success, as in the instance of the great Seven-Thirty Loan, which is now all in the hands of the loyal people, and deemed by them the most desirable security ever issued by the government." For the campaign, see Larson, *Jay Cooke*, 152–75; and Oberholtzer, *Jay Cooke*, 1:425–629.

41. Scrapbook, Jay Cooke Papers. There is also much material on the marketing of the loans in Larson, *Jay Cooke*, 96–175; and Oberholtzer, *Jay Cooke*, 1:212–325, 425–658. The latter reprints many newspaper items, broadsides, and letters.

42. To the Editor from Peasle & Co., n.d., Scrapbook, Jay Cooke Papers.

43. *New York Tribune*, July 17, 1865 ("hunerd thalers," "Troth"), "The Best Way to

Put Money Out at Interest," *Philadelphia Ledger*, March 28, 1865, and *Fitzgerald City Stern*, May 7, 1863, all in Scrapbook, Jay Cooke Papers. As with other aspects of government finance, Britain was the point of reference also in discussions of the safety of investing in securities. For example, one paper noted, "As we know that in England, the safest and most desirable investment is in its public stocks, which vary less than anything else in value, so we shall find in this country that the public debt is not only safe and permanent, but also convenient as an investment." *St. Louis Daily Union*, May 20, 1863, in ibid. For a stimulating analysis of the ideology of Cooke's campaigns, see Melinda Lawson, *Patriot Fires: Forging a New American Nationalism in the Civil War North* (Lawrence: University Press of Kansas, 2002), 40–64.

44. *New York Tribune*, March 7, 1865 ("weave," "this fist," "white man's war") reprinted in Oberholtzer, *Jay Cooke*, 585–87, 589–94; *Fitzgerald City Stern*, May 7, 1863 ("sublime") and *New York Tribune*, July 17, 1865 ("all sorts," "shop-keepers") in Scrapbook, Jay Cooke Papers. The *Tribune* also gave a brief description of the business of the night office agencies: "The machinery of the agency is simple—a few desks and a table—a corps of experienced clerks and tellers—the exchange of the registered 7-30 bond for each individual loan—and the applicant at the Nation's Savings Bank becomes at once the Nation's creditor and beneficiary."

45. *Daily Illinois State Journal*, January 10, 1863 ("solemn duty") and "Seven-Thirty Facts and Figures" (1865) ("Your Sons"), in Scrapbook, Jay Cooke Papers; *Media (PA) American*, April 1, 1865 ("All day long"), reprinted in Oberholtzer, *Jay Cooke*, 1:596–97; *Philadelphia Inquirer*, September 13, 1861 ("money bags"); *St. Louis Daily Evening News*, May 19, 1863 ("great power . . . contributes"), quoted in Oberholtzer, *Jay Cooke* 1:160, 251.

46. *New York Times*, May 9, 10 ("Something Wonderful," "Choctaw"), 12, 13 ("Great Day"); see also ibid., March 20, May 16, 17, 18, 23, 28, and July 4, 15, 17, 18, and 19. For some examples of a similar strategy for 5-20s, see *New York Times*, March 22, April 19, and May 12, 1863; *Sandusky Register*, April 29, 1863; and *Fitzgerald City Stern*, May 7, 1863, in Scrapbook, Jay Cooke Papers.

47. *New York Times*, July 21, 1865; *Constitutional Union*, April 5, 1865, in Scrapbook, Jay Cooke Papers.

48. *Economist* 22, no. 1063 (January 9, 1864): 34.

49. Act of August 5, 1861, ch. 45, *US Statues at Large*, 12:292–313; Richardson, *Greatest Nation of the Earth*, 110–15; Flaherty, *Revenue Imperative*, 61–79; Hammond, *Sovereignty and an Empty Purse*, 271. For passage of these measures through Congress, see Cong. Globe, 37th Cong., 1st sess., 229, 246–52, 268–74, 280–87, 299–308, 323–31 (H.R. 71), and 152, 171–77, 202–5, 208, 253–55, 278–79, 313–23, 335–36, 344, 354, 365, 395–400, 415–16, 428 (H.R. 54).

50. Report of the Secretary of the Treasury on the State of the Finances, for the Year Ending June 30, 1861, Sen. Ex. Doc. 2, 37th Cong., 2d sess., 13–16, 20; Cong. Globe, 37th Cong., 2d sess., 344–49. When the bill was debated in Congress, the *New York Times*, April 21, 1862, commented that new tax measures "should leave no question about the security of the public debt."

51. Cong. Globe, 37th Cong. 2d sess., 1194–95; H.R. 312, 37th Cong., 2d sess.; Richardson, *Greatest Nation of the Earth*, 115–26; Flaherty, *Revenue Imperative*, 91–99;

Hammond, *Sovereignty and an Empty Purse*, 261–82. For the passage of H.R. 312 through Congress, see Cong. Globe, 37th Cong., 1st sess., 1041–41, 1194–1215, 1217–28, 1236–45, 1252–59, 1273–79, 1286–96, 1303–14, 1322–30, 1342–47, 1360–69, 1383–90, 1403–15, 1432–43, 1452–64, 1480–89, 1508–14, 1527–36, 1544–51, 1564–66, 1576–77, 1603, 1614, 1966, 2254–62, 2278–88, 2308–21, 2329–41, 2344–56, 2367–79, 2396–2408, 2419–30, 2443–51, 2454–77, 2479–94, 2508–26, 2540–60, 2572–87, 2598–2611, 2620, 2671, 2675, 2680–82, 2708, 2873–77, 2890–91. A sentiment similar to Morrill's had been expressed by the *New York Times* on January 8, 1862: "For the present . . . we must bid adieu to the golden era of our history in which we were scarcely conscious that we had a Government, so lightly did its burdens rest upon us."

52. Cong. Globe, 37th Cong. 2d sess., 1194. In its report on the bill, the *New York Times*, March 4, 1862, noted that "the agricultural interest is spared as much as possible." As a result, the protests from members of Congress from western states could be expected to be muted.

53. Cong. Globe, 37th Cong., 2d sess., 1407; *Economist* 20, no. 970 (March 29, 1862): 341–42; Gladstone quoted Smith with reference to the British budget in the spring of 1862. A reprint of the London *Times* report of the speech was published in the *New York Times*, April 19, 1862. The *Economist* article was reprinted as far away as Australia; see Melbourne *Argus*, June 28, 1862, and Sydney *Empire*, July 1, 1862.

54. Cong. Globe, 37th Cong., 2d sess., 1407; *Economist* 20, no. 986 (July 19, 1862): 787; *New York Times*, March 5, 1862.

55. Cong. Globe, 37th Cong., 2d sess., 2606. The *New York Times* consistently criticized the Ways and Means Committee for not following British practice in devising its fiscal measures. "Taxes should be levied upon as few subjects as possible. The tendency of the English system is to constantly reduce the number of articles upon which they are imposed. The great bulk of the English revenues are collected from about a dozen subjects. We should do well to study the example set us." *New York Times*, March 5, 1862. The paper had already drawn attention to British practice on January 21. The message was repeated after the bill had gone to the Senate on April 19 and again on April 30, May 3 (when the paper listed eight "flaws" in H.R. 312), and May 27 (when the bill was called a "monstrosity"). In later years and after the close of the war, the paper again pointed to Britain as the most appropriate model for American taxation; see *New York Times*, January 18, 1864, and August 14, 1865.

56. Cong. Globe, 37th Cong., 2d sess., 1308–10.

57. Cong. Globe, 37th Cong., 2d sess., 1406–10.

58. Act of July 1, 1862, ch. 19, *US Statutes at Large*, 9:432–89; Act of July 14, 1862, ch. 158, *US Statutes at Large*, 9:543–61; Cong. Globe, 37th Cong., 2d sess., 1196; Report of the Secretary of the Treasury on the State of the Finances, for the Year Ending June 30, 1863, H.R. Ex. Doc. 3, 38th Cong., 1st sess., 3; Report of Commissioner of Internal Revenue, November 30, 1863, in Report of the Secretary of the Treasury on the State of the Finances for the Year Ending June 30, 1863, H.R. Ex. Doc. 3, 38th Cong., 1st sess., 70.

59. Report of the Secretary of the Treasury on the State of the Finances, for the Year Ending June 30, 1863, H.R. Ex. Doc. 3, 38th Cong., 1st sess., 9–10; Chase to Cyrus Vance, February 22, 1864, SPCP, 4:295; Chase to Horace Greeley, April 6, 1864, ibid., 4:367; Chase to Fessenden, April 12, 1864, ibid., 4:373; Chase to Jesse Baldwin, May 18, 1864,

ibid., 4:383; Chase to Fessenden, June 20, 1864, ibid., 4:399–400; Chase to Lincoln, June 30, 1864, ibid., 4:410; Chase to William Curtis Noyes, July 11, 1864, ibid., 4:418.

60. Act of June 30, 1864, ch. 173, *US Statutes at Large*, 13:223–306; Richardson, *Greatest Nation of the Earth*, 126–33; Dewey, *Financial History*, 302–5; Flaherty, *Revenue Imperative*, 114–16; Studenski and Krooss, *Financial History*, 150–53. For passage of H.R. 405 through Congress, see Cong. Globe, 38th Cong., 1st sess., 1532, 1697, 1715–33, 1755–61, 1784–91, 1814–27, 1832–40, 1848–54, 1875–84, 1901–8, 1934–39, 1940–43, 2015, 2344, 2437–47, 2459–70, 2486–2501, 2512–21, 2522–26, 2545–51, 2554–75, 2589–99, 2601–6, 2625–36, 2654–63, 2665–71, 2698–2715, 2730–41, 2754–70, 2810, 2995, 2996–3001, 3018–21, 3024–28, 3039, 3055, 3056–57, 3078, 3254–56, 3266, 3267, 3275–78, 3378.

61. Cong. Globe, 39th Cong., 1st sess., 2438.

62. *New York Times*, May 11, June 15, and July 30, 1865; To the Editor from Peasle & Co., June 28, 1865; Wilkeson, *How Our National Debt May Be a National Blessing*, 3; *New York Herald*, June 19 and 23, 1865, in Scrapbook, Jay Cooke Papers. Wilkeson's pamphlet was reprinted in *New York Tribune*, June 16, 1865; *New York Times*, June 19, 1865; *Philadelphia Inquirer*, June 19, 1865; and *Albany Argus*, June 19, 1865. A more successful publication put out by Cooke was William Elder, *How Our National Debt Can Be Paid: The Wealth, Resources, and Power of the People of the United States* (Philadelphia: Sherman, 1865).

63. Report of the Secretary of the Treasury on the State of the Finances for the Year 1865, H.R. Ex. Doc. 3, 39th Cong., 1st sess., 16; Report of the Secretary of the Treasury on the State of the Finances for the Year 1866, H.R. Ex. Doc. 4, 39th Cong., 2d sess., 8; Carter et al., *Historical Statistics of the United States: Millennial Edition*, 5:80, table Ea586.

64. This and the following paragraph are based on Dewey, *Financial History*, 331–58; Studenski and Krooss, *Financial History*, 161–75; and Carter et al., *Historical Statistics of the United States: Millennial Edition* 5:80–81, table Ea587.

65. Report of the Secretary of the Treasury on the State of the Finances for the Year 1865, H.R. Ex. Doc. 3, 39th Cong., 1st sess., 5, 14.

66. Ephraim Douglass Adams, *Great Britain and the American Civil War*, 2 vols. (London: Longmans, 1925); Lynn M. Case and Warren F. Spencer, *The United States and France: Civil War Diplomacy* (Philadelphia: University of Pennsylvania Press, 1970); Crook, *The North, the South, and the Powers*; Jenkins, *Britain and the War for the Union*; Howard Jones, *Union in Peril: The Crisis over British Intervention in the Civil War* (Chapel Hill: University of North Carolina Press, 1992); Jones, *Blue and Gray Diplomacy: A History of Union and Confederate Foreign Relations* (Chapel Hill: University of North Carolina Press, 2010).

67. Alexander J. Beresford Hope, *A Popular View of the American Civil War* (London: James Ridgway, 1861), 37; Baron de Brunow to Prince Gortchakov, January 1, 1860, quoted in Adams, *Great Britain and the American Civil War*, 1:36.

68. Kenneth Bourne, *Britain and the Balance of Power in North America, 1815–1908* (London: Longmans, 1967); C. P. Stacey, *Canada and the British Army, 1846–1871: A Study in the Practice of Responsible Government* (Toronto: University of Toronto Press, 1963); Robin W. Winks, *Canada and the United States: The Civil War Years* (Baltimore: Johns Hopkins University Press, 1960).

69. Lord Lyons to Earl Russell, received May 9, 1865, "Report by Captain Goodenough, RN, on the Naval Resources of the United States," in Kenneth Bourne, ed., *British Documents on Foreign Affairs: Reports and Papers from the Foreign Office Confidential Print. Part I, From the Mid-Nineteenth Century to the First World War. Series C, North America, 1837–1914* (Frederick, MD: University Publications of America, 1986), vol. 6, doc. 402, 303–9; "Dispatch 788. Lord Lyons to Earl Russell," November 3, 1863, in James J. Barnes and Patience P. Barnes, eds., *The American Civil War through British Eyes* (Kent, OH: Kent State University Press, 2005), 105–4; Lt. Col. Thomas L. Gallwey to Lord Lyons, May 27, 1864, enclosed in Dispatch 467. Lord Lyons to Earl Russell, July 4, 1864, ibid., 189–93; Robinson quoted in Bourne, *Balance of Power*, 281.

70. Bourne, *Balance of Power*, 251–312; Peter Burroughs, "Defence and Imperial Disunity," in Andrew Porter, ed., *The Oxford History of the British Empire*. vol. 2, *The Nineteenth Century* (Oxford: Oxford University Press, 1999), 320–43, Commons resolution quoted at 328; Stacey, *Canada and the British Army*, 172–201; Seymour Fitzgerald, Speech to the House of Commons, February 20, 1865, *Parl. Deb.*, Commons, 3d ser., vol. 177 (1865), cols. 1552–53 ("formidable artillery"); Robert Lowe, Speech to the House of Commons, April 6, 1865, ibid., vol. 178 (1865), col. 809.

71. Letter to the Secretary of State for War with Reference to the Defence of Canada, by Colonel Jervois, Deputy Director of Fortifications, 1865, Command Paper 3434, *Parliamentary Papers*, 37:429; Robert Lowe, Speech to the House of Commons, February 20, 1865, *Parl. Deb.*, Commons, 3d ser., vol. 177 (1865), cols. 1579–86 ("trained, disciplined"); Chicester Fortescue, ibid., cols. 1591–95; Lord Cecil, ibid., cols. 1613–14; Lord Elcho, Speech to the House of Commons, April 6, 1865, ibid., vol. 178 (1865), cols. 801 ("grave"); Charles Buxton, Speech to the House of Commons, April 6, 1865, ibid., cols. 805–12 ("unparalleled artillery"); J. B. Smith, ibid., cols. 825–29;. Thomas Gallwey to Lyons, May 27, 1864, in Barnes and Barnes, *American Civil War through British Eyes*, 3:191.

72. Bourne, *Balance of Power*, 206–412; Burroughs, "Defence and Imperial Disunity," 320–43; W. L. Morton, *The Critical Years: The Union of British North America, 1857–1873* (London: McClellan and Stewart, 1964); Charles Perry Stacey, *Canada and the British Army: A Study in Responsible Government* (Toronto: University of Toronto Press, 1963); Robin W. Winks, *Canada and the United States: The Civil War Years* (Baltimore: Johns Hopkins University Press, 1960).

73. London *Times*, December 2, 1871.

74. *New York Times*, April 11, 1871.

CONCLUSION

1. John Brewer, *The Sinews of Power: War, Money, and the English State, 1688–1783* (London: Unwin Hyman, 1989); Steve Pincus, *1688: The First Modern Revolution* (New Haven, CT: Yale University Press, 2009); Charles Tilly, ed., *The Formation of National States in Western Europe* (Princeton, NJ: Princeton University Press, 1975), 42 (quotation); Tilly, *Coercion, Capital, and European States, AD 990–1990* (Oxford: Blackwell, 1990). Michael Mann provides comparative data on central state expenditure in his work on the nineteenth-century state. Although government expenditure as share of GDP

or national income was around six to seven times higher in Britain and around four to five times higher in France than in the United States, the federal government's spending on the military as a share of total spending was more than twice that of the British central government and slightly less than twice that of the French central government; see Mann, *Sources of Social Power*, vol. 2, *The Rise of Classes and Nation-States, 1760–1914* (New York: Cambridge University Press, 1993), 366–67, table 11.3, and 373–74, table 11.4.

2. James Madison, "Federalist 41," in *Federalist*, 272; Andrew Jackson, Farewell Address, in *Messages and Papers*, 3:296. For an analysis of the eighteenth-century critique of the "war system" and the European state, see Herbert E. Sloan, *Principle and Interest: Thomas Jefferson and the Problem of Debt* (New York: Oxford University Press, 1995), 86–124.

3. James Madison, quoted in Sloan, *Principle and Interest*, 86.

4. Thomas Jefferson to Samuel Kercheval, July 12, 1816, in Andrew A. Lipscomb et al., eds., *Writings of Thomas Jefferson*, , 20 vols. (Washington, DC: Thomas Jefferson Memorial Association), 15:39–40.

5. Jefferson to William Ludlow, September 6, 1824, in Lipscomb et al., *Writings of Thomas Jefferson*, 16:76.

6. *New York Herald*, February 4, 1848.

7. Report by the Secretary of the Treasury on the Finances, Containing Estimates of the Public Revenue and Public Expenditures, and Plans for Improving and Increasing the Revenue, Sen. Ex. Doc. 2, 37th Cong, 1st sess., 6–7.

8. Alexander Hamilton, "First Report on the Further Provision Necessary for Establishing Public Credit," *PAH*, 7:233; "State of the Finances," *ASP: Finance*, 2:497; "State of the Finances," ibid., 3:10; "Treasury Report," *Register of Debates*, 20th Cong., 2d sess., 21.

9. Richard Rush, "Annual Treasury Report," in *Register of Debates*, 20th Cong., 2d sess., appendix, 18.

10. Report of the Secretary of the Treasury on the State of the Finances, For the Year Ending June 30, 1861, Sen. Ex. Doc. 2, 37th Cong., 2d sess., 18, lists the loans outstanding on July 1, 1861.

11. Davis Rich Dewey, *Financial History of the United States*, 12th ed. (1934; repr., New York: Augustus M. Kelley, 1968 [1934]), 268. On the military buildup, coastal fortifications, and internal improvements, see, respectively, Michael Fitzgerald, "Europe and the United States Defense Establishment: American Military Policy and Strategy, 1815–1821" (PhD diss., Purdue University, 1990); Mark Smith, "The Army Corps of Engineers," (PhD diss., University of Alabama, 2004); and John Lauritz Larson, *Internal Improvements: National Public Works and the Promise of Popular Government in the Early United States* (Chapel Hill: University of North Carolina Press, 2001).

12. Hamilton, "Federalist 36," in *Federalist*, 228.

13. On the structure of British taxation, see Brian R. Mitchell, *British Historical Statistics* (Cambridge: Cambridge University Press, 1988), 576–77, 581–82.

14. Maurice C. Baxter, *Henry Clay and the American System* (Lexington: University Press of Kentucky, 1995); Richard E. Ellis, *The Union at Risk: Jacksonian Democracy*,

States' Rights and the Nullification Crisis (New York: Oxford University Press, 1987); William W. Freehling, *Prelude to Civil War: The Nullification Controversy in South Carolina, 1816–1836* (New York: Harper and Row, 1966), 253–86; Nicholas Onuf and Peter Onuf, *Nations, Markets, and War: Modern History and the American Civil War* (Charlottesville: University of Virginia Press, 2006); Brian Schoen, "Calculating the Price of Union: Republican Economic Nationalism and the Origins of Southern Sectionalism, 1790–1828," *Journal of the Early Republic* 23, no. 2 (2003): 173–206.

15. Dewey, *Financial History*, 247, 249–51, 262; Paul Studenski and Herman E. Krooss, *Financial History of the United States: Fiscal, Monetary, Banking, and Tariff, Including Financial Administration and State and Local Finance* (New York: McGraw-Hill, 1952), 90–92, 98–99, 117, 122; Frank Taussig, *The Tariff History of the United States*, 8th ed. (1931; repr., New York: Augustus Kelley, 1967), 18–115.

16. Report of the Secretary of the Treasury on the State of the Finances, For the Year Ending June 30, 1861, Sen. Ex. Doc. 2, 37th Cong., 2d sess., 13.

17. Studenski and Krooss, *Financial History*, 162–63, 174; Sidney Ratner, *American Taxation: Its History as a Social Force in Democracy* (New York: Norton, 1942), 111–399; Cong. Globe, 37th Cong., 2d sess., 1404.

18. On the expenditure of central governments, see Mann, *Sources of Social Power*, 2:366–67, table 11.3.

19. See references cited in note 9 in the introduction.

20. John Holroyd, Earl of Sheffield, *Observations on the Commerce of the American States with Europe and the West Indies* (London, 1783), 68; Lord Harlington quoted in London *Times*, March 24, 1865.

21. *Economist* 21, no. 1017 (February 21, 1863): 201.

22. Edward Burke, *There's a Heap of Work to Do* (New York: J. Wrigley, 1866); *The Annexation of Mexico the Means of Paying the National Debt. Letter to President Johnson from Andrew J. Wilcox* (Baltimore, 1865).

23. Peter Burroughs, "Defence and Imperial Disunity," in Andrew Porter, ed., *The Oxford History of the British Empire*, vol. 2, *The Nineteenth Century* (Oxford: Oxford University Press, 1999), 320–43; Kenneth Bourne, *Britain and the Balance of Power in North America, 1815–1908* (London: Longmans, 1967); Brian Jenkins, *Britain and the War for the Union*, 2 vols. (Montreal: McGill-Queen's University Press, 1980), 2:367–74; C. P. Stacey, *Canada and the British Army, 1846–1871: A Study in the Practice of Responsible Government* (Toronto: University of Toronto Press, 1963); Robin W. Winks, *Canada and the United States: The Civil War Years* (Baltimore: Johns Hopkins University Press, 1960).

24. Arnold Blumberg, *The Diplomacy of the Mexican Empire, 1863–1867* (Philadelphia: American Philosophical Society, 1971); Henry Blumenthal, *France and the United States: Their Diplomatic Relations, 1789–1914* (Chapel Hill: University of North Carolina Press, 1970), 74–116; Michele Cunningham, *Mexico and the Foreign Policy of Napoleon III* (New York: Palgrave, 2001); Alfred H. Hanna and Kathryn A. Hanna, *Napoleon III and Mexico: American Triumph over Monarchy* (Chapel Hill: University of North Carolina Press, 1971); William E. Hardy, "South of the Border: Ulysses S. Grant and the French Intervention," *Civil War History* 54, no. 1 (March 2008): 63–86.

25. Thomas A. Bailey, "Why the United States Purchased Alaska," *Pacific Historical*

Review 3 (1934): 39–49; Benjamin P. Thomas, *Russo-American Relations, 1815–1867* (Baltimore: Johns Hopkins University Press, 1930); Ilya Vinkovetsky, *Russian America: An Overseas Colony of a Continental Empire, 1804–1867* (New York: Oxford University Press, 2011), 181–88; Albert A. Woldman, *Lincoln and the Russians* (Cleveland: World, 1952).

INDEX

Page numbers in italics refer to illustrations.

Adams, Henry, 5
Adams, John: and image of Hercules, 2; Quasi War, 111, 116; *Thoughts on Government*, 22
Adams, John Quincy, 142, 229, 235
Alaska Purchase of 1867, 7, 146, 147, 251, 256n10
alcohol: import duties on, 76, 246; internal taxes on, 75, 76, 115, 206, 208–9, 211; state taxes on, 54–55
American Almanac and Repository of Useful Knowledge for the Year 1847, The, 151–52, 153
American Cottage Library, 151, 154
American Indian nations: aggressive policies of Republicans against, 87; demise of Great Plains nations with Mexican War, 11; reservation system, 8, 9, 11; territorial dispossession and ethnic cleansing of, 7, 8, 9, 147, 223, 235, 247; treaties regulating Indian land cessions, 8
American Peace Society, 151
"American System" economic plan, 242
Ames, Fisher, 50, 90, 95, 100–101, 103, 107, 275n29, 275n30
Amsterdam, international securities market, 90
Annapolis Convention, 30–31
antistatism, 224, 229
Aranda, Count de, 2, 3
army notes, 61
Arrillaga, Mariana Paredes y, 169

Articles of Confederation, 19, 20, 222; attempts to reform, prior to 1787, 28–30; compact of union between sovereign states, 21; goals of independence and union, 21; lack of enforcement powers for congressional resolutions, 25–26; method of apportioning expenditures between the states, 40; and powers of commercial intercourse, 22; and powers of foreign relations and war making, 21–22, 23, 24; and powers of intrastate relations, 22; and powers to regulate relations with American Indians, 22
assignats, 193
Astor, John Jacob, 129
Augustín I, 168–69

Bancroft, George, 148
Bank of England, 122
Barbary states, wars with, 10, 26, 116
Baring Brothers of London, 113, 121, 164
Barker, Jacob, 130, 132
Bates, Edward, 185
Beckwith, George, 151
Belmont, August, 187
bills of credit, 54, 59, 60, 191
Bingham, William, 75
Black Hawk War of 1832, 2
Blackstone, William, 101
Boudinot, Elias, 90
Braxton, Carter, 23
Brock, Isaac, 218

308   INDEX

Buchanan, James, 150, 174
Buel, Richard, 274n26
buffalo hunters, 11
Bull Run, Battle of, 178
Burke, Edmund, "There's a Heap of Work to
   Do," 249
Burke, Thomas, 23
Burr, Aaron, 105

California, US acquisition of, 145, 147, 149
Campbell, George W., 130, 131, 132
Canadian Confederation: British military
   withdrawal from, 219-21, 250; given
   dominion status by Great Britain, 12,
   220; view of American territorial aggression, 3-4
Canton, American bombardment of coastal
   fortifications, 10
capitation (poll) taxes, 47, 54, 66, 169
Carleton, Guy, 218
Cass, Lewis, 159-60
central government expenditure: comparative
   data on, 246, 302n1; security costs, 223
Chase, Samuel P., 16, 228; British criticism
   of financial measures, 295n15; Civil War
   war finance plan, 183, 186-89, 196-97,
   210, 215; on debt, 245; hard-money
   advocate, 188, 191, 192-93; inexperience and lack of knowledge of monetary
   history, 185-86; proposed import duties
   on coffee, tea, and sugar, 186; resignation
   as Treasury secretary, 198; rooted in past
   practice, 186
Chataigner, Alexis, 2
"Choctaw" (one million dollars), 204
civil list (nonmilitary expenses), 113
Civil War: attack on Fort Sumter, 178; Battle
   of Antietam, 216; Battle of Bull Run, 178,
   188; began as war to preserve Union,
   178, 179, 248; cost of, 16; and cotton
   famine, 215; eradication of slavery as
   most important outcome, 179; international dimensions, 11-12, 215-21,
   248-49; number of deaths in, 293n2;
   number of enlisted men in, 179; resource
   mobilization, 15-16, 181; role of money
   in Union victory, 181-82; Trent crisis,
   188, 216, 217; US rite of passage to great-
   power status, 181, 182, 247-48; views of
   European observers on, 179-80. See also
   financing war: Civil War

Clay, Henry, "American System" economic
   plan, 242
Collection Act, 50
Collin, Nils (Nicholas), 1-2
common currency, 19
Compromise Tariff, 244
Concert of Europe, 219
Confederate States of America, 174, 194
Congress. See Continental Congress; First
   federal Congress
Connecticut Compromise, 20, 31
conscientious objectors, fines levied
   against, 54
"consols," 140-41
Constitutional Convention: Article VII
   debate, 38-40, 41; ban on national export
   taxes, 38-40, 48; battle over principle
   of representation, 34-35; and bills of
   credit, 191; and centralization of fiscal
   power, 37; Committee of Detail, 34, 37,
   38; Committee of Style and Arrangement, 43; compromise over slavery, 39,
   45; creation of national government
   acting directly on American people
   without state assistance, 20, 31-32;
   delegates acting as representatives of
   their constituents, 48; early attempt to
   enumerate powers of national government, 34; historical reinterpretation of,
   18-19; issue of assumption of state debt,
   41-43; issue of direct taxation, 30; letter
   accompanying transmission of Constitution to Congress, 43; priority of effective
   foreign relations capability, 50; priority
   of overcoming requisitions system, 50;
   restriction of federal fiscal power to
   protect interest of southern states, 38-39;
   sectional tensions, 38-40, 43; three-fifths
   rule for apportioning representatives in
   the House and direct taxes, 40-41, 48
Constitution of the United States: Revolutionary debt as major impetus behind
   drafting of, 230; state ratifying conventions, 44, 49. See also Constitutional
   Convention
consuls, 9
Continental Army, reliance on expropriation to obtain services and supplies for
   troops, 25
Continental Congress, 21; only nominal
   control over inhabitants of the West, 17;

rejection of idea of federal veto power over state laws, 35–36. *See also* First federal Congress
Continentals, 24–25, 125, 193
Cooke, Jay, 213; appeal to patriotism in bond campaigns, 202–3; daily publication of bond sales, 203–4; 1863 campaign to sell long-term bonds (5-20s), 184, 197–98, 297n35; 1865 campaign to sell long-term bonds (7-30s), 200–204, 297n40; "Facts About the 7-30s—The Advantage they Offer," 201; on public debt, 245; sale of 7-30 Treasury notes in 1861, 197; 7-30 night office agencies, 201, 203, 299n44; use of press in bond campaigns, 201-4
Cooper, Thomas: *Lectures on the Elements of Political Economy*, 152–53; *Manual of Political Economy*, 152
Corcoran, William, 164
Corcoran & Riggs, 156, 160–61, 164
Corning, Erastus, 205
Cornwallis, Charles, 25
Cortés, Hernán, 156
Country Whig doctrine, 43, 84–85, 105
Cowper, William, 154
Crawford, William, 142
Crimean War, 219, 250
Cumberland County petition, 44
"currency finance," 24–25, 41–42, 125, 141, 144, 190–94
customs duties: customs, imports, and GDP, 1789-1861, *243*; customs receipts in four major ports, 1785–1788 and 1792–1795, 77–78; exceeded income from internal revenue up to early twentieth century, 246; growth of revenues during Polk administration, 165; growth of revenues from 1800 to 1808, 116; growth of revenues in 1790s, 79–80, 239; as mainstay of federal fiscal regime, 37, 52–53, 69–70, 77, 91, 227–28, 229
Customs Service, 47, 237
customs union, 19

Dallas, Alexander, 122–23, 132–33, 135, 228–29
Davis, William, 209
debt. *See* public debt, US; War of Independence, debt
Declaration of Independence, 19, 21
Democratic Party: opposition to intermingling of public finances and banks, 149; opposition to protectionism of Whigs, 148; ridicule of Whig objections to loans, 159
Díaz, Porfirio, 169
direct taxes
—apportioned between states and federal income tax during Civil War, 186, 205, 245
—difficulty of collecting, 56–57
—issue of, at Constitutional Convention, 30, 41
—levied by state governments: average annual tax rates in southern states, 1785–1795, 65–66; burden of, in confederation period, 58–61, 238; cause of hardship and protests in 1780s, 238; could be paid in bills of credit or indents, 60, 61, 63, 66; could be paid in part in depreciated paper, 61, 64; decrease in years after adoption of Constitution, 66, 238; levied in northern and middle states between 1785 and 1795, 61–65, 62, 64; penalties for nonpayment, 57–58; taxes on property and persons, 54, 56–57
—replaced with indirect taxes as source of government revenue, 51, 53, 69, 238
—and three-fifths rule for apportioning, 40–41, 48
Disraeli, Benjamin, 181
Duer, William, 163

Economist, 180–81, 297n35; attempt to identify American idea of Union, 248; on Union war finance, 194, 196, 204, 208
embargo of 1807, 117, 118, 124
Eppes, John, 125
Era of Good Feelings, 142
Essex Results, 22
European governments: anticipated breakdown of US Union, 180–81; concern over US hegemony in North America, 180; funding systems, 88–90; turbulence of 1850s and 1860s, 249
exceptionalism, ideas of, 5
Exchequer bills, Great Britain, 127
Excise Act of 1791, 76
excise taxes, 47, 151, 158; constitutional right of Congress to levy, 41, 238; and first fiscal system, 71, 75–76, 77–78, 91; levied by state governments; levied during Civil War, 186, 189, 206; on manufacturers, 206, 210, 211, 214; as proportion of federal revenue, 239, 242

export duties: constitutional ban on, 38–40, 48; state governments, 54, 56

"Facts About the 7-30s—The Advantage they Offer," 201
Falkland Islands, American occupation of, 10
Farías, Valentín Goméz, 172, 173
federal government: Americans' distrust of, 224, 225, 226–27, 229; created to act directly on American people without state assistance, 31–32; and need for defense of national independence, 223; responsibility for foreign affairs, 19. *See also* fiscal system, federal; public debt, US
federal indents, 60–61
Federalist, The, 17, 20, 44–48, 51, 81, 207
Federalists: criticism of requisition system, 238; efforts to establish central government, 18, 44; opposition to discriminating between original and subsequent owners of securities, 91; and Revolutionary debt redemption policy, 100, 102, 104–5; support for public credit as instrument of modern war, 105; on tax collection, 68–69; view of trade duties as most acceptable tax to Americans, 228, 238; warning of dissolution of Union if Constitution was not adopted, 224–25
Fessenden, William P., 185, 191, 192, 198, 200, 208
fiat currency. *See* paper currency
financing war
—Civil War, 182–83; certificates of deposit, 183; Chase plan, 183, 186–89, 196–97, 210, 215; creation of internal revenue administration, 184, 185; debt retrenchment in decades after war, 184, 213–14, 215; direct tax apportioned between states and federal income tax, 186, 205, 245; foreign investors' lack of interest in loans to Union, 187; four different methods of finance, 183–84; historiography of, 294n14; increase in customs duties, 184, 210; increasing expenditures and decreasing revenues by late 1862, 188; internal taxation, 184, 205, 206–10; introduction of "greenbacks" by Congress, 183–84, 189, 190–91; long-term bonds, 186–87, 190, 191–92, 197–98, 200–204, 297n40; major sources of government revenue, 1862–1863, *195*; major sources of government revenue, 1863–1864, *199*; major sources of government revenue, 1865–1866, *212*; major sources of government revenue per quarter, 1862–1866, *183*; "national loan" marketed toward citizens, 187; new excise duties on manufacturers, 206, 210, 211; resulting federal debt, 16, 179, 182, 183, 245; revenue act of 1864, 189, 205–15; suspension of specie conversion in 1861, 189, 190, 193, 205; transformation of federal fiscal regime, 229–30; treasury notes, 183, 188
—Albert Gallatin's war finance plan, 117, 119–26, 136–37, 280n23; and debt repayment, 125, 142, 282n32; dependence on rechartered Bank of the United States, 123; opposition to paper money, 125–26; on pattern of war bond emissions, 140; reliance on long-term bonds, 126, 127–28, 129; taxation as critical part of, 123, 124–25; and Treasury notes, 126–27, 191
—Mexican War, 15; 1846 loan act, 154; increase in import duties, 150–51, 157–58; Mexican tax assessment, 157, 162; sale of long-term bonds, 147, 155–61, 163–64, *165*, 184; sale of Treasury notes, 154, 155, 165
—War of 1812, 14–15, 126–44; borrowing, 107, 126, 232; debt repayment, 142–44, *143*, 231, 286n56; fiscal system in January 1815, *134–35*; friction among states over distribution of burdens of war, 222; issuance of short-term Treasury notes, 126–27, 133, 141, 282n34; new duties and property taxes, 132–33, 281n31; passage of five loan acts by Congress, 127; revision of finance plan in 1814, 113, 126, 144; sale of long-term securities, 119–20, 126, 127–32, *138–39*, 140–41, 184, 285n51
—War of Independence, 23, 24–26; "currency finance," 24–25, 125, 141, 144; economic consequences, 15, 78; expropriation, 25; foreign loans, 25; "military" or "depreciation" certificates, 25; suspension of interest-bearing bond sales, 141
First Bank of the United States, 111, 121–23, 127, 136, 232
First federal Congress: agreement about powers of, among founders, 23; Collection Act, 50; creation of national revenue administration, 14, 222–23; debate and

passage of Impost Act, 30, 51, 69–70, 71–74, 269n34, 269n49; debate and passage of Tonnage Act, 50, 71, 72–73, 269n34; designation of customs duties as mainstay of fiscal system, 37, 52–53, 69–70; discussion of Bill of Rights, 50; and federal assumption of state debts, 41, 52, 68 (*see also* Funding Act); language of states' rights in fiscal debates, 72; members' perceived duty to protect interests of their states, 48, 227; and question of intersectional symbiosis, 72, 73; replacement of direct taxes with indirect, 51, 53, 69, 238; sectional rift between North and South, 72–73; tax exemption on slave imports, 73; willingness to compromise, 73

First World War, income tax legislation to finance, 246

fiscal system, federal: apportionment of direct taxes by population, 40–41, 48; ban on export taxes, 38–40, 348; conflict over tariff, 242–43; creation of (*see* First federal Congress); customs duties as mainstay of, 37, 52–53, 69–70, 77, 91, 227–28, 229; dual sovereignty over taxation, 238; effects of states' rights ideology on, 227, 229; fear of monarchy among opponents of, 43–44; federal borrowing, 231–32, 233–34; historical reinterpretation of, 19; limitations of, 246; origins of (*see* Constitutional Convention); provided authority for national government acting independently from states, 13, 19; reform of, 237–39; shift of tax burden from property to trade, 46–48, 66, 228, 238; strong element of continuity in, 239–42, 278n52; and supremacy clause, 36; tied government to commercial sector, 244; transformation of, during Civil War, 229–30, 245–46. *See also* public debt, US; revenues, federal, and federal fiscal system; spending, federal, and federal fiscal system

Fisher, David, 163
Fiske, John, 5
Fitzsimons, Thomas, 52, 70–71, 73
Florida Cession, 3, 236, 256n10
foreign affairs: delegation of responsibility to national government, 19; power of, under Articles of Confederation, 21–22, 23, 24; priority of, for Constitutional Convention, 50
Fort Sumter, attack on, 178

France: demand that American states ratify treaties individually, 27; intervention in Mexico, 170, 174, 217, 248, 249, 250; refusal to open markets to American merchants, 26; Second Empire, 219; withdrawal from North America, 12, 250
Franco-Prussian War, 249
Franklin, Benjamin, 2
free traders, 243–44
French and Indian War, 24, 220
French Revolution, 1–2, 5, 78, 101, 119
Fries's Rebellion, 79, 94
frontier myth, 247
Funding Act: and contemporary European debt management practices, 83; debate and passage of, 81, 92; and deferred debt, 96, 98; failed to ensure repayment of principal of debt, 82, 230; and federal assumption of state debt, 83, 93; impetus for, 81–82; nationalization of the Revolutionary debt, 82, 223; and original security holders' right to compensation, 82–83; provoked split between Federalists and Republicans, 83; supported by both Madison and Jefferson, 106; and timetable for debt retirement, 99, 230–31. *See also* funding and assumption program, Alexander Hamilton's
funding and assumption program, Alexander Hamilton's: assumption plan for state debts, 66, 68, 230; attempt to adapt European debt management principles to America, 90, 230; change from fixed-term securities to securities without maturation date, 95–96; "The Continentalist No. IV," 87; and debt redemption, 99, 100; "Defense of the Funding System," 87; denial of Jefferson's charges against his funding plan, 85–86; dilemma of servicing a debt with insufficient revenue, 94; disagreement with Jefferson about public debt, 81; estimate of domestic and foreign debts, 91; estimate of interest on federal debt, 91; ideas on public credit, 45, 81, 86–87, 88, 91, 104, 274n19, 274n20; origins of plan, 81; placed responsibility for debt servicing and taxation in same hands, 81; plan for debt redemption, 99–104; plan for retirement of foreign debt and domestic loans, 231; and public creditors, 95–96, 97–98, 230; reduction of interest rate, 96; *Report on a Plan for the*

funding and assumption program, Alexander Hamilton's (*continued*)
Further Support of Public Credit, 99, 102–3, 273n14, 277n46; *Report on Funds for the Payment of the Interest on the States' Debts*, 76–77, 82; *Report on Public Credit*, 74–77, 82, 85, 88–91, 96, 98, 99, 100, 110; restoration of public credit, 80, 81–104; transformation of public debt from liability to asset, 13–14; view of plan as means to improve economy, 86; view that some wealth should be held in reserve for national exigencies, 93

Gadsden Purchase, 146, 174, 256n10
Gallatin, Albert, 15, 104, 107, 109, 116, 143, 228; admission that Federalist and Jeffersonian debt policy were the same, 112; criticism of Federalist finance practices, 109–10; criticism of Washington's failure to balance budget, 111; definition of public credit, 123–24; on funding of Revolutionary debt, 110–11; on Jefferson's reduction of taxes, 115; mistrust of public creditors, 113; objection to assumption of state debts, 111; object of debt reduction to improve national security, 111–12; opposition to debt for reasons of political economy, 113; opposition to high military expenditure, 153; peace mission to London, 131, 133; *A Sketch of the Finances of the United States*, 110–11, 113; understanding of role of public debt in modern statecraft, 113; on war, 118–19. *See also* financing war: Albert Gallatin's war finance plan
Gaynor, James, 249
German unification, 249
Gerry, Elbridge, 73, 93–94, 113, 275n30
Gettysburg Address, 178
Girard, Stephen, 129
Glorious Revolution of 1688, 84, 86
gold in currency in New York City, price of, 1862–1865, *193*
Goodenough, James, 217
Gorham, Nathaniel, 40
Great Britain: adoption of national paper currency during Napoleonic Wars, 191; barring of American traders from West Indies, 26, 28, 39; expected implosion of the United States with Civil War, 216–17; expulsion of American colonies from common market, 17; fear of US attack on Canada, 217–19; funding of Napoleonic Wars, 296n25; interest in maintaining autonomous Indian territory as barrier to US growth, 11, 17; military withdrawal from Canada, 12, 219–21; more diverse fiscal system than that of the United States, 241–42; post-Revolution military posts in the United States, 17, 26; principles of war finance, 194; public debt consisting of "consols," 86, 94, 98, 101, 102, 140–41; recognition of American military capacity as result of Civil War, 217–19; securities investments, 127–28, 298n43; Sixtieth Rifle Corps, 220, 221; view of US Civil War as US bid for continental domination, 180
Great Plains, destruction of ecological foundations of economy, 11
greenbacks, 183–84; comparisons to Bank of England notes, 296n25; depreciation of, 193, 197; difference from Continentals, 194; introduced by Congress during Civil War, 189, 190–91, 194, 196, 198; remained in place after Civil War, 214

Hamilton, Alexander, 30, 79, 141–42, 223; advice against military conflict, 118; belief that war would recur in the future, 45; borrowing from Bank of the United States, 122; on constitutional shift of tax burden from property to trade, 46–48, 66; on customs duties, 70; definition of funded debts, 276n35; discussion of Constitution in *The Federalist*, 44–48; discussion of importance of fiscal powers in times of war, 45–46; on essential points that Federalists should try to achieve, 105–6; "The Examination," 114, 115, 117; and image of Hercules for the United States, 2; on inefficiency of requisitions system, 46; limited impact on fiscal policy, 51; opposition to tax on alienation of securities, 275n30; on role of fiscal matters in framing of Constitution, 17; on status of United States in 1780s, 27; on taxation in the 1780s, 52; tax reform proposals, 74–77; warning that American people would not be willing to pay for a war, 274n24. *See also* funding and assumption program, Alexander Hamilton's
Harper, Robert Goodloe, 102

INDEX 313

Hartington, Marquess of, 248
Hartley, Thomas, 275n32
Hercules, legend of, as metaphor for United States, 1–2
Hidalgo revolt, 168
Hope, Alexander Beresford, 216
Horsman, Reginald, 285n51
House of Representatives: power to enact fiscal legislation, 51; report on Second Bank of the United States, 137; three-fifths rule for apportioning representatives to, 41; Ways and Means Committee, 185
House of Rothschild, 187
Hume, David, 96, 101, 102

Imperial Fortress, Quebec City, 218, 220, 250
import duties, 47; on alcohol, 75, 76, 79, 208–9, 211, 246; customs, imports, and GDP, 1789–1861, 243; and finance of Mexican War, 150–51, 157–58; as share of GDP, 1789–1861, 243, 244–45; and state governments, 54, 56
Impost Acts, 30, 50, 51, 71–74, 76, 206, 269n34
income tax, 227; legislation of, in 1917, 246; levied during Civil War, 186, 205; reduced in 1867 and abolished in 1872, 214
indirect taxes, replaced direct taxes as most acceptable to American people, 51, 53, 69, 228
internal revenue service: creation of during Civil War, 189, 210; revenue from, 211, 212
international commerce: and need for federal powers, 18; promotion of, 9–10. *See also* customs duties
international securities market, 90
intersectional symbiosis, 72, 73
interstate conflicts, and need for federal powers, 18
interstate contracts, 19
intraunion relations, federal responsibility for, 19
Italian unification, 249, 250

Jackson, Andrew, 133, 142, 170; expenditures, 235; Indian removal, 9, 235; opposition to Second Bank of the United States, 149; portrayal of United States as peaceful nation, 4; use of public credit to acquire territory, 14; warning against disunion, 225
Jackson, James, 73–74

Japan, opening of, 10
Jay, John, 23
Jay-Gardoqui negotiations, 27
Jay Treaty, 5, 103
Jefferson, Thomas: abolishment of all internal taxes in 1801, 114–15, 117; administration of Federalist repayment plan for Revolutionary debt, 104, 107, 109; attitude toward public debt, 105, 226; comparison of debt in Europe and America, 94; Country Whig rhetoric, 271n5; criticism of Federalist administrations, 108; critique of Hamiltonianism, 81, 84–85, 271n5; customs income growth during administration, 116; and Declaration of Independence, 21; difference of administration from those of Federalists, 108–9; "Empire of Liberty," 87; expenditures during administration, 116, 237; fiscal success built upon reforms of Federalists, 109, 116; and Funding Act, 83, 271n5; inaugural address, 108; portrayal of United States as peaceful nation, 4; and public credit, 14, 113–14; and "Revolution of 1800," 108, 115; shaped government to limit choices open to future administrations, 115, 117; support for loans over taxes, 280n24; use of public credit for territorial expansion, 13, 232
Jervois, Drummond, 218
Johnson, Andrew, 249
Johnson, Reverdy, 159
Jones, William, 120–21, 126, 130
Juarez, Benito, 249
Judiciary Act of 1789, 36

Kellogg, William, 208–9
King, Rufus, 41
Kipling, Rudyard, 7
Krooss, Herman E., 285n51
Kuala Batee, Sumatra, 7

Langdon, John, 41
Law, John, 208, 209
Lee, Robert E., surrender at Appomattox, 181, 249
legal-tender act: authorization of 5-20 bonds, 191–92; led to active demand and full credit of all government securities, 198; required payment of import duties and interest on government bonds in specie, 192. *See also* greenbacks

Lincoln, Abraham, 216; appointing of rivals to administration, 185; assassination of, 249; call for massive mobilization, 178; commitment to preserve the Union at all costs, 178, 179; Gettysburg Address, 178; signing of new tax law, 196, 210
List, Friedrich, *National System of Political Economy*, 153
Locke, John, 22
long-term securities, sale of, to finance war, 13, 15, 68; in Britain, 122; and Civil War, 186–87, 190, 191–92, 197–98, 200–204, 297n40; and Mexican War, 147, 155–61, 163–64, *165*, 184; and War of 1812, 119–20, 126, 127–32, *138–39*, 140–41, 184, 285n51
Louisiana Purchase, 3, 13, 107, 112, 121, 232, 236, 256n10
Lyon, Matthew, 118
Lyons, Lord, 217–18

Madison, James, 30, 106, 225, 281n30; argument that good of the Union moderated states' rights, 72; borrowing to finance War of 1812, 107, 232; defense of constitutional compromise over slavery, 45; discussion of fiscal policy in First Congress, 50, 52, 70, 71, 271n4; failure to obtain aims of War of 1812, 143; and issue of state compliance with Congress, 29–30, 36; military expenditures during presidency, 116; on nature of constitutional reform of 1787, 20; position on funding of debt, 82–83, 91; and reform of organizational structure of federal union, 31–33, 34, 35; tax reform proposals, 75, 76; on Tonnage Act and importance of navy, 72; use of public credit to acquire territory, 14; on war and taxation, 225–26
Manifest Destiny, 146
Mann, Michael, 302n1
Marcy, William, 157
maritime expansion, 9–10, 247
Martin, Luther, 37, 39
Mason, James, 35, 36, 37, 188
Massachusetts Constitution of 1778, 22
Maximilian I, 170, 174, 217, 248, 249, 250
McCulloch, Hugh, 213–14, 215
McGee, Thomas D'Arcy, 4
Mediterranean Fund, 116
Mercer, John, 39
Mexican Cession, 8, 9, 11, 145, 175, 256n10

Mexican War, 5, 11, 145–77, 172, 247; Battle of Buena Vista, 161; Battle of Palo Alto, 172; congressional declaration of war, 150; and demise of Great Plains Indian nations, 11; number of men serving in, 178; opening of second front, 156; outcomes for the United States, 175–76; and public debt, 166, 231–32; Scott's victory at Cerro Gordo, 173; total costs of, 164–65, 291n46; Treaty of Guadalupe Hidalgo, 161, 164, 172, 174, 175, 176, 177; US attempts to arrive at peace treaty, 156, 161–63; US indemnity payments to Mexico, 165, 174; US occupation of California and New Mexico, 156; viewed as inevitable by American historians, 146. *See also* financing war: Mexican War
Mexico: American views on national feeling among Mexican people, 157, 289n73; Augustín administration, 168, 169, 172; border conflict with Texas, 149; default on foreign debt, 169, 170; disordered public finances and political instability after independence, 148, 167, 169–70, 171, 174; French invasion and occupation, 170, 174, 217, 248, 249, 250; Hidalgo revolt, 168; inability to mobilize for war with the United States, 15, 148, 166–69, 172–73; involuntary loans and expropriations, 169, 172, 173; *Junta Instituyente*, 169; national income in 1845, 167; presidency of Guadalupe Victoria, 169; regional discontent, 171–72; richness in natural resources, 166–67; view of American territorial aggression (*The Other Side*), 3–4, 145–46
"military" or "depreciation" certificates, 25
molasses, duty on, 73, 227
Monroe, James: and repayment of Revolutionary debt, 107; spending, 232, 235; use of public credit to acquire territory, 14
Montesquieu, Baron de, 22
Mormons, 223
Morrill, Justin S., 185, 196, 206, 209, 246
Morris, Robert, 25, 35–36, 37, 39–40, 41, 43, 197
Mortimer, Thomas, 141

Napoleon III, 12, 187, 219, 248–49, 250
Napoleon Bonaparte, 131
Napoleonic Wars, 88, 118, 136, 141, 168
National Banking Act, 296n22
national government. *See* federal government

Native Americans. *See* American Indian nations
New Jersey Plan, 33–34, 37

Oregon settlement, 9, 147, 150, 256n10, 288n11
Other Side, The, 3, 4, 145–46

Paine, Thomas, 224; *The Decline and Fall of the English System of Finance*, 101, 276n42
Palfrey, John Gorham, 158
Panic of 1837, 231
paper currency: Continentals, 24–25, 125, 141, 144, 193; greenbacks, 183–84, 189, 190–91, 193, 296n25; state currency, 61
Parish, David, 129
Paris Peace Treaty of 1783, 7, 11
Parker, Josiah, 73–74
Parrot, William S., 149
Paterson, William, 37
Peace of Amiens, 119
Peace of Paris, 222, 251
Peasle & Co., 201, 213
Perkins, Edwin J., 278n52, 282n34
Perry, Matthew, 10
"Philadelphia system" or "peace pact," contemporary views of, 5
Pinckney, Charles, 34, 38, 39, 40
Pitt, William, 101, 277n43
Plantou, Julia, *The Peace of Ghent 1814 and the Triumph of America*, 2
Playfair, William, 101, 102, 276n42
Polk, James, 161; and acquisition of California and New Mexico, 149; creation of independent Treasury Department, 149; demand that Mexico recognize Texas annexation and Rio Grande border, 149; demand that Mexico repay debts to American citizens, 150; and financing of Mexican War, 150, 154, 156–57, 162–63, 232; minimalist vision of national government, 153–54, 176; on outcomes of war with Mexico, 175–76; platform of foreign policy, tariff reduction, and Treasury reform, 148; portrayal of United States as peaceful nation, 4; on protectionism of Whigs, 148–49; and treaty with Britain over Oregon, 288n11; use of public credit to acquire territory, 14; view of public debt and debt retrenchment, 151, 156–57, 176–77

poll (capitation) taxes, 47, 54, 66, 169
Porfiriato, 168–69
Postlethwayt, Malachy, *Universal Dictionary of Trade and Commerce*, 95–96, 272n8
property taxes: difference from poll or capitation taxes, 47; levied by state governments, 54, 56–57; levied during War of 1812, 132–33, 281n31; shift away from to taxation on trade, 46–48, 66, 228, 238
protectionism, 49, 71, 148–49, 163, 243–44
Prussia, 249
public bankruptcies, 89
public credit: five reasons for federal borrowing, 232; restoration of, 81–104; use of, for territorial expansion, 14, 87, 232; use of, to finance Civil War, 16, 232
public creditors, 97–98, 113; original and subsequent owners of securities, 91; and reduction of interest rate, 96, 275n32; right of, to transfer securities, 95–96, 230; state creditors, 93–94
public debt, US, 41–43, 60; decreasing interest rates on, in eighteenth century, 89–90; effect of Mexican War on, 166; in 1865, 213; in 1866, 16; 1791–1861, 231–32; European funding systems, 88–90; managed by Treasury Department, 122; periodic reductions of, up to New Deal, 246; popular American views of, 147–48, 151–53; post–Civil War debt, 179, 182, 183; practice of not making repayments of principal, 90; problems with paying off or repudiating, 89; retrenchment in decades after Civil War, 184, 213–15; in 1780s, 59; in 1795 and 1801, 104; state assumption of, in mid-1780s, 41, 52, 60–61, 68. *See also* War of Independence, debt

Quasi War, 5, 79, 88, 104, 111, 247

Ramirez, José Fernando, 166, 171, 173
Randolph, Edmund, 32, 33, 36, 37, 41
Republicans: aggressive policy against Indian nations and European states, 87; creation of fiscal system that undermined nation's self-determination, 117; debt as theme in opposition to Federalist administration, 100, 104, 105, 107; given credit by historians for paying off Revolutionary debt, 104; management of debt after assumption of power in 1801, 83, 107; Revolution of 1800, 87; war finance principles, 123–24

republics, regarded as unstable political entities, 174–75, 180
requisitions system, 23, 26, 28, 29–30, 34, 35, 36–37, 46, 50, 66–67, 68, 238
reservation system, for American Indians, 9, 11
revenues, federal, and federal fiscal system: customs duties as 69 percent of total income from 1789 to 1861, 241; increase in, as result of Walker tariff, 240; increase in 1835 and 1836 as result of public land sales, 240, 241; loan revenues in five periods, 241; total revenue, customs revenue, and loan revenue, 1792–1861, 239–41; total tax revenue, per capita tax revenue, and tax revenue as share of GDP, 1789–1861, 240–41
revenue sources, of state governments, 54, 55, 56; bills of credit, 54; court fees, 54; direct taxes, 56–57; excise taxes, 54, 55, 56, 60; export and import duties, 54, 56; sources other than taxation, 53–54; structure of revenue, 1785–1787, 55; types of taxes in 1780s, 54–55. *See also* direct taxes: levied by state governments
Revolutionary War. *See* War of Independence, debt
Robinson, Robert Spencer, 218
Rush, Richard, 229
Russell, Lord, 180
Russia: sale of Alaska, 12, 251; support of Union in Civil War, 250
Russian American Company, 251

Santa Anna, Antonio López de, 161, 173
Scott, Winfield, 8–9, 161, 167, 170, 173
"scrip" (subscription), 128
Second Bank of the United States, 126, 232; congressional refusal to renew charter in 1837, 149; establishment of, 142; House Committee of Ways and Means report on, 137
Second German Empire, 249
Second Schleswig War, 219, 249
Seven Years' War, 167
Sevier, Ambrose, 159
Seward, William, 185, 216, 250
Seybert, Adam, *Statistical Annals of the United States of America*, 207
Shays, Daniel, 33
Shays's Rebellion, 51, 52, 63, 92
Sheffield, Lord, *Observations on the Commerce of the American States*, 248

Sherman, John, 194, 196
Sherman, Roger, 19, 33, 36, 37, 74
Sherman, William Tecumseh, 180, 200
sinking fund, 27n43, 101–2, 205
slave imports, tax exemption on, 73
slave tax, 54, 66
Slidell, John, 150, 188
Smith, Adam, 89, 101
Smith, Caleb Blood, 158
Smith, J. B., 181, 219
Smith, Sydney, 207–8
Smith, William, 73
southern states: and ban on export duties, 38–40, 48; and ban on interference with slave trade, 39–40; and constitutional restrictions on federal fiscal powers, 38–39; linking of direct taxes to representation, 40–41; taxes on land and slaves, 54
Spain: closure of Mississippi to American commerce, 26; interest in maintaining autonomous Indian territory as barrier to US growth, 11; loss of American dominions, 2–3, 11; revenue system in American possessions in late colonial period, 167–68
Spanish-American War, 5, 215
Spaulding, Elbridge G., 185, 296n24
"special indents," 61, 66
specie conversion, suspension of, 122–23, 137, 140, 142, 189, 190, 193, 205
spending, federal, and federal fiscal system, 232–37; average annual expenditure per administration, 235; four-fifths of spending between 1789 and 1860 for war, 237; for internal improvements, 237; per capita expenditures, 1792–1861, 236–37; for territorial acquisitions, 236, 237
Speight, Jesse, 159
Staël, Madame de, 112
state creditors, 93–94
state currency, 61
state governments: early securities market, 59–60; expenses, 1785–1787, 66–68, 67; federal assumption of debts, 41–43, 52, 68, 83, 93; individual actions to defend and promote their interests, 27; interest payments on debts as percentage of total expenses, 268n28; noncompliance with congressional resolutions, 25–26, 29–30. *See also* direct taxes: levied by state governments; revenue sources, of state governments

states' rights ideology, 18, 23, 41, 72–73, 208, 227, 229, 245
Stephens, Thaddeus, 185
Stone, Michael Jenifer, 88–89, 273n14
Studenski, Paul, 285n51
Sully, Robert, 2
supremacy clause, 36

tariff: of 1832, 244; Compromise Tariff, 244; conflicts over, 242–43; effects of reforms between 1816 and 1861, 243–44; first protectionist of 1824, 244; Tariff of Abominations, 242, 244; during War of 1812, 142, 244
tax arrears, in 1780s, 57–58
taxation: constitutional shift of burden from property to trade, 46–48, 238–39; distinction between property taxes and poll or capitation taxes, 47; eighteenth-century ideas of, 47; fear of, in American political thought, 225–27; reduction of, after Civil War, 184; taxation without representation, 24
taxes: on alcohol, 54–55, 75, 76, 79, 115, 206, 208–9, 211; income tax, 186, 205, 214, 246; indirect, 51, 53, 69, 228; poll (capitation) taxes, 47, 54, 66, 169. *See also* direct taxes; excise taxes; import duties
tax resistance, 51, 52, 63, 79, 92, 97, 117, 245
Taylor, Zachary, 156, 157, 161, 167
territorial expansion, United States: Alaska Purchase of 1867, 7, 146, 147, 251, 256n10; Gadsden Purchase, 146, 174, 256n10; Mexican Cession, 8, 9, 11, 145–46, 175, 256n10; Oregon Territory, 147, 150; through power politics, diplomacy, and war, 5–9, 12, 147, 247; romantic notion of expansion achieved by settlers, 146; through territorial dispossession and ethnic cleansing of American Indian nations, 7, 8, 9, 146–47, 223, 235; and transformation of natural environment, 6; use of public credit for, 13, 14, 232; views of, by Mexican and Canadian writers, 3–4
Texas annexation, 9, 11, 146, 147, 149, 256n10
Texas revolt of 1835, 171
Thatcher, George, 73
Thomas, George H., 200
Tilly, Charles, 223–24
Tonnage Act, 50, 71, 72–73, 206, 269n34
trade: federal promotion, regulation, and protection of, 9–10, 19, 21, 23, 28, 29, 32, 34; free trade position, 38, 71, 151, 155, 160, 163, 243–44; protectionism, 49, 71, 148–49, 163, 243–44; rising volume from 1802 to 1807, 116–17; shift of tax burden from property to trade, 46–48, 66, 228, 238; West Indies trade, 26, 28, 38, 49
Trade and Intercourse Act of 1790, 8
trade duties, 47–48. *See also* customs duties; import duties
Treasury notes (Exchequer bills): and Civil War finance, 183, 187, 188, 197; and Mexican War finance, 154, 155, 165; and War of 1812 finance, 126–27, 133, 141, 191, 282n34
Treaty of Guadalupe Hidalgo, 161, 164, 172, 174, 175, 176, 177
Trent crisis, 188, 216, 217, 218
Tripartite Convention, 170
Tucker, Thomas, 72–73, 74

United States Congress. *See* Continental Congress; First federal Congress
United States Navy, international policing and diplomatic activity, 9–10, 247

Van Buren, Martin, 149, 235
Victoria, Guadalupe, 169, 174
Vinton, Samuel Finley, 163
Virginia House of Delegates, protest against Funding Act, 85
Virginia Plan, 32–37; proposal of veto power over state laws, 35; and representation issue, 40; resistance from small states' delegates, 33; solutions to problem of state delinquency, 34–35

Walker, Robert J., 15, 137, 186; and financing of Mexican War, 148–49, 150–51, 154–57; projections of future greatness for the United States, 145, 175; "revenue tariff" (Walker tariff), 148–49, 154–55, 163; sale of long-term bonds, 160–61, 163–64, 165
Walters, Raymond, Jr., 285n51
war: as accepted instrument of statecraft, 224; coupled with disunion by Federalists, 224–25; as means of US expansion, 2–9, 10–12, 147
War of 1812, 5, 88, 108–44; and control of trans-Appalachian West, 10; cost of, 16, 232; invasion of New Orleans, 131; number serving in, 178, 293n2; peace talks,

War of 1812 (continued)
131, 133; per capita expenditures during, 236; poor preparation and execution of, 119, 136, 143–44; sack of Washington, 131. *See also* financing war: Albert Gallatin's war finance plan; financing war: War of 1812

War of Independence, debt, 14, 41, 81–104, 141, 230, 265n7; change in political debate on, from 1790 to 1795, 100; motives behind, as identified by modern historians, 84–87; repayment of the foreign debt, *107*; repayment of the 6 percent debt, *105*; repayment of the 6 percent deferred debt, *106*. *See also* financing war: War of Independence; Funding Act; funding and assumption program, Alexander Hamilton's

Washington, George, 51, 99; borrowing mostly to reform Revolutionary debt, 232; and image of Hercules, 2; portrayal of United States as peaceful nation, 4

Webster, Noah, 25, 26, 31, 262n14

Webster, Pelatiah, 27–28, 29, 31, 36, 69–70; *An Essay on Credit*, 90

Westcott, James, 159

western United States, management of, and need for federal powers, 18

West Indies trade: closure of, to American ships, 26, 28, 38; lifting of restrictions on, 49

Whigs, opposition to Polk's policies, 154–55, 158, 159, 163

Whiskey Rebellion, 79, 94, 122, 223

White, Leonard, 278n50

Wilcox, Andrew Jackson, "The Annexation of Mexico the means of paying the National Debt," 249

Wilkerson, Samuel, *How Our National Debt May Be a National Blessing*, 182, 213

Wilkes, Charles, 188

Williamson, Hugh, 39, 92

Wilmot Proviso, 162

Wilson, James, 41

Wolcott, Oliver, Jr., 52, 103, *106*, *107*, 111, 119

Wolfe, James, 218, 220

Woodbury, Levi, 142